The *New* Meaning of Educational Change

The Meaning of Educational Change

SECOND EDITION

Michael G. Fullan

with
Suzanne Stiegelbauer

The Ontario Institute
for Studies in Education

Teachers College
Columbia University

Published by Teachers College Press, 1234 Amsterdam Avenue
New York, NY 10027

Library of Congress Cataloging-in-Publication Data

Fullan, Michael.
    The new meaning of educational change / Michael G. Fullan with Suzanne
Stiegelbauer.—2nd ed.
        p. cm.
    Rev. ed. cf: The meaning of educational change. 1982.
    Includes bibliographical references (p.) and index.
    ISBN 0-8077-3061-0 (alk. paper).
    ISBN 0-8077-3060-2 (pbk. alk. paper)

    1. Educational change—Canada. 2. Educational change—United States.
3. Education and state—Canada. 4. Educational and state—United States.
I. Stiegelbauer, Suzanne M. II. Fullan, Michael. Meaning of educational
change. III. Title.
LA412.F85   1991   379.73—dc20   90-21681

Canadian Cataloging-in-Publication Data

Fullan, Michael, 1940–
    The new meaning of educational change

2nd ed.
First ed. published under title: The meaning of
educational change.
Includes bibliographical references.
ISBN 0-7744-0357-8

1. Educational innovations—Canada. 2. Educational
innovations—United States. 3. Educational
planning. I. Title. II. Title: The meaning of
educational change.

LB1027.F85 1990   379.1'54   C90-094766-7

Printed on acid-free paper

Manufactured in the United States of America

98 97 96 95   8 7 6 5 4

To
Chris, Maureen, Josh, and Bailey

Contents

vii

PART II: EDUCATIONAL CHANGE AT THE LOCAL LEVEL

PART III: EDUCATIONAL CHANGE AT THE REGIONAL AND NATIONAL LEVELS

Preface

The issue of central interest in this book is not how many new policies have been approved or how many restructuring efforts are being undertaken, but rather what has actually changed in practice—if anything—as a result of our efforts. Has the cumulative effect of attempted reform been positive, or neutral or are we losing ground? How do we know when change is worthwhile? What can teachers, administrators, parents, or policy-makers do when they know that something is desperately wrong in our schools? Can rejecting a proposed educational program be more progressive than accepting it? Why are we so often unclear and ambivalent about new ways of doing things?

Underlying the above questions is the problem of finding meaning in change. If reforms are to be successful, individuals and groups must find meaning concerning *what* should change as well as *how* to go about it. Yet it is exceedingly difficult to resolve the problem of meaning when large numbers of people are involved. And often we find meaning only by trying something. Successful innovations and reforms are usually clear after they work, not in advance.

We have witnessed over the last 30 years numerous attempts at planned educational change. The benefits have not nearly equaled the costs, and all too often the situation has seemed to worsen. We have, however, gained clearer and clearer insights over this period about the do's and don'ts of bringing about change. I have attempted in this book to distill from these experiences the most powerful lessons about how to cope with and influence educational change. In compiling the best of theory and practice my goal has been to explain why change processes work as they do and to identify what would have to be done to improve our success rate.

It is essential to understand both the small and the big pictures. We have to know what change looks like from the point of view of the teacher, student, parent, and administrator if we are to understand the actions and reactions of individuals; and if we are to comprehend the big picture, we must combine the aggregate knowledge of these individual situations with an understanding of organizational and institutional factors that influence the process of change as government departments, universities, teacher federations, school systems, and schools interact.

One of the most promising features of this new knowledge about change is that successful examples of innovation are based on what might be most accurately labeled "organized common sense." It may not be easy to organize common sense—or rather to prevent other factors from overcoming it when the going gets tough—but explanations of success and of failure as described in this book do make sense. The difficulty in using this knowledge to improve other situations is that it requires contending with several factors at once: leadership, staff development, values and ideas, as well as who benefits from them, quality of materials and programs, and the demands from all quarters for evidence that the new way is desirable and effective. Managing social change is indeed a multivariate business that requires us to think of and address more than one factor at a time. While the theory and practice of successful educational change do make sense, and do point to clear guidelines for action, it is always the case that particular actions in particular situations require integrating the more general knowledge of change with detailed knowledge of the politics, personalities, and history peculiar to the setting in question.

Emphasizing the integration of the general and the specific is another way of saying that in the final analysis each individual must decide on a course of action for herself or himself. To help in guiding these decisions, I have written this book for individuals at all levels in the educational system. They will find a chapter on their own roles, as well as chapters on other roles and agencies with which they have direct and indirect contact. It is necessary to reflect on and understand both one's own situation and the situations of relevant others in order to plan or cope with change. Part I—"Understanding Educational Change"—provides an overview of the sources, processes, and outcomes of change, and the implications for dealing with change. Part II contains chapters on each of the main roles at the local level, examining the day-to-day situations people face and how change is part of these daily realities. In Part III, I return to the larger scene to consider the role of governments, teacher and administrator preparation and professional development, and the future of educational change. Each of the 16 chapters can be read and understood on its own, although the underlying theme and total picture depend on the combined chapters.

There is not very much jargon in the book: One cannot claim that meaning is the answer and then proceed to write an abstruse treatise on the subject. On the other hand, the main findings are amply referenced. For the student of change who wishes to delve into the topic, the references contain some 500 items, many of which are new. For those less interested in the research base, the chapters can be read without attention to the references cited. In short, the book is intended for professionals (policy-makers and practitioners) interested in education and change at the school, local, regional, and national levels, as well as for university students and professors on faculties of education seeking a textbook on theories and practices of planned educational change.

The focus is on "planned" change. I do not dwell on unplanned or naturally occurring changes, although these are obviously important in any long-term perspective on the evolution of social change. My goal is to highlight the problems and possibilities in bringing about educational change through some deliberate means. The basic question is how to get good at change—that is, how to increase the *capacity* of individuals and organizations to know when to reject certain change possibilities, to know when and how to pursue and implement others, and to know how to cope with policies and programs that are imposed on them.

Dissatisfaction with and interest in the prospects for educational reform is a worldwide phenomenon. Although most of the material I draw on comes from North American sources, any discussion with those involved in educational innovation and reform in other countries quickly reveals that the nature of problems and many of the principles of success and failure have a great deal in common.

Ten years ago we "studied innovations"; today we are "doing reform." There has been a shift from passivity to action, and from narrowness to comprehensiveness of solutions. We may know more, but we are also taking on more. Restructuring is a good example. There are currently many reform initiatives from school to district to state aimed at changing the structures of school work and the norms and practices within them. Unfortunately, structural changes are easier to bring about than normative ones. If we are not careful we can easily witness a series of non-events and other superficial changes that leave the core of the problem untouched.

The forces reinforcing the status quo are systemic. The current system is held together in many different crosscutting ways. Confronting the isolationism and privatism of educational systems is a tall order. It requires intensive action sustained over several years to make it possible both physically and attitudinally for teachers to work naturally together in joint planning, observation of each other's practice, and seeking, testing, and revising teaching strategies on a continuous basis. Reform is not putting into place the latest policy. It means changing the cultures of the classrooms, the schools, the districts, the universities, and so on. There is much more to educational reform than most people realize. This book honors that complexity but also identifies the most powerful levers for reform at our disposal. These levers must have the strength to influence complex webs of factors, while having the virtue of clarity if not simplicity. We need powerful usable strategies for powerful recognizable change.

If a healthy respect for and mastery of the change process does not become a priority, even well-intentioned change initiatives will continue to create havoc among those who are on the firing line. Careful attention to a small number of key details during the change process can result in the experience of success, new commitments, and the excitement and self-satisfaction of accomplishing something that is important. More fundamentally, reducing the number of failures and realizing new successes can lead to the revitalization of teaching and learning that is so desperately needed in the lives of educators and students today.

It isn't that people resist change as much as they don't know how to cope with it. My purpose is to provide multifaceted insights into the knowledge, the will, and the skill necessary to engage in more changes more profitably, while minimizing the intrusion of unwanted change. The answer is for individuals, armed with knowledge of the change process, to take responsibility and action to exploit the many opportunities for bringing about improvements. If we know one thing about innovation and reform, it is that it cannot be done successfully *to* others. It is not as if we have a choice whether to change or not. Demands for change will always be with us in complex societies; the only fruitful way ahead is to carve out our own niche of renewal and build on it.

I have benefited enormously from a large international group of students and doers of educational change with whom I have worked and who have freely provided me with insights and support. This network of academics, policy-makers, and practitioners has expanded greatly over the past 10 years. They now number in the hundreds, to the point that it is no longer possible to thank them in one place. I can only say that they know who they are and I thank them sincerely for the privilege of learning from them and with them. I would like to thank my new colleagues on the faculty of education of the University of Toronto, who have opened up the whole new dimension of teacher education. Confronting the relationship between theory and practice in teacher development is one of the more fertile quagmires for developing a practical theory of planned change.

Typing the manuscript was itself no easy task. Dolora Harvey, almost always in the evening hours, produced it with impressive speed and accuracy. Thank you for meeting all those deadlines. Ron Galbraith, Nina George, and all the editorial staff at Teachers College Press were professionally expert and humanly flexible, improving the manuscript along the way with countless helpful suggestions. Suzanne Stiegelbauer, recognized as assistant author, and an expert in the change process herself, was very helpful in compiling resources and helping to set the direction of the text.

Wendy and Bailey were great and fun supporters throughout, even when they kept asking, "How many more pages left?" Even they will tell you that I can't thank them enough.

To all these people, I hope the final product contributes some sense of new meaning and value commensurate with at least a fraction of their support.

Part I

UNDERSTANDING
EDUCATIONAL
CHANGE

CHAPTER 1

The Purpose and Plan
of the Book

Everything must change at one time or another or else a static society will evolve.

—Anonymous first-year university student
on an English language proficiency test

One person claims that schools are being bombarded by change; another observes that there is nothing new under the sun. A policy-maker charges that teachers are resistant to change; a teacher complains that administrators introduce change for their own self-aggrandizement and that they neither know what is needed nor understand the classroom. A parent is bewildered by a new practice in reading and by the relevance of education to future jobs. Some argue that restructuring schools is the only answer, while others decry that this, too, is just a pipedream diverting our attention from the core curriculum changes that are desperately needed. One university professor is convinced that schools are only a reflection of society and cannot be expected to bring about change; another professor is equally convinced that schools would be all right if only superintendents and principals had more "vision" as educational leaders, and teachers were more motivated to learn new approaches to improving the curriculum. A governor works hard to get major new legislation passed to reform education; a principal thinks, "this too shall pass." Change agents at all levels wonder how to get more and more programs institutionalized, while teachers think that it is these same promoters of change who should be institutionalized, not their programs. Students are too distracted by a host of other matters to pay much attention to all the uproar.

This book is concerned with educational change affecting elementary and secondary schools. Those involved with schools are constantly embroiled in small- and large-scale change. In Canada this means some 5 million elementary and secondary school students and their parents, 300,000 teachers, and 30,000 school and district administrators, not to mention the thousands of government and university personnel working on educational programs. There are approximately 15,000 schools across Canada and 1,000 local school systems in the 10 provinces plus the Northwest Territories and the Yukon. In the United States there are close to 45 million students enrolled in public elementary and secondary schools, over 2 million teachers, 200,000 school and district administrators, and tens of thousands of regional, state, federal, and university-based personnel; the 88,000 schools are organized into over 15,000 school districts.

It is impossible to estimate the number of innovative programs. In New York City's board of education, for example, 781 innovative programs were piloted between 1979 and 1981 (Major's Management Report, Supplement, 1980, cited in Mann, 1981). And that was a quiet period compared with the innovation boom since 1983 following the release of *A Nation at Risk*. If we broaden the term innovation to include all educational changes occurring through legislation, new and revised curricula, and special projects—in short, any practice new to the person attempting to cope with an educational problem—it is clear that change is common fare for school people. For example, California's School Bill 813, enacted in 1983, contains over 80 major components. Say Odden and Marsh (1988), "Its dozens of provisions, if fully implemented would alter curriculum and instruction in virtually every school in the state" (p. 593). After reviewing the current era of reform, Murphy (in press) observes that "the scope and momentum of the movement are unparalleled," and have "spawned more activity than at any time in the past" (p. 4).

Implicit in discussions of educational reform, but rarely recognized, is the confusion between the terms *change* and *progress*. Resisting certain changes may be more progressive than adopting them, but how do we know? The key to understanding the worth of particular changes, or to achieving desired changes, concerns what I call "the problem of meaning." One of the most fundamental problems in education today is that people do not have a clear, coherent sense of *meaning* about what educational change is for, what it is, and how it proceeds. Thus, there is much faddism, superficiality, confusion, failure of change programs, unwarranted and misdirected resistance, and misunderstood reform. What we need is a more coherent picture that people who are involved in or affected by educational change can use to *make* sense of what they and others are doing.

The problem of meaning is central to making sense of educational change. In order to achieve greater meaning, we must come to understand both the small and the big pictures. The small picture concerns the subjective meaning or lack of meaning for individuals at all levels of the educational system. Neglect of the phenomenology of change—that is, how people actually experience change as distinct from how it might have been intended—is at the heart of the spectacular lack of success of most social reforms. It is also necessary to build and understand the big picture, because educational change after all is a sociopolitical process. This book will have succeeded or failed to the extent that people who are involved in education can read the account and conclude that it makes sense of their individual situations, enables them to understand the broader social forces influencing change and—above all—points to some action that they and others around them can take to improve their immediate situation.

In the process of examining the individual and collective situations, it is necessary to contend with both the *what* of change and the *how* of change. Meaning must be accomplished in relation to both these aspects. It is possible to be crystal clear about what one wants and be totally inept at achieving it. Or to be skilled at managing change but empty-headed about what changes are most needed. To make matters more difficult, we often do not know what we want, or do not know the actual consequences of a particular direction, until we try to get there. Thus, on the one hand, we need to keep in mind the values and goals and the consequences associated with specific educational changes; and on the other hand, we need to comprehend the dynamics of educational change as a sociopolitical process involving all kinds of individual, classroom, school, local, regional, and national factors at work in interactive ways. The problem of meaning is one of how those involved in change can come to understand what it is that should change and how it can be best accomplished, while realizing that the what and how constantly interact and reshape each other.

We are not only dealing with a moving and changing target; we are also playing this out in social settings. Solutions must come through the development of *shared meaning*. The interface between individual and collective meaning and action in everyday situations is where change stands or falls.

Remarkably, the history of the careful study of the educational change process is quite young. It is only since the 1960s that we have come to understand how educational change works in practice. I see four phases in this evolution of the study and practice of planned educational change, which I will label adoption (1960s), implementation failure (1970–77), implementation success (1978–82), and intensification vs. restructuring (1983–90). The exact time periods are loosely represented around the margins, but the distinct themes are evident. These trends are more pronounced in the United States than in Canada, where there are similar tendencies but the lines are less sharply drawn.

The post-Sputnik crisis in the 1960s spawned the development of large-scale curriculum innovations and the advocacy of inquiry-oriented and student-centered instruction. It was a period of new math, radical revisions in chemistry and physics, open education, individualized instruction, and so forth. We have come to call this decade the *adoption* era, because people were preoccupied with how many innovations of the day were being "taken on," or adopted. Innovations, the more the better, became the mark of progress.

Around 1970, almost overnight, innovation got a bad name. The term implementation—what was happening (or not happening) in practice—came into use. Goodlad and his colleagues' *Behind the Classroom Door*, Sarason's *The Culture of the School and the Problem of Change*, Gross and associates' *Implementing Organizational Innovations*, and Smith and Keith's *Anatomy of Educational Innovation*, all published in 1970 or 1971, exposed the problem. Innovations were being adopted without anyone asking why (change for the sake of change), and no forethought was being given to follow-through. This first phase of implementation (roughly 1970–77) can be called failure because that is what people were experiencing and that is what researchers were writing about.

Up to this point, then, one could say that in the 1960s educators had been busy developing and introducing innovations, while in the first half or so of the 1970s they were busy failing at putting them into practice. The negative lessons of these first two periods were not lost, and a number of more positive though hitherto unrelated themes began to converge in the late 1970s. It would be stretching the point to characterize this period (1978–82) as universal implementation success, but compared with what preceded it, we see more and more pockets of success. Our confidence in their validity was buoyed by the fact that the evidence was coming from a variety of research and practice traditions that were compatible but were arrived at seemingly independently. Implementation research and practice, school improvement, effective schools, staff development (e.g., coaching), and leadership (e.g., the role of the principal) all more or less independently documented success stories and provided lists of key factors and processes associated with these accomplishments.

It would be nice to say that the story ended on this positive note. But something was wrong. European educators, engaged in large-scale societal reform efforts (not any more successful than our efforts in North America, but that is another story), had long claimed that Americans were too inclined to look for the quick fix and too preoccupied with ad hoc, small-scale, piecemeal innovations, instead of tackling more basic structures and more comprehensive reforms.

Apparently others agreed. The futility of attempting to implement one innovation at a time, even serious ones, was attacked with force by the National Commission on Excellence in Education in the watershed document *A Nation at Risk* (1983). Its subtitle contained the new call to arms—"The imperative for educational reform." The report was an attention getter and both galvanized and reinforced a number of major developments. The Carnegie Forum's (1986) *A Nation Prepared: Teachers for the 21st Century*, and the National Governors' Association's (1986) *A Time for Results* were two among several high-powered, nationwide mandates for the action that followed, not to mention the even more prolific omnibus reform efforts at the state level across the United States. While everyone seemed to agree that comprehensive reform was essential, the direction of change took two very different forms.

One wave of reform, which had been emerging at the state level for some time, but never with such legislative force, I have called "intensification." Increased definition of curriculum, mandated textbooks, standardized tests tightly aligned with curriculum, specification of teaching and administrative methods backed up by evaluation, and monitoring all serve to intensify as exactly as possible the what and how of teaching (see Wise, 1988; Corbett & Wilson, 1990; Firestone, Fuhrman, & Kirst, 1989b). The other wave, which lagged only slightly behind, goes by the label of "restructuring": It takes many forms, but usually involves school-based management; enhanced roles for teachers in instruction and decision making; integration of multiple innovations; restructured timetables supporting collaborative work cultures; radical reorganization of teacher education; new roles such as mentors, coaches, and other teacher leadership arrangements; and revamping and developing the shared mission and goals of the school among teachers, administrators, the community, and sometimes students (see Harvey & Crandall, 1988; Elmore, 1989; Murphy [in press]).

At least since 1986 there has been a tug-of-war of national proportions between intensification and restructuring advocates. We will see in later chapters how this battle is currently playing itself out. For our purposes here, three points stand out. First, unlike previous attempts, the new waves of reforms are comprehensive. Their intent is to bring about *systematic* change from top to bottom or vice-versa. Second, the two approaches are philosophically and politically at odds, although since politics makes strange bedfellows we can expect combinations of elements of the two approaches to be integrated in some situations (Firestone et al., 1989b). Third, because the stakes are so high, it is all the more important to pay attention to the process of change. While previous change initiatives were not as comprehensive in scope and required less energy for implementation, there has been a steady accumulation of knowledge about the change process. There is indeed a strong base of evidence available about how and why educational reform fails or succeeds.

Much of this evidence has been developed over the past decade and is dispersed in a variety of published and unpublished sources. I draw heavily on this growing body of research in order to provide a comprehensive picture to aid understanding and action by those in roles at all levels of the system. I will endeavor to show the factual basis for claims made and to provide more specific explanations for why change works as it does. However, this book is not about research in the sense of complicated statistics, jargon, and reams of information without explanation. Good research derives from practice, and I use it to depict and to help explain social reality. Kurt Lewin's well-known saying puts it best: "There is nothing so practical as good theory." Or, if you prefer, there is nothing so theoretical as good practice. Conversely, there is nothing so impractical as bad theory, or so atheoretical as bad practice.

In setting the stage for describing the ongoing relationship between theory and practice pertinent to each of the particular roles and agencies involved in educational change, the next section outlines the plan of the remaining chapters. I close the chapter with a brief discussion of "What is school reform for?"—a question that all too frequently gets lost when we are immersed in promoting or resisting given change efforts. Fighting for or against change can easily become an end in itself.

THE PLAN OF THE BOOK

I do not attempt to survey the content or substance of all the latest educational innovations and reforms. I do, however, use a wide range of specific innovations to explain the practical meaning of educational change. Included in the studies on which I draw are changes in various curriculum areas (e.g., reading, mathematics, science, social studies), microcomputers, school–work programs, cooperative learning, special education, school restructuring, teacher education, and so on. Locally initiated changes are well represented along with those sponsored at the provincial/state and national levels. The materials used derive mainly from attempts at educational reform in Canada and the United States, although several studies concerning problems of educational innovation in other countries, indicate that the basic problems and principles of educational reform are quite widespread.

The book is divided into three main parts. Part I, "Understanding Educational Change" (Chapters 1 through 6), provides a detailed overview of how educational change works. Chapter 2 addresses the issues of what the main sources and purposes of educational change are. It raises questions about who benefits from what types of changes, and about the bases on which decisions to change are made. Evidence is analyzed that leads to the conclusion that many decisions about the kinds of educational innovations introduced in school districts, are biased, poorly thought out, and unconnected to the stated purposes of education. The sources of innovation and the quality of decisions made indicate that change is not necessarily progress. Change must always be viewed in relation to the particular values, goals, and outcomes it serves. This is frequently difficult to assess in education, because rhetoric differs from reality, and consequences cannot easily be determined or measured.

Whether or not the sources of change are suspect, what does it mean to change? Chapter 3 depicts the subjective reality of coping with change, both involuntary and desired change, and makes explicit the objective reality of what we mean when we refer to something as having changed. This chapter defines what change is. Combined with Chapter 2, it suggests that not all proposed educational changes either should or could be implemented.

Chapter 4 identifies the main factors that relate to adoption or decisions to initiate change. There are a variety of reasons why individuals or groups decide to embark on a change—personal prestige, bureaucratic self-interest, political responsiveness, concern for solving an unmet need. This chapter raises questions about how and why decisions on particular educational changes are made. How these decisions are made strongly influences what will happen at the follow-up or implementation stage.

Implementation and continuation (or the extent to which change actually occurs and is sustained) is the focus of Chapter 5. Since implementation refers to what really happens in practice (as distinct from what was supposed to happen), it is a central theme that runs through all chapters. The history of implementation research is not pleasant. It shows that planned change attempts rarely succeed as intended. As some old sayings go, "There's many a slip 'twixt the cup and the lip," "the proof is in the pudding," and "the road to hell is paved with good intentions." Honorable motives are even more problematic when we attempt to get others to heaven as well as ourselves—when social rather than individual change is at stake. In fact, I will show that, ironically, in many ways the more committed an individual is to the specific form of change, the less effective he or she will be in getting others to implement it. While the above sayings have been around a long time, it is only in the last 20 years that educators have come to realize that "the proof is in the *putting*": how change is put into practice determines to a large extent how well it fares. As we shall see, some of the most recent evidence indicates that we may be getting better at planning and implementing not only specific innovations, but also more complex organizational reforms. Certainly there is greater clarity about what factors need to be addressed and how to address them.

Chapters 4 and 5 together cover the process of change: from how changes become initiated to how or whether they get put into practice and become institutionalized. What happens at one stage has powerful consequences for subsequent stages. In the final analysis, Chapter 5 provides an overview of the dynamics of how educational changes get implemented/nonimplemented and institutionalized/discontinued.

It is one thing to know the events and situations that cause change or prevent change from happening; it is an entirely different question to know what to do about it. Chapter 6 delves into the complex issues of planning and coping with educational change. Many attempts at change fail because no distinction is made between theories of change (what causes change) and theories of chang*ing* (how to influence those causes). And when solutions are attempted, they often create their own problems, which are more severe than the original ones. Fatal remedies co-exist with progress (Sieber, 1979). Understanding the causes of change in societies as complex as ours should lead us to be much more modest in our expectations of change; understanding the difficulties of changing these causes will make us downright discouraged. Nonetheless, Chapter 6 contains examples of both failure and success at planned change. At a minimum this knowledge offers certain psychological and practical advantages simply through allowing us to become more clear about the process and meaning of change and more realistic about what can be accomplished. By making explicit the problems of planning and coping with change, we gain further understanding of why certain plans fail and others succeed. I also identify some guidelines for how change can be approached or coped with more effectively.

Part I, then, provides the overall framework for thinking about and doing something about educational change. It shows, incidentally, that "rationally planned" strategies are not that rational when it comes to dealing with people and the problem of meaning. Part I does not differentiate in detail what it all means for the everyday teacher, principal, parent, and so on. This is the purpose of Part II, "Educational Change at the Local Level," which consists of six chapters (7 through 12) in which I examine what is known about the role of people in different positions at the local-school and school-district levels. In each case, I bring to bear the body of research knowledge (particularly concrete, experiential evidence) on a given role in order to address two sets of questions. The first set concerns the meaning of change for people in the role under discussion—what their experience is and their relationship to the process of educational change. Then, when we have some understanding of the meaning of change for given role incumbents, the second set of questions is directed at generating ideas for what they could or should do about it. These guidelines will range from general suggestions to specific steps to be taken, depending on the circumstances.

The six chapters in Part II are organized into these two main themes: "what is" and "what could or should be." In each chapter, I use the framework from Part I to illuminate the meaning of change and the change process in a way that explains why seemingly rational strategies for change do not work. The chapters are designed so that individuals within these roles can gain greater understanding of their place in the context of changes around them. These chapters also enable individuals in one role to gain an understanding of the realities of participants in other roles and thereby a clearer view of the sociology of educational change in the society as a whole.

Chapters 7 to 9 examine change within the school by analyzing the roles of key participants and their organizational relationships. As implementation is the essence of change, it follows that the teacher as implementer is central. Chapter 7 examines the concrete situation of the teacher and shows that change is only one among many problems the teacher faces—in fact, that the conditions for change as well as strategies employed by central policy-makers and administrators provide many more disincentives than benefits. Sociologically speaking, few of us, if placed in the current situation of teachers, would be motivated or able to engage in effective change. Obvious strategies do not seem to work. Teacher participation in curriculum development has not been effective when it comes to other teachers' use of the results. In-service training of teachers has been ineffective and wasteful more times than not. Building on earlier chapters, Chapter 7 explains why many approaches to change do not work for teachers and suggests some remedies.

More lip service than mind service has been given to the pivotal role of the principal as gatekeeper or facilitator of change. However, the research evidence is mounting, and we have much to go on in sorting out the role of school leadership. Chapter 8 describes the situation of the principal and his or her current role in facilitating or inhibiting change. As before, to understand what is, we examine specific evidence and situations. It is only through specificity that we can go beyond the generalities of leadership qualities found in much of the literature. In deriving implications for what the role of the principal could or should be, the emphasis will be on the formulation of specific guidelines that deal with the total reality faced by the principal.

People think of students as the potential beneficiaries of change. They think of achievement results, skills, attitudes, and the need for various improvements for the good of the children. They rarely think of students as *participants* in a process of change. Consequently, there is little evidence on what students think about changes and their role regarding them. It is interesting and worthwhile to attempt to develop the theme of what the role of students is and what it could be. Naturally there will be differences according to the age of students, but Chapter 9 will elaborate on the possible meaning of change for children and adolescents.

The remaining three chapters of Part II address the immediate local environment of the school—district administrators, consultants or resource people at the district level, and the parents, community, and school board. A considerable amount of evidence exists that the superintendent and other district administrators are as crucial for determining change within the district as the principal is within the school. Again it will be necessary to examine evidence that will allow us to determine in which ways this is specifically true. What is it that the district administrator does? What is the actual process of events, and what are the results? Chapter 10 analyzes the role of the district administrator as an actual and potential manager of educational change.

There are many different consultants in education, variously called curriculum coordinators or consultants, resource teachers, internal change agents, external agents, organization development specialists, disseminators, linking agents, and so on. Chapter 11 considers the role of consultants, broadly divided into two categories—those internal to the district and those external. The intricacies of being a consultant are considerable; the consultant needs to combine subject-matter knowledge, interpersonal skills in working with individuals and groups, and planned change skills for designing and implementing larger change efforts. Evidence from major studies in recent years, combined with the framework for understanding educational change, enables us to draw some conclusions about how and why some consultants are effective and others are not, and how the roles of internal and external consultants can be better conceptualized and practiced.

In Chapter 12 the roles of parents and school boards are examined. The problem of meaning is especially acute for these groups, who are vitally concerned about and responsible for educational decisions but who often have limited knowledge. Case-study materials and other research evidence will be used to clarify what communities do vis-à-vis questions of initiating, rejecting, supporting, or blocking particular changes in their schools, and will illustrate the dilemma that schools face about whether or not to involve parents in decisions about change. I will especially take up the questions of the role of the individual parent in instruction, decision making, and otherwise relating to the school and to the education of his or her child.

As Part II analyzes what happens at the local level, the four chapters in Part III return to the regional and national levels. If we are to understand the realities of change at the local level, we must discover how societal agencies, for better or worse, influence change in schools. The role of government agencies represents another dilemma for understanding educational change. On the one hand, important social reforms would not be launched without federal or state/provincial impetus. On the other hand, external reforms frequently are not successful and are seen as interfering with local autonomy. We now have enough evidence from governmental change efforts since 1960 to understand why this source of reform is necessary, why it often doesn't work, and what the implications are for altering the approach. Common principles and research findings will be used to analyze how federal and state agencies in the United States, and how provincial governments in Canada (where education is virtually the responsibility solely of the 10 provinces and the territories), function in the realm of education. Chapter 13 assesses these issues and formulates guidelines for governmental action.

In Chapters 14 and 15 the education and continuing professional development of school personnel are examined. Nothing is more central to reform than the selection and development of teachers and administrators. The initial preparation of teachers, including induction and alternative certification, is the purview of Chapter 14. Attention is currently being riveted on teacher education as a major strategy for improvement. The preservice education of teachers has not prepared them at all for the complexities of educational change. And, until recently the plight and the potential of the beginning teacher have been ignored. While reversal of these traditions is not yet in evidence, I will present considerable data to demonstrate that teacher education is finally receiving the critical attention it deserves.

Career-long professional development for teachers and administrators, which I take up in Chapter 15, has not fared much better. In-service education or ongoing staff development explicitly directed at change has failed, in most cases, because it is ad hoc, discontinuous, and unconnected to any plan for change that addresses the set of factors I have identified in earlier chapters. Factors affecting change function in interaction and must be treated as such; solutions directed at any one factor in isolation will have minimal impact. Nevertheless, if there is a premier strategy for reform it would involve the continuum of teacher and administrator selection and development, and its link to school improvement. Fortunately, some of the best and most recent research and practice is in this very area of professional preparation and in-service education. Chapters 14 and 15 analyze these developments in some detail, demonstrating that success hinges on how well these new potentialities are realized.

In the final chapter of the book (Chapter 16) I reflect on the problem of change in the context of future trends and expectations for educational change. In many ways we now know what works. Unfortunately this formulation itself is partly a theory of change rather than of changing—to know what works in some situations does not mean we can get it to work in other situations. The basis for hope, however, lies somewhere among the naivete of the 1960s, the cynicism of the 1970s, and the partial successes of the 1980s. Going beyond hope, this book will identify and point to action steps that each and every one of us can take to bring about significant improvements.

As we approach the 1990s we are in the midst of an educational reform movement the likes of which we have never before seen. This time reform efforts are more comprehensive *and* backed up by more resources and follow-through. We should find out over the course of the next decade whether our now considerable knowledge about the do's and dont's of implementing educational improvements can be put to good use. Working more effectively with the change process means not losing sight of what school reform is for—a deceptively complex question.

WHAT IS SCHOOL REFORM FOR?

What are schools supposed to do? Does educational change help do it? What are the prospects for improvement? These basic questions run through the entire book, but they deserve special emphasis from the beginning.

What Are Schools For?

What schools are supposed to do is a complicated question. However, the main espoused purposes can be identified. There are at least two major purposes to schooling: to educate students in various academic or cognitive skills and knowledge, and to educate students in the development of individual and social skills and knowledge necessary to function occupationally and sociopolitically in society (see Bowles & Gintis, 1976, Ch. 2; Sarason, 1990; Schlechty, 1990). Let us label these, respectively, the cognitive/academic and the personal/social-development purposes of education. Superimposed on these two main purposes in democratic societies is the goal of equality of opportunity and achievement—in John Dewey's (1916) phrase, "the opportunity to escape from the limitations of the social group" in which one is born (p. 20).

To assess whether schools are doing their job it would be necessary to have certain *internal* and *external* information. The former refers to how students do in terms of achievement while they are in and as they end their schooling. The latter refers to how students fare occupationally and socially once they leave school. We would want to know how family background relates to performance both internal to schools and in society after schooling has been completed.

I do not intend to answer the question of school performance very thoroughly at this stage. Much has been written about it over the past 25 years since the Coleman (1966) report. The short answer is that family background correlates strongly with educational performance and occupational achievement. There are some who claim that this is inevitable in capitalist society (Bowles & Gintis, 1976; Jencks, Smith, Ackland, Bane, Cohen, Gintis, Heyns, & Micholson, 1972). The claim is that students from more privileged family backgrounds are educationally advantaged by the time they start school and are favored even more strongly by the middle-class bias of schools as they progress through the grade levels. In any case, students from more privileged family backgrounds do perform better academically. The personal/social-development goals may be even more radically affected because they are embedded in the "hidden curriculum." According to these arguments, the hierarchical social order of the school is inimical to many of the espoused personal/social-development goals related to living and working in a democratic society (e.g., personal and group decision-making abilities). Some authors go so far as to say that even if schools were good at academic and personal development, it might not make a great deal of difference in occupational success (Jencks et al., 1972). Others claim that many educational innovations and reforms, however unwittingly, serve to reinforce the status quo and make conditions worse for teachers and students (Apple, 1988; Apple & Jungck, 1991).

Countering these gloomy prognoses is a growing body of evidence that schools can and sometimes do make a difference, at least for some educational objectives. The so-called "school effectiveness" research shows that schools in poor areas can and do (depending on their characteristics) help students make significant gains in relation to basic academic achievement (see Brookover, 1981; Lezotte et al., 1980; Edmonds, 1979). In a landmark longitudinal research study in the United Kingdom, whose findings we will report in subsequent chapters, Mortimore, Sammons, Stoll, Lewis, and Ecob (1988) proved rather conclusively that "school matters." Some schools facing similar problems and with similar resources do better in both academic and social terms. The key question of course, for those interested in educational reform (and the theme of this book), is how can we deliberately set out to improve classrooms and schools by managing change more effectively. There are still major dilemmas because of multiple and competing purposes of schooling, but it is precisely within this morass that educational reform must find its way.

What Is Reform For?

In theory, the purpose of educational change presumably is to help schools accomplish their goals more effectively by replacing some structures, programs and/or practices with better ones. Throughout the book I will be pursuing this question in terms of whether, how, and under what conditions educational change improves schools. Change for the sake of change will not help. New programs either make no difference, help improve the situation, or make it worse. The difference between change and progress,[1] can be most forcefully brought home if we ask: What if the majority of educational changes introduced in schools, actually made matters worse, however unintentionally, than if nothing had been done? (see Chapter 2). Behind this theme is also the matter of the relationship between educational and societal change. There are certainly limits to what education can do for the life chances of individuals. Educational reform is no substitute for societal reform. However, in this book we are most interested in the performance of the educational system. The question is whether it can influence, respond to, or otherwise make a contribution to societal reform. The failure of educational change may be related just as much to the fact that many innovations and reforms were never implemented in practice (i.e., real change was never accomplished) as to the fact that societal, political, and economic forces inhibit change within the educational system.

What are the prospects for making school reform more effective?

While opportunities can be squandered, we have never been in a better position to make a difference. Current reforms, as I have stated, are much more comprehensive both vertically (across classroom, school district, and state) and horizontally (incorporating more wholistic elements of reform within each level). There is more wisdom available about the change process, and more school people in leadership positions employing this wisdom. Without question, it will be a struggle as the forces of intensification and restructuring interact in determining the nature of reform that will occur. We are in an era where more is being attempted than ever before. We need powerful reforms and powerful strategies to obtain powerful change. The information presented in subsequent chapters suggests that individuals and groups at all levels of the system can accomplish major improvements if they pay attention to both the content and the process of educational change (see also Barth, 1990; Schlechty, 1990).

Through the trial and error of constantly experiencing attempts at school reform, we have learned that the process of planned educational change is much more complex than had been anticipated. As the following chapters indicate, we have also learned that implementing effective reforms is just as much a matter of good common sense as of fancy theories. We need to immerse ourselves in the fascinating world of educational change where the simplicity of common sense and the complexity of personal and political forces intermingle. Our task, as Alfred North Whitehead said about science, is "to seek the simplest explanations of complex facts [but] seek simplicity and distrust it." While we should be wary of simple explanations, our goal is to render complex phenomena understandable.

I pursue complexity but seek simplicity at both the micro and macro levels of the educational system. In understanding and in coping with educational change it is essential to find out what is happening at the classroom, school, and local levels of education as well as at the regional and national levels. Neither set of levels can be understood in isolation from the other. The process of educational change in modern society is so complex that the greatest initial need is to comprehend its dynamics. Paradoxically, the road to understanding complex social phenomena is through simple and concrete explanations, since the main criterion for *understood complexity* is the extent to which it is meaningful. A minimum of jargon is used in favor of explanations that are understandable to those participating in the educational enterprise. The chapters are written to be useful for any of the participants mentioned in the book, in their quest to make sense not only of their own immediate situations but also of the totality of educational change and how it can become more meaningful individually and collectively. But, we will not be seeking passive understanding. It is only by considering and *taking action* that deeper meaning can be achieved.

CHAPTER 2

Sources of
Educational Change

Entrepreneurs exploit innovation
–Peter Drucker (1985)

The nature of educational and social change must first be understood in terms of its sources and purposes. One does not have to be a historian to accept the fact that a number of major external and internal forces over time create pressures for change. For our purposes we do not even have to understand fully how these pressures specifically come about. At this level, it is sufficient to agree with Levin (1976) that there are three broad ways in which pressures for educational policy change may arise:

1. through natural disasters such as earthquakes, floods, famines, and the like;
2. through external forces such as imported technology and values, and immigration; and
3. through internal contradictions, such as when indigenous changes in technology lead to new social patterns and needs, or when one or more groups in a society perceive a discrepancy between educational values and outcomes affecting themselves or others in whom they have an interest.

We can take it as a given that there will always be pressures for educational change in pluralistic societies. These pressures increase as society becomes more complex.

What interests us is the more specific manifestations of why people in education decide to push for or promote particular changes. It is no denial of the possible good intentions of promoters of educational change to say that a close look at how decisions about change are made, and what decisions are made, will inspire little confidence that the majority of recommended changes are worthwhile or that the most needed changes are being proposed. In examining how and what decisions are made we should keep in mind two critical questions: who benefits from the change (the values question), and how sound or feasible are the idea and ap-

FIGURE 2.1.   Types of Implementation Outcomes of Adopted Changes

Actual implementation of the change

		YES	NO
Value and technical quality of the change	YES	I	II
	NO	III	IV

proach (the capacity for implementation question). Both are complex and difficult questions to answer.

To facilitate the discussion, Figure 2.1 presents a condensed and simplified picture of four possible outcomes. "Actual implementation" refers to whether or not there has been a real change in practice. "Value and technical quality" collapse the two factors related to who benefits and whether or not the program has been technically well developed.[1] The four possible outcomes illustrate why educational changes should be examined closely. Type I, for example, represents what we are presumably striving for: the actual implementation of a quality program that we value. Type II reflects a planning problem in that a valued, technically sound program is not being implemented for certain reasons (which Chapter 5 identifies). We do not, however, often conceive of types III and IV. In type III a change that is not technically well developed or is not valued (by whatever reference group we use) is being put into practice. In short, a bad change is being introduced. Even if a certain idea is valued because of its goal direction, it may not be sufficiently developed and tested to be practically usable. Far too many innovations, even those with laudable (valued) goals, have been rushed into practice without any clear notion and corresponding resources related to how they could be used in practice (or, more charitably, the technical requirements or means of implementation have been underestimated). Type IV, interestingly, is a form of success in that a poorly valued or poorly developed change is being rejected in practice. It is a success except for the time, energy, and frustration involved in the course of attempting to implement it (or of combating it). Many of the bandwagon changes of the 1960s have been of this type, as have many of the state-mandated, competency-based reforms of the 1980s that have attempted to "legislate learning" (Corbett & Wilson, 1990; Wise, 1979, 1988).

We make no attempt to list the content of educational innovations and reforms that abound in society today. Reforms, as I have noted in Chapter 1, seem to have gone through at least four phases since 1960—adoption, implementation failure, implementation success, and intensification vs. restructuring. There is no question that the consumer of educational change faces an infinitely more complex and confusing set of choices in 1990 than ever before. First, the changes of the 1980s and 1990s involve more complex and multilevel innovations. Second, the battle between standardization and restructuring can be bewildering as one attempts to sort out the questions of value and technical soundness. And reforms may have unintended consequences that contradict or outweigh their intended outcomes (Corbett & Wilson, 1990).

My point is not that we should expect a clearer and more rational system of innovations. The generation of innovations is after all a political and entrepreneurial process. Thus, innovations are less a source of rational ideas, and more an array of possibilities. Pluralistic societies produce many competing versions of change, which offer choices as well as impositions.

THE SOURCES OF INNOVATION

The examination of a range of different educational innovations should establish without any doubt that it is at least an open question whether the sources of educational change are to be trusted on grounds either of who benefits or of technical soundness. Two major problems stand out: the appropriateness of innovations that are introduced, and the bias of neglect vis-à-vis needed changes that are never so much as proposed.

The Appropriateness of Adopted Innovations

Gross, Giacquinta, and Bernstein (1971) and Smith and Keith (1971) have written the two classic case studies that signaled the problems of implementing educational reform even among people who seemingly desire the change. Both cases illustrate the problems just discussed. The authors concentrate on the failure to develop an adequate design for implementation—technical problems in the management of change and questions about the developmental soundness of the innovations themselves. However, it is more revealing of the assumptions of the time (the late 1960s, when change was assumed to be good) that the authors themselves treat the innovations as givens. Both "innovations" pertained to open education in elementary schools. Gross and associates studied the implementation of a new teacher role to facilitate self-motivation of children; Smith and Keith examined a new open-education elementary school. In both cases, the innovations came from broad external forces—generally influenced by the British primary open education model, fueled in the United States by university-based supporters of open education, and adopted willingly by school boards at the request of key progressive superintendents. Gross, Smith, Keith, and their colleagues never question whether the innovations concerned were appropriate for the communities that the two schools served. They simply assumed without any reflection that these "progressive innovations" were good, and that only problems of delivery interfered.

Gross and associates say nothing about the role or rights of the community other than that the school is inner city (and thereby they assume that a certain open-education role model for teachers is good for this community). Nor do Smith and Keith analyze the innovation in terms of whether it is right for the community. Furthermore, when we consider how the decisions were made and how the main promoters of the change behaved, we have every reason to believe that the changes were adopted by superintendents who were on their way up the career ladder largely as a result of their innovation record. These superintendents could have been (and probably were) convinced that the innovations in question would solve a great many problems. Intentions do not matter, however, if the quality or appropriateness of the innovation is not fully considered, or if the main sponsors of the program do not remain on the scene for more than a couple of years. One of the main consequences of introducing innovations is career advancement for the sponsor and subsequent failed implementation of the innovation (see also Carlson, 1972; Huberman & Miles, 1984).

One might say that since the soundness of many innovations is questionable, it is fortunate that there is little implementation in such cases. This is true except for the fact that a great deal of time and frustration is expended, to the longer-term detriment of the morale of school people. Their justifiable lack of enthusiasm will make it even more unlikely that any kind of changes will be adopted in the future, even worthwhile ones. Negative attitudes accumulate, as do positive ones in cases of success.

While we consider these examples of open education, I want to reiterate that I am raising two possible types of problems (which become compounded when they interact). One problem relates to whether open education is the most effective reform for particular communities in which it is introduced. The other and equally problematic issue is whether its lack of technical development and failed implementation harmed rather than helped children. It may very well be the case that open education—an innovation "adopted" across North America in the 1960s by nearly all school boards—was harmful (at least as it was implemented) to the educational interests of lower-class children.[2] For example, Sharp and Green (1975) conducted an intensive case study of a progressive primary school in England and demonstrated how the assumptions of open education worked against lower-class children. Some teachers interpreted open education to mean that since all children have potential, they should choose their own learning experiences. When some children (e.g., those from working-class backgrounds) failed to develop, their home background was blamed. The teachers faced with such problem children tended to neglect them, and certainly did not put pressure on them to achieve "because to do so would be to violate the integrity of the child" (see Whiteside, 1978, p. 28). If failure continued, in the final analysis it would be parental background that would be blamed rather than the possible inappropriateness of the new educational practices being used.

In addition to case studies of individual schools and districts, the nature of decisions at the local level has also been well researched in larger comparative studies. The best known is the study of U.S. federally sponsored educational programs carried out by Berman, McLaughlin, and associates at Rand (see Berman & McLaughlin, Vols. VII–VIII, 1977–78). They investigated 293 change projects, including 29 field studies. They found that school-district decisions to engage in particular reforms were of two types: those reflecting *opportunism*, in which districts were motivated primarily by the desire "to reap federal funds," and those characterized by *problem solving*, in which the main motivation emerged in response to locally identified needs. As might be expected, projects characterized by the latter orientation tended to be much more successful at achieving desired outcomes and at continuation after federal funds were terminated. The main point, however, is that school districts sometimes adopt innovations that are not intrinsically related to their educational needs.

> Local school officials may view the adoption of a change agent project primarily as an opportunity to garner extra, short term resources. In this instance the availability of federal funds rather than the possibility of change in educational practice motivates project adoption. Or, school managers may see change agent projects as a "low cost" way to cope with bureaucratic or political pressures. Innovation *qua* innovation often serves the purely bureaucratic objective of making the district appear up-to-date and progressive in the eyes of the community. Or a change agent project may function to mollify political pressures from groups in the community to "do something" about their special interests. Whatever the particular motivation underlying opportunistic adoption there was an absence of serious educational concerns. (Berman & McLaughlin, 1978a, p. 14)

Staff development, which as we shall see in Chapter 15, has enjoyed considerable success as a strategy for implementing instructional improvements, also evidences many instances of inappropriate practice. Pink's (1989) review of 4 staff development-based change projects identified 12 major problems that were overlooked, resulting in failed implementation. They included: district tendencies toward faddism and quick-fix solutions; too many competing demands or overload; failure to understand

and take into account differences among schools; underfunding projects or trying too much with too little.

The effective schools movement provides another widespread example of potentially useful innovations that can go wrong (Duttweiler, 1988; Fullan, 1985; Purkey & Smith, 1985; Rosenholtz, 1987). Effective schools research takes a highly complex phenomenon and represents it in a simplified manner by citing factors such as strong leadership focusing on instruction, high expectations for students, clear goals, an orderly atmosphere, frequent monitoring, parental involvement, school improvement teams, and so on. The popularity of this innovation is indicated by the number of districts adopting effective schools programs. Miles, Farrar, and Neufeld (1983) located effective schools projects operating in 25 states and covering 875 school districts. The Education Commission of the States reported in 1985 that eight states had incorporated the findings of effective schools research into school improvement policy (Purkey & Smith, 1985). While the effective schools movement differs in some important ways from other educational panaceas—emphasizing both instructional and school-wide change—it has mostly focused on narrow educational goals, and the research itself tells us almost "nothing about how an effective school got that way" and if it stayed effective (Fullan, 1985).

Not only are questions about the dependability of decisions and sources of innovation evident at the school and school-district level, but they permeate all levels. Thus, the great curriculum reform movement of the 1960s came from a combination of university professors interested in upgrading the quality of discipline-based teaching (usually representing inquiry-oriented teaching) and government sponsorship preoccupied with the importance of producing better scientists and mathematicians. One of the main sources of the impetus (or reinforcement, depending on one's viewpoint) was the launching of Sputnik, which called U.S. technological capacities into question. Sarason (1982) analyzes the experience of the new math and concludes: "There are no grounds for assuming that any aspect of the impetus for change came from teachers, parents or children. The teachers were not 'hurting' because of the existing curriculum" (p. 49).

A major review of education in 1970 draws a similar conclusion: that the reason the reform movement failed was "the fact that its prime movers were distinguished university scholars"; what was assumed to be its greatest strength turned out to be its greatest weakness (Silberman, 1970, p. 179). The specific reasons cited by Silberman are revealing because they show that well-intentioned, intelligent university authorities and "experts" on education can be dead wrong. The reforms failed because of faulty and overly abstract theories not related or relatable to practice, limited or no contact with and understanding of the school, ignorance of the lessons of experiences of the reformers in the 1920s and 1930s, and above all the failure to consider explicitly the relationship between the nature of the proposed innovations and the purposes of schools. Innovations became ends in themselves as the reformers lost sight of the supposed central questions of the purpose of change: "What is education for? What kind of human beings and what kind of society do we want to produce? What methods of instruction and classroom organization as well as what subject matter do we need to produce these results? What knowledge is of most worth?"(Silberman, 1970, p. 182).

Curriculum reform in Canada has suffered similar problems. Changes come in the form of curriculum guidelines and programs produced in each of the 10 provinces by the respective ministries of education. Although there is provincial autonomy, the guidelines are remarkably similar from province to province in their orientation: inquiry-oriented science and social studies, Canadian studies, "back to basics" via a core curriculum, etc. We can only infer where the ideas contained in the guidelines originated, but they seem to be a strange blend of public, political pressures (emphasizing core curriculum and basic skills) and the pet theories and ideas of progressive university professors and school teachers (emphasizing, e.g., inquiry-oriented learning). The latter groups were heavily influenced by the "theoretical" developments of the university-based curriculum reform efforts in the 1960s in the United States, reviewed by Silberman (1970). The results are the same—the premature adoption of programs that turn out to be questionable on the grounds of need, feasibility, or technical soundness. Studies of the implementation of language arts curriculum (Simms, 1978) and social studies (Aoki and associates, 1977; Downey and associates, 1975) in Canada contain ample documentation of the lack of clear need for and/or limitations in the technical development of new curricular policies. This conclusion was confirmed in a sweeping review of Canadian curriculum by Tomkins (1986).

Similarly, the role of the governments raises questions about the source of innovation. While at later stages I will argue that pressures for educational reform do need to come from government levels and are legitimate, there is enough evidence to show that the educational basis for decisions is often questionable. Boyd (1978) reviews Daniel Moynihan's characterization of "professionalization of reform." This is an interesting phenomenon to consider, because unlike some of the curriculum changes reviewed above, the federal reforms were directed explicitly at improving conditions for the poor and disadvantaged. Boyd quotes Moynihan in referring to the professional policy-makers' advisers as people who "tended to measure their success by the number of things they got started." "The war on poverty was not declared at the behest of the poor;

it was declared in their interest by persons confident of their own judgment in such matters" (quoted in Boyd, 1978, pp. 590–91). Boyd himself observes

> A more complete, and charitable interpretation of the professionalization of reform would acknowledge that professionals positioned in national organizations and agencies have an important responsibility to attend to, and anticipate, national needs. . . but it nevertheless is hard to deny that the generally liberal-activist ideology of these professionals, in combination with their self-interest in career advancement and the maintenance and enhancement needs of their organizations, must influence their policy recommendations. (p. 590)

House (1974, Ch. 8) also seriously questions depending on the federal government as a source of innovations. Referring to the federal "doctrine of transferability" and political turnover, House quotes Gallagher, former Director of the U.S. Bureau for Education of the Handicapped, who writes

> The credibility of the Federal government is under serious and justified attack because of its failure to follow through on programs once they have begun. In the second or third year of their efforts—their political glamour worn off—their favored place was taken in the Administration by new, bright, and shiny programs that are polished by hope and unsullied by experience. (p. 207)

As state and provincial governments have become increasingly interventionist over the past five years, the problem as well as the potential for governments as sources of innovation and reform have become more acute. Relative to "intensification" type reforms, Corbett and Wilson's (1990) study of the impact of statewide testing in Maryland and Pennsylvania is a case in point. They found that new statewide testing mandates caused action at the local level, but in ways that narrowed the curriculum and created conditions adverse to reform:

> coping with the pressure to attain satisfactory results in high-stakes tests caused educators to develop almost a "crisis mentality" in their approach, in that they jumped quickly into "solutions" to address a specific issue. They narrowed the range of instructional strategies from which they selected means to instruct their students; they narrowed the content of the material they chose to present to students; and they narrowed the range of course offerings available to students. (Corbett & Wilson, 1990, p. 207)

Corbett and Wilson also identified other unintended consequences including the diversion of attention and energy from more basic reforms in the structure and practice of schools, and reduced teacher motivation, morale, and collegial interaction necessary to bring about reform. They conclude: "when the modal response to statewide testing by professional educators is typified by practices that even the educators acknowledge are counterproductive to improving learning over the long term, then the issue is a 'policymaking problem'" (p. 321).

I am not just picking on statewide testing. Reforms in the restructuring domain like site-based management, and career ladders can also have unintended negative consequences that far outweigh their benefits (for site-based management see Lindquist & Mauriel, 1989, Levine & Eubanks, 1989 and Chapter 10; for career ladders see Bellon, Bellon, Blank, Brian & Kershaw, 1989b, Hart, 1987, Timar, 1989 and Chapter 15). The general conclusion is that one must be wary of innovation and reform, not because the intention of reformers is evil, but because the solution might be wrong, unimplementable or create adverse side-effects.

Bias by Neglect

Not only are questionable innovations promoted, but needed changes can also be systematically ignored for decades, as Sarason and Doris (1979) document in their historical analysis of the treatment of immigrants and the mentally handicapped during the past 140 years in the United States. The basis of educational reform originated with the initial purposes of the common school, which was devised "to develop the cognitive skills, and the moral and ethical character that would, according to the leading thought of the time, ensure citizens capable of participating in a complex, ever more industrialized society as productive, law abiding, and socially responsible members" (Sarason & Doris, 1979, p. 7). Immigrants and the handicapped were seen as creating problems for the system in fulfilling its main mandate. In examining the history of attempts to deal with mental retardation, Sarason and Doris note that the "same" speech about the inhumane conditions in institutions for the mentally retarded was given in 1843 and again in 1967 in the same state legislature. They comment

> The fact is that a lot of things have changed in a century, and a lot of well meaning people have devoted themselves to improving the residential care of the mentally retarded as well as other dependent or handicapped groups, but the end result was another example of the more things change, the more they remain the same. (p. 18)

The authors make similar points in their investigation of the treatment of immigrants, who were disproportionately selected as mentally retarded in need of special education through segregation. Reflecting the subtleties of the change process and the need to distinguish between change and progress, Sarason and Doris write: "No one consciously sought to create conditions that were sadistic or evil, and yet time and again the results were inhumane" (p. 18). Indeed, policy-makers were convinced that they were doing the right and proper thing. Sarason and Doris are perhaps overstating the case, because policies have changed (although it took over a hundred years) with recent legislation in both the United States and Canada. As they themselves amply describe, these policy changes represent the cumulative results of special-interest groups and responsive policy-makers. However, policy change is not practice change—but that is another matter, to be analyzed in Chapter 5.

Other examples of innovation bias by neglect can easily be cited. For example, the majority of curriculum innovations are directed at cognitive/academic goals rather than personal/social-development goals. The former are more concrete, easier to implement and measure, and probably more elitist (academic) in their consequences. Individual, interpersonal, and social attitudes and skills appropriate for a democratic society do not receive the equal attention that Dewey (1916) so clearly argued they should and that the rhetoric of formal goal statements of schools and governments implies. Even within certain goal areas that receive emphasis and are desired, there are serious problems pertaining to the bias of relative neglect. For example, the major current emphasis on basic skills (factual content, reading, mathematics, etc.) and testing raises all kinds of questions about relative neglect (Corbett & Wilson, 1990). The emphasis on basic skills and factual knowledge may be preempting the rest of the curriculum, including higher order cognitive skills (e.g., problem-solving and other thinking skills); moreover, it may be leading to the almost wholesale neglect of personal and social-development goals (see Wise, 1979, 1988; Galton, Simon, & Croll, 1980). Educational changes are adopted piecemeal without any thought as to whether the sum total of what is expected can feasibly be implemented. If it cannot, as is certainly the case, the more obvious, most easily measured, minimal objectives will be the de facto curriculum. Or, with an impossibly large number of priorities, the choice of emphasis may be based on the personal preferences and ideologies of individual teachers and administrators. Relative neglect is central to many issues: whether schools equally address the needs of female students (e.g., in science, mathematics and career education); whether secondary schools have an academic bias; whether schools provide equal programs for minority groups, and so forth.

The increased state-driven standardization and specification of tests since 1983 has produced a more pervasive bias of neglect.[3] According to Wise (1988), tests and monitoring alter the curriculum in undesirable ways.

Some effects are obvious. Testing takes time, and preparing students for testing takes even more time. And all of this time is time taken away from real
teaching.

Less obvious, however, are the distortions introduced into the curriculum by testing. Some teachers begin to emphasize the content as it will be
tested. They begin to teach in a format that will prepare students to deal with
the content as it will be tested. Some even teach items that are likely to appear
on the test. Meanwhile, the rest of the curriculum is deemphasized. (p. 330)
(See also Corbett & Wilson's 1990 study.)

Apple and Jungck's (1991) case study of the introduction of a new curriculum mandate to develop computer literacy in a particular school district
provides an "up-close" look at the consequences of increased specification
of curricula. Prepackaged textual and worksheet material, prespecified
lists of behaviorally defined competencies, pretests and posttests, record-
keeping and reporting requirements all conspired to what Apple calls the
"intensification of labor" (Apple, 1988). Getting done takes precedence
over getting the job done well, says Apple.

In highlighting the problem of meaning in educational change, the
main implication is that innovations should not be taken for granted.
What values are involved? Who will benefit from the change? How much
of a priority is it? How achievable is it? Which areas of potential change
are being neglected? All are important questions about the sources and
consequences of change.

In summary, innovations get generated through a mixture of political and educational motives. Writ large, educational reform is very much
a political process (see Sarason, 1990). I do not use the term *political* pe-
joratively, but only to recognize the process for what it is. Politically motivated change is accompanied by greater commitment of leaders, the
power of new ideas, and additional resources; but it also produces overload, unrealistic time-lines, uncoordinated demands, simplistic solutions,
misdirected efforts, inconsistencies, and underestimation of what it takes
to bring about reform. If one is on the receiving end, as nearly all of us
are, the main piece of advice is *caveat implementer*.

INNOVATIONS ARE NOT ENDS IN THEMSELVES

It may seem to the reader that I set out in this chapter to destroy the
credibility of educational change. This is not true. There are some excellent innovations available, depending on the specific need and on the
approach taken in deciding whether and how to use them. And many of
the innovations represent important steps along the way to more successful change. In subsequent chapters I will describe examples of successful

change and conclude that we have come to know a great deal more about what makes for success. I have attempted here, however, to put the sources of change in perspective by suggesting that innovations are not neutral in their benefits and that there are many reasons other than educational merit that influence decisions to change. A closer examination reveals that innovations can be adopted for symbolic political or personal reasons: to appease community pressure, to appear innovative, to gain more resources. All of these forms represent *symbolic* rather than *real* change. The incentive system of public schools with abstract and unclear goals, lack of performance scrutiny, and a noncompetitive market makes it more profitable politically and bureaucratically to "innovate" without risking the costs of real change. "For the schools' purposes, verbal adoption of innovations may be entirely sufficient" (Pincus, 1974, p. 125). Further, the purported neutrality of technical experts obscures

> the fact that innovations are still means by which some people organize and control the lives of other people and their children according to their conceptions as to what is preferable. It disguises the reality that some people helped to plan the changes, that some people benefited from them while others did not, and that some consequences were intended while others were not. (Whiteside, 1978, p. 20)

Even good ideas may represent poor investments on a large scale if the ideas have not been well developed or if the resources to support implementation are unavailable.

There are two major lessons contained in this chapter. First, it has served to highlight the problem of meaning in educational change. The worth of particular policies or innovations cannot be taken for granted, because we cannot be sure about the purposes, possibilities of implementation, or actual outcomes of proposed changes. We should neither accept nor reject all changes uncritically. Nisbet (1980) claims that the "metaphor" of growth and progress in Western thought has seduced us into falsely assuming that change is development. He shows that actual historical events and processes do not sustain the notion of the linearity and inevitability of progress. The corrective is not a counter-metaphor of decay. Rather, the nature of educational changes should be examined according to the specific values, goals, events, and consequences that obtain in concrete situations. Educational innovations are not ends in themselves. We should strive to find meaning in assessing specific innovations and be suspicious of those that do not make sense—a task made no easier but all the more necessary by the fact that the goals of education in contemporary society and the best means of achieving them are simply not that clear or agreed upon. The good news is that there is a vast array of innovations in the environment to draw upon in forging meaning.

The second implication is more subtle. We are beginning to get a sense that the challenge of reform is not simply to master the implementation of single innovations. Like Cuban (1988b) we might ask the question: "How can it be that so much school reform has taken place over the last century yet schooling appears pretty much the same as it's always been?" (see also Sarason, 1990). His categorization of innovations into first- and second-order changes offers some further insights into why some changes have been more successful than others. *First-order changes* are those that improve the efficiency and effectiveness of what is currently done, "without disturbing the basic organizational features, without substantially altering the way that children and adults perform their roles" (p. 342). *Second-order changes* seek to alter the fundamental ways in which organizations are put together, including new goals, structures, and roles (e.g., collaborative work cultures). Most changes since the turn of the century have been first-order changes, aimed to improve the quality of what already existed. Second-order reforms largely failed.

> Most reforms foundered on the rocks of flawed implementation. Many were diverted by the quiet but persistent resistance of teachers and administrators who, unconvinced by the unvarnished cheer of reformers, saw minimal gain and much loss in embracing second-order changes boosted by those who were unfamiliar with the classroom as a workplace. Thus first-order changes succeeded while second-order changes were either adapted to fit what existed or sloughed off, allowing the system to remain essentially untouched. The ingredients change, the Chinese saying goes, but the soup remains the same. (Cuban, 1988b, p. 343)

The challenge of the 1990s will be to deal with more second-order changes—changes that affect the culture and structure of schools, restructuring roles and reorganizing responsibilities, including those of students and parents. In the past we have often worked on the notion that if we just "fix it" and if all perform their roles better, we will have improved education.

We have our work cut out for us. In the meantime we may very well take solace in the fact that proposed educational changes that we do not desire will probably not get adequately implemented anyway. But this also means that educational reforms we value do not stand much of a chance either.

CHAPTER 3

The Meaning of
Educational Change

*If there is no meaning in it, that saves a world of trouble, you know, as
we needn't try to find any.*

–King of Hearts in *Alice in Wonderland,* after
reading the nonsensical poem of the White Rabbit

We have become so accustomed to the presence of change that we rarely
stop to think what change really means as we are experiencing it at the
personal level. More important, we almost never stop to think what it
means for others around us who might be in change situations. The crux
of change is how individuals come to grips with this reality. We vastly
underestimate both what change is (the topic of this chapter) and the
factors and processes that account for it (discussed in Chapters 4 and 5).
In answering the former question, let us put aside for the moment the
problem of the reliability of the sources and the purpose of change
(Chapter 2) and treat change for what it is—a fact of life. The clarification
process that I propose to follow has four parts. The first task is to consider the more general problem of the meaning of individual change in
society at large, not as confined to education. Second, I elaborate on the
subjective meaning of change for individuals. Third, I organize these ideas
more comprehensively to arrive at a description of the *objective* meaning
of change, which more formally attempts to make sense of the components of educational change. The test of the validity of this objective description will indeed be whether it orders and makes sense of the confusion and complexity of educators' subjective realities. Last, I elaborate on
the implications of subjective and objective realities for understanding
educational change.

THE GENERAL PROBLEM OF THE MEANING OF CHANGE

The titles of some of the more general accounts of individual change
and reality in modern society provide us with as succinct an introduction

to the problem as any—*Loss and Change* (Marris, 1975), *Beyond the Stable State* (Schön, 1971), *The Social Construction of Reality* (Berger & Luckmann, 1967), *The Micro Millennium* (Evans, 1979), *Future Shock* (Toffler, 1970), *The Third Wave* (Toffler, 1980), *Thriving on Chaos* (Peters, 1987), *Riding the Waves of Change* (Morgan, 1989).

While there is a difference between voluntary and imposed change, Marris (1975) makes the case that *all* real change involves loss, anxiety, and struggle. Failure to recognize this phenomenon as natural and inevitable has meant that we tend to ignore important aspects of change and misinterpret others. As Marris states early in his book, "Once the anxieties of loss were understood, both the tenacity of conservatism and the ambivalence of transitional institutions became clearer" (p. 2).

According to Marris, "Whether the change is sought or resisted, and happens by chance or design; whether we look at it from the standpoint of reformers or those they manipulate, of individuals or institutions, the response is characteristically ambivalent" (p. 7). New experiences are always initially reacted to in the context of some "familiar, reliable construction of reality" in which people must be able to attach personal meaning to the experiences regardless of how meaningful they might be to others. Marris does not see this "conservative impulse" as incompatible with growth: "It seeks to consolidate skills and attachments, whose secure possession provides the assurance to master something new" (p. 22).

Change may come about either because it is imposed on us (by natural events or deliberate reform) or because we voluntarily participate in or even initiate change when we find dissatisfaction, inconsistency, or intolerability in our current situation. In either case, the meaning of change will rarely be clear at the outset, and ambivalence will pervade the transition. Any innovation "cannot be assimilated unless its *meaning* is shared" (Marris, 1975, p. 121, my emphasis).

I quote at some length a passage from Marris (1975) that is most revealing and fundamental to our theme.

> No one can resolve the crisis of reintegration on behalf of another. Every attempt to pre-empt conflict, argument, protest by rational planning, can only be abortive: however reasonable the proposed changes, the process of implementing them must still allow the impulse of rejection to play itself out. When those who have power to manipulate changes act as if they have only to explain, and when their explanations are not at once accepted, shrug off opposition as ignorance or prejudice, they express a profound contempt for the meaning of lives other than their own. For the reformers have already assimilated these changes to their purposes, and worked out a reformulation which makes sense to them, perhaps through months or years of analysis and debate. If they deny others the chance to do the same, they treat them as puppets dangling by the threads of their own conceptions. (p. 166)

Schön (1971) has developed essentially the same theme. All real change involves "passing through the zones of uncertainty . . . the situation of being at sea, of being lost, of confronting more information than you can handle" (p. 12). "Dynamic conservatism" in both Marris' and Schön's formulation is not simply an individual but a social phenomenon. Individuals (e.g., teachers) are members of social systems (e.g., schools) that have shared senses of meaning.

> Dynamic conservatism is by no means always attributable to the stupidity of individuals within social systems, although their stupidity is frequently invoked by those seeking to introduce change. . . . The power of social systems over individuals becomes understandable, I think, only if we see that social systems provide . . . a framework of theory, values and related technology which enables individuals to make sense of their lives. Threats to the social system threaten this framework. (Marris, 1975, p. 51)

The implications of the principles and ideas described by Marris and others are profound in relation to our understanding of educational change in two senses—one concerning the meaning of change, and the other regarding the process of change. In the rest of this chapter, I will begin to apply these principles to specific examples of the meaning of educational change by introducing concepts pertaining to different dimensions and degrees of change. In Chapters 4 through 6 the implications for the management of change will be documented in an examination of a large body of evidence on the causes and processes of change.

Real change, then, whether desired or not, represents a serious personal and collective experience characterized by ambivalence and uncertainty; and if the change works out it can result in a sense of mastery, accomplishment, and professional growth. The anxieties of uncertainty and the joys of mastery are central to the subjective meaning of educational change, and to success or failure—facts that have not been recognized or appreciated in most attempts at reform.

THE SUBJECTIVE MEANING OF EDUCATIONAL CHANGE

The details of the multiple phenomenologies of the different role incumbents in the educational enterprise will be taken up in each of the relevant chapters in Parts II and III. In this section, my purpose is to establish the importance and meaning of the subjective reality of change.[1] For illustration I will use examples taken from the world of the teacher, but the reader should refer to Chapter 7 for a more complete treatment of the teacher's situation, and to other chapters for the various relevant realities of other participants.

The daily subjective reality of teachers is very well described by House and Lapan (1978), Huberman (1983), Jackson (1968), Lortie

(1975), and Rosenholtz (1989). The picture is one of limited development of technical culture: Teachers are uncertain about how to influence students, especially about noncognitive goals, and even about whether they are having an influence; they experience students as individuals in specific circumstances who, taken as a classroom of individuals, are being influenced by multiple and differing forces for which generalizations are not possible; teaching decisions are often made on pragmatic trial-and-error grounds with little chance for reflection or thinking through the rationale; teachers must deal with constant daily disruptions, within the classroom in managing discipline and interpersonal conflicts, and from outside the classroom in collecting money for school events, making announcements, dealing with the principal, parents, central office staff, etc.; they must get through the daily grind; the rewards are having a few good days, covering the curriculum, getting a lesson across, having an impact on one or two individual students (success stories); they constantly feel the critical shortage of time.

Huberman, based on his own investigations and reviews of other research, summarizes the "classroom press" that exerts daily influences on teachers.

- the press for *immediacy and concreteness*: Teachers engage in an estimated 200,000 interchanges a year, most of them spontaneous and requiring action.
- the press for *multidimensionality and simultaneity*: Teachers must carry on a range of operations simultaneously, providing materials, interacting with one pupil and monitoring the others, assessing progress, attending to needs and behavior.
- the press for *adapting to everchanging conditions or unpredictability*: Anything can happen. Schools are reactive partly because they must deal with unstable input—classes have different "personalities" from year to year; a well-planned lesson may fall flat; what works with one child is ineffective for another; what works one day may not work the next.
- the press for *personal involvement with students*: Teachers discover that they need to develop and maintain personal relationships and that for most students meaningful interaction is a precursor to academic learning (Huberman, 1983, pp. 482–83; see also Crandall et al., 1982).

This "classroom press," according to Huberman and to Crandall and associates, affects teachers in a number of different ways: It draws their *focus to day-to-day effects* or a short-term perspective; it *isolates them from other adults*, especially meaningful interaction with colleagues; it *exhausts their energy*—"at the end of the week, they are tired; at the end of the year, they are exhausted" (Crandall et al., 1982, p. 29); it *limits their opportunities for sustained reflection* about what they do—"teachers tend to function intuitively and rarely spend time reasoning about how they carry out their jobs" (Crandall et al., 1982, p. 29). Further, it tends to increase the dependence of teachers on the experiential knowledge necessary for day-to-day coping, to the exclusion of sources of knowledge beyond their own classroom experience.

The concerns expressed by Huberman and by Crandall and associates about teacher isolation and its negative effect on response to change are echoed by Rosenholtz (1989) in her study of the teacher's workplace. Rosenholtz studied 78 schools in 8 districts in the state of Tennessee. She classified the schools as "stuck," "in-between," or "moving." Rosenholtz describes teachers' subjective construction of reality as part and parcel of their everyday activities. Her study indicates that schools in which teachers have a shared consensus about the goals and organization of their work are more likely to incorporate new ideas directed to student learning. In contrast, teachers that worked in "low-consensus schools" more commonly "skirted the edge of catastrophe alone," learning the lesson that they must shoulder classroom burdens by themselves, not imposing on one another. Within this there is little room for other than individual interpretations of change or anything else. In Rosenholtz' study "shared meaning" among teachers and others characterized those schools that were continually improving.

Enter "the hyperrationalization of change" (Wise, 1977, 1988), and the possibilities for achieving meaning become nearly impossible. The rational assumptions, abstraction, and descriptions of a proposed new curriculum do not make sense in the capricious world of the teacher: "Many proposals for change strike them as frivolous—they do not address issues of boundedness, psychic rewards, time scheduling, student disruption, interpersonal support, and so forth" (Lortie, 1975, p. 235).

In short, there is no reason for the teacher to believe in the change, and few incentives (and large costs) to find out whether a given change will turn out to be worthwhile. As House (1974) explains,

> The personal costs of trying new innovations are often high . . . and seldom is there any indication that innovations are worth the investment. Innovations are acts of faith. They require that one believe that they will ultimately bear fruit and be worth the personal investment, often without the hope of an immediate return. Costs are also high. The amount of energy and time required to learn the new skills or roles associated with the new innovation is a useful index to the magnitude of resistance. (p. 73)

Predictably, "rational" solutions to the above problems have backfired because they ignore the culture of the school (Sarason, 1982). Two of the most popular, but in themselves superficial, solutions consist of the use of general goals (on the assumption that teachers should specify the change according to their own situation) and of voluntary populations (on the assumption that people who choose to participate will implement the change). The result has been two forms of nonchange: *false clarity* without change and *painful unclarity* without change. As to the former, Goodlad, Klein, and associates (1970) comment on the presence of specific educational reforms (e.g., team teaching, individualization) in 158 classrooms that they examined across the United States. They found

> A very subjective but nonetheless general impression of those who gathered and those who studied the data was that some of the highly recommended and publicized innovations of the past decade or so were dimly conceived, and, at best, partially implemented in the schools claiming them. The novel features seemed to be blunted in the effort to twist the innovation into familiar conceptual frames or established patterns of schooling. For example, team teaching more often than not was some form of departmentalization. . . . Similarly, the new content of curriculum projects tended to be conveyed into the baggage of traditional methodology. . . . [Principals and teachers] claimed individualization of instruction, use of a wide range of instructional materials, a sense of purpose, group processes, and inductive or discovery methods when our records showed little or no evidence of them. (pp. 72–73)

Other studies of attempted change show that not all teachers experience even the comfort of false clarity. Gross and associates (1971), Charters and Pellegrin (1973), and Huberman and Miles (1984) all found that abstract goals combined with a mandate for teachers to operationalize them resulted in confusion, frustration, anxiety, and abandonment of the effort.

Thus, false clarity occurs when people *think* that they have changed but have only assimilated the superficial trappings of the new practice. Painful unclarity is experienced when unclear innovations are attempted under conditions that do not support the development of the subjective meaning of the change. Loucks and Hall's (1979) research clearly shows that the assumptions of introducers of change are out of whack with the "stages of concerns" of teachers. At initial stages, teachers are often more concerned about how the change will affect them personally, in terms of their in-classroom and extra-classroom work, than about a description of the goals and supposed benefits of the program. In brief, change is usually not introduced in a way that takes into account the subjective reality of teachers.

Essential to the discussion in this section are three themes. *First*, the typical situation of teachers is one of fixity and a welter of forces keeping things that way. As Lortie (1975) states, "The teacher ethos is conservative, individualistic, and focused on the present" (p. 212). *Second*, there is little room, so to speak, for change. When change is imposed from outside, it is bitterly resented. Cooper (1988, p. 45) reminds us that it is important that we recognize that "outside looking in" is different from "inside looking out." Even when voluntarily engaged in, change is threatening and confusing. *Third*, there is a strong tendency for people to adjust to the "near occasion" of change, by changing as little as possible—either assimilating or abandoning changes that they were initially willing to try, or fighting or ignoring imposed change. Marris (1975, p. 16) gives a good description of the fundamental meaning of the threat of change.

> Occupational identity represents the accumulated wisdom of how to handle the job, derived from their own experience and the experience of all who have had the job before or share it with them. Change threatens to invalidate this experience robbing them of the skills they have learned and confusing their purposes, upsetting the subtle rationalizations and compensations by which they reconciled the different aspects of their situation.

The extent to which proposals for change are defined according to only one person's or one group's reality (e.g., the policy-maker's or administrator's) is the extent to which they will encounter problems in implementation.[2] This is not to say that subjective realities *should* define what is to change, but only that they are powerful constraints to change or protections against undesirable or thoughtless change (depending on your viewpoint and the particular change). Ultimately the transformation of subjective realities is the essence of change.

Defining the objective reality of innovations will move us one step closer to an understanding of the nature of educational change, which in my view is an essential precondition for formulating our own subjective response to the question of when change is progress.

THE OBJECTIVE REALITY OF EDUCATIONAL CHANGE

People do not understand the nature or ramifications of most educational changes. They become involved in change voluntarily or involuntarily and in either case experience ambivalence about its meaning, form, or consequences. I have implied that there are a number of things at stake—changes in goals, skills, philosophy or beliefs, behavior, etc. Subjectively these different aspects are experienced in a diffuse, incoherent manner. Change often is not conceived of as being *multidimensional*. Objectively, it is possible to clarify the meaning of an educational change by identifying and describing its main separate dimensions. Ignorance of these dimensions explains a number of interesting phenomena in the field of educational change: for example, why some people accept an innovation they do not understand; why some aspects of a change are implemented and others not; and why strategies for change neglect certain essential components.

The concept of objective reality is tricky (see Berger & Luckmann, 1967). Reality is always defined by individuals and groups. But individuals and groups interact to produce social phenomena (constitutions, laws, policies, educational change programs), which exist outside any given individual. There is also the danger that the objective reality is only the reflection of the producers of change and thus simply a glorified version of *their* subjective conceptions. As Berger and Luckmann (1967) put it, we can minimize this problem by following the practice of posing double questions: "What is the existing conception of reality on a given issue?" Followed quickly by "Says who?" (p. 116). With this caution in mind, I would now like to turn to the possibility of defining educational change.

What Is Change in Practice?

The implementation of educational change involves "change in practice." But what exactly does this mean? Although change in practice can occur at many levels—the teacher, the school, the school district, etc.—I will use as an illustration the classroom or teacher level because this level is closest to instruction and learning. When we ask which aspects of current practice would be altered, if given educational changes were to be implemented, the complexity of defining and accomplishing actual change begins to surface. The difficulty is that educational change is not a single entity even if we keep the analysis at the simplest level of an innovation in a classroom. Innovation is *multidimensional*. There are at least three components or dimensions at stake in implementing any new program or policy: (1) the possible use of new or revised *materials* (direct instructional resources such as curriculum materials or technologies), (2) the possible use of new *teaching approaches* (i.e., new teaching strategies or activities), and (3) the possible alteration of *beliefs* (e.g., pedagogical assumptions and theories underlying particular new policies or programs).[3]

All three aspects of change are necessary because together they represent the means of achieving a particular educational goal or set of goals. Whether or not they do achieve the goal is another question depending on the quality and appropriateness of the change for the task at hand. My point is the logical one that the change has to *occur in practice* along the three dimensions in order for it to have a chance of affecting the outcome. As Charters and Jones (1973) observe, if we do not pay careful attention to whether change in practice has actually occurred, we run "the risk of appraising non-events."

It is clear that any individual may implement none, one, two, or all three dimensions. A teacher could use new curriculum materials or technologies without altering the teaching approach. Or a teacher could use the materials and alter some teaching behaviors without coming to grips with the conceptions or beliefs underlying the change.

Before we turn to some illustrations of the dimensions, three diffi-culties should be noted. First, in identifying the three aspects of change, there is no assumption about who develops the materials, defines the teaching approaches, and decides on the beliefs. Whether these are done by an external curriculum developer or a group of teachers is an open question (see Chapters 4 and 5). Second, and partly related, there is a dilemma and tension running through the educational change literature in which two different emphases or perspectives are evident: the fidelity perspective and the mutual-adaptation or evolutionary perspective. The fidelity approach to change, as the label indicates, is based on the assump-tion that an already developed innovation exists and the task is to get individuals and groups of individuals to implement it faithfully in prac-tice—that is, to use it as it is "supposed to be used" as intended by the developer. The mutual-adaptation or evolutionary perspective stresses that change often is (and should be) a result of adaptations and decisions made by users as they work with particular new policies or programs, with the policy or program and the user's situation mutually determining the outcome.[4] Third, we can see that it is very difficult to define once and for all exactly what the objective dimensions of change are with respect to materials, teaching approach, and beliefs, because they may get trans-formed, further developed, or otherwise altered during implementation (this indeed is the essence of the evolutionary perspective). Nonetheless, there is value in conceptualizing change (in order to define it over time) in terms of the three dimensions. Some examples illustrate this point.

In considering examples, it should be recognized that individual in-novations or programs vary in terms of whether they entail significant change on the three dimensions in relation to the current practices of particular groups of individuals; but I suggest that the majority of edu-cational innovations extant in the field involve substantial changes with regard to these criteria. In fact, innovations that do not include changes on these dimensions are probably not significant changes at all. For ex-ample, the use of a new textbook or materials without any alteration in teaching strategies is a minor change at best—an example of "the more things change the more they remain the same" (Sarason, 1982). Put in terms of the theme of this book, real change involves changes in concep-tions and role behavior, which is why it is so difficult to achieve.

Numerous examples could be used to illustrate the objective reality of the dimensions of change. I will draw on three studies—one on a province-wide curriculum for language arts, one on open education, and one on mainstreaming. Considering these innovations in the light of the dimensions puts us in a better position to argue the desirability of the content of change because we can argue concretely.

Simms (1978) conducted a detailed study in one of the provinces in Canada on the use of an elementary language arts program. A few of the main objectives of the program are stated as follows:

- developing students' competencies in receiving information (critically) through listening, reading, viewing, touching, tasting, smelling;
- understanding the communication process as well as their role as receivers, processors or expressers in that process. (quoted in Simms, 1978, p. 96)

The three dimensions of potential change can be illustrated by reference to the basic document. For example, implications for pedagogical *beliefs* are contained in the following passage:

The basic focus is on the child as a flexible user of language. If language is to be truly useful (functional) we must begin with the present experience and competence of the child and fit our teaching into the natural language situation, which is an integrated, whole situation. It should be emphasized that the developing philosophy is one of total integration of all aspects of language arts. In this sense, integration refers to the treatment of all the communication skills as closely interrelated. (Simms, 1978, pp. 90–91)

References to possible alterations in *teaching approaches* are stated throughout the document. Recommended teaching methodologies include providing opportunities for active involvement of the child, using a variety of resources and techniques (viewing, reading, speaking, informal drama, mime, photography, etc.), and using "the inductive method . . . frequently in small groups and individual teaching situations" (pp. 366–77). We need not describe the content of *curriculum materials and resources*—the third dimension—but the difficulties of clarifying and accomplishing changes in practice involving the interrelationship of beliefs, teaching approaches, and resources should be clear.

By employing the distinction between surface curriculum and deep structure in analyzing open education, Bussis, Chittenden, and Amarel (1976) have played right into our theme. They found that open-education teachers differed fundamentally in their use of open-education dimensions. Some teachers operated at the level of surface curriculum, focusing on materials and seeing that students were "busy." They tried to address open-education goals *literally*, but they did not comprehend the underlying purpose. For example, they wanted to ensure that children were "learning to share materials, to take turns, to respect the property of others, and so on—with the focus of concern being the manifestation of these behaviors rather than concomitant attitudes and understanding" (Bussis et al., 1976, p. 59). It was these teachers who reacted to the problem of ambiguity by requesting further guidance on "what exactly has to be covered." Other teachers had developed a basic understanding of the principles of open education and concrete activities that reflected them. They were "able to move back and forth between classroom activities and organizing priorities, using a specific encounter to illustrate a broader concern and relating broader priorities back to specific instances" (p. 61). Reflectivity, purposefulness, and awareness characterized these teachers, but not in a linear way; for example, they would do something out of intuition and then reflect on its meaning in relation to overall purpose. Assumptions about and orientations to children varied similarly. Teachers ranged from those who felt that children's ability to choose was unreliable and idiosyncratic (some could, others couldn't) to those who assumed and experienced that *all* children have interests and who were able to relate individualized interests to common educational goals across the curriculum (pp. 95–98).

In the pages of quotes from teachers and in their own analysis, Bussis and associates clearly demonstrate (although not using the same words) the nature of the dimensions of change at work. Some examples: teachers who saw open education as literally covering subject content but who had no underlying rationale (p. 57); those "who were reasonably articulate in indicating priorities for children [but] were more vague in describing concrete connections between these priorities and classroom activities" (p. 69); still others who "may provide the classroom with rich materials *on the faith* that they will promote certain learning priorities" (p. 74, their emphasis).

In the words of our dimensions, it is possible to change "on the surface" by endorsing certain goals, using specific materials, and even imitating the behavior *without specifically understanding* the principles and rationale of the change. Moreover, with reference to beliefs, it is possible to value and even be articulate about the goals of the change without understanding their implications for practice: ". . . action based on valuing and faith is not very likely to lead to an enlargement or strengthening of the teacher's own understanding. The potential informational support available in feedback to the teacher is not received because it is not recognized" (Bussis et al., 1976, p. 74).

Joyce and Showers (1988) make the same point: Innovation is multidimensional, involving changes in skills, practice, and theory or conceptions. Joyce and Showers found that few staff development programs get beyond short-term superficial manifestations of the changes they are addressing.

In summary, for our purposes there are three critical lessons to be learned. First, change is multidimensional and can vary accordingly within the same person as well as within groups. Second, there are some deep changes at stake, once we realize that people's basic conceptions of education and skills are involved—that is, their occupational identity, their sense of competence, and their self-concept. The need and difficulty for individuals to develop a sense of meaning about change is manifest. Third, compounding the second lesson is the fact that change consists of a sophisticated and none-too-clear *dynamic interrelationship* of the three dimensions of change. Beliefs guide and are informed by teaching strategies and activities; the effective use of materials depends on their articulation with beliefs and teaching approaches and so on. Many innovations entail changes in some aspects of educational beliefs, teaching behavior, use of materials, and more. Whether or not people develop meaning in relation to all three aspects is fundamentally the problem.

Special education legislation and policies in Canada and the United States emphasize every child's right to a full education. The practice known as mainstreaming provides another example of the misunderstood complexities and multiple components of change (see Sarason & Doris, 1979, for a detailed account). Sarason and Doris recognize the problem in the first lines of their chapter on mainstreaming.

> The speed with which mainstreaming as a concept, value and public policy has emerged in our society is little short of amazing. Indeed, the change has come about so fast and with such apparent general approbation as to raise a question about what people understand about mainstreaming and its implications for schools. . . . Because we may think mainstreaming is desirable is no excuse for assuming that institutional realities will accommodate our hopes. (p. 355)

It is not necessary to give a complete litany of the dimensional implications of mainstreaming for schools, but some of the philosophical, role-change, and materials consequences both inside and outside the classroom are evident in the following excerpts from Sarason and Doris:

> For effective mainstreaming, regular classroom teachers must have the strong and coordinated backing of special education teachers and support personnel. (Ryor, quoted in Sarason & Doris, p. 372)
> The law mandates the involvement of parents and lay groups in "overseeing, evaluating, and operating special education programs" through regional and state advisory committees, a majority of whose members are parents of handicapped children. (p. 376)
> Success requires "integrated diagnosis, prescription, and follow through" with "an individual education prescription for each handicapped child," and "to be done well this not only requires time but harmonious relationships among school personnel." (p. 389)

Mainstreaming is one of the more complex changes on the current educational scene, and as such it highlights the dimensions of change and the magnitude of the task in bringing about major educational reform—valuing new beliefs; cognitively understanding the interrelationship between the philosophical principles and concrete diagnosis and treatment; changing the roles and role relationships between regular classroom teachers and special education teachers, and between school personnel and community members and professionals outside the school.

We could take other educational changes to illustrate the significance of the different dimensions of change. Virtually every program change states or implies all three aspects, whether we refer to language arts, social studies, school-work programs, microcomputers, Head Start or Follow Through programs, special education, restructuring and so on. Working on the meaning and definition of change is all the more important these days because more complex and frequently more vague reforms (like restructuring) are being attempted. More is at stake. The point is that educational change programs have an objective reality that may be more or less definable in terms of what beliefs, teaching practices, and resources they encompass.

Why worry about all three aspects of change? Why not be content to develop quality innovations and provide access to them? The answer is simply that such an approach does not adequately recognize how individuals come to confront or avoid behavioral and conceptual implications of change. The innovation as a set of materials and resources is the most visible aspect of change, and the easiest to employ, but only literally. Change in teaching approach or style in using new materials presents greater difficulty if new skills must be acquired and new ways of conducting instructional activities established. Changes in beliefs are even more difficult: they challenge the core values held by individuals regarding the purposes of education; moreover, beliefs are often not explicit, discussed, or understood, but rather are buried at the level of unstated assumptions. And the development of a clear belief system is essential because it provides a set of criteria for overall planning and a screen for sifting valuable from not-so-valuable learning opportunities that inevitably arise during instruction (recall Bussis et al., 1976). The ultimate question, of course, is how essential are all three dimensions of change. The use of new materials by themselves may accomplish certain educational objectives, but it seems obvious that developing new teaching skills and approaches and understanding conceptually what and why something should be done, and to what end, represents much more fundamental change, and as such will take longer to achieve but will have a greater impact once accomplished. I will leave the whole matter of strategies of change until later chapters. How best to deal with conceptions (e.g., beliefs) and behavior (e.g., teaching approaches) is complicated, but some of the implications include the need for addressing them on a *continuous* basis during implementation and the possibility that beliefs can be most effectively discussed *after* people have had at least some behavioral experience in attempting new practices (see Chapter 5).

Specific educational programs and policies differ in how great a change is at stake. The extent of change must always be defined with reference to concrete situations and individuals, because the degree of potential change is a function of the discrepancy between the state of existing practice on the part of particular individuals and the future state where a change might take them. The large-scale Study of Dissemination Efforts Supporting School Improvement (DESSI) demonstrates the critical importance of defining the extent of change in terms of individuals' starting points (Crandall et al., 1982). This study found that teachers, under the right supportive conditions, used new materials and altered teaching practices consistent with innovations adopted by their schools or districts.

In summary, the purpose of acknowledging the objective reality of change lies in the recognition that there are new policies and programs "out there" and that they may be more or less specific in terms of what they imply for changes in materials, teaching practices, and beliefs. The real crunch comes in the relationships between these new programs or policies and the thousands of subjective realities embedded in people's individual and organizational contexts and their personal histories. How these subjective realities are addressed or ignored is crucial for whether potential changes become meaningful at the level of individual use and effectiveness. It is perhaps worth repeating that changes in actual practice along the three dimensions—in materials, teaching approaches, and beliefs, in what *people do and think*—are essential if the intended outcome is to be achieved.

IMPLICATIONS OF THE SUBJECTIVE AND OBJECTIVE REALITIES

As we integrate the ideas of this chapter and Chapter 2, there are six major observations to be made concerning

1. the soundness of proposed changes;
2. understanding the failure of well-intentioned change;
3. guidelines for understanding the nature and feasibility of particular changes;
4. the realities of the status quo;
5. the deepness of change; and
6. the question of valuing.

First, as we have seen in Chapter 2, not all change proposals are "authentic." There may be a variety of reasons why change decisions are made, not all of which represent sustained commitments. Moreover, if the subjective and objective implications of implementing real change are as profound as I have suggested, there is no way that even a fraction of the changes coming down the pike could be implemented. All new programs could not possibly be fully implemented and developed to the point that they become meaningful. And if they were, it might be discovered that some were unsound, meaningless ideas in the first place. As the King of Hearts says (cited at the beginning of this chapter), we needn't try to find any meaning if there is no meaning in it—good advice for maintaining sanity when change seems senseless. Change strategies or strange chatter-ies? Sometimes it is difficult to discern the difference.

Second, another version of the inauthenticity of change relates to new programs or policies that are very sincerely hoped for, and adopted naively, with their adopters not realizing—perhaps never realizing—the implications. This phenomenon accounts for the false clarity in Goodlad, Klein, and associates' (1970) findings that teachers *thought* they were using a new approach but actually were not. It also accounts for Sarason and Doris' (1979) observation about mainstreaming where a large number of people endorse an innovation because of value agreement without real-izing what specific changes might be involved. Watzlawick, Weakland and Fisch (1974, p. 79) quote Laing, "If I don't know I don't know, I think I know." Knowing the subjective and objective dimensions of change helps us to understand these occurrences.

Third, the objective dimensions can be and have been used to analyze given changes in order to understand what they are and how feasible and desirable they might be (see Crandall et al., 1982; Hall & Hord, 1987; Leithwood, 1981). For example, we might examine a particular curricu-lum change or direction and discover that (a) the goals are specific and clear, but the means of implementation are vague, or (b) the beliefs and goals are abstract, vague, and unconnected with other dimensions (e.g., teaching strategies), or (c) the number of changes implied (e.g., the num-ber of different teaching activities) is overwhelming or the changes, when taken together, are incoherent. Such an analysis could lead to any one of a number of conclusions—the proposed change is hopelessly incoherent; the proposed change is *too* coherent (i.e., too prescriptive); the change has possibilities but needs further development and/or resources during implementation, and if they are not available further work is unfeasible.

Fourth, the status quo is so fixed that it leaves little room for change. We must understand the *existing* realities of the major participants in re-lation to the feasibility of any change. In Parts II and III we will see that understanding the *different* realities of the main groups of participants goes a long way in explaining the total picture; that is, the sum total of subjective meanings provides a more comprehensive picture of educa-tional change as a whole.

Fifth, change can be very deep, striking at the core of learned skills and beliefs and conceptions of education, and creating doubts about purposes, sense of competence, and self-concept. If these problems are ignored or glossed over, superficial change will occur at best; at worst, people will retreat into a self-protective cocoon, unreflectively rejecting all proposed changes. Even changes that do not seem to be complex to their promoter, may raise numerous doubts and uncertainties on the part of those not familiar with them.

Sixth, there is the question: How do we know if a particular change is valuable, and who decides? Sarason and Doris (1979) give some indication of the difficulty and indeed impossibility of coming up with a definitive answer.

> Institutional custom and practice are effective bulwarks to forces for change and this, we too easily forget, has both good and bad features. On the one hand, we do not want our institutions to change in response to every new fad or idea and, on the other hand, we do not want them blindly to preserve the status quo. In regard to mainstreaming, how one regards the oppositional stance of our schools and university training centers will depend on how one feels about mainstreaming. If one is for mainstreaming, then one will tend to view opposition as another instance of stoneage attitudes. If one is against mainstreaming, one will tend to view it as another misguided effort that will further dilute the quality of education of everyone. (p. 361)

The short answer is that a change is good depending on one's values, whether or not it gets implemented, and with what consequences. Some people blindly support certain changes that they value, oblivious to questions of implementation and consequences. Others are unsure of the value of change because they are only too well aware of the lack of clarity and uncertainty that permeates the transition from values to goals, to adoption, through implementation, to outcomes.

What I have been saying has nothing to do with the *intentions* of promoters of change. It is mainly that no matter how honorable the motives, each and every individual who is necessary for effective implementation will experience some concerns about the meaning of new practices, goals, beliefs, and means of implementation. Clear statements at the outset may help, but do not eliminate the problem; the psychological process of learning and understanding something new does not happen in a flash (or for most educational changes, in several flashes). The presence or absence of mechanisms to address the ongoing problem of meaning—at the beginning and as people try out ideas—is crucial for success, because it is at the individual level that change does or does not occur.

This principle is true whether change is imposed on individuals or whether they voluntarily decide to do something new. Basic to this process is the reality that learning a new skill and entertaining new conceptions create doubts and feelings of awkwardness or incompetence, especially when we first try something (see, for example, Joyce & Showers, 1988). Of course, in saying that change occurs at the individual level, it should be recognized that organizational changes are often necessary to provide supportive or stimulating conditions to foster change in practice.

Finally, while this may seem obvious, to say that meaning matters is to say that people matter—change works or doesn't work on the basis of individual and collective responses to it. Shared meaning, "shared cognition," or "interactive professionalism," as I have called it, goes a long way in making significant change a reality (Joyce & Showers, 1988; Rosenholtz, 1989).

So far I have dwelt on the problem of meaning in relation to the content of innovations. I have suggested that individuals and groups working together have to become clear about new educational practices that they wish (and/or someone else wishes them) to implement. This is meaning, if you will, about the content and theory of educational practice. Affecting the likelihood of obtaining meaning about the desirability and workability of specific educational practices is the question of *how* new practices are introduced. The latter concerns the theory of change— a complex social process in which people have just as many problems understanding what is happening and why. I mentioned in Chapter 1 that educational change involves two main aspects: what changes to implement (theories of education) and how to implement them (theories of change). There are dangers in separating these two aspects, because they interact and shape each other. But it is helpful to realize this distinction in planning or analyzing specific reform efforts. In short, we have to understand *both* the change and the change process.

I start in Chapter 4 near the beginning of the process, with how educational changes get decided on or initiated in the first place.

CHAPTER 4

The Causes and Processes
of Initiation

*The pressures [for change] seem to subside with the act of adoption
followed by the appearance of implementation.*
— Berman and McLaughlin (1979), p. 1

There is no shortage of recommendations about how the ills of education
should be rectified. But the remedies remain pie in the sky as long as competing "shoulds" fight it out without an understanding of how to get
started and how to keep going. The next two chapters contain a description of the educational change process and an explanation of why it works
as it does.

The number and dynamics of factors that interact and affect the process of educational change are too overwhelming to compute in anything
resembling a fully determined way. We do know more about the processes
of change as a result of the research of the 1970s and 1980s, only to
discover that there are no hard-and-fast rules, rather a set of suggestions
or implications given the contingencies specific to local situations. In fact,
as Firestone and Corbett (1987); Fullan (1985); Clark, Lotto, and Astuto
(1984); Huberman and Miles (1984), and others, suggest, the uniqueness
of the individual setting is a critical factor—what works in one situation
may or may not work in another. This is not to say that there are not
guidelines, and we will get to some of them. Research findings on the
change process should be used less as instruments of "application" and
more as means of helping practitioners and planners "make sense" of
planning, implementation strategies, and monitoring. It is also important
to say that this is a possible task: "Schools, classrooms, and school systems
can and do improve and the factors facilitating improvement are neither
so exotic, unusual, or expensive that they are beyond the grasp of . . .
ordinary schools" (Clark, Lotto, & Astuto, 1984, pp. 59, 66).

Most researchers now see three broad phases to the change process.
Phase I—variously labeled initiation, mobilization, or adoption—consists
of the process that leads up to and includes a decision to adopt or proceed
with a change. Phase II—implementation or initial use (usually the first
two or three years of use)—involves the first experiences of attempting to

FIGURE 4.1.   A Simplified Overview of the Change Process

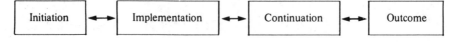

put an idea or reform into practice. Phase III—called continuation, incorporation, routinization, or institutionalization—refers to whether the change gets built in as an ongoing part of the system or disappears by way of a decision to discard or through attrition (see Berman & McLaughlin, 1978a; Huberman & Miles, 1984). Figure 4.1 depicts the three phases and adds the concept of outcome to provide a more complete overview of the change process.

In simple terms, someone or some group, for whatever reasons, initiates or promotes a certain program or direction of change. The direction of change, which may be more or less defined at the early stages, moves to a phase of attempted use (implementation), which can be more or less effective in that use may or may not be accomplished. Continuation is an extension of the implementation phase in that the new program is sustained beyond the first year or two (or whatever time frame is chosen). Outcome, depending on the objectives, can refer to several different types of results and can be thought of generally as the degree of school improvement in relation to given criteria. Results could include, for example, improved student learning and attitudes; new skills, attitudes, or satisfaction on the part of teachers and other school personnel; or improved problem-solving capacity of the school as an organization.

Figure 4.1 presents only the general image of a much more detailed and snarled process. First, there are numerous factors operating at each phase. Second, as the two-way arrows imply, it is not a linear process but rather one in which events at one phase can feed back to alter decisions made at previous stages, which then proceed to work their way through in a continuous interactive way. For example, a decision at the initiation phase to use a specific program may be substantially modified during implementation, and so on. A useful distinction to keep in mind is whether the process is characterized more by a programmatic or fidelity emphasis or more by a mutually adaptive or evolutionary mode (Berman, 1981).

The third set of variables, which are unspecified in Figure 4.1, concerns the scope of change and the question of who develops and initiates the change. The scope can range from large-scale externally developed innovations to locally produced ones. In either of these cases the teacher as user may or may not be centrally involved in development and/or decisions to proceed. Thus, the concept of "initiation" leaves open the question of who develops or initiates the change. The question is taken up at various places in the rest of this chapter and in relevant chapters on particular roles.

The fourth complication in Figure 4.1 is that the total time perspective as well as subphases cannot be precisely demarcated. The initiation phase may be in the works for years, but even later specific decision-making and pre-implementation planning activities can be lengthy. Implementation for most changes takes two or more years; only then can we consider that the change has really had a chance to become implemented. The line between implementation and continuation is somewhat hazy and arbitrary. Outcomes can be assessed in the relatively short run, but we would not expect many results until the change had had a chance to become implemented. In this sense implementation is the *means* to achieving certain outcomes; evaluations have limited value and can be misleading if they provide information on outcomes only (Charters & Jones, 1973; Fullan, 1987).

The total time frame from initiation to institutionalization is lengthy; even moderately complex changes take from three to five years, while major restructuring efforts can take five to ten years. Of course, information can and should be gathered and assessments made throughout the process. The single most important idea arising from Figure 4.1 is that *change is a process, not an event* (Fullan & Park, 1981; Hall & Loucks, 1977)—a lesson learned the hard way by those who put all their energies into developing an innovation or passing a piece of legislation without thinking through what would have to happen beyond that point.

So far we have been talking as if schools adopted one innovation at a time. This single innovation perspective largely reflects the lessons learned from the 1970s and early 1980s, and can be very useful for examining individual innovations. The broader reality, of course, is that schools are in the business of contending simultaneously with *multiple innovations* (Anderson, 1989). Thus, when we identify factors affecting successful initiation and implementation, we should think of these factors operating across many innovations—and many levels of the system (classroom, school, district, state, nation). This multiplicity perspective, as I stated in Chapter 1, inevitably leads us to look for solutions at the level of individual roles and groups, which we do in the chapters in Part II. This is so, because it is only at the individual and small group level that the inevitable demands of overload can be prioritized and integrated. Such integration will not happen at the political level, which, by its very nature, generates more innovations than can be handled.

What happens at one stage of the change process strongly affects subsequent stages, but new determinants also appear. Because the processes are so entangled, I will endeavor to identify a list of the main factors and to describe their influence at each stage. The ideas in this chapter and Chapter 5 will be used to help explain why the processes of initiation, implementation, and continuation function as they do. This discussion will set the stage for Chapter 6, in which the difficult questions of the relationships among broad strategies of change, the processes, and in-

FIGURE 4.2.   Factors Associated with Initiation

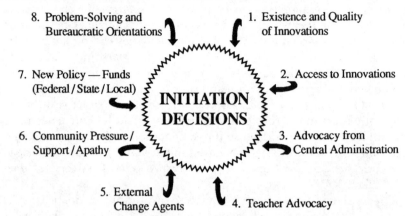

tended and unintended outcomes will be explored: What can we say about the impact of educational change (both intended and unintended) on attitudes, achievement, and capacities for further change? What are some guidelines and alternatives for approaching and coping with educational change more effectively?

The most immediate question, however, is which factors influence whether or not changes get initiated in the first place. Answering this question will provide an important basis for understanding the subsequent course of the changes.

FACTORS AFFECTING INITIATION

Initiation is the process leading up to and including the decision to proceed with implementation. It can take many different forms, ranging from a decision by a single authority to a broad-based mandate. At a general level, we might assume that specific educational changes are introduced because they are desirable according to certain educational values and meet a given need better than existing practices. As we have seen, however, this is not the way it always or even usually happens.

There are countless variables potentially influencing whether a change program gets started. We concentrate in this chapter on those factors associated with planned or action-oriented change, leaving aside the question of tracing the origin of the change. Figure 4.2 depicts eight sources affecting initiation, which have been derived from recent literature. I make no claim that the list is exhaustive, only that there is evidence of support across many studies. The order is not important, although different combinations are. For example, community pressure combined with a problem-solving orientation will have quite different consequences than community pressure combined with a bureaucratic orientation. The main point is that innovations get initiated from many different sources and for different reasons. The matter of the need for change can be embedded in any one or several of the factors, depending on whose viewpoint one takes.

Existence and Quality of Innovations

Educational innovations exist in plentiful numbers. The question is what innovations are out there. It is well beyond the scope of this study to investigate the world of invention and development. Therefore, it will be impossible to draw systematic data-based conclusions about the content of available changes. The answer probably is that there are all kinds of innovations in existence, which could address a wide range of values, as we would expect in any pluralistic or heterogeneous society.

Innovations are usually developed in response to the incentive system of the society. Market conditions (federal or state tenders, government-sponsored development, salability in terms of values, cost, etc.) serve to delimit the educational changes likely to be generated. Boyd (1978, pp. 370–71) states that conflict avoidance is a major market determiner in the school textbook industry in the United States. Consequently, publishers try to please the national or state market, being careful to exclude material that might offend given communities or subgroups in the country. In this way, material appropriate for many other communities or subgroups with different values is less likely to be produced, and controversial material, which might form the very basis of addressing some of the social goals of education (e.g., in social studies curriculum), is less likely to be developed. Boyd also points out that many teachers and local districts do not have the resources to produce their own curriculum and therefore are dependent on available materials. A counter-tendency, as Boyd indicates, occurs when government agencies and foundations sponsor the development of new materials; for example, a variety of policies and programs for disadvantaged groups are sponsored directly or indirectly by government agencies.

Since 1983 the struggle between standardization and restructuring has produced changes that both limit (or focus, depending on your viewpoint) and liberate change possibilities. Relative to the former, for example, many states have begun to prescribe textbooks and link them to standardized state tests (Wise, 1988). On the other hand, restructuring initiatives have resulted not only in numerous local efforts, but also several high-profile national projects in the United States, including the Coalition of Essential Schools, Re-Learning, the National Network for Educational Renewal, the National Education Association Mastery in

Learning Project Schools, the Holmes Group, the Carnegie Task Force on Teaching as a Profession, and the American Federation of Teachers' reform efforts (see references section, and Harvey & Crandall, 1988).

Along with the question of what innovations are available is the issue of the quality of new programs. I have stated that program clarity and quality have been a major problem since the innovation boom of the 1960s. The situation has improved immensely in some program areas (e.g., the teaching of basic skills at the elementary school level). In the United States, the National Diffusion Network (NDN) contains a catalogue of validated innovations judged to be of proven quality (Crandall et al., 1982). Quality, at least in the case of NDN innovations, refers to programs that could be shown to cause positive observable change, in a number of different settings. The Research and Development Utilization Project (R&DU) found that quality was rated high by teachers and other school personnel who adopted a number of R&D products in seven program areas (Louis & Rosenblum, 1981). The large-scale Study of Dissemination Efforts Supporting School Improvement (Crandall et al., 1982), which included NDN innovations, found many examples of the adoption of educational programs perceived by adopters to be of high quality.

Quality, of course, is difficult to assess and agree on. It does seem, however, that quality is improving, as we would expect it to after years of trial and error and continuing development. Because of the importance of the problem of meaning, it is interesting to consider the relationship between clarity and the adoption of innovations. Given what I have said up to this point, it should not be surprising that perceived clarity of an innovation bears no necessary relationship to initiation (although it does to implementation); in other words, many educational changes have been "adopted" without any clear notion as to their specific meaning. The lessons of the past have made people in education more careful in taking on unproven new change programs; and limited resources force them to be even more selective. Thus, in addition to quality, clarity and perceived advantage are increasingly important, especially if teachers are the decision-makers.

None of this discussion assumes that innovations are simply "out there." Many innovations are locally developed or "interpreted." Improvement activities based on school effectiveness research are one example. District implementation plans for translating curriculum guidelines to the classroom, as so often happens in Canadian provinces, are another (Fullan, Anderson, & Newton, 1986). In both cases the original "innovation" might be said to be high on philosophical purpose but low on specificity or prescriptiveness. Schools and school systems must design their own versions, given what they know or understand about how the innovation might best work in practice. Needless to say, caution is warranted in that too often the innovations are not "debugged" (Crandall et al., 1986) and lack the clarity and program characteristics necessary to help users know what to do. Even for those interested in particular solutions who turn to externally developed programs, implementation can mean significant modifications (e.g., in materials, in specific instructional activities) as people adapt them to their own situations. Others may simply develop their own programs, based on their own assessment of the best approach.

Leaving aside for the moment the question of who develops or initiates change, and reflecting on the question of existence of innovations, we may conclude that the universe of innovations is rather plentiful as a result of pluralistic sponsors, but not as unrestricted and as equitable as might be necessary to address the educational needs of various groups in society. And many people (e.g., teachers, parents) who have particular needs that are currently unmet do not have the time, skills, or resources to develop solutions.

Access to Information

A second factor related to initiation is the selectivity that occurs as a result of differential access to information. The primacy of personal contact in the diffusion of innovations has been known for years (Katz, Lewin, & Hamilton, 1963), and its importance in education is concisely summarized by House (1974, Ch. 1). District administrators and other central office personnel such as coordinators and consultants spend large amounts of time at conferences and workshops within ongoing professional networks of communication among their peers (Carlson, 1972; House, 1974, Ch. 3 on the "educational entrepreneur"). Individual teachers are less likely to come into contact with new ideas, for they are restricted to the classroom and have a limited network of ongoing professionally based interaction within their schools or with their professional peers outside (see Chapter 7).[1] Teachers do receive information literature, and most attend workshops here and there, but they do not have the opportunity for *continuous personal* contact, which would be necessary for becoming aware of and following up on innovative ideas (House & Lapan, 1978, p. 177; Huberman & Miles, 1984).

All communities, and especially those whose members have limited formal education, are at a double disadvantage: They are unfamiliar with and not confident about technical matters, and they have almost no personal contact (or time and energy to develop contact) with even a small part of the educational universe. School boards have more direct responsibility in this realm but also are dependent on central administrators. (This does not mean that boards are unable to put pressure on administrators.) Finally, access to innovations, as is obvious but rarely emphasized, depends on an infrastructure of communication—ease of transportation, resources, and density of population and ideas in the geographical area. Urban school districts and large school districts enjoy favorable conditions; rural and small school districts do not. House (1974, Ch. 2) uses a mathematical model and data on the spread of the Illinois Program for Gifted Children, which show exactly this pattern over a number of years. Research on the U.S. federally funded Experimental Schools (ES) program involving 10 rural school districts corroborates the problem of lack of access and difficulties of communication about new ideas faced by such districts (Herriott & Gross, 1979; Rosenblum & Louis, 1979, pp. 305–59). Daft and Becker (1978) found also that district size was related to adoption of innovations in 13 high school districts. On reflection, all of this is common sense, but it is seldom recognized as biasing the initiation process from the beginning.

Advocacy from Central Administrators

Initiation of change never occurs without an advocate, and one of the most powerful is the chief district administrator, with his or her staff, especially in combination with school board support or mandate. In some circumstances, the district administration may not be interested in innovation, and little may happen. But when there is an interest, for whatever reason—mandate from a board, or a reform-minded or career-oriented administrator—it is the superintendent and central staff who combine access, internal authority, and resources necessary to seek out external funds for a particular change program and/or to obtain board support. Numerous studies have found this to be the case: the ES rural district program (Rosenblum & Louis, 1979); the Rand Change Agent study (Berman & McLaughlin, 1977); Berman, McLaughlin, and associates (1979) more intensive study of five school districts; Miles' (1987) research on new schools; Huberman and Miles' (1984) case studies of 12 districts; Carlson's (1972) and Havelock and Havelock's (1973) investigations of the school superintendent; and LaRocque & Coleman's (1989a) study of district ethos in British Columbia. All of these studies show that the chief district administrator and central district staff are an extremely important source of advocacy, support, and initiation of new programs.

For example, Huberman and Miles (1984) found that "central office administrators were at the locus of decision-making in 11 of the 12 cases" (p. 55). Hidden in these findings is the message that district administrators are often an important source of district-wide changes that favor groups that might otherwise be neglected (see Purkey & Smith, 1985). Moreover, some of the more radical restructuring efforts have been initiated at the district level as distinct from the state or school level (David, 1989b; Firestone, Fuhrman, & Kirst, 1989a,b).

By the same token administrators can be equally powerful at blocking changes they do not like. Sarason (1982) reminds us that we do not have much knowledge about change proposals that *never get to the adoption stage*—a fairly high proportion, according to principals and teachers with whom Sarason talked. Whatever the case, district administrators and staff are often powerful advocates and can sponsor or block initiation and adoption of change programs (see also Chapter 10).

Teacher Advocacy

While teachers as a group have less opportunity to come into contact with new ideas and less time and energy to follow through on those that they do become aware of, most teachers do innovate. In fact, the "innovation paradigm," which in effect traces the development and implementation of *formally* initiated innovations, is biased because it misses the thousands of small innovations that individual and small groups of teachers engage in every day. There is a strong body of evidence that indicates that other teachers are often the preferred source of ideas. On the other hand, the evidence is equally strong that opportunities to interact with other teachers is limited, and that when good ideas do get initiated by one or more teachers, it requires the support of others if the ideas are to go anywhere (Crandall et al., 1982).

The power of teachers working together is well illustrated in Little's 1982 in-depth research of improvement and work conditions in six schools. She found that school improvement occurred when

1. teachers engaged in frequent, continuous, and increasingly concrete talk about teaching practice;
2. teachers and administrators frequently observed and provided feedback to each other, developing a "shared language" for teaching strategies and needs; and
3. teachers and administrators planned, designed, and evaluated teaching materials and practices together.

When schools come to have "norms of continuous improvement" teachers constantly search for new ways of making improvements (Fullan, 1990; Little, 1982). Rosenholtz (1989) found the same thing in her larger study involving 78 schools. All these researchers, however, also found that the working conditions of teachers in the vast majority of schools are not conducive to sustained teacher innovation (see Chapter 7). On a more global level, national teacher unions have lately become strong advocates of reforms (see Shanker, 1988, 1990; National Education Association, 1988; McDonnell & Pascal, 1988).

These findings taken together indicate that many teachers are willing to adopt change at the individual classroom level and will do so under the right conditions (e.g., an innovation that is clear and practical, a support-ive district administration and principal, opportunity to interact with other teachers, and outside resource help). There are several qualifiers: Most teachers do not have adequate information access, time, or energy; the innovations they do adopt will be individualistic (and unlikely to spread to other teachers); advocacy from district administrators and/or union leaders is necessary for district-wide changes.

External Change Agents

Change agents or facilitators external to the district, that is, in re-gional, state, or national roles, play an important part in initiating change projects (see Chapter 11). Many roles at these levels are formally charged with the responsibility of stimulating and supporting change. The impor-tance of these roles, especially at the initiation stage, has been docu-mented over a number of years. For example, research on the Pilot State Dissemination Program, in which field agents were used to stimulate knowledge utilization in seven areas of the United States, demonstrates the impact of outside facilitators on teacher adoption of new ideas (Louis & Sieber, 1979). In the larger DESSI study of 80 external assisters who worked with 97 local schools, Cox (1983a) reports that the external facil-itators: made people aware of the existence of new practices; helped school people choose among a range of new practices; sometimes helped arrange funding; worked with local facilitators to develop plans for im-plementation; arranged and conducted initial training; and sometimes played a continuing support and evaluation role. External facilitators are most influential at the early (i.e., initiation) stages of change and when they work in combination with local leaders (see also Corbett, Dawson, & Firestone, 1984).

Community Pressure/Support/Opposition/Apathy

Since communities vary and characteristics of school districts differ greatly, different combinations of factors will result in various initiation patterns—a perennial problem in understanding change processes. But when some of the main combinations are examined, we can make sense of the paradox that some communities support innovation, others block it, most are apathetic, and even more are all of those things at one time or another.

In general terms, and depending on the circumstances, communities can either (1) put pressure on district administrators (directly or through school boards) to "do something" about a problem, (2) oppose certain potential adoptions about which they become aware, or (3) do nothing (passive support or apathy). The meaning of these patterns is clarified by considering some evidence.

The most predictable initial pressure for change from the community is likely to come as a result of population shifts. The Berman, McLaughlin, and associates (1979) study of five school districts demonstrates that major demographic changes (rapid growth in population, or a change in composition that results in different social-class and cultural mixes) lead to the development of community efforts and demands for change. How the demands are handled depends very much on the problem-solving vs. bureaucratic orientations to be discussed below. In other words, demands may or may not result in initiation, depending on a combination of factors—but the point is that communities can instigate educational change. (In one of the Berman and McLaughlin cases, for example, population growth led to community activism in a previously stagnant school system, election of new board members, hiring of an innovative superintendent, facilitation of change by other central staff, principals, teachers, etc.)

Schaffarzick's study of 34 San Francisco Bay area districts is also very revealing. He found that 62 percent of the curriculum decision cases in his sample did not involve lay participation (cited in Boyd, 1978, p. 613). Community apathy and indifference characterized these decisions. However, in the 19 cases that involved conflict and bargaining, the community groups nearly always prevailed. Boyd (1978) indicates that conflict avoidance is a major orientation of school boards and administrators. Innovations that involve major value differences (e.g., the teaching of evolution, sex education) can easily be blocked by a local minority at the initiation stage or shortly thereafter if the minority play up the controversiality of the change (regardless of whether their claims are accurate). Concerning the selective role of communities, Daft and Becker (1978) found that highly educated ones correlated substantially with the adoption of innovations for college-bound students, but less well educated communities did *not* correlate with the greater likelihood of programs of benefit to high school terminating students. Bridge (1976, p. 370) makes a similar point: "It is easier to organize parents, particularly lower class parents, to resist perceived threats than it is to organize them to achieve long term positive goals."

In putting these findings together, we can conclude that the role of the community in the initiation process is not straightforward, but it is understandable when we break it down into the following components:

1. Major demographic changes create turbulence in the environment, which may lead to initiation of change or irreconcilable conflict, depending on the presence of other factors listed in Figure 4.2.

2. Most communities do not actively participate in change decisions about educational programs.
3. More highly educated communities seem to put general pressure on their schools to adopt high-quality, academic-oriented changes. They also can react strongly and effectively against proposed changes that they do not like.
4. Less well educated communities are less likely to initiate change or put effective pressure on educators to initiate changes on their behalf. They are also less likely to become activated against changes because of lack of knowledge, but once activated they too can become effective.

There is a very powerful message implicit in the above statements: *In relatively stable or continuous communities there is a tendency for innovations favoring the least advantaged not to be proposed (the bias of neglect) and there is a greater likelihood that educators can introduce innovations (which they believe in) unbeknownst to the community.* Moreover, demographic shifts create strong demands for initiation of change, but what the demands result in is anyone's ball game, for they interact with other factors in the situation. Chapter 12 examines the role of parents and the community in educational change in more detail.

New Policy and Funds

Most federal projects in the United States are voluntary, but we need to distinguish these projects from new legislation or policy that *mandates* adoption at the local district level. Increasingly, state and provincial governments are mandating new programs and procedures (see Chapter 13). Since we are talking just about "causes of adoption," we need make only two points. First, without the existence of state and federal lobby groups and reform-minded policy-makers, many new social change programs would never even get formally adopted. Many major educational initiatives are generated through government policy making and legislation in areas in greatest need of reform, such as special education, desegregation, basic skills, teacher education, and the like.

The second point is more of a dilemma. On the one hand, policies are often left ambiguous and general; it is easier in this case for local districts to adopt the policy in principle, but problems such as lack of implementation emerge at later stages (Elmore, 1980; Williams, 1980). On the other hand, in the 1980s policies became increasingly prescriptive in many states, which results in resistance or pro forma implementation (Wise, 1988).

In any case, new policies, especially if accompanied by funds, stimulate and sometimes require initiation of change at the local level. One major example of incentive grants through state legislation, which we will examine in more detail later, is California's School Improvement Program (SIP) (Marsh & Bowman, 1988). Schools are given substantial funds contingent upon their submitting a plan for improvement that conforms to the guidelines set by the state department of education. California has attempted to address the dilemma of centralization vs. decentralization by striving to cause "bottom-up" change through "top-down" initiative.

In Canada, provincial governments, through the cyclical production of curriculum guidelines and government-sponsored task forces on major policy issues, stimulate new initiatives. Major reforms, for example, in British Columbia and Ontario are described in Chapter 13. The federal government, on the other hand, plays virtually no role constitutionally and practically in Canadian school systems. In effect, in Canada each provincial government is the central government for education for school systems within its jurisdiction.

Problem-Solving and Bureaucratic Orientations

The orientation that school districts take to external policy and funds is another story. Berman and McLaughlin (1977) discovered that adoption decisions of school districts were characterized by either an opportunistic (bureaucratic) or problem-solving orientation. Districts welcome external funds and/or policies either as an opportunity to obtain extra resources (which they use for other purposes and/or which represent a symbolic act of appearing to respond to a given need) or as a chance to solve particular local problems. In more recent research carried out by the Center for Policy Research in Education, Fuhrman, Clune, and Elmore (1988) found that many districts use new policies to go beyond minimal requirements when they favor the policy directions. In case studies of four school districts in Ontario, Fullan, Anderson, and Newton (1986) found that district administrators sometimes welcomed new curriculum policies because they provided a stimulus or reminder to work in a desired direction.

We do not know the proportions of problem-solvers and bureaucrats in the school districts of North America. Pincus (1974) would have us believe that the properties of public school systems *qua* systems make them more bureaucratic than problem-oriented. Pincus claims that compared with competitive firms,

1. public schools are less motivated to adopt cost-reducing innovations unless the funds so saved become available for other purposes in the district;
2. they are less likely to adopt innovations that change the resource

mix or the accustomed authority roles (e.g., that involve behavioral changes in role); and

3. they are more likely to adopt new instructional processes that do not significantly change structure, or to adopt new wrinkles in administrative management, because such innovations help to satisfy the demands of the public without exacting heavy costs (1974, pp. 117–18).

That is, in terms of the multidimensionality of implementation (Chapter 3) schools are more likely to implement superficial changes in content, objectives, and structure than changes in role behavior, conceptions of teaching, etc.—a conclusion also reached by Cuban (1988b,c) when he noted that first-order changes in content are more likely than second-order changes in roles and culture.

Three factors favorable to adoption are identified by Pincus (1974, p. 120).

1. *bureaucratic safety,* as when innovations add resources without requiring behavioral change;
2. *response to external pressure* (in which "adoption" may ease the pressure); and
3. *approval of peer elites* (in the absence of clearly defined output criteria, whatever is popular among leading professional peers is sometimes the determining criterion).

In other words, "schools tend voluntarily to adopt innovations which promote the schools' self-image" as "up-to-date . . . efficient . . . professional . . . responsive" (p. 122). Stated differently again, it is relatively easy for schools to *adopt* complex, vague, inefficient, and costly (especially if someone else is paying) innovations as long as they do not have to *implement* them.

Pincus' review is analytically rather than empirically based (although he does use illustrations), so we do not know how pervasive these bureaucratic practices are empirically. Certainly both bureaucratic and problem-solving orientations exist, depending on the school district. Berman and McLaughlin (1977, 1978a) found that opportunistic (as distinct from problem-solving) adoption decisions were more frequent in the school districts in their large sample. These authors also give detailed case examples that describe both processes at work: the "illusion of change" approach, in which "the pressures [for change] seem to subside with the act of adoption," and the developmental pattern in which particular pressures were responded to by analysis and adoption of needed changes (Berman, McLaughlin, and associates, 1979).

Nelson and Sieber (1976) found interesting adoption patterns in their survey of 32 innovations in urban secondary schools. Using a sample of 679 principals (with an 82% response rate) in all U.S. cities with a population of 300,000 or over, Nelson and Sieber discovered that

1. the publicity value of innovations and faddism were major reasons for adoption;
2. one-fourth of the schools adopted many innovations, but few were of relatively high quality (quality was assessed by a panel of experts);
3. cost was not a barrier to adoption (the two were *positively* correlated); and
4. cost was inversely related to quality (i.e., the more costly the innovation, the lower the quality—as judged by a panel of experts).

Bureaucratically speaking, then, the political and symbolic value of initiation of change for schools is often of greater significance than the educational merit and the time and cost necessary for implementation followthrough. However, the symbolic value is not unimportant. Such decisions may be necessary for political survival, may be needed first steps that set the preconditions for real change in practice, or may represent the only change possible in certain situations.

In assessing the nature of initiation decisions, we should remember that all research studies are *time bound.* Much of the above research was conducted in the early 1970s, when failure and confusion were widespread. In more recent research there is a glimmer of hope in that some educators seem to be getting better at adopting sounder changes tied more closely to real need (Crandall et al., 1982; Marsh & Bowman, 1988). But it is only a glimmer, because this research is based on samples that are not necessarily representative of the total population. Whatever the situation, we need to understand that there are different ways of making initial decisions about educational change; some of these ways are effective, and others result in the illusion and disillusion of reform.

THE INITIATION PROCESS

We have presented an amalgam of different factors that influence the initiation of change projects. The first message is that change does and will always be initiated from a variety of different sources and combination of sources. This presents constant opportunity for or imposition of change, depending on the innovation and one's role in the setting. The second matter, which we have not teased out, is what we know about the *initiation process*—that is, what happens by way of mobilization, and planning to prepare for change. In particular, what do we know about *success-*

ful initiation; that is, what do we know about startups that have a better chance of mobilizing people and resources toward the implementation of desired change?

There is no easy answer as to what represents successful initiation because, as with so many aspects of the change process, those contemplating change are faced with a series of dilemmas. Should we have a short or long time period for starting? Should we go for internal development or import external innovations? Should we work with volunteers or a more representative group? Should we go with large numbers or small numbers? Should we focus on instruction or on the organization, or on both? Should we try major change or start with minor change? Should we have lots of participation at the early stages or not? (See Crandall, et al., 1986.) I take up some of these issues in Chapter 6 on planning. In the meantime, I will discuss some insights into the initiation process.

First, changes adopted for symbolic or opportunistic reasons, with little likelihood of follow-through; large-scale change projects that bite off too much and/or are inherently vague; narrow prescriptive changes that constrain the curriculum and the teacher; decentralized school-based changes that lack definition and support; or imposed change of any kind that teachers find meaningless all have served over the past 30 years to give change and innovation a deservedly bad name.

Second, we are beginning to see more examples of successful initiation. Miles (1987), in reviewing a number of major research studies, found that a combination of strong advocacy, need, active initiation, and a clear model for proceeding characterized the more successful startups. The combination of advocacy and active initiation raises one of the most perplexing issues related to how changes get started, namely, what is the role of participation in the early stages of change projects? There is some evidence that large-scale participation at the initiation phase is sometimes counterproductive (Huberman & Miles, 1984). Elaborate needs assessments, endless committee and task force debates, and the like often consume large amounts of energy and time, and ironically can create confusion and alienation in the absence of any action. There is even the not unlikely situation where elaborate pre-action discussions exhaust the energy needed for implementation, so that by the time the innovation reaches the action stage, people are "burnt out."

Participation can also be deceptive when representatives of large groups are involved. For example, the production of provincial curriculum guidelines in Canada, or school district curricula decision making, usually involves selected teachers as participants in work groups or committees. While selected teachers thus do develop materials, once the materials are ready for use they are no more meaningful to rank-and-file teachers (who are seeing them for the first time) than if they had been

FIGURE 4.3.   Considerations in Planning for Adoption

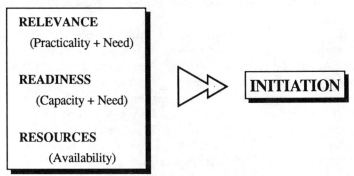

produced by publishers or district curriculum specialists. It is the *members of the committee* who have developed their subjective meaning of the change, not anyone else.

I am not saying that early participation is unimportant, only that it must be seen in the context of the early stages of a very long process of mobilization and meaning. It might be more helpful, as I suggest in Chapter 5, to conceive of participation as something that begins during initiation, and grows and grows through action, i.e., through implementation (see Louis & Miles, 1990).

Ideally, the best beginnings combine the three R's of relevance, readiness, and resources (Figure 4.3). *Relevance* includes the interaction of need, clarity of the innovation (and practitioner's understandings of it), and utility, or what it really has to offer teachers and students. Surprisingly, "simple changes are the ones school systems are least likely to adopt and implement successfully" (Clark, Lotto, & Astuto, 1984, p. 56), largely because they are not perceived to be worth the effort. By contrast, "the greatest success is likely to occur when the size of the change is large enough to require noticeable, sustained effort, but not so massive that typical users find it necessary to adopt a coping strategy that seriously distorts the change" (Crandall et al., 1986, p. 26). Relevance and importance do matter.

Readiness involves the school's practical and conceptual capacity to initiate, develop, or adopt a given innovation—what Firestone (1989) calls the school's "capacity to use reform." Readiness may be approached in terms of "individual" and "organizational" factors. For individuals: Does it address a perceived need? Is it a reasonable change? Do they possess the requisite knowledge and skills? Do they have the time? For organizations: Is the change compatible with the culture of the school? Are facilities, equipment, materials, and supplies available? Are there other crises or other change efforts in progress? The greater the number of "no's," the more reason to take another look at readiness (Crandall et al., 1986, p. 37).

Resources concern the accumulation of and provision of support as a part of the change process. Just because it is a good and pressing idea, doesn't mean that the resources are available to carry it out. People often underestimate the resources needed to go forward with a change. While resources are obviously critical during implementation, it is at the initiation stage that this issue must first be considered and provided for.

I said above that "ideally" a combination of relevance, readiness, and resources should exist at the launch stage, but it is not always possible to sort out the three elements in advance. It may be necessary to start on a small scale and use this as leverage for further action.

The relationship between initiation and implementation is loosely coupled and interactive. The process of initiation can generate meaning or confusion, commitment or alienation, or simply ignorance on the part of participants and others affected by the change. Poor beginnings can be turned into successes depending on what is done during implementation. Promising startups can be squandered by what happens afterwards.

There are many good innovations around. The difficulty is determining the match between local needs and available innovations, given the reality of funding, personnel, and other changes in progress. As I said at the beginning, there are many reasons for adopting innovations, some of them sound, some of them not so sound. Further, change in the 1980s and 1990s often means multiple change, systems change, change in basic structures and meanings. Such restructuring changes require an especially careful look at what the reform is and its capacity to deliver in relation to the setting in question.

At this point we know that initiation decisions occur all the time and come through a variety of sources. We have some inkling that—depending on the sources, the process followed, and the combination of contextual conditions in the situation—what happens after the initiation phase will be all over the map. We can now turn to the next critical phase in the process. Implementation is where the action is. The two key questions are: *What is the relationship between the initiation process and subsequent implementation? What other factors emerge during implementation that determine what change in practice actually occurs?*

CHAPTER 5

Causes/Processes
of Implementation and Continuation

*Well, the hard work is done. We have the policy passed; now all you have
to do is implement it.*

—Outgoing deputy minister of education to colleague

Educational change is technically simple and socially complex. While the
simplicity of the technical aspect is no doubt overstated, anyone who has
been involved in a major change effort will intuitively grasp the meaning
of and concur with the complexity of the social dimension. A large part
of the problem of educational change may be less a question of dogmatic
resistance and bad intentions (although there is certainly some of both)
and more a question of the difficulties related to planning and coordinating a multilevel social process involving thousands of people.

As I described in Chapter 4, a great majority of the curriculum development and other educational change "adoptions" during the last 25
years did not get implemented in practice even where implementation
was desired. Implementation consists of the process of putting into practice an idea, program, or set of activities and structures new to the people
attempting or expected to change. The change may be externally imposed or voluntarily sought; explicitly defined in detail in advance or developed and adapted incrementally through use; designed to be used uni-
formly or deliberately planned so that users can make modifications
according to their perceptions of the needs of the situation.

In this chapter I identify those factors that affect whether or not an
initiated or decided-upon change happens in practice. The processes beyond adoption are more intricate, because they involve more people, and
real change (as distinct from verbal or "on-paper" decisions) is at stake.
Many attempts at policy and program change have concentrated on product development, legislation, and other on-paper changes in a way that
ignored the fact that what people did and did not do was the crucial
variable. This neglect is understandable, for people are much more unpredictable and difficult to deal with than things. They are also essential
for success.

The positive side is that the persistence of people-related problems in educational change has forged greater knowledge about what makes for success. If we constantly remind ourselves that educational change is a *learning experience for the adults involved* (teachers, administrators, parents, etc.) as well as for children, we will be going a long way in understanding the dynamics of the factors of change described in this chapter.

We must start by restating where implementation fits and why it is important. The simple implementation question is: "What types of things would have changed if an innovation or a reform were to become fully implemented?" As discussed in Chapter 3, several definable aspects of classroom or school life would be altered. Sticking with the classroom for the sake of simplicity, we suggested that changes would likely occur in (1) curriculum materials, (2) teaching practices, and (3) beliefs or understandings about the curriculum and learning practices. Implementation is critical for the simple reason that it is the *means* of accomplishing desired objectives. Recalling Charters and Jones' (1973) concern about the risk of appraising "non-events," implementation may turn out to be nonexistent (i.e., no real change in the desired direction), superficial, partial, thorough, and so on. In a word, implementation is a variable, and if the change is a potentially good one, success (such as improved student learning or increased skills on the part of teachers) will depend on the degree and quality of change in actual practice.

It is not quite that simple, but the logic of the change process depicted earlier, in Figure 4.1, is essentially straightforward: However changes get initiated, they proceed or not to some form of implementation and continuation, resulting in some intended and/or unintended outcomes. In this chapter we are interested in the factors and processes that affect implementation and continuation. Our goal is to identify the critical factors that commonly influence change in practice, and to obtain insights into how the implementation process works.

FACTORS AFFECTING IMPLEMENTATION

The idea of implementation and of the factors affecting actual use seems simple enough, but the concept has proven to be exceedingly elusive. Examples of successful improvement described in the research of the last 20 years seem to make common sense. More and more, the evidence points to a small number of key variables. It is obvious that they work, yet how they work is not necessarily clear. Intrinsic dilemmas in the change process, coupled with the intractability of some factors and the uniqueness of individual settings, make successful change a highly complex and subtle social process. Effective approaches to managing change call for

> combining and balancing factors that do not apparently go together—simultaneous simplicity-complexity, looseness-tightness, strong leadership-

participation (or simultaneous bottom up-top downness), fidelity-adaptivity, and evaluation-nonevaluation. More than anything else, effective strategies for improvement require an understanding of the process, a way of thinking that cannot be captured in any list of steps or phases to be followed. (Fullan, 1985, p. 399)

While there is convergence on many of the findings, the sheer complexity of the change process has led researchers to search for different ways to best characterize implementation (see Berman, 1981; Clark, Lotto, & Astuto, 1984; Cohen, 1987; Crandall et al., 1982; Firestone & Corbett, 1987; Hall & Hord, 1987; Huberman & Miles, 1984; Louis & Miles, 1990 for the best examples). One method involves identifying a list of key factors associated with implementation success, such as the nature of the innovation, the roles of the principal, the district role, and so on. Another way is to attempt to depict the main themes, such as vision, empowerment, and the like. Both make important contributions: The former has the advantage of isolating and explaining specific roles; the latter is more likely to capture the dynamics of the change process.

We are going to use both methods in this chapter, labeled, respectively, key factors and key themes. In either case, one overriding qualification should be kept in mind. Describing educational change as a general phenomenon hides variations in large-scale change as compared with small-scale change, differences in units of analysis (e.g., individual classrooms vs. schools, districts, or whole countries), and so on. To understand the basic flow of change, we need not be concerned with these specifications at this time. But if we were interested in a particular change, we would have to make the necessary adjustments, depending on the unit of our interest, as we do in the appropriate chapters in Parts II and III.

We should keep in mind that we are interested in factors or themes to the extent that they causally influence implementation (or more specifically the extent to which teachers and students change their practices, beliefs, use of new materials, etc.) in the direction of some sought after change. If any one or more factors or themes are working against implementation, the process will be less effective. Put positively, the more factors supporting implementation, the more change in practice will be accomplished. Finally, we should avoid thinking of sets of factors or themes in isolation from each other. They form a *system of variables* that interact to determine success or failure. Above all, educational change is a dynamic process involving interacting variables over time, regardless of whether the mode of analysis is factors or themes.

KEY FACTORS IN THE IMPLEMENTATION PROCESS

Figure 5.1 lists 9 critical factors organized into 3 main categories relating to (1) the characteristics of the innovation or change project, (2)

FIGURE 5.1.   Interactive Factors Affecting Implementation

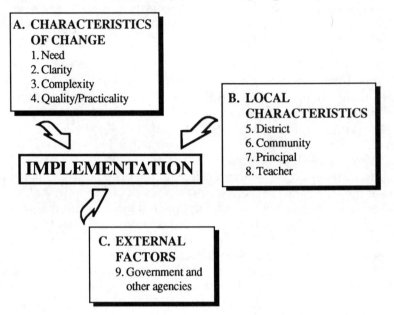

local roles, and (3) external factors. In describing the roles I have tried to emphasize aspects that can be altered rather than those that are fixed or givens. The list is necessarily oversimplified. Each factor could be "unpacked" into several subvariables, as I do in later chapters. At this time the goal is to obtain an overview and feel for the roles in the change process.

Factors Related to Characteristics of the Change

Earlier research on the initiation and implementation process stressed the impact of the nature of the change itself on potential users, i.e., teachers in their classrooms. The characteristics of the change, its size, complexity, prescriptiveness, and practicality for teachers were considered in the light of the teachers' response, most often in hindsight. While the innovations considered in such research were largely curriculum- or classroom-focused changes, the lessons they offer hold true for multidimensional, systemic changes as well.

In Chapter 4, we touched on the relevance of innovation characteristics as part of the initiation process. We found that the potential problems of need, clarity, complexity, and quality neither were nor could be resolved at this early stage. This lack of resolution carries over into implementation and becomes much more visible.

Need. As noted earlier, many innovations are attempted without a careful examination of whether or not they address what are perceived to be priority needs. Teachers, for example, frequently do not see the need for an advocated change. Several large-scale studies in the United States confirm the importance of relating need to decisions about innovations or change directions. In the Experimental Schools (ES) project, Rosenblum and Louis (1979) found that "the degree to which there was a formal recognition within the school system of unmet needs" (p. 12) was one of the four "readiness factors" associated with subsequent implementation. The Rand Change Agent study identified problem solving/ orientation (i.e., identification of a need linked to selection of a program) as strongly related to successful implementation. The Research & Development Utilization Project reports that perceived relevance of products is correlated significantly with extent of implementation. Other studies have discovered that implementation is more effective when it is relatively focused or specific needs are identified (e.g., Emrick & Peterson, 1978; Louis & Sieber, 1979). Complex or multifaceted reforms, such as those addressed in restructuring initiatives can also be focused, but they require a great deal of effort to clarify the nature of the needs being addressed (see David, 1989b; Murphy, in press).

While the importance of perceived or felt need is obvious, its role is not all that straightforward. There are at least three complications. First, schools are faced with overloaded improvement agendas. Therefore, it is a question of not only whether a given need is important, but also how important it is relative to other needs. Needless to say, this prioritizing among sets of desirables is not easy, as people are reluctant to neglect any goals, even though it may be unrealistic to address them all. This is why the themes approach, which are discussed in the next section, is valuable. The theme of vision, for example, provides a screening mechanism for helping groups sort out and integrate competing priorities. Second, precise needs are often not clear at the beginning, especially with complex changes. People often become clearer about their needs only when they start doing things, that is, during implementation itself. Third, need interacts with the other eight factors to produce different patterns. Depending on the pattern, need can become further clarified or obfuscated during the implementation process.

In summary, the "fit" between a new program and district and/or school needs is essential, but it may not become entirely clear until implementation is underway. Huberman and Miles (1984) also remind us that by this early implementation stage, people involved must perceive both that the needs being addressed are significant *and* that they are making at least some progress toward meeting them. Early rewards and some tangible success are critical incentives during implementation.

Clarity.   Clarity (about goals and means) is a perennial problem in the change process. Even when there is agreement that some kind of change is needed, as when teachers want to improve some area of the curriculum or improve the school as a whole, the adopted change may not be at all clear about what teachers should do differently. Gross et al. (1971) found that the majority of teachers were unable to identify the essential features of the innovation they were using. Problems related to clarity have been found in virtually every study of significant change (e.g., Aoki et al., 1977; Charters & Pellegrin, 1973; Huberman & Miles, 1984; Mortimore et al., 1988; Weatherley, 1979). And, the more complex the reform (as is presently the case), the greater the problem of clarity. In short, lack of clarity—diffuse goals and unspecified means of implementation—represents a major problem at the implementation stage; teachers and others find that the change is simply not very clear as to what it means in practice.

Legislation and many other new policies and programs are sometimes deliberately stated at a general level in order to avoid conflict and promote acceptance and adoption. Such policies often do not indicate how implementation is to be addressed (Elmore, 1980; Sarason & Doris, 1979; Weatherley, 1979). Curriculum guidelines in Canada have also suffered from vagueness of goals and especially of means of implementation (Downey et al., 1975; Robinson, 1982; Simms, 1978).

There is little doubt that clarity is essential, but its meaning is subtle; too often we are left with *false clarity* instead. False clarity, as I indicated in Chapter 3, occurs when change is interpreted in an oversimplified way; that is, the proposed change has more to it than people perceive or realize. For example, an approved textbook may easily become *the* curriculum in the classroom, yet fail to incorporate significant features of the policy or goals that it is supposed to address. Reliance on the textbook may distract attention from behaviors and educational beliefs critical to the achievement of desired outcomes. In Canada, new or revised provincial curriculum guidelines may be dismissed by some teachers on the grounds that "we are already doing that"; but this is another illustration of false clarity if the teachers' perception is based only on the more superficial goal and content aspects of the guidelines to the neglect of beliefs and teaching strategies. Similarly, many of the latest curriculum guidelines in Canada contain greater specificity of objectives and content than previous guidelines, with the result that teachers and others welcome them as "finally providing direction"; however, these guidelines may be used in a literal way without the realization that certain teaching strategies and underlying beliefs are essential to implementing the guidelines effectively.

On the other hand, I have cited evidence above that not everyone experiences the comfort of false clarity. Unclear and unspecified changes can cause great anxiety and frustration to those sincerely trying to implement them. Clarity, of course, cannot be delivered on a platter. It is accomplished or not depending on the *process*. Nor is greater clarity an end in itself: Very simple and insignificant changes can be very clear, while more difficult and worthwhile ones may not be amenable to easy clarification. This brings me directly to the third related factor—complexity.

Complexity. Complexity refers to the difficulty and extent of change required of the individuals responsible for implementation. The actual amount depends on the starting point for any given individual or group, but the main idea is that any change can be examined with regard to difficulty, skill required, and extent of alterations in beliefs, teaching strategies, and use of materials. Many changes, such as open education (Bussis et al., 1976), systematic direct instruction (Gersten, Carnine, Zuref, & Cronin, 1981), inquiry-oriented social studies (Aoki et al., 1977), special education (Weatherley, 1979), effective schools (Louis & Miles, 1990; Mortimore et al., 1988; Wilson & Corcoran, 1988), parent involvement (Chapter 12), and restructuring experiments (David, 1989b; Murphy, in press) require a sophisticated array of activities, structures, diagnoses, teaching strategies, and philosophical understanding if effective implementation is to be achieved.

While complexity creates problems for implementation, it may result in greater change because more is being attempted. Berman and McLaughlin (1977) found that "ambitious projects were less successful in absolute terms of the percent of the project goals achieved, but they typically stimulated more teacher change than projects attempting less" (p. 88). Those changes that did occur were more thorough as a result of the extra effort that the project required or inspired. As Berman (1980) stated elsewhere, "little ventured, nothing gained." Crandall and associates (1982) also found that those attempting major changes accomplished more—the more tried for, the more accomplished. However, Crandall and his colleagues emphasize that the magnitude of change must be defined in terms of the starting points of individuals.

We face here another dilemma in the change process. On the one hand, we have evidence to suggest that the "larger the scope and personal 'demandingness' of a change, the greater the chance for success" (Crandall, et al., 1986, p. 25). On the other hand, attempting too much can result in massive failure. Huberman and Miles (1984) found that schools often attempt to implement innovations that are beyond their ability to carry out, a phenomenon they call "overreaching" and one we have seen since the 1960s.

In summary, simple changes may be easier to carry out, but they may not make much of a difference. Complex changes promise to accomplish more, which is good news given the kinds of changes in progress in the

1980s and 1990s, but they also demand more effort, and failure takes a greater toll. The answer seems to be to break complex changes into components and implement them in a divisible and/or incremental manner.

Yin, Herald, and Vogel, (1977, p. 61), for example, studied 140 technological innovations across the criminal, justice, fire, health, education, transportation, and planning sectors. They classified the innovations according to whether they could be used/tested on a limited basis. Those cases where divisibility existed were associated with a higher frequency of success (improvement plus eventual incorporation). Rosenblum and Louis (1979) examined divisibility in their study of comprehensive (complex) system-wide changes in the ES program. Three of the four districts that scored high on implementation had undertaken changes with a greater number of components and these components were highly differentiated (Rosenblum & Louis, 1979, p. 269). Each component was targeted to a specific part of the problem (a grade level, a curriculum, etc.). Huberman and Miles (1984) also describe how ambitious change projects were implemented incrementally, but they caution, as I have in this chapter, that success depends on the presence of other conditions as well, such as sustained assistance (see the subsequent section on key themes).

Quality and practicality of program. The last factor associated directly with the nature of change concerns the quality and practicality of the change project—whether it is a new curriculum, a new policy, a restructured school, or whatever. The history of the quality of attempted changes relative to the other three variables (need, clarity, complexity) is revealing. To say that the importance of the quality of the change is self-evident is to underestimate how initiation decisions are made. Inadequate quality and even the simple unavailability of materials and other resources can result when adoption decisions are made on grounds of political necessity, or even on grounds of perceived need without time for development. Put differently, when adoption is more important than implementation, decisions are frequently made without the follow-up or preparation time necessary to generate adequate materials. Ambitious projects are nearly always politically driven. As a result the time line between the initiation decision and startup is typically too short to attend to matters of quality. In the DESSI study the median length of time from awareness to adoption was 9.5 months, while the time from adoption to startup (implementation) was only 3.5 months. The shorter the latter time line, the more problems there were (Huberman & Miles, 1984). The more complex the change, the more work there is to do on quality.

Changes in schools must also pass the test of the "practicality ethic" of teachers (Doyle & Ponder, 1977–78). Practical changes are those that address salient needs, that fit well with the teachers' situation, that are focused, and that include concrete how-to-do-it possibilities (Mortimore et al., 1988). Practical does not necessarily mean easy, but it does mean the presence of next steps. Again we can see a dilemma in the change process. Changes that are practical, even though of good quality, may be trivial or offensive, while changes that are complex may not be practically worked out.

It is possible, indeed necessary, to combine ambitious change and quality. I have maintained that it is what people develop in their minds and actions that counts. People do not learn or accomplish complex changes by being told or shown what to do. Deeper meaning and solid change must be born over time. With particular changes, especially complex ones, one must struggle through ambivalence before one is sure that the new vision is workable and right (or unworkable and wrong). Good change is hard work; on the other hand, engaging in a bad change or avoiding needed changes may be even harder on us.

Local Factors

This section analyzes the social conditions of change; the organization or setting in which people work; and the planned and unplanned events and activities that influence whether or not given change attempts will be productive. The local school system represents one major set of situational constraints or opportunities for effective change. The same program is often successful in one school system and a disaster in another. Some districts have a track record of continual innovative achievement; others seem to fail at whatever they attempt.

The research on the role of organizations in change indicates that "planned change has become a matter of both motivating from without and orchestrating from within" (Firestone & Corbett, 1987, p. 321). The individual school may be the unit of change, but frequently change is the result of system initiatives that live or die based on the strategies and supports offered by the larger organization. This is especially true of multilevel, complex system-oriented innovations where what is being changed is the organizational culture itself.

The school district. I have suggested that adoption decisions are frequently made without adequate follow-through, and that the difficulties (subjective realities) inherent in the process of change are not well understood. Most attempts at collective change in education seem to fail, and failure means frustration, wasted time, feelings of incompetence and lack of support, and disillusionment. Since introducing innovations is a way of life in most school systems, districts build up track records in managing change. Whatever the track record at a given point in time, it represents a significant precondition relative to the next new initiative. The importance of the district's history of innovation attempts can be stated in the form of a proposition: The more that teachers or others have had negative experiences with previous implementation attempts in the district or elsewhere, the more cynical or apathetic they will be about the next change presented regardless of the merit of the new idea or program. Districts, provinces or states, and countries can develop an incapacity for change as well as a capacity for it.

There isn't much direct research on the prehistory of innovative attempts, but it doesn't take a historian to conclude that history in the educational change field has been made with remarkable alacrity and intensity. And it is not good history. In general, teachers and others have become skeptical about the purposes and implementation support for educational change.

On the other hand, nothing is more gratifying psychologically than attempting a change that works and benefits students. Success can beget more success. If the subjective meaning of change is so central, it is worth stressing that people carry meanings from one experience to the next. This psychological history of change is a major determinant of how seriously people try to implement new programs. To predict and to understand individuals' and groups' responses to particular innovative programs, one must know their immediate past history.

The role of the district administration and central staff is the subject of Chapter 10; it will be sufficient here to summarize the main findings. Individual teachers and single schools can bring about change without the support of central administrators, but district-wide change will not happen. Although it has always been said that the superintendent and the principal are critical to educational change, it is only recently that we are beginning to understand more specifically what that means in practice. All of the research cited in this chapter shows that the support of central administrators is critical for change in district practice. It also shows that general support or endorsement of a new program has very little influence on change in practice (for example, verbal support without implementation follow-through). Teachers and others know enough now, if they didn't 20 years ago, not to take change seriously unless central administrators *demonstrate through actions* that they should. Berman, McLaughlin, and associates (1979, pp. 84–95) give an excellent description of how one new superintendent with a mandate from the board "transformed the organization" by actively supporting new proposals, by visiting schools to see what was happening, by following through on decisions, and so on.

One of the more interesting analyses was carried out by Rosenblum and Louis (1979, p. 179). They investigated the relative effects on implementation of superintendent authority on the one hand and classroom autonomy of the teacher on the other hand. They found that superintendent authority (number of decision areas influenced by the superintendent) was *positively* associated with implementation of a new district-wide program, and classroom autonomy (number of classroom decisions made by the teacher on his or her own) was *negatively* related to implementation. They suggest that a degree of centralization is necessary for implementing comprehensive changes across schools, and that strong norms of individual classroom autonomy in some districts may actually inhibit organizational and district-wide changes.

All major studies show that the local implementation process at the district level is essential if substantial improvement is the goal (Louis, 1989; Marsh, 1988; Rosenholtz, 1989). The chief executive officer and other key central administrators set the conditions for implementation to the extent that they show specific forms of support and active knowledge and understanding of the realities of attempting to put a change into practice. To state it most forcefully, district administrators affect the quality of implementation to the extent that they understand and help to manage the set of factors and the processes described in this chapter.

Board and community characteristics. It is very difficult to generalize about the role of communities and school boards vis-à-vis implementation. Corwin (1973) found that community support of the school was correlated positively with innovativeness. Smith and Keith (1971) and Gold and Miles (1981) tell the painful sagas of what happens when middle-class communities do not like the innovations they see in their schools. School boards can indirectly affect implementation by hiring or firing reform-oriented superintendents. Demographic changes often put increasing pressure on schools to adopt, if not implement, new policies (Berman, McLaughlin, and associates, 1979). For example, a case study of the Toronto school system shows how the school board was central to the initial development of new multicultural policies and programs that were not necessarily welcomed by many schools (see Toronto Board of Education, 1976). Rosenblum and Louis (1979, p. 111) found that "the degree to which environmental changes external to the school were impinging on it to change" was one of four readiness factors related to subsequent implementation. Major conflicts sometimes incapacitate districts in bringing about actual change; in a sense, certain adoption decisions have to be settled before energy can be turned to implementation. In situations where the school board and the district are *actively* working together, substantiated improvements can be achieved, compared to conflictful or uninvolved boards (LaRocque & Coleman, 1989b). Whatever the case, as Miles (1987) asserts, attending to political stabilization in relation to the community is one of the primary tasks of planning and implementing new programs. In contemplating or introducing innovations, districts frequently ignore the community and/or the school board (see Gold & Miles, 1981; Smith & Keith, 1971).

There is also some evidence that rural districts not only have less access to innovations (House, 1974) but often are too distant geographically from needed sources of assistance during implementation (Bass & Berman, 1979, 1981; Rosenblum & Louis, 1979).

In short, the role of communities and school boards is quite variable ranging from apathy to active involvement—with the latter varying from conflictful to cooperative modes depending on the conditions (see Chapter 12).

The principal. As we shift from the district to the school level, the meaning of the phrase "the school is the unit or center of change" will become evident (Goodlad, 1975; Sirotnik, 1987). While we talk about the potential role of students in Chapter 9, the main agents (or blockers) of change are the principals and teachers.

All major research on innovation and school effectiveness shows that the principal strongly influences the likelihood of change, but it also indicates that most principals do not play instructional or change leadership roles. Berman and McLaughlin (1977) found that "projects having the *active* support of the principal were the most likely to fare well" (p. 124, their emphasis). Principals' actions serve to legitimate whether a change is to be taken seriously (and not all changes are) and to support teachers both psychologically and with resources. Berman, McLaughlin, and associates (1979, p. 128) note that one of the best indicators of active involvement is whether the principal attends workshop training sessions. If we recall the earlier dimensions of change (beliefs, teaching behavior, curriculum materials), we might speculate that unless the principal gains some understanding of these dimensions (not necessarily as an expert or an instructional leader) he or she will not be able to understand teachers' concerns—that is, will not be able to provide support for implementation. Such understanding requires interaction.

There is an abundance of other evidence cited in Chapter 8 that describes how and why the principal is necessary for effective implementation. The principal is the person most likely to be in a position to shape the organizational conditions necessary for success, such as the development of shared goals, collaborative work structures and climates, and procedures for monitoring results.

While the principal can have a major impact on implementation, there is also considerable research that indicates that he or she frequently does not in fact play an active role. Berman and McLaughlin (1978a, p. 131) report that one-third of the teachers thought that their principal functioned primarily as an administrator. Teachers rated these principals as ineffective and uninvolved in change. At the other end of the scale, Leithwood and Montgomery (1986) estimate that only about 1 in 10 principals were systematic problem-solvers—the highest of four categories in their principal profile.

The subjective world of principals is such that many of them suffer from the same problem in "implementing a new role as facilitator of change" as do teachers in implementing new teaching roles: What the principal should do *specifically* to manage change at the school level is a complex affair for which the principal has little preparation. The psychological and sociological problems of change that confront the principal are at least as great as those that confront teachers. Without this sociological sympathy, many principals will feel exactly as teachers do: Other people simply do not seem to understand the problems they face.

The role of teachers.   Both individual teacher characteristics and collective or collegial factors play roles in determining implementation. At the individual level, Huberman (1988), Hopkins (1990), McKibbin and Joyce (1980), and others have found that the psychological state of a teacher can be more or less predisposed toward considering and acting on improvements. Some teachers, depending on their personality and influenced by their previous experiences and stage of career, are more self-actualized and have a greater sense of efficacy, which leads them to take action and persist in the effort required to bring about successful implementation.

Psychological state can be a permanent or changeable trait, depending on the individual and on the conditions. Several researchers have found that some schools have a much higher proportion of change-oriented teachers than others (Little, 1982; Rosenholtz, 1989). Some of this is no doubt through selection, but it also seems to be the case that the culture or climate of the school can shape an individual's psychological state for better or for worse.

In the final analysis it is the actions of the individual that count. Since interaction with others influences what one does, relationships with other teachers is a critical variable. The theory of change that we have been evolving clearly points to the importance of peer relationships in the school. Change involves learning to do something new, and interaction is the primary basis for social learning. New meanings, new behaviors, new skills, and new beliefs depend significantly on whether teachers are working as isolated individuals (Goodlad, 1984; Lortie, 1975; Sarason, 1982) or are exchanging ideas, support, and positive feelings about their work (Little, 1982; Mortimore et al., 1988; Rosenholtz, 1989). The quality of working relationships among teachers is strongly related to implementation. Collegiality, open communication, trust, support and help, learning on the job, getting results, and job satisfaction and morale are closely interrelated. There is a vast difference between the "learning-impoverished" schools and the "learning-enriched" schools described by Rosenholtz (1989). Only 13 of the 78 schools in Rosenholtz' sample were classified as "learning enriched," but they provide powerful models of work environments that stimulate continuous improvements.

No words could sum up this discussion of school-level factors more accurately than those of Judith Little (1981), based on her study of work practice in six urban schools.

School improvement is most surely and thoroughly achieved when:

Teachers engage in frequent, continuous and increasingly concrete and precise *talk* about teaching practice (as distinct from teacher characteristics and failings, the social lives of teachers, the foibles and failures of students and their families, and the unfortunate demands of society on the school). By such talk, teachers build up a shared language adequate to the complexity of teaching, capable of distinguishing one practice and its virtue from another.

Teachers and administrators frequently *observe* each other teaching, and provide each other with useful (if potentially frightening) evaluations of their teaching. Only such observation and feedback can provide shared *referents* for the shared language of teaching, and both demand and provide the precision and concreteness which makes the talk about teaching useful.

Teachers and administrators *plan, design, research, evaluate and prepare teaching materials together.* The most prescient observations remain academic ("just theory") without the machinery to act on them. By joint work on materials, teachers and administrators share the considerable burden of development required by long-term improvement, confirm their emerging understanding of their approach, and make rising standards for their work attainable by them and by their students.

Teachers and administrators *teach each other* the practice of teaching. (pp. 12–13, her emphasis)

Only two of the six schools in Little's study evidenced a very high percentage of these practices, but no more convincing picture of the conditions for developing *meaning* on the part of individual teachers and administrators could be portrayed than in the passage just quoted.

External Factors

The last set of factors that influence implementation places the school or school district in the context of the broader society. In Canada this means primarily the offices of the department or ministry of education of each province, faculties of education, and other regional institutions. In the United States the main authorities consist of state departments of education and federal agencies. Other agencies such as regional R&D laboratories and centers also attempt to support educational implementation across the country. The relationship of the school to these various outside agencies is quite complicated, but necessary to analyze in order to understand the forces that impinge on school personnel. This section provides an overview of the influence of this outside set of forces.

I have already discussed the importance of unmet needs at the local level. But what does the larger society think of its educational system? Provincial/state and national priorities for education are set according to the political forces and lobbying of interest groups, government bureaucracies, and elected representatives. Legislation, new policies, and new program initiatives arise from public concerns that the educational system is not doing an adequate job of teaching basics, developing career-relevant skills for the economic system, producing effective citizens, meeting the needs of at-risk children—recent immigrants or handicapped children or cultural minorities—and so on. These "sources" of reform put pressure on local districts (sometimes to the point of force) and also provide various incentives for changing in the desired direction: New provincial guidelines are established as policy, new federal and state legislation is passed, new federally sponsored projects are developed. We have no reason whatsoever to imagine that these actions in their own right are related to implementation. Whether or not implementation occurs will depend on the congruence between the reforms and local needs, and how the changes are introduced and followed through.

Government agencies have been preoccupied with policy and program initiation, and until recently they vastly underestimated the problems and processes of implementation. We have a classic case of two entirely different worlds—the policy-maker on the one hand, and the local practitioner on the other hand. ("Divergent worlds" as Cowden & Cohen, 1979, call them.) To the extent that each side is ignorant of the *subjective* world of the other, reform will fail—and the extent is great. The quality of relationships across this gulf is crucial to supporting change efforts when there is agreement, and to reconciling problems when there is conflict among these groups: between provincial ministries and local school boards, administrators, and teachers; between state departments and local districts; and between federal project officers and local authorities.

The most straightforward way of stating the problem is to say that local school systems and external authority agencies have not learned how to establish a *processual* relationship with each other. The relationship is more in the form of episodic events than processes: submission of requests for money, intermittent progress reports on what is being done, external evaluations—paper work, not people work. More recently, in the United States, through resource support, standardization, and closer monitoring, state departments of education have had some direct influence on implementation of specific objectives. Some states have had strong impacts in interaction with favorable local conditions (Odden & Marsh, 1988). Mostly, however, lack of role clarity, ambiguity about expectations, absence of regular interpersonal forums of communication, ambivalence between authority and support roles of external agencies, and solutions that are worse than the original problems combine to erode the likelihood of implementation.

The difficulties in the relationship between external and internal groups are central to the problem and process of meaning. Not only is meaning hard to come by when two different worlds have limited inter-action, but misinterpretation, attribution of motives, feelings of being misunderstood, and disillusionment on both sides are almost guaranteed.

Government agencies have become increasingly aware of the impor-tance and difficulty of implementation and are allocating resources to establishing implementation units, to assessing the quality of potential changes, to supporting staff development, to monitoring implementation of policies, and to addressing other factors discussed in this chapter. Whether they will be successful is a relative matter, related partly to the resources required to address problems and partly to the capacity of local school systems to use these resources effectively.

The offer by governments of additional resources for educational reform is embedded in the U.S. educational system, even with recent ma-jor cutbacks in federal expenditures. These resources provide the margin required for implementation support in many school districts. As one might predict, whether they are used for better implementation depends on the characteristics of local systems. The larger issue of compliance with federal and state policies raises a host of questions, which are taken up in Chapter 13. (See Elmore, 1980, for an excellent brief account of the prob-lem.)

Technical assistance for implementation (materials, consultancy, staff development, etc.) is frequently available in federal- or state-sponsored innovative programs. We have learned a great deal in the past few years about the conditions under which external help is needed and effective (see Chapter 11; also Louis & Rosenblum, 1981; Crandall et al., 1982). The simplest observation at this juncture is that outside assistance or stim-ulation can influence implementation greatly, provided that it is inte-grated with the factors at the local level described above.

To conclude the discussion of external factors, the multiplicity of post-adoption decisions after educational legislation or new policies in-volves several layers of agencies. That success is achieved in many in-stances is a reflection that some people "out there" know what they are doing. Sharing and developing this know-how should be a major goal of those interested in educational change.

KEY THEMES IN THE IMPLEMENTATION PROCESS

Innovations have become increasingly more wholistic in scope as reformers have realized that introducing single curriculum changes amounts to tinkering. As these changes have become more organic and multilevel, it has been necessary to rethink the change process. Discussing individual roles and lists of factors, while helpful to a point, seems no longer adequate. Researchers and initiators of change have reconceptualized and studied change projects by identifying key themes in successful improvement efforts. This has resulted in a much more dynamic and vivid picture of the change process.

Miles (1987) captures this new approach as he summarizes findings from a study of successful urban high schools:

> The need for a vision of what the school should look like is affected by two preconditions: the principal must exercise leadership in promoting a vision, but the staff must also be cohesive enough to be willing to buy some shared set of goals. Having a vision leads indirectly to good implementation by creating an enthusiasm that increases willingness and initiative, but also by creating an environment in which a long term vision of the future permits program evolution that is always purposive, but reflects growth of activities rather than limiting implementation. Putting it another way: a good vision provides shared criteria for judging movement. Such evolution also leads, characteristically, to organizational change: new structures and procedures that in turn promote institutionalization. (p. 7)

There are a number of recent studies that provide clear descriptions of the main themes in successful change at the school level (Louis & Miles, 1990; Marsh, 1988; Wilson & Corcoran, 1988). The message is consistent in this research that a small number of powerful themes in combination make a difference.

The most fully developed conceptualization of this new approach is contained in Louis and Miles (1990) study of how urban high schools improve. They identify five major themes: vision-building, evolutionary planning and development, initiative-taking and empowerment, resource and assistance mobilization, and problem-coping. I used Louis and Miles' scheme as the starting point for developing Figure 5.2. I see six themes as paramount. Five are contained in Louis and Miles' study (I have relabeled resource and assistance mobilization as staff development and resource assistance, and problem-coping as monitoring/problem–coping). I have added a sixth theme, namely, restructuring, because it is clear that altering the organizational arrangements and roles in schools is essential to reform.

Vision–Building

Vision-building feeds into and is fed by all other themes in this section. It permeates the organization with values, purpose, and integrity for both the what and how of improvement. It is not an easy concept to

FIGURE 5.2.   Key Themes in Improvement

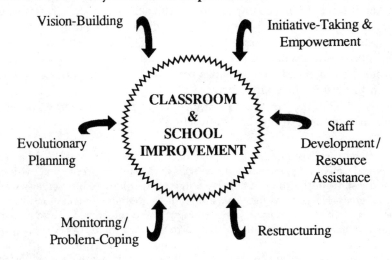

work with, largely because its formation, implementation, shaping, and reshaping in specific organizations is a constant process.

Bennis and Nanus (1985) make it clear that vision formation is a dynamic interactive process.

> All of the leaders to whom we spoke seemed to have been masters at selecting, synthesizing, and articulating an appropriate vision of the future. . . . If there is a spark of genius in the leadership function at all, it must lie in this transcending ability, a kind of magic, to assemble—out of all the variety of images, signals, forecasts and alternatives—a clearly articulated vision of the future that is at once single, easily understood, clearly desirable, and energizing. (p. 101)

Miles (1987) stresses that vision involves two dimensions: "The first is a sharable, and shared vision of what the *school* could look like; it provides direction and driving power for change, and criteria for steering and choosing. . . . The second type is a shared vision of the *change process* . . . what will be the general game plan or strategy for getting there?" (p. 12) (their emphasis). Note the emphasis on *shared* sense of purpose concerning both the content and the process of change.

As reforms become more complex and directed to transforming the educational system, strategies for building a shared vision have to reflect a broader agenda. Anderson and Cox (1987, pp. 8, 9) suggest the following: be open to different views and perspectives, maintain a core of well-regarded and capable people to keep synthesizing and articulating the evolving view of the system, as much as possible allow for direct experiences with elements of the change (don't let people become passive observers), broaden the number of people aware of and committed to the change through communicating about it, build credibility through the use of symbols and public dialogue, legitimate emerging viewpoints in support of a new vision, be aware of shifts in the change process having an effect on the organization, implement partial solutions when necessary to act as building blocks for the larger effort, broaden political support, and, finally, find ways to dampen the opposition.

While virtually everyone agrees that vision is crucial, the practice of vision-building is not well understood. It is a highly sophisticated dynamic process, which few organizations can sustain. Most of the literature on vision talks about what should or could be; the research reported in this section is based on actual examples of vision development in schools. (In addition to Louis and Miles, 1990, see Rosenholtz, 1989, and Wilson and Corcoran, 1988, for good descriptions of successful vision-building in elementary and secondary schools, respectively.)

Evolutionary Planning

Once implementation was underway toward a desirable direction, the most successful schools in Louis and Miles' (1990) study adapted their plans as they went along to improve the fit between the change and conditions in the school to take advantage of unexpected developments and opportunities. Blending top-down initiative and bottom-up participation is often a characteristic of successful multilevel reforms that use what amounts to evolutionary planning approaches (Marsh, 1988).

For major change, says Miles (1987), "tight forward scenarios" are undesirable: "Those steering school improvement need good data on what is happening, and the capacity to take advantage of unexpected developments in the service of vision" (p. 13). Have a plan, but learn by doing is the message, one strongly echoed in the business literature (Kanter, 1989). As Tom Peters (1987) advises: "Invest in applications-oriented small starts," "pursue team development of innovations," "encourage pilots of everything," "practice 'creative swiping,'" "practice purposeful impatience," "support fast failures." All of these are designed to foster an atmosphere of calculated risk-taking and constant multifaceted evolutionary development. (See also Chapter 6 on planning.)

Initiative-Taking and Empowerment

Since implementation is doing, getting and supporting people who are acting and interacting in purposeful directions is a major route to change. Louis and Miles (1990) found that initiative can come from different sources, but when it comes to implementation "power sharing" is crucial. In their study, leaders in successful schools supported and stimulated initiative-taking by others; set up cross-hierarchical steering groups consisting of teachers, administrators, and sometimes parents and students; and delegated authority and resources to the steering groups, while maintaining active involvement in or liaison with the groups. Louis and Miles note that the leadership skills relative to this theme are difficult—such as giving up power without losing control, taking active initiative without shutting out others, and supporting others' initiative without becoming patronizing (see also Barth, 1990). Extending involvement and influence to clients (students and parents) is very much part of this theme (see Chapters 9 and 12).

Developing collaborative work cultures is also clearly central to this theme. It helps reduce the professional isolation of teachers, allowing the codification and sharing of successful practices and the provision of support (see Fullan, 1990; Hargreaves, 1989; and Little, 1990b for a discussion of the pros and cons of collaboration). Working together has the potential of raising morale and enthusiasm, opening the door to experimentation and increased sense of efficacy (Cohen, 1988; Rosenholtz, 1989). Constant communication and joint work provide the continuous pressure and support necessary for getting things done. As Peters and Waterman (1982) observe: "Nothing is more enticing than the feeling of being needed, which is the magic that produces high expectations. What's more, if it's your peers that have those high expectations of you, then there's all the more incentive to perform well" (p. 240). Implementation is very much a social process.

Staff Development and Resource Assistance

The essence of educational change consists in learning new ways of thinking and doing, new skills, knowledge, attitudes, etc. It follows that staff development is a central theme related to change in practice. But, as with all the variables I am considering, the use of staff development can be grossly misapplied unless it is understood in relation to the meaning of change and the change process taken as a whole (Fullan, 1990). One of the great problems in educational reform is that there is too much well-intentioned "ad hoc-ism"—the use of single, segmented solutions unconnected or unintegrated with their systemic realities. The result is more participation here, more materials production there, more in-service training everywhere—more, more, more. Well, when it comes to implementation, more is sometimes less.

The amount of staff training is not necessarily related to the quality of implementation, but it can be if it combines pre-implementation training with assistance during implementation, and uses a variety of trainers (see Huberman & Miles, 1984; Louis & Rosenblum, 1981). Most staff development does not incorporate these follow-through features (see Chapter 15). Pre-implementation training in which even intensive sessions are used to orient people to new programs does not work (Berman & Mc-Laughlin, 1978a, p. 27; Huberman & Miles, 1984; Joyce & Showers, 1988). One-shot workshops prior to and even during implementation are not very helpful. Workshop trainers and program consultants are frequently ineffective. Consultants inside the district are often unclear about their roles. Teachers say they learn best from other teachers, but research shows that they interact with each other infrequently (Lortie, 1975). When teachers are trained as staff developers, they can be very effective in working with other teachers (see Stallings, 1989). Teachers also say that they need direct outside help, if it is practical and concrete; and they find those qualities to be the exception rather than the rule. Researchers report that concrete and skill-specific training is effective, but "only for the short run" (Joyce & Showers, 1988; McLaughlin & Marsh, 1978, p. 76).

The theory and meaning of change employed in this book explain why the above attempts at training are not effective. Simply put, most forms of in-service training are not designed to provide the ongoing, interactive, cumulative learning necessary to develop new conceptions, skills, and behavior. Failure to realize that there is a need for in-service work *during implementation* is a common problem. No matter how much advance staff development occurs, it is when people actually try to implement new approaches and reforms that they have the most specific concerns and doubts. It is thus extremely important that people obtain some support at the early stages of attempted implementation. Getting over this initial critical hump represents a major breakthrough for working toward more thorough change (Huberman, 1981). McLaughlin and Marsh (1978) stress that skill-specific training by itself has only a transient effect because the use of new materials and methods is often mechanical without the underlying ideas becoming assimilated. Similarly, the learning of new skills through demonstration and practice does not necessarily include the learning of the conceptual underpinnings necessary for lasting use (Bussis et al., 1976; Hall & Loucks, 1978; Joyce & Showers, 1988; McLaughlin & Marsh, 1978).

The dilemmas and inconsistencies in trying to understand why the "obvious" strategy of staff development fails more often than it succeeds are easy to resolve. Implementation, whether it is voluntary or imposed, is nothing other than a process of *learning something new.* One foundation of new learning is *interaction.* Learning by doing, concrete role models, meetings with resource consultants and fellow implementers, practice of the behavior, and the fits and starts of cumulative, ambivalent, gradual self-confidence all constitute a process of coming to see the meaning of change more clearly. Once this is said, examples of successful training approaches to implementation make sense (Huberman & Miles, 1984; Joyce & Showers, 1988; Louis & Miles, 1990; Marsh, 1988; Stallings,

1989). They are effective when they combine concrete, teacher-specific training activities, ongoing continuous assistance and support during the process of implementation, and regular meetings with peers and others. Research on implementation has demonstrated beyond a shadow of a doubt that these processes of sustained *interaction and staff development* are crucial regardless of what the change is concerned with. The more complex the change, the more interaction is required *during* implementation. People can and do change, but it requires social energy. School districts and schools can help generate extra energy by developing or otherwise supporting continuous staff development opportunities for teachers, administrators, and others.

Monitoring/Problem-Coping

The monitoring theme is not evaluation in the narrow sense of the term. It includes information systems, resources, and acting on the results through problem-coping and solving. Monitoring the *process* of change is just as important as measuring outcomes. As Peters (1987) states, successful organizations "measure what is important." And they do it in a certain way through

1. simplicity of presentation,
2. visibility of measurements,
3. everyone's involvement,
4. undistorted collection of primary information,
5. the straight forward measurement of what's important, and
6. achievement of an overall feel of urgency and perpetual improvement. (Peters, 1987, p. 484)

Monitoring serves two functions. First, by making information on innovative practices available it provides access to good ideas. Many good practices go unreported because of the isolation of teachers, schools, and districts from each other. Second, it exposes new ideas to scrutiny, helping to weed out mistakes and further develop promising practices. According to Peters, the best "systems" to ensure correct choices are

1. a clear vision,
2. sharing stories that illustrate how others, at all levels, have reacted to novel situations consistent with the vision, and
3. recognition for jobs well done. (p. 486)

The result, claims Peters, is "a *control system* in the truest sense of that term" (p. 486, his emphasis).

Formal monitoring procedures by themselves do not produce better results. The "intensification" of educational reform, which I referred to in Chapter 1, fails because it either does not measure what is most important or its findings are not linked to a process of improvement that incorporates and interrelates the six themes described in this section.

Monitoring the results and the process of change is especially important at the school level. All research on effective schools shows that paying constant attention to students' academic, personal, and social development is essential for success (Mortimore et al., 1988; Odden & Marsh, 1988).

Gathering data on implementation issues is also crucial. The success of implementation is highly dependent on the establishment of effective ways of getting information on how well or poorly a change is going in the classroom and school. The crux of the matter is getting the right people talking together on a regular basis with the right information at their disposal. Getting information about implementation progress needs to be channeled into provisions for additional in-service and assistance, materials support, and possible modification in plans, organizational arrangements, and the innovation itself—in short, carrying out organizational problem solving.

Louis and Miles (1990) stress that "all serious improvement programs have problems" (p. 268). In their research unsuccessful sites used shallow coping strategies such as avoidance, denial, procrastination, and people-shuffling, while successful sites engaged in deep problem solving such as redesign, creating new roles, providing additional assistance and time, and the like.

Evaluation and monitoring progress is probably one of the most difficult and complex strategies for change "to get right." It is frequently misused or not used (Wise, 1988). It is usually the last component of a change initiative that gets effectively, if at all, put in place (Fullan, Anderson, & Newton, 1986). In the early stages of attempts at change, people are usually wary of gathering information. On the other hand, it is revealing to note that once an improvement process of the type described in this section is underway, teachers and others close to implementation are those most insistent on gathering and examining the results of their efforts. Good change processes develop trust, relevance, and the desire to get better results. Accountability and improvement can be effectively interwoven, but it requires great sophistication (see also McLaughlin & Pfeiffer, 1988).

Restructuring

I will not take on here the big question of restructuring school, district, and state systems (David, 1989b; Elmore, 1989; Harvey & Crandall, 1988; Murphy, in press). I refer more directly to how the school as a workplace is organized. I use structure in the sociological sense to include organizational arrangements, roles, finance and governance, and formal policies that explicitly build in working conditions that, so to speak, support and press for improvement. Time for individual and team planning, joint teaching arrangements, staff development policies, new roles such as mentors and coaches, and school improvement procedures are examples of structural change at the school level that are conducive to improvement. There is a strong conceptual rationale for the importance of restructuring schools, but there is not much empirical evidence of its positive effects. We are still at the early stages of restructuring experiments, which should serve to help clarify the concept and debug how it might best be implemented. I include restructuring as a theme for implementation because of its obvious importance and potential, and because much of the action in the 1990s will center on attempts to restructure schools and the relationships of schools to external forces.

In summary, these six themes—leadership and vision, evolutionary planning, initiative-taking and empowerment, staff development and assistance, monitoring/problem-coping, and restructuring—provide a dynamic and powerful image of the complexity and excitement of the implementation process. They feed into and on each other. All six themes in concert are required for substantial change to occur.

FACTORS AFFECTING CONTINUATION

Implementation is the big hurdle at the level of practice, but the question of the continuation of initiated reforms should be considered in its own right. In a sense continuation represents another adoption decision, which may be negative, and even if positive may not itself get implemented. Berman and McLaughlin (1978a, pp. 166–83) found that projects that were not implemented effectively were discontinued (as would be expected), but they also found that only a minority of those that were well implemented were continued beyond the period of federal funding. The reasons for lack of continuation were in the main the same ones that influenced implementation, except that their role became more sharply defined. Lack of interest or inability to fund "special projects" out of district funds, and lack of money for staff development and staff support for both continuing and new teachers, signaled the end of many implemented programs. Lack of interest and support at the central district office (e.g., on the part of those who had taken on the project for opportunistic reason) was another reason for noncontinuation. Similarly, at the school level

The principal was the key to both implementation and continuation. . . . After the end of the federal funding, the principal influenced continuation in . . . direct ways. Often because of turnover in the original cadre of project teachers, projects would have decayed without active efforts by principal to bring on new staff. . . . It was extremely difficult for teachers to go on using project methods or materials without the principal's explicit support. (Berman & McLaughlin, 1977, p. 188)

Berman and McLaughlin identified a small number of cases in which continuation was sustained. In addition to the specific factors just cited (active leadership, staff development, etc.), the authors noted

District officials paid early attention to mobilizing broad-based support for the innovation. And after federal funding ended, mobilization efforts were increased to pave the way for the project's transition from its special status to its incorporation into key areas of district operations: the budget, personnel assignment, curriculum support activities, and the instruction program. In short, the groundwork and planning for sustaining a change agent project had the early, active, and continued attention of school district managers. (Berman & McLaughlin, 1978a, p. 20)

As a cautionary note, Berman and McLaughlin (1977, pp. 185–86) emphasize that the "meaning of continuation" can be misleading. For example, a district may officially decide to continue a project, but teachers may not implement it (i.e., in terms of the dimensions of implementation). Or a district may decide to discontinue the program, but many of the teachers may have already assimilated it. In other words, the program may leave its mark on the district in ways that may be overlooked. Direct assistance from external authorities may be helpful for initial implementation; but when it comes to institutionalization, the larger the external resource support, the *less likely* the effort will be continued after external funds terminate, because the district will not be able to afford to incorporate the costs into its regular budget (Yin et al., 1977, p. 16).

The problem of continuation is endemic to all new programs irrespective of whether they arise from external initiative or are internally developed. Huberman and Miles (1984) stress that continuation or institutionalization of innovations depends on whether or not the change gets embedded or built into the structure (through policy, budget, timetable, etc.), has (by the time of the institutionalization phase) generated a critical mass of administrators and teachers who are skilled in and committed to the change, and has established procedures for continuing assistance (such as a trained cadre of assisters), especially relative to supporting new teachers and administrators. Corbett and associates (1984) also found that availability of support and incorporation of the change into policy or guidelines varied and was related to the likelihood of continuation. They did not find that the availability of evaluation data from effectiveness instruments was much of a factor in the decision to continue (mainly because few schools in their sample had collected such data).

We talk about continuation as the third phase in a planned change process, but it should be clear that the process is not simply linear and that all phases must be thought about from the beginning and continually thereafter. For example, one of the most powerful factors known to take its toll on continuation is staff and administrative turnover (Berman & McLaughlin, 1977; Huberman & Miles, 1984). Very few programs plan for the orientation and in-service support for new members who arrive after the program gets started. And arrive they do, chipping away, however unintentionally, at what is already a fragile process.

One final distinction is critical. How might we best think of the relationship between continuation of a specific project and "future improvements" that go beyond the innovation or reform being attempted? This question can be profitably examined by considering both the case of single innovations and that of more ambitious reform projects at the school level.

With respect to single innovations, Crandall and associates (1986), drawing on the work of Hall and Loucks (1977), help us to understand that institutionalizing a given innovation is not an end in itself. The process "begins with the individual user not even interested in attending to the innovation, but ends with the user so proficient that he or she is riding new winds, modifying the original innovation so that it in fact works better, or even looking for a practice that represents an improvement over the one just mastered" (Crandall et al., 1986, p. 44). Improvement of practice is thus a continuous process of renewal.

Similarly, schools that engage in major effectiveness or restructuring efforts are presumably interested in going beyond the original projects. Put more powerfully, school effectiveness projects are in the business of institutionalizing the long-term capacity for continuous improvement. We need to make this goal more explicit because one can succeed in the short run in establishing an exciting, innovative, effective school, only to find that it doesn't last (Little, 1988). Deeper changes in the very culture of the school and its relationship to outside agencies are at stake if we are to develop this generic capacity for improvement.

PERSPECTIVES ON THE CHANGE PROCESS

As we have seen, the implementation process is complex and dilemma ridden, but we have accumulated considerable knowledge and insight into the process of change over the past decade. Some of these lessons were not self-evident at the outset, although they make common sense once discovered. The main revelations in this journey include a combination of elements that we usually think of as mutually exclusive or as not operating in the manner that they do. There are four main insights that were not predictable, but have turned out to be important.

1. active initiation and participation,
2. pressure and support,
3. changes in behavior and beliefs, and
4. the overriding problem of ownership.

The first issue is how can reform get started when there are large numbers of people involved. There is no single answer, but it is increasingly clear that changes require some impetus to get started. There is no evidence that widespread involvement at the initiation stage is either feasible or effective. It is more likely the case that small groups of people begin and, if successful, build momentum. Active initiation, starting small and thinking big, bias for action, and learning by doing are all aspects of making change more manageable, by getting the process underway in a desirable direction. Participation, initiative-taking, and empowerment are key factors from the beginning, but sometimes do not get activated until a change process has begun.

Second, it is increasingly clear that both pressure and support are necessary for success. We usually think of pressure as a bad thing, and support as good. But there is a positive role for pressure in change. There are many forces maintaining the status quo. When change occurs it is because some pressure has built up that leads to action. During the change process interaction among implementers serves to integrate both pressure and support. One of the reasons that peer coaching (Chapter 15) works so effectively is that it combines pressure and support in a kind of seamless way. Successful change projects always include elements of both pressure and support. Pressure without support leads to resistance and alienation; support without pressure leads to drift or waste of resources.

Third, the relationship between changes in behavior on the one hand, and changes in beliefs or understanding on the other hand requires careful consideration. Returning to the theme of meaning, it seems that most people do not discover new understandings until they have delved into something. In many cases, changes in behavior precede rather than follow changes in belief (Fullan, 1985). Moreover, when people try something new they often suffer what I call "the implementation dip." Things get worse before they get better and clearer as people grapple with the meaning and skills of change (Joyce & Showers, 1988). We see then that the relationship between behavioral and belief change is reciprocal and ongoing, with change in doing or behavior a necessary experience on the way to breakthroughs in meaning and understanding.

The role of ownership is the fourth subtlety in the change process. Clearly, deep ownership of something new on the part of large numbers of people is tantamount to real change, but the fact is that ownership is not acquired that easily. And when people are apparently in favor of a particular change, they may not "own it" in the sense of understanding it and being skilled at it, that is, they may not know what they are doing. Ownership in the sense of clarity, skill, and commitment is a progressive process. True ownership is not something that occurs magically at the beginning, but rather is something that comes out the other end of a successful change process.

In summary, the broad implications of the implementation process have several interrelated components. The first is that the crux of change involves the development of meaning in relation to a new idea, program, reform, or set of activities. But it is *individuals* who have to develop new meaning, and these individuals are insignificant parts of a gigantic, loosely organized, complex, messy social system that contains myriad different subjective worlds.

The causes of change also become more easily identifiable and understood once we possess an underlying conception of what constitutes change as a process over time. The factors of implementation and continuation reinforce or undercut each other as an interrelated system. Single-factor theories of change are doomed to failure. Arguments that product quality is more important than teacher attitude, or that external factors are more important than internal ones, or that teachers are more central than administrators, are pointless. Effective implementation depends on the *combination* of all the factors and themes described in this chapter. The characteristics of the nature of the change, the make-up of the local district, the character of individual schools and teachers, and the existence and form of external relationships interact to produce conditions for change or nonchange. The six critical themes co-exist or work at cross-purposes. It takes a fortunate combination of the right factors—a critical mass—to support and guide the process of re-learning, which respects the maintenance needs of individuals and groups and at the same time facilitates, stimulates, and prods people to change through a process of incremental and decremental fits and starts on the way to institutionalizing (or, if appropriate, rejecting) the change in question.

Moreover (as if we could stand more quandaries), there is frequently no definitive "change in question" at the beginning of the process of implementation, especially for complex reforms. Situations vary, and we never fully know what implementation is or should look like until people in particular situations attempt to spell it out through use. Implementation *makes* further policy; it does not simply put predefined policy into practice (see Farrar, DeSanctis, & Cohen, 1979; Majone & Wildavsky, 1978; Berman, 1980).

We understand that not all change is progress, or even meant to be. As individuals react incorrectly to pressures, so do school districts and societies. There are many motivations and origins for educational change, and in retrospect only a fraction of them seem to be based on the identification of a clear and important educational need and on the development of a quality idea and program. Even if we get the need and the idea right, the sheer complexity of the process of implementation has, as it were, a sociological mind of its own, which frequently defies management even when all parties have the best of intentions. After 25 years of ripping off and ripping into the system, we have learned "the pathos of implementation": Faithful implementation is sometimes undesirable (because the idea is bad), sometimes impossible (because power won't permit), and often unforeseeable (because it depends on what people bring to it as well as what's in it) (Majone & Wildavsky, 1978, p. 25).

The odds against successful planned educational change are not small. Increasing our understanding of implementation may alter them. We will see examples of how change can work when the factors of initiation, implementation, and continuation are combined in certain ways. The theory of the meaning of change and the change process provides us with an underlying conception of what should be done. This guide to change enables us to locate specific factors, to observe how they work in concrete situations, and to explain why they function as they do, and with what consequences for school improvement.

The "solution" to the management of educational change is straightforward. All we need to do in any situation is to take the factors and themes described in this chapter (and all their subvariables and interactions), change them in a positive direction, and then orchestrate them so that they work smoothly together. The mind may be excused for boggling.

If the theory of change emerging at this point leads us to conclude that we need better implementation plans and planners, we are embarking on the infinite regress that characterizes the pursuit of a theory of "changing." To bring about more effective change, we need to be able to explain not only what causes it but how to influence those causes. To implement programs successfully, we need better implementation plans; to get better implementation plans, we need to know how to change our planning process; to know how to change our planning process, we need to know how to produce better planners and implementers and on and on. Is it any wonder that the planning, doing, and coping with educational change is the "science of muddling through" (Lindblom, 1959)? But it is a *science*. All of which is another way of saying that Chapter 6 is ready to begin.

CHAPTER 6

Planning, Doing,
and Coping with Change

*When I remember how many of my private schemes have miscarried . . .
how the things I desperately strove against as a misfortune did me im-
mense good—how while the objects I ardently pursued brought me little
happiness when gained . . . I am struck with the incompetence of my
intellect to prescribe for society. There is a great want of this practical
humility in our political conduct.*

—Herbert Spencer, "Over Legislation," *The Westminster Review*
(July 1853)

For the growing number of people who have attempted to bring about
educational change, "intractability" is becoming a household word. Being
ungovernable, however, is not the same as being impervious to influence.
And the inability to change *all* situations we would ideally like to reform
does not lead to the conclusion that *no* situation can be changed. (To com-
plicate matters even further, to conclude that a situation can be changed
in a certain way does not mean that it should be.)

The picture of change that has been evolving in the previous chapters needs to be considered from the point of view of what, if anything,
can be done about it. To do this, I treat four major aspects of the problem
of planning educational change: "Why planning fails," "Success is possible," "Planning and coping," and "The scope of change."

WHY PLANNING FAILS

Understanding why most attempts at educational reform fail goes far
beyond the identification of specific technical problems such as lack of
good materials, ineffective in-service training, or minimal administrative
support. In more fundamental terms, educational change fails partly because of the assumptions of planners and partly because some "problems"
are inherently unsolvable. These two issues are explored in the next two
subsections.

Faulty Assumptions and Ways of Thinking About Change

In a word, the assumptions of policy-makers are frequently *hyperrational* (Wise, 1977, 1979, 1988). One of the initial sources of the problem is the commitment of reformers to see a particular desired change implemented. Commitment to *what should be changed* often varies inversely with knowledge about *how to work through a process of change*. In fact, as I shall claim later, strong commitment to a particular change may be a barrier to setting up an effective process of change, and in any case they are two quite distinct aspects of social change. The adage "Where there's a will there's a way" is not always an apt one for the planning of educational change. There is an abundance of wills, but they are *in* the way rather than pointing the way. As we have seen, a certain amount of vision is required to provide the clarity and energy for promoting specific changes, but vision by itself may get in the way if it results in impatience, failure to listen, etc. Stated in a more balanced way, promoters of change need to be committed and skilled in the *change process* as well as in the change itself.

Lighthall's (1973) incisive critique of Smith and Keith's (1971) famous case study of the failure of a new open-concept elementary school provides strong support for the hypothesis that leadership commitment to a particular version of a change is negatively related to ability to implement it. Lighthall states, as I do throughout this book, that educational change is a process of coming to grips with the *multiple* realities of people, who are the main participants in implementing change. The leader who presupposes what the change should be and acts in ways that preclude others' realities is bound to fail. Lighthall describes Superintendent Spanman's first speech to the Kensington school faculty.

> Spanman's visit to Kensington School was to make a "presentation" to the twenty-one member faculty. It was not for the purpose of discussing with them their joint problems of creating a whole new kind of education. His purpose was to express to the faculty parts of his reality; it was not to exchange his for theirs. Inasmuch as it was the faculty who were to carry the educational goals and images of his reality into action, that is to make much of his reality their realities too, and inasmuch as no person responds to realities other than his own, Spanman's selection of a one-way form of communication was self-defeating. In order for his reality to become part of theirs he would have to have made part of theirs his. (p. 263)

Innovators who are unable to alter their realities of change through exchange with would-be implementers can be as authoritarian as the staunchest defenders of the status quo. This is not to say that innovators should not have deep convictions about the need for reform or should be prepared to abandon their ideas at the first sign of opposition. It is to say that, for reasons that should be very clear from Chapters 2 through 5, innovators need to be open to the realities of others: sometimes because the ideas of others will lead to alterations for the better in the direction of change, and sometimes because the others' realities will expose the problems of implementation that must be addressed and at the very least will indicate where one should start.

Lighthall clearly documents how the superintendent and principal at Kensington continually imposed only their own realities and how their stance led in a relatively short time to disastrous results. Lighthall (1973) observed: "The tendency is widespread for problem solvers to try to jump from their private plans to public implementation of these plans without going through the [number of realities] necessary to fashion them in accordance with problems felt by the adult humans whose energy and intelligence are needed to implement the plans" (p. 282). Sarason (1971) states it another way: "An understandable but unfortunate way of thinking confuses the power (in a legal or organizational chart sense) to effect change with the process of change" (p. 29). In short, one of the basic reasons why planning fails is that planners or decision-makers of change are unaware of the situations that potential implementers are facing. They introduce changes without providing a means to identify and confront the situational constraints and without attempting to understand the values, ideas, and experiences of those who are essential for implementing any changes.

But what is wrong with having a strong belief that a certain aspect of schooling should be changed? Is it not appropriately rational to know that a given change is necessary, and to make it policy, if one is in a position to do so? Aside from the fact that many new programs do not arise from sound considerations (Chapters 2 and 4), there are other more serious problems. The first problem is that there are many competing versions of what should be done, with each set of proponents equally convinced that their version is the right one. Forceful argument and even the power to make decisions do not at all address questions related to the process of implementation. The fallacy of rationalism is the assumption that the social world can be altered by seemingly logical argument. The problem, as George Bernard Shaw observed, is that "reformers have the idea that change can be achieved by brute sanity."

Wise (1977) also describes several examples of excessive rationalization, as when educational outcomes are thoroughly prescribed (e.g., in competency-based education) without any feasible plan of how to achieve them. Wise characterizes the behavior of some policy-makers as wishful thinking: "When policy makers require by law that schools achieve a goal which in the past they have not achieved, they may be engaged in wishful thinking. Here policy makers behave as though their desires concerning what a school system should accomplish, will, in fact, be accomplished if the policy makers simply decree it" (p. 45). Wise goes on to argue that even if rational theories of education were better developed—with goals clearly stated, means of implementation set out, evaluation procedures stated—they would not have much of an impact, because schools, like any social organization, do not operate in a rational vacuum. Some may say that they should, but Wise's point is that they do not, and wishing them to do so shows a misunderstanding of the existing culture of the school (see Sarason, 1982; Lortie, 1975).

In fact it might be more useful to accept the nonrational quality of social systems and move on from there. Patterson, Purkey, and Parker (1986) suggest that organizations in today's society do not follow an orderly logic, but a complex one that is often paradoxical and contradictory, but still understandable and amenable to influence. They contrast the assumptions of the rational conception with those of a nonrational conception on five dimensions. *First,* goals: School systems are necessarily guided by multiple and sometimes competing goals, as we have said in Chapters 2 through 4. *Second,* power: In school systems, power is distributed throughout the organization. *Third,* decision making: This is inevitably a bargaining process to arrive at solutions that satisfy a number of constituencies. *Fourth,* external environment: The public influences school systems in major ways that are unpredictable. *Fifth,* teaching process: There are a variety of situationally appropriate ways to teach that are effective.

For Patterson and his colleagues the central difference between rational and nonrational models lies in their interpretation of reality: Proponents of the rational model believe that a change in "procedures" will lead to improvement. When their "if–then" procedures don't work, they become "if–only" procedures, tightening up rules to influence what is seen as a deficiency in response. Proponents of nonrational models recognize that organizations do not behave in a logical, predictable manner, and try to work this to their advantage. Wishing for, waiting for, and urging the system to become more rational is in itself irrational—it won't happen.

Another faulty assumption, ironically, is the problem of how to implement the implementation plan. Many people have responded to the research of the 1970s, which documented implementation problems, by developing elaborate implementation plans designed to take into account factors known to affect success. Designed to help, but actually adding insult to injury, complex implementation plans themselves become another source of confusion and burden on those carrying out change. Levine and Leibert (1987) identify this very problem in their discussion of how to improve improvement plans at the school and district levels. They observe that "comprehensive or semicomprehensive planning requirements often have the unintended effect of overloading teachers and administrators" (p. 398) and provide excuses at the school level by directing blame toward the plan. Among other guidelines, Levine and Leibert suggest: "Do not overload schools or allow them to overload themselves as part of a futile bureaucratic attempt to 'demonstrate' that they are doing everything possible to improve achievement" (p. 406); and "assistance from the central office must be furnished primarily through technical support from persons, not forms to fill out and deadlines to meet on paper" (p. 407). I will discuss specific guidelines for better implementation planning later in this chapter.

In short, implementation planning is itself a process of innovation. Planners, whether a teacher in a coaching project or a leader of a large-scale reform effort, have to combine expertise and knowledge about the direction and nature of the change they are pursuing, with an understanding of and an ability to deal with the factors and strategies inherent in the process of change.

Unsolvable Problems

More disturbing is the conclusion reached by several people who have attempted to understand or combine theory and practice in their daily work: that some problems are so complex that in the final analysis and final action they are simply not amenable to solution (Lindblom & Cohen, 1979; Sarason, 1978, 1983, 1990; Schön, 1971; Sieber, 1979). This is not to say that our efforts to solve them cannot be improved. But let us admit the hypothetical possibility that some social problems in a complex diverse society contain innumerable interacting "causes" that cannot be fully understood. Nor can we necessarily change those factors that we do understand as causes. Further, there is such an overload of problems that it is not possible to solve very many of them with the time, energy, and resources at our disposal.

Wise (1977) refers to the ways in which statements of goals for education frequently ignore this more basic question of whether the goals can be attained: "To create goals for education is to will that something occur. But goals, in the absence of a theory of how to achieve them, are mere wishful thinking. If there is no reason to believe a goal is attainable—as perhaps evidenced by the fact that it has never been attained—then a rational planning model may not result in goal attainment" (p. 48).

In solving educational problems, it is not just the number of factors to be understood but the reality that these factors sometimes change during the process; for example, people's attitudes change. Sarason (1978) reviews the expectation for social science.

Just as the natural sciences had developed laws about the nonhuman world, the social sciences would seek the laws of human society, not only for the purposes of explaining the workings of society but for controlling it. They would be the embodiment of Plato's philosopher-kings. Apparently, they were not impressed with the fact that Plato saw the problems of social living as so difficult to understand and cope with, requiring of philosopher-kings such a fantastic depth of learning and wisdom that one could not entrust social responsibility to them until they were well along in years. (p. 375)

Of course, Plato's solution was a "theory of change" that claimed that the world would be better off *if* we could develop and install philosopher-rulers with certain characteristics. It was not a theory of *how* to arrive at and maintain such a state.

Lindblom (1959) also claims that it is patently impossible to manage social action by analyzing all possible alternatives and their consequences.

Although such an approach can be described, it cannot be practical except for relatively simple problems and even then only in a somewhat modified form. It assumes intellectual capacities and sources of information that men simply do not possess, and it is even more absurd as an approach to policy when the time and money that can be allocated to a policy problem is limited, as is always the case. (p. 156)

There are two issues running through the above comments. The first is that with complex social problems the total number of variables (and their interactive, changing nature) is so large that it is logistically infeasible to obtain all the necessary information, and cognitively impossible for individuals to comprehend the total picture even if the information is available (see Schön, 1971, p. 215). The second is that even if some experts were able to comprehend the total picture themselves, our theories and experiences with meaning and implementation suggest that they would have a devil of a time getting others to act on their knowledge—partly because others will not easily understand the complex knowledge, and partly because the process of implementation contains so many barriers that have nothing to do with the quality of knowledge available.

In sum, to return to the opening paragraph of this section, planning fails partly because of the assumptions of planners and partly because the problems may not be solvable. The hubris of the change agent becomes the nemesis of implementers and others affected by new programs. The first form of hubris occurs when policy-makers assume that the solutions that they have come to adopt are unquestionably the right ones. We have seen that those solutions are bound to be questioned on grounds of competing values or technical soundness.

The second and related form of hubris, which compounds the problem, occurs when planners of change introduce new programs in ways that ignore the factors associated with the process of implementation—factors that are only partly controllable, but that are guaranteed to be out of control if ignored. The more the planners are committed to a particular change, the *less* effective they will be in getting others to implement it if their commitment represents an unyielding or impatient stance in the face of ineluctable problems of implementation. Commitment to a particular program makes it less likely that the planners will set up the necessary time-consuming procedures for implementation, and less likely that they will be open to the transformation of their cherished program and tolerant of the delays that will inevitably occur when other people begin to work with it. If we react to delays and transformations by assuming that they arise from the incompetence or bullheadedness of those implementing the program, we will add one more major barrier to the considerable number already operating. The solution is not to be less committed to what we perceive as needed reforms, but to be more sensitive to the possibility that our version of the change may not be the fully correct one, and to recognize that having good ideas may be less than half the battle compared with establishing a process that will allow us to use the ideas and discover additional ones along the way.

SUCCESS IS POSSIBLE

Recognizing the limitations of planning is not the same thing as concluding that effective change is unattainable. But in order to conclude that planned educational change is possible, it would not be sufficient to locate situations where change seems to be working. We would need to find examples where a setting has been *deliberately transformed* from a previous state to a new one that represents clear improvement. We need to know about the causes and dynamics of how change occurs.

Over the past decade there have been a number of increasingly clear examples of how school districts and schools dramatically transformed and improved the quality of education through a process of deliberate change. Berman, McLaughlin, and colleagues' (1979) description of Lakeville district (a pseudonym) is a concise but comprehensive account of how major changes transpired over a several-year period. The key factors were: hiring a new superintendent, creating a new role for central district personnel, transferring school principals and establishing new expectations and training for the role of principals, creating incentives and opportunities for teachers to obtain resources for changes that they proposed, establishing a teachers' center and other activities to stimulate teacher interaction and professional development, and obtaining added resources through federal innovative programs.

Wilson and Corcoran (1988) examine the tough domain of reforming high schools. Their synthesis of findings derived from documentation on 571 secondary schools recognized as unusually successful, along with case studies of a subgroup of schools, tells a dramatic story of how some of these high schools brought about substantial turnarounds in performance. Wilson and Corcoran found familiar themes at work: active leadership, professional work environments, positive learning opportunities, broad community involvement, continuous improvement, and service to all students.

Several other research studies describe success stories involving multiple schools and districts (Anderson et al., 1987; David, 1989b; Louis & Miles, 1990; Odden & Marsh, 1988, to name just a few). Direct research investigations on what makes schools effective or ineffective are even more convincing in proving that some schools are much more successful than others even when they face similar problems. Rosenholtz (1989) provides a very clear picture of the difference between "learning enriched" and "learning impoverished" schools in her study of 78 elementary schools.

Even more compelling is Mortimore and associates' (1988) longitudinal investigation of 50 "junior" schools (ages 7–11) in inner-city London. Fifty schools were matched on background characteristics, and their performance was traced over a four-year period. Mortimore and his colleagues found that students did better over the four-year period in the most effective compared with the least effective schools on a variety of cognitive and noncognitive outcomes, including reading, mathematics, writing, oracy, self-concept, behavior, attendance, and attitude to school. In addition to finding that schools tend to be effective or ineffective for all groups of children, they found that "a child whose parents are in manual employment and who attends an effective junior school is likely to attain more highly in reading and mathematics than a child who has the advantage of a nonmanual background, but also attends an ineffective school" (p. 215). The distinguishing characteristics of more effective schools included several "givens" (as Mortimore and associates call them) like size of school and status and stability of teaching staff; but they also found 12 key "policy factors," that is, factors amenable to alteration through strategic action. (I commented on these factors in Chapter 5. They involved, among other things, purposeful leadership by the principal, intellectually challenging teaching, record keeping, parental involvement, etc.)

The point of all this is that successful change is possible in the real world, even under difficult conditions. And many of the reasons for the achievements can be pinpointed. By and large, those reasons relate to the factors and themes analyzed in Chapter 5. I am not by any means implying that these factors can be inserted like pieces in a puzzle. However, there are classrooms, schools, communities, districts, and states that have altered the conditions for change in more favorable, workable directions. Not every situation is alterable, especially at certain periods of time; but it is a good bet that major improvements can be accomplished in many more settings than is happening at present.

The central, practical question is how best to plan for and cope with change in settings that are not now enjoying success. This takes us into the vicissitudes of theories of changing in which improvement rather than resolution is the name of the game.

PLANNING AND COPING

Many have dreamed up republics and principalities which have never in truth been known to exist; the gulf between how one should live and how one does live is so wide that a man who neglects what is actually done for what should be done paves the way to self-destruction rather than self-preservation.

—Machiavelli, *The Prince* (1514)

We have come to the most difficult problem of all. When all is said, what can we actually do to plan for and to cope with educational change? This section contains an overview of the assumptions, elements, and guidelines for action. Additional specific implications for particular roles and agencies (teacher, principal, superintendent, federal or state/provincial agencies, etc.) are left for the appropriate chapters in Parts II and III. First, I introduce the topic by indicating some of the basic issues and by noting that advice will have to vary according to the different situations in which we find ourselves. Second, I provide some advice for those who find that they are forced to respond to and cope with change introduced by others. Third, the bulk of the section is addressed to the question of how to plan and implement change more effectively.

Change is full of paradoxes. Being deeply committed to a particular change in itself provides no guidelines for attaining the change, and may blind us to the realities of others that would be necessary for transforming and implementing the change effectively. Having no vision at all is what makes for educational bandwagons. In the final analysis, either we have to give up and admit that effective educational change is impossible, or we have to take our best knowledge and attempt to improve our efforts. We possess much knowledge that could make improvement possible. Whether this knowledge gets used is itself a problem of change, part of the infinite regression that, once we have gained some knowledge of the process of change, leads us to ask how we get that knowledge—of the process of change—used or implemented.

A framework for planning and/or coping with educational change

FIGURE 6.1.   Change Situations According to Authority Position and Relation to the Change Effort

Authority position

		YES	NO
Relation to change effort	Initiator or promoter	I Planner (e.g., policy-maker)	II Planner (e.g., developer)
	Recipient or responder	III Coper (e.g., principal)	IV Coper (e.g., teacher)

has been implicit throughout this book. I do not think that a detailed technical treatment on how to plan for change is the most profitable route to take, although such a treatment may have some benefit. The most beneficial approach consists in our being able to understand the process of change, locate our place in it, and act by influencing those factors that are changeable and by minimizing the power of those that are not. All of this requires a way of thinking about educational change that has not been characteristic of either planners or victims of past change efforts.

In general, there are four logical types of change situations we could face as individuals. These are depicted in Figure 6.1. There are many different specific roles even within a single cell, which cannot be delineated here, but people generally find themselves in one of the four situations depending on whether they are initiating/promoting a change or are on the receiving end, and whether or not they are in authority positions. I start with coping, or being on the receiving end of change (cells III and IV), because this is the most prevalent situation.

Coping with Change

Those in situations of having to respond to a particular change should assume neither that it is beneficial nor that it is useless; that much is clear from the previous analysis. The major initial stance should involve *critical assessment* of whether the change is desirable in relation to certain goals and whether it is "implementable"—in brief, whether it is worth the effort, because it will be an effort if it is at all worthwhile. Several criteria would be applied: Does the change address an unmet need? Is it a priority in relation to other unmet needs? Is it informed by some desirable sense of vision? Are there adequate (not to say optimal) resources committed to support implementation (technical assistance, leadership support, etc.)? If the conditions are reasonably favorable, knowledge of the change process outlined in previous chapters could be used to advantage; for example, pushing for technical assistance, opportunities for interaction among teachers, and so on. If the conditions are not favorable or cannot be made favorable, the best coping strategy consists of knowing enough about the process of change so that we can understand why it doesn't work, and therefore not blame ourselves; we can also gain solace by realizing that most other people are in the same situation of nonimplementation. In addition, we can realize that implementation, in any case, cannot be easily monitored; for most educational changes it is quite sufficient to *appear* to be implementing the change, such as by using some of the materials. In sum, the problem is one of developing enough meaning vis-à-vis the change so that we are in a position to implement it effectively or reject it, as the case may be.

Those who are confronted with unwanted change and are in authority positions (cell III) will have to develop different coping mechanisms from those in nonauthority positions (cell IV). For the reader who thinks that resisting change represents irresponsible obstinacy, it is worth repeating that nonimplementable programs and reforms probably do more harm than good when they are attempted. The most responsible action may be to reject innovations that are bound to fail and to work earnestly at those that have a chance to succeed. Besides, in some situations resistance may be the only way to maintain sanity and avoid complete cynicism. In the search for meaning in a particular imposed change situation, we may conclude that there is no meaning, or that the problem being addressed is only one (and not the most important or strategic) of many problems that should be confronted. The basic guideline is to work at fewer innovations, but do them better—because it is probably not desirable, and certainly not humanly possible, to implement all changes expected, given what we know about the time and energy required for effective implementation.

We should feel especially sorry for those in authority positions (middle management in district offices, principals, intermediate government personnel in provincial and state regional offices) who are responsible for leading or seeing to implementation but do not want or do not understand the change—either because it has not been sufficiently developed (and is literally not understandable) or because they themselves have not been involved in deciding on the change or have not received adequate orientation or training. The psychiatrist Ronald Laing captures this situation in what he refers to as a "knot."

> There is something I don't know
> that I am supposed to know.
> I don't know what it is I don't know,
> and yet am supposed to know,

And I feel I look stupid
  if I seem both not to know it
  and not know *what* it is I don't know.
Therefore, I pretend I know it.
  This is nerve-wracking since I don't
  know what I must pretend to know.
Therefore, I pretend I know everything.
                    –R. D. Laing, *Knots* (1970)

A ridiculous stance to be sure, as painful as it is unsuccessful. It can, of course, be successful in the sense of maintaining the status quo. Depending on one's capacity for self-deception, it can be more or less painful as well. In any case, teachers know when a change is being introduced by or supported by someone who does not believe in it or understand it. Yet this is the position in which many intermediate managers find themselves, or allow themselves to be. Those in authority have a need for meaning too, if for no other reason than the change will be unsuccessful if they cannot convey their meaning of it to others.

Planning and Implementing Change

The implications for those interested in planning and implementing educational change (cells I and II) are very important, because we would all be better off if changes were introduced more effectively. It is useful to consider these implications according to two interrelated sets of issues: What *assumptions* about change should we note? How can we plan and implement change more effectively?

Assumptions about change. The assumptions we make about change are powerful and frequently subconscious sources of actions. When we begin to understand what change is as people experience it, we begin also to see clearly that assumptions made by planners of change are extremely important determinants of whether the realities of implementation get confronted or ignored. The analysis of change carried out so far leads me to identify 10 "do" and "don't" assumptions as basic to a successful approach to educational change.

1. Do not assume that your version of what the change should be is the one that should or could be implemented. On the contrary, assume that one of the main purposes of the process of implementation is to *exchange your reality* of what should be through interaction with implementers and others concerned. Stated another way, assume that successful implementation consists of some transformation or continual development of initial ideas. (Particularly good discussions of the need for this

assumption and the folly of ignoring it are contained in Lighthall, 1973; Marris, 1975, Ch. XVIII; Schön, 1971, Ch. 5; Louis & Miles, 1990).

2. Assume that any significant innovation, if it is to result in change, requires individual implementers to work out their own meaning. Significant change involves a certain amount of ambiguity, ambivalence, and uncertainty for the individual about the meaning of the change. Thus, effective implementation is a *process of clarification*. It is also important not to spend too much time in the early stages on needs assessment, program development, and problem definition activities—school staff have limited time. Clarification is likely to come in large part through *practice* (see Cohen, 1987; Loucks-Horsley & Hergert, 1985).

3. Assume that conflict and disagreement are not only inevitable but fundamental to successful change. Since any group of people possess multiple realities, any collective change attempt will necessarily involve conflict. Assumptions 2 and 3 combine to suggest that all successful efforts of significance, no matter how well planned, will experience an implementation dip in the early stages. Smooth implementation is often a sign that not much is really changing (Huberman & Miles, 1984).

4. Assume that people need pressure to change (even in directions that they desire), but it will be effective only under conditions that allow them to react, to form their own position, to interact with other implementers, to obtain technical assistance, etc. Unless people are going to be replaced with others who have different desired characteristics, relearning is at the heart of change.

5. Assume that effective change takes time. It is a process of "development in use." Unrealistic or undefined time lines fail to recognize that implementation occurs developmentally. Significant change in the form of implementing specific innovations can be expected to take a minimum of two or three years; bringing about institutional reforms can take five or more years. Persistence is a critical attribute of successful change.

6. Do not assume that the reason for lack of implementation is outright rejection of the values embodied in the change, or hard-core resistance to all change. Assume that there are a number of possible reasons: value rejection, inadequate resources to support implementation, insufficient time elapsed.

7. Do not expect all or even most people or groups to change. The complexity of change is such that it is impossible to bring about widespread reform in any large social system. Progress occurs when we take

steps (e.g., by following the assumptions listed here) that *increase* the number of people affected. Our reach should exceed our grasp, but not by such a margin that we fall flat on our face. Instead of being discouraged by all that remains to be done, be encouraged by what has been accomplished by way of improvement resulting from your actions.

8. Assume that you will need a *plan* that is based on the above assumptions and that addresses the factors known to affect implementation (see the section below on guidelines for action). Evolutionary planning and problem-coping models based on knowledge of the change process are essential (Louis & Miles, 1990).

9. Assume that no amount of knowledge will ever make it totally clear what action should be taken. Action decisions are a combination of valid knowledge, political considerations, on-the-spot decisions, and intuition. Better knowledge of the change process will improve the mix of resources on which we draw, but it will never and should never represent the sole basis for decision.

10. Assume that changing the culture of institutions is the real agenda, not implementing single innovations. Put another way, when implementing particular innovations, we should always pay attention to whether the institution is developing or not.

Effective planning. Assumptions, whether consciously or unconsciously held, constitute our philosophy of change. The purpose of this section is to make this philosophy more explicit in the forms of the conceptions and skills that underpin successful planning, that is, planning that results in improvement in practice.

In order to engage in successful change, we need to develop a way of thinking about change based on a thorough understanding of the processes analyzed in Chapters 4 and 5. Such knowledge, once obtained, is far more powerful as a resource than a memorized list of specific steps that we should follow. The fundamental goal for planners is to achieve a feel for the change process and the people in it, which entails a blend of research and experiential knowledge. As Cohen (1987, p. 485) says, we should "use research findings to supplement . . . professional experience and wisdom, not to supplant it." Lindblom and Cohen (1979) make a more complete argument for the necessity of combining knowledge from "professional inquiry" with what they call "ordinary knowledge." Both types of knowledge are necessary for solving problems.

In other words, change is not a fully predictable process. The answer is found not by seeking ready-made guidelines, but by struggling to understand and modify events and processes that are intrinsically complicated, difficult to pin down, and ever changing. Sarason (1971) explains that change agents do not confront their own conceptions of how to go about change and thus do not learn to improve their approaches: "I confess that I find it somewhat amusing to observe how much thought is given to developing vehicles for changing target groups and how little thought is given to vehicles that protect the agent of change from not changing in his understanding of and approach to that particular instance of change" (p. 217).

Concentrating on a way of thinking about planning is far from an abstract exercise in theorizing. It helps us identify which factors need to be addressed. It helps us recognize that concentrating on one or two sets of factors while neglecting others is self-defeating. It provides ideas for formulating a "plan" designed to address and review how these factors are operating in a given instance. I have frequently stated that good ideas, while necessary, are not sufficient for influencing others to change. To the extent that good ideas or visions of change are not combined with equally good conceptualizations of the process of change, the ideas will be wasted. Just as meaning about the substance of change is necessary, so is the development of a sense of meaning and competence about how best to approach it.

Rational planning models, as we have seen, do not work. Patterson, Purkey, and Parker (1986) argue for strategic planning appropriate for the "nonrational" world of school systems—planning that takes into account ever changing external factors, integrates these with internal organizational conditions, is medium or short range rather than long range, and uses qualitative as well as quantitative data. In their words,

> The goal of strategic planning is to produce a stream of wise decisions designed to achieve the mission of the organization. Emphasis shifts from product to process. Just as the planning process builds in flexibility for adaptation to changing conditions in and out of the organization, it also accepts the possibility that the final product may not resemble what was initially intended. (p. 61)

Louis and Miles (1990) provide a clear analysis of this evolutionary planning process in action in their study of urban high schools. They first stress that a small number of themes are interrelated: vision-building, evolutionary planning, resource assistance, and problem-coping. In effective schools these themes feed on each other. The planning theme is the one of interest here.

> The evolutionary perspective rests on the assumption that the environment both inside and outside organizations is often chaotic. No specific plan can last for very long, because it will either become outmoded due to changing external pressures, or because disagreement over priorities arises within the

organization. Yet, there is no reason to assume that the best response is to plan passively, relying on incremental decisions. Instead, the organization can cycle back and forth between efforts to gain normative consensus about what it may become, to plan strategies for getting there, and to carry out decentralized incremental experimentation that harnesses the creativity of all members to the change effort.

This approach is evolutionary in the sense that, although the mission and image of the organization's ideal future may be based on a top-level analysis of the environment and its demands, strategies for achieving the mission are frequently reviewed and refined based on internal scanning for opportunities and successes. Strategy is viewed as a flexible tool, rather than a semi-permanent expansion of the mission. (Louis & Miles, 1990, p. 193)

Louis and Miles draw several key conclusions from the cases.

- Effective evolutionary planning must be built on the direct involvement of the principal or some other key leader in the school (p. 199).
- Action precedes planning as much as follows it: "In 'depressed schools' one of the few ways of building commitment to a reform program is for successful action to occur that actualizes hope for genuine change. Effective action . . . often stimulates an interest in planning rather than vice versa" (p. 204).
- Multiple themes often precede mission statements: "The more successful of our schools had no *a priori* mission statements. Instead, multiple improvement efforts coalesced around a theme or set of themes only after the activity had begun" (p. 206). In one school, for example, initial themes focused on improvements in facilities and climate; moved to serve the needs of the whole student, incorporating social service agencies; and shifted gradually to a general vision.
- It is best to start small, experiment, and expand the successful while contracting the less successful: "The objective of evolutionary planning is to capitalize on the 'low risk' quality of smaller scale innovation to increase certainty. This in turn increases motivation and the possibility of concerted, more 'tightly coupled' action across the school" (p. 211). This approach also "permits schools to take advantage of unanticipated opportunities" (pp. 210–211).
- Leadership-dominated early planning must shift to shared control with teachers and others. The control base expands as evolutionary planning unfolds (p. 214).

While Louis and Miles' focus is at the school level, the principles of effective planning are being found and advocated in a wide range of organizations in business (Morgan, 1989; Peters, 1987) and in school systems (Crandall et al., 1986; Patterson et al., 1986). Complex change means facing a paradox. On the one hand, the greater the complexity, the greater the need to address implementation planning; on the other hand, the greater the thoroughness of implementation planning, the more complex the change process becomes. People get better at the change process by continuously acting and reflecting on the principles of effective implementation planning.

THE SCOPE OF CHANGE

There are many dilemmas and no clear answers to the question of where to start. The reader who by now has concluded that the theory of educational change is a theory of unanswerable questions will not be too far off the mark. Harry Truman (and later Pierre Trudeau) said, "We need more one-armed economists," because they were frustrated at the advice they kept getting: "on the one hand . . . on the other hand." The same can be said about the scope of educational change efforts. No one knows for sure what is best. We are engaged in a theory of probing and understanding the meaning of multiple dilemmas in attempting to decide what to do.

Sarason (1971), as usual, identifies many of the underlying issues.

A large percentage of proposals of change are intended to affect all or most of the schools within a system. The assumption seems to be that since the change is considered as an improvement over what exists, it should be spread as wide as possible as soon as possible. The introduction of new curricula is, of course, a clear example of this. What is so strange here is that those who initiate this degree of change are quite aware of two things: that different schools in the system can be depended on differentially to respond to or implement the proposed change, and that they, the sources . . . do not have the time adequately to oversee this degree of change. What is strange is that awareness of these two factors seems to be unconnected with or to have no effect on thinkings about the scope of the change. (pp. 213–14)

In a more recent work, Sarason (1990) maintains that we still have not learned to focus our efforts on understanding and working with the culture of local systems:

Ideas whose time has come are no guarantee that we know how to capitalize on the opportunities, because the process of implementation requires that you understand well the settings in which these ideas have to take root. And that understanding is frequently faulty and incomplete. Good intentions married to good ideas are necessary but not sufficient for action consistent with them (p. 6.1).

Above all, planning must consider the pre-implementation issues of whether and how to start, and what readiness conditions might be essential prior to commencing. Implementation planning is not a matter of establishing a logical sequence of steps deriving from the innovation or reform at hand.

Several additional points put the problem of scope in perspective. First, in some situations it may be more timely or compatible with our priorities to concentrate on getting a major policy "on the books," leaving questions of implementation until later. In other words, the first priority is initiation, not implementation. Major new legislation or policies directed at important social reforms often fit this mode—for example, new legislation on desegregation, special education, or restructuring. There is no answer to the question of whether this is more effective than a more gradual approach to legislation, but it should be recognized that implementation is then an immediate problem. Sarason and Doris (1979), in commenting on special education legislation, warn us: "To interpret a decision . . . as a 'victory' is understandable but one should never underestimate how long it can take for the spirit of victory to become appropriately manifested in practice" (p. 358). Much social policy legislation is vague on implementation; some vagueness may be essential in order to get the policy accepted, but nonetheless it means that implementation can be easily evaded (see Weatherley & Lipsky, 1977; Sarason & Doris, 1979, Ch. 19). In the face of major value or power resistance, it is probably strategically more effective in the short run to concentrate our energies on establishing new legislation, hoping that in the long run the pressure of the law, the promotion of implementation through incentives and disincentives, and the emergence of new implementers will generate results.

Second, significant change, as we have seen, can be accomplished by taking a developmental approach, pursuing multiple lines simultaneously. Given that universal reform cannot succeed (and may do more harm than good), Sarason (1971) wonders: "Why not pick one's spots, learn from experience, and then take up the tactics of extension? What if the schools that were not to receive the service were part of an ongoing group to discuss and evaluate what was going on in the schools receiving service?" (p. 214). Even changes that are quite explicit and clear face the problem of scope of coverage when they are attempted with larger numbers than the support system (such as staff development and other forms of assistance) can handle.

A third possibility, not always appropriate, is to concentrate efforts on working intensively with those schools or school districts that are interested in the particular change effort. It is a testimony to the complexities of implementation that even programs that involve apparently volunteer groups frequently fail. As to nonvolunteers, Sarason observes, "One may decide *to start nowhere,* that is, the minimal conditions required for that particular change to take hold . . . are not present" (p. 218, emphasis in the original). Far from being an evasion, says Sarason, such a decision forces one to consider "what other kinds of change have to take place before the minimal conditions can be said to exist" (p. 218). It is important to recognize that if the obstacles to change in particular situations are ignored, the experience with implementation can be harmful to the adults and children directly involved—*more harmful* than if nothing had been done.

Understanding the central importance of "meaning" for those who are implementing change, gives us hints about the processes that may be required and makes sense of the assumptions and guidelines for action contained in this chapter. It also reveals why the usual approaches to change fail. Many of those concerned with educational reform have been preoccupied with developing and advocating the goals of change, as if all that is needed are good intentions and the power to legislate.

It is easier—more tangible, clear, and satisfying in the short run—to concentrate on *developing* a new program than to enter the conflict-filled, ambiguous, anxious world of seeing what others think of the idea. But what is understandable is not necessarily right. The subtleties of change are once again evidenced when we point out that efforts to bring about change have failed regardless of whether they were engineered by university professors, federal or state/provincial departments of education, or local teacher committees. The main reason for failure is simple—developers or decision-makers went through a process of acquiring *their* meaning of the new curriculum. But when it was presented to teachers, there was no provision for allowing them to work out the meaning of the changes for themselves. Innovations that have been succeeding have been doing so because they combine good ideas with good implementation decision and support systems.

It is necessary to dwell on the subtleties of managing change because even the distinction between the content and the process of change is not sufficient. Concentrating on the process of change may turn out to be only a theory of what *should* change. In keeping with the theme of this book, a theory of change should be judged only in terms of whether it is successfully implemented—whether it actually alters factors it sets out to change—not for what it claims to be. Otherwise, there is no real difference between those who claim that educational problems would be solved if only schools would adopt this or that *program change,* and those who argue that problems would be solved if only schools would follow this or that *process of change.* Both are engaged in wishful thinking—the former about the substance of change and the latter about the form.

Constant attention to both the content and process of reform and their complex interrelationship is required. This can be done effectively only when it is grounded in particular roles in particular situations. Success depends on people. Understanding the orientations and working conditions of the main actors in schools and school systems is a prerequisite for planning and coping with educational change effectively. The chapters in Part II portray the social realities of those most directly involved in attempting to balance stability and change in education in their daily work lives.

Part II

EDUCATIONAL CHANGE
AT THE LOCAL LEVEL

CHAPTER 7

The Teacher

If a new program works teachers get little of the credit; if it fails they get most of the blame.

—Anonymous

Educational change depends on what teachers do and think—it's as simple and as complex as that. It would all be so easy if we could legislate changes in thinking (Sarason, 1971, p. 193). Whether significant educational change is possible is a moot point; easy it certainly isn't.

Classrooms and schools become effective when (1) quality people are recruited to teaching (see Chapter 14), and (2) the workplace is organized to stimulate and reward accomplishments (Conley, Bacharach, & Bauer, 1989). The two are intimately related. Professionally rewarding workplace conditions attract and retain good people. Using sustained improvement as the criterion, this chapter progresses from the negative—the situation for most teachers—to the positive—conditions where teaching thrives.

The conditions of teaching appear to have deteriorated over the past two decades. Reversing this trend, as I shall argue in this chapter, must be at the heart of any serious reform effort. Leaving aside the question of blame, it is a fact that teachers have become devalued by the community and the public. Teacher stress and alienation from the profession, as discussed later in this chapter, are at an all time high, judging from the increasing demand for workshops on coping with stress and the numbers of teachers leaving or wanting to leave the profession. The range of educational goals and expectations for schools and the transfer of family and societal problems to the school, coupled with the ambivalence of youth about the value of education, present intolerable conditions for sustained educational development and satisfying work experiences. The review of the status of teaching put forth by the Carnegie and Holmes groups (both 1986) reinforces the need to strengthen teachers and teaching as a "profession." For both stability and change, the mental health and attitudes of teachers are absolutely crucial to success.

If educational change is to happen, it will require that teachers understand themselves and be understood by others. As Nisbet (1969) has argued, in order to consider change, we must first understand stability and order. For this reason, I start with a sketch of where teachers are. From there I move to the phenomenon of the introduction of change— in 9 cases out of 10 a gross mismatch, as far as the world of the teacher is concerned. Third, I focus on what makes change work, especially on the classroom and workplace conditions necessary for success. In the fourth section—guidelines for teachers—I make recommendations for how teachers might assess and cope with wanted and unwanted change. Finally, I take up the matter·of professionalism at the crossroads, for teaching is at a critical juncture in its evolution as a profession.

WHERE TEACHERS ARE

Starting where teachers are means starting with routine, overload, and limits to reform, because this is the situation for most teachers. As we shall see there are notable exceptions to this modal pattern, which represent glimpses of what could be, but for most teachers daily demands crowd out serious sustained improvements.

It is clearly not possible to describe in a few pages the school lives of two-and-one-half million teachers in diverse settings across North America. Not even a sociologist could do that. The following, written by a teacher, provides a composite picture that, despite the flamboyance of the language, captures the experience of many high school teachers.

> Teachers routinely have to teach over 140 students daily. On top of that, we have lunch duty, bus duty, hall duty, home room duty. . . . We go to parents' meetings, teachers' meetings, in-service meetings, curriculum meetings, department meetings, county-wide teachers' meetings, school board meetings, and state teachers' conferences. We staff the ticket booths and concession stands at football and basketball games. We supervise the production of school plays, annuals, newspapers, dances, sports events, debates, chess tournaments, graduation ceremonies. We go on senior trips. . . . We go on field trips to capital buildings, prisons, nature centers, zoos, courtroom trials. We choke down macaroni and cheese and USDA peanut butter at lunch (and have to pay for it). We search lockers during bomb threats. We supervise fire drills and tornado alerts. We write hall passes, notes to the principal, the assistant principal, parents and ourselves. We counsel. We wake up every morning to the realization that the majority of our students would far rather be someplace else. On top of that everyone's yelling at us—state legislatures, parents, and SAT scores. . . . To add injury to insult, colleges and universities are getting all huffed up and grumpy and indignant over the increasingly poor preparation of the students we're sending them. Well, just who do they think taught us how to teach? How much support and prestige do they accord their own schools of education? (Wigginton, 1986, p. 191)

The situation of elementary school teachers is different, but no more attractive. Most urban teachers in North America, for example, increasingly face ethnic and language diversity, special needs children, one-parent families, and a bewildering array of social and academic expectations for the classroom. After reviewing the goals of education—mastery of basic skills, intellectual development, career education, interpersonal understandings, citizenship participation, enculturation, moral and ethical character development, emotional and physical well-being, creativity and aesthetic self-expression, and self-realization—Goodlad (1984, Ch. 2) concludes *we want it all.*

The circumstances of teaching, then, ask a lot of teachers in terms of daily maintenance and student accountability, and give back little in the time needed for planning, constructive discussion, thinking, and just plain rewards and time for composure. The central tendency of these conditions, as I will describe in this section, is decidedly negative in its consequences. Only by recognizing these negative conditions can we hope to transform them (see the section below on "what makes change work for teachers"). But first, let us examine more systematically the predominant themes.

One of the most respected and widely quoted studies of what teachers do and think was conducted by Lortie (1975). Lortie based his study on 94 interviews with a stratified sample of elementary and secondary school teachers in the greater Boston area (called the Five Town sample), questionnaires to almost 6,000 teachers in Dade County, Florida, and various national and local research studies by others. His findings can be best summarized in point form.

1. Teacher training (see also Chapter 14) does not equip teachers for the realities of the classroom. Nor could it be expected to do so in light of the abruptness of the transition. In September, the young teacher (who typically was a student in June) assumes the same responsibility as the 25-year teacher veteran. For both the beginning and experienced teacher, issues of classroom control and discipline are one of the major preoccupations. Lortie claims that for most teachers there is always a tension between the task-oriented controlling aspect of a teacher role and the relational reaching-the-student aspect.

2. The cellular organization of schools means that teachers struggle with their problems and anxieties privately, spending most of their time physically apart from their colleagues.

3. Partly because of the physical isolation and partly because of norms of not sharing, observing, and discussing each other's work, teachers do not develop a common technical culture. The picture is not one of "colleagues who see themselves as sharing a viable, generalized body of knowledge and practice" (p. 79). In many ways student learning is seen

as determined either by factors outside the teachers' control (family background) or by unpredictable and mysterious influences. According to Lortie, the lack of a technical culture, an analytic orientation, and a serious sharing and reflection among teachers creates ambiguity and ad hocness: "The teacher's craft. . . . is marked by the absence of concrete models for emulation, unclear lines of influence, multiple and controversial criteria, ambiguity about assessment timing, and instability in the product" (p. 136). A teacher is either a good teacher or a bad one; a teacher has either a good day or a bad one. It all depends.

4. When teachers do get help, the most effective source tends to be fellow teachers, and secondly administrators and specialists. Such help is not frequent and is used on a highly selective basis. For example, teachers normally do not relate objectives to principles of instruction and learning outcomes of students. Rather, "they describe the 'tricks of the trade' they picked up—not broader conceptions that underlie classroom practice" (p. 77). As to the frequency of contact, 45% of the Five Town teachers reported "no contact" with other teachers in doing their work, 32% reported "some contact," and 25% reported "much contact" (p. 193). There is some indication that teachers desire more contact with fellow teachers—54% said that a good colleague is someone who is willing to share (p. 194). Again, this refers more to "tricks of the trade" than to underlying principles of teaching and to the relationship of teaching to learning.

5. Effectiveness of teaching is gauged by informal, general observation of students—50% of the teachers in Dade County responded in this vein; the next most frequent choice related to the results of tests—a very distant 13.5%. In short, teachers rely heavily on their own informal observations.

6. The greatest rewards mentioned by teachers were what Lortie labels "psychic rewards": "the times I reached a student or group of students and they have learned" (p. 104). Over 5,000 (86%) of the 5,900 teachers in Dade County mentioned this source of gratification. The next most frequent response—respect from others—was selected by 2,100, or 37% of the sample.

7. Lortie also found that "striking success with one student" here and one student there was the predominant source of pride (as distinct from raising test scores of the whole group) (p. 121). For secondary school teachers, the success stories often did not become visible until one or more years after graduation, when a former student returned to thank a teacher. In comparing single successes with group results, it is revealing

that 64% of the Five Town teachers mentioned the former category, and only 29% mentioned the latter, as a major source of satisfaction.

8. One of the predominant feelings that characterize the psychological state of teachers and teaching is *uncertainty*—teachers are not sure whether they have made any difference at all.[1] Intangibility, complexity, and remoteness of learning outcomes, along with other influences (family, peer, and societal) on the students, make the teacher's assessment of his or her impact on students endemically uncertain (Ch. 6): 64% of the Five Town teachers said that they encountered problems in assessing their work; two-thirds of them said the problem was serious (p. 142).

9. Of particular relevance to innovation, when Lortie asked teachers how they would choose to spend additional work time, if they received a gift of 10 hours per week, 91% of the almost 6,000 teachers in Dade County selected classroom-related activities (more preparation, more teaching with groups of students, more counseling). "It is also interesting," writes Lortie, "that 91 percent of the first choices are *individualistic*; they are all tasks which teachers normally perform alone" (p. 164, my emphasis). Second, the lack of time and the feeling of not having finished one's work is a perennial problem experienced by teachers. Unwanted or unproductive interruptions, Lortie observes, "must be particularly galling" (p. 177). Among the Five Town teachers, Lortie found that 62 of the 98 reasons for complaints given by teachers "dealt with time erosion or the disruption of work flow" (p. 178). One can immediately see how unwanted innovations can be another source of annoyance.

There are many other details one could add concerning what teachers do, particularly if we could examine differences between grade levels, types of communities, and so on; but as a basic characterization of common problems faced by most teachers, Lortie's description seems amazingly accurate and complete in light of the confirmation of his main conclusions in numerous other studies. House and Lapan (1978), Clark and Yinger (1977), Jackson (1968, 1980), and Huberman (1978, 1983) all corroborate Lortie's analysis. For example, House's description of his first year of teaching is reminiscent of Lortie's findings:

> The other striking feature of my first year of teaching, besides the strong feelings of my own failure and despair, was that I was entirely alone. There was no senior partner in the firm from whom I could solicit advice on my first case. . . . Professionally I was alone. It was sink or swim by myself. There were some people who might have helped. I was teaching in a combined junior and senior high school so both the principals theoretically were supervisors of instruction. . . . Of course this is far removed from the truth. Help

from sources where one might have expected it—from the common culture of teachers, from discussions in the teachers' lounge, from talks with a few colleagues—was almost totally absent. . . . The information [that was] transferred tends to be more personal than professional. (House & Lapan, 1978, pp. 16–17)

There is no need to repeat the details of House and Lapan's other observations; they represent a litany of the issues raised by Lortie—uncertainty and guilt about whether what they are doing has any value, the isolated joys of reaching individual students, the lack of reflexivity on either an individual or a collective basis, the perennial frustration of lack of time and unwanted interruptions, the complexity of the teaching act in a crowded classroom with management problems, interacting with one or more students while others are waiting, and the unpredictability of a well-planned lesson falling flat, an unplanned session connecting, and so on.

Further research, much of it sophisticated and systematic, over the past five years has confirmed and elaborated many of Lortie's findings. Goodlad (1984) and his colleagues studied a national sample of 38 schools, including over 8,000 parents, 17,000 students, and 1,350 teachers and their classrooms. Goodlad's conclusions about the modal patterns of classroom life are not inspiring:

- The dominant pattern of classroom organization is a group to which the teacher most frequently relates as a whole.
- Each student essentially works and achieves alone within a group setting.
- The teacher is virtually autonomous with respect to classroom decisions—selecting materials, determining class organization, choosing instructional procedures.
- Most of the time the teacher is engaged in either frontal teaching, monitoring students' seatwork, or conducting quizzes. Relatively rarely are students actively engaged in learning directly from one another or initiating processes of interaction with teachers.
- There is a paucity of praise and correction of students' performance, as well as of teacher guidance in how to do better next time.
- Students generally engage in a rather narrow range of classroom activities—listening to the teacher, writing answers to questions, and taking tests and quizzes.
- Large percentages of the students surveyed appeared to be passively content with classroom life.
- Even in the early elementary years there was strong evidence of students not having time to finish their lessons or not understanding what the teacher wanted them to do.

• The teacher has little influence or involvement in school-wide and other extra-classroom matters (Goodlad, 1984, pp. 123–24, 186).

Goodlad proceeds to analyze the conditions under which teachers work. The theme of autonomous isolation stands out. Although teachers functioned independently, "their autonomy seemed to be exercised in a context more of isolation than of rich professional dialogue" (p. 186). Inside schools, "teacher-to-teacher links for mutual assistance or collaborative school improvement were weak or non-existent" (p. 186). A large majority said that they never observed another teacher teaching, although 75 percent at all levels of schooling stated that they would like to observe other teachers at work (we shall return to the potential of this latter finding later in this chapter). Teachers also reported that they were not involved in addressing school-wide problems. Outside the school, aside from casual contacts at in-service workshops and meetings, Goodlad found that "there was little. . . .to suggest active, ongoing exchanges of ideas and practices across schools, between groups of teachers, or between individuals even in the same schools" (p. 187).

Rosenholtz' study of 78 schools in Tennessee (1989) corroborated many of Goodlad's observations. The majority of schools (65 of the 78) were classified by Rosenholtz as relatively "stuck" or "learning impoverished" for both teachers and students. She described these schools as showing little or negative attention to school-wide goals, isolation among teachers, limited teacher learning on the job, teacher uncertainty about what and how to teach, and low commitment to the job and the school. This constellation of factors functioned in these schools as a vicious negative cycle to suppress teacher and student desire and achievement. Rosenholtz says "stuck schools" are characterized by

> Little attachment to anything or anybody. Teachers seemed more concerned with their own identity than a sense of shared community. Teachers learned about the nature of their work randomly, not deliberately, tending to follow their individual instincts. Without shared governance, particularly in managing student conduct, the absolute number of students who claimed teachers' attention seemed greater. . . . teachers talked of frustration, failure, tedium and managed to transfer those attributes to the students about whom they complained. (p. 208)

It would be wrong to conclude that the majority of teachers actively dislike being teachers. For most it is a never ending mixture of satisfying and stressful experiences. King, Warren, and Peart's (1988) study of almost 6,000 high school teachers in Ontario reports the 10 most satisfying and 10 most stressful aspects of being a teacher (see Figure 7.1)—aspects similar to those found by Goodlad (1984).

A further component of the status and working conditions of teach-

FIGURE 7.1. Stressful and Satisfying Aspects of Being a Teacher
(Ranked in Order of Most Frequent Mention)

Satisfying	*Stressful*
1. working with young people, rapport/relationship	1. time demands, too much marking, lesson preparation, "administrivia," deadlines
2. times when the "light goes on" and a student suddenly understands, student enjoyment, immediate feedback	2. discipline/attendance problems, student confrontations
3. student success, achievement	3. student lack of motivation, apathy, negative attitudes
4. interaction with/support from colleagues	4. lack of administrative support, poor administration
5. influencing the growth, character, and attitudes of students	5. colleagues' negative attitudes, incompetent/poor teachers
6. involvement with extracurricular activities, coaching, drama	6. working conditions, lack of equipment/texts, low budget
7. subject matter taught, developing curriculum	7. lack of security, redundancy, declining enrollments
8. teaching, a lesson taught well	8. large class size
9. helping students individually with personal academic problems	9. Ministry directive, changing curriculum/course content
10. feedback from students at the end of the year and after graduation	10. lack of public/parental support, negative attitude toward education

Adapted from King et al., 1988.

ers concerns salaries. In the United States during the 1970s teacher salaries declined relative to many other occupations and to purchasing power. Accompanying the reform efforts in the 1980s has been a widespread boost in teacher salaries. From 1981 to 1986 average salaries increased by 31 percent, from approximately $19,200 to $25,200, an increase considerably higher than inflation, although "these increases only restored teachers to the real value of average teacher salaries in 1971–72" (Darling-Hammond & Berry, 1988, p. 39). There is an increased recognition that compensation for teachers must be improved. In many cases financial increases are linked explicitly to new expectations for school improvement (Darling-Hammond & Berry, 1988).

In Canada, teachers are comparatively better paid, reflecting a higher status and greater incentive for those entering the teaching profession. For example, the average salary for teachers in Ontario in 1988–89 was over $42,000, and the starting salary was over $26,000, which places first-year teachers close to the average salary of all teachers in the United States, albeit in Canadian dollars.

Another revealing aspect of where teachers are is to consider how the career of teaching unfolds. There is surprisingly little research on the career cycle of teachers, and most of it is recent (see Bacharach et al., 1987; Burke et al., 1987; Huberman, 1988, 1991). Huberman in an in-depth study of 160 teachers in Switzerland found several subpatterns, but in general terms his findings show that teachers go from survival and discovery (the first three years), to stabilization (years 4–6), to experimentation and diversity (years 7–18), to focusing down (19 or more years). Huberman (1988) found three subpatterns in the latter group, which he labeled "positive focusing" (doing my own thing), "defensive focusing" (withdrawn and critical), and disenchantment (withdrawn and bitter). As Huberman states, there are individual exceptions to the pattern and the dividing lines are approximate, but he wonders what the findings say about how change is being managed if we are producing a lot of older teachers who are bitter or worn out. Note also that Huberman's study involved those who stayed with the career of teaching. It does not say anything about those who left teaching or became administrators.

To anticipate a theme we take up later in this chapter, Huberman (1991) observes that "there are schools in which staff members do not disengage later in their careers, do not end up tending uniquely their own gardens, do not feel the stale breath of routine after only 8–10 years into the profession" (p.16).

Other studies go beyond career stages to observe life-cycle (age as well as career) and gender differences. Krupp (1989) and Levine (1989) make it very clear that there are major differences between men and women, and across the age cycle (for example, between the 20s and 40s), which must be taken into account. They argue for the necessity for appreciating the whole person and recognizing differences according to life situations.

One final indicator of the seriousness of the problem is whether teachers see teaching as their career of choice. National polls indicate that teaching was not the first choice of as much as a third of the teaching force (more so at the secondary level). The percentage of teachers who approach their career with ambivalence, both before and while on the job, is significant. In a sample of Ontario teachers, Rees and associates (1989) found that teaching was the reported first choice of occupation for 71% of female elementary teachers, 64% of male elementary teachers, 56% of female secondary teachers, and only 37% of male secondary teachers. For three of the four groups about one in every five teachers on the job has thought about leaving teaching, and almost two of five secondary male teachers have considered leaving.

In addition, somewhere between one-third and one-half of new teachers leave the profession by the time they reach the seventh year of teaching (Metropolitan Life, 1985). We have a complicated set of variables operating. To the extent that some of the wrong people are coming into the profession (see Chapter 14), we can be just as happy that many are leaving (although this is a very expensive way of going about selection). To the extent that working conditions are forcing good people out of teaching, or wearing down good people who stay, we are witnessing the fundamental deterioration of schools.

Teacher stress and burnout have become common terms in the professional and public media. Cherniss's (1980) characterization of burnout among professionals (including teachers) captures the pervasive malaise associated with this phenomenon:

> Burnout involves a change in attitude and behavior in response to a demanding, frustrating, unrewarding work experience. The dictionary defines "to burn out" as "to fail, wear out, or become exhausted by making excessive demands on energy, strength, or resources." This term all too aptly describes the experience of many human service professionals. However, the term "burnout" has come to have an additional meaning in recent research and writing on the topic; it refers to negative changes in work-related attitudes and behavior in response to job stress. What are these negative changes? A major one is loss of concern for the client and a tendency to treat clients in a detached, mechanical fashion. Other changes include increasing discouragement, pessimism, and fatalism about one's work; decline in motivation, effort, and involvement in work; apathy; negativism; frequent irritability and anger with clients and colleagues; preoccupation with one's own comfort and welfare on the job; a tendency to rationalize failure by blaming the clients or "the system," and resistance to change, growing rigidity, and loss of creativity. . . .
>
> In addition to these negative changes in thought and behavior related to the job, there are physical and behavioral signs. These include chronic fatigue, frequent colds, the flu, headaches, gastrointestinal disturbances, and sleeplessness; excessive use of drugs; decline in self-esteem; and marital and family conflict. Of course, not all of these symptoms need to be present to say that a person is burning out. Some may be present and some not in any particular case. However, when there are several of these signs and changes in a professional, the work situation is all too likely the source of this burnout. (cited in Sarason, 1982, pp. 6–7)

Under the conditions described in the past several pages, innovation can be a two-edged sword. It can either aggravate the teachers' problems or provide a glimmer of hope. It can worsen the conditions of teaching, however unintentionally, or it can provide the support, stimulation, and pressure to improve.

ENTER CHANGE

Although educational change is all around the teacher at any given time, each new policy or curriculum, psychologically speaking, "enters" when it is first proposed or arrives on the scene. This is true *even when innovations are voluntarily undertaken or are developed by other teachers.*

One of the great mistakes over the past 30 years has been the naive assumption that involving *some* teachers on curriculum committees or in program development would facilitate implementation, because it would increase acceptance by *other* teachers. Of course, it was such an automatic assumption that people did not use the words "some" and "other." It was just assumed that "teachers" were involved because "teachers" were on major committees or project teams. Well, they were not involved, as the vast majority of classroom teachers know. Once again there was a failure to distinguish between "the change" and "the change process." As far as most teachers were concerned, when the change was produced by fellow teachers it was just as much *externally experienced* as if it had come from the university or the government. In fact, it could be more aggravating, if teachers who had developed the change were seen as getting special rewards and recognition, or if the teacher-developers saw themselves as innovative and their colleagues as somewhat resistant or slow to catch on to the great new ideas they had produced.

Change is a highly personal experience—each and every one of the teachers who will be affected by change must have the opportunity to work through this experience in a way in which the rewards at least equal the cost. The fact that those who advocate and develop changes get more rewards than costs, and those who are expected to implement them experience many more costs than rewards, goes a long way in explaining why the more things change, the more they remain the same. If the change works, the individual teacher gets little of the credit; if it doesn't, the teacher gets most of the blame.

Innovations and reforms, then, can make matters worse or better. For example, teacher appraisal and clinical supervision schemes (see Chapter 15) can alter teachers' work in narrow and superficial ways (Gitlin & Smyth, 1989) or it can result in significant improvements (McLaughlin & Pfeiffer, 1988). On balance, the evidence suggests that change attempts fail more often than not, because of the neglect of the factors we have been discussing.

The problem of the meaning of change for teachers can be understood most directly if we examine the criteria teachers use in assessing any given change. These pertain to the balance of rewards and costs, or, more simply, "Why should I put my efforts into this particular change?" The research discussed in the previous section, as well as some to be introduced shortly, shows that teachers use four main criteria:

1. Does the change potentially address a need? Will students be interested? Will they learn? Is there evidence that the change works, i.e., that it produces claimed results?

2. How clear is the change in terms of what the teacher will have to do?
3. How will it affect the teacher personally in terms of time, energy, new skill, sense of excitement and competence, and interference with existing priorities?
4. How rewarding will the experience be in terms of interaction with peers or others?

Teachers have had little opportunity to believe that such rewards will be forthcoming. A fifth criterion—chance for promotion—has sometimes been cited as an important motivator; but I discount this, because by definition it cannot apply to very many teachers. My interest is in the motivation to implement for all teachers, not just the few who see it as a stepping stone.

Most teachers, according to Doyle and Ponder (1977–78), are governed by "the practicality ethic."

> The essential features of this ethic can be summarized briefly as follows. In the normal course of events teachers receive a variety of messages intended to modify or improve their performance. If one listens carefully to the way teachers talk about these messages, it soon becomes clear that the term "practical" is used frequently and consistently to label statements about classroom practices. (pp. 1–2)

The label "practical" in Doyle and Ponder's terms is an expression of "the taken-for-granted world of the practitioner." They suggest that there are three aspects to this ethic, which they designate as congruence, instrumentality, and cost. These three criteria parallel the first three suggested above: need/evidence, procedural clarity, and personal costs and benefits.

Congruence refers to the teachers' best estimate (based on the evidence presented) of how students will react to the change (student interest, learning, etc.) and how well the innovation appears to fit the teachers' situation. Instrumentality concerns the procedural content and clarity of the proposal (i.e., the hows of implementation). Statements of theory, philosophy, general principles, or even clearly specified student outcomes "are not practical because they lack the necessary procedural referents" (Doyle & Ponder, 1977–78, p. 7). Central to the theme of this book, teachers have to have some understanding of the *operational meaning* of the change before they can make a judgment about it. To repeat an earlier point, clear specification of an innovation at the outset does not seem to resolve the problem. Clarification is a process. Full understanding can come only after some experience with the change.

Finally, the question of cost can be defined as the ratio of investment to return as far as the individual is concerned. Money is a very small part;

personal costs in time, energy, and threat to sense of adequacy, with no evidence of benefit in return, seem to have constituted the major costs of changes in education over the past 30 years. On the other hand, when the changes involve a sense of mastery, excitement, and accomplishment, the incentives for trying new practices are powerful (Huberman & Miles, 1984).

In sum, the balance of incentives and disincentives from the perspectives of individual teachers helps explain the outcome of change efforts. Need, clarity, and the personal benefit/cost ratio must be favorable on balance at some point relatively early in implementation. Ambivalence about whether the change will be favorable is nearly always experienced before the change is attempted. It is only by trying something that we can really know if it works. The problem is compounded because first attempts are frequently awkward, not providing a fair test of the idea. Support during initial trials is critical for getting through the first stages, as is some sign of progress.

The above notions have been further confirmed through the extensive work of Hall and colleagues at the University of Texas on the reaction of teachers to innovations (Hall & Hord, 1987). Building on the earlier work of Frances Fuller, Hall and others have found that different teachers have different "concerns" in relation to innovations, as well as concerns about an innovation's impact on or benefit to students. Depending on how the innovation is introduced, these concerns may be abated or exacerbated.

Let us now see how the history of innovative attempts measures up to this practicality ethic. Not very well. In Chapter 2, I suggested that educational innovations are unreliable at least as often as they are reliable—that is, they do not work out either because they have been ill conceived (they are inappropriate or underdeveloped) or because resources to support implementation are missing, or too frequently for both reasons. House (1974, p. 73) summarizes the situation of teachers viewing most innovations: Personal costs are high, and benefits are unpredictable.

In other words, teachers get the worst of all worlds—student benefit and procedural clarity are low, and personal costs are high. Moreover, House claims that there is a strong tendency to "oversell" innovations in order to obtain funding or to get them adopted by policy-makers, teachers, and others. The gap between the benefits promised and those received is usually very large, even in situations where good intentions exist. The difficulty of learning new skills and behavior and unlearning old ones is vastly underestimated. As we have seen in Chapter 3, changes in educational beliefs, teaching styles, and other practices represent profound changes affecting the teacher's professional self-definition. The "oversold" innovation, moreover, may often be promoted on the basis of an oversimplification of what implementation involves, and the supporting resources provided on a scale suited to the oversimplification—as though the change for the teacher consisted of no more than a superficial alteration in routine activities.

In any case, changes are often introduced to teachers with the emphasis on the wonderful benefits of the innovation in general or on long-term goals. Yet even when the innovation is thoroughly "explained" at the beginning, it cannot be absorbed, for teachers like anybody else do not learn new ideas all at once. Change is a process, not an event. On top of all this, even potentially good changes do not fare well because far too many changes are in front of teachers at any one time. Regardless of the reasons, there are more changes being proposed than are humanly possible to implement—if by implementation we mean changes in behavior and thinking. Nor does giving teachers the opportunity to develop their own innovations work, unless they are also given some support and external assistance (Charters & Pellegrin, 1973; Huberman & Miles, 1984).

In summary, the strategies commonly used by promoters of changes, whether by legislators, administrators, or other teachers, frequently do not work because they are derived from a world or from premises different from that of the teachers. Innovations are "rationally" advocated from the point of view of what is rational to the promoter, not the teachers. Sometimes innovations are rationally sold on the basis of sound theory and principles, but they turn out not to be translatable into practice with the resources at the disposal of teachers. Or innovations may contain many good ideas and resources, but assume conditions different from those faced by teachers. Other times, innovations are strongly advocated in terms of the supposed benefits for students, without clear evidence that the particular teacher's students would share the benefit. The credibility of the claim for student benefits cannot be assumed. The DESSI study found that if another teacher or some other trusted person vouches for the benefits of the innovation, teachers are willing to try it. But even then, some early success or progress must be experienced (Crandall et al., 1982). Some proposals are not clear about the *procedural* content (the how to implement); others fail to acknowledge the personal costs, the meaning of change to teachers, and the conditions and time it will take to develop the new practices. Stated another way, teachers' reasons for rejecting many innovations are every bit as rational as those of the advocates promoting them. Wise (1977) has called the promoters of change "hyperrational" in their assumptions, an idea that accurately captures what proposed changes look like from the vantage point of the everyday teacher (although I am sure that a few other adjectives more readily come to teachers' minds).

WHAT MAKES CHANGE WORK FOR TEACHERS

Change is necessary because high proportions of students are alienated, performing poorly or below par or dropping out. Their life in schools and after schooling is far less than it should be (see Chapter 9). But here we are talking about teachers. Change is needed because many teachers are frustrated, bored, and burnt out. Good change processes that foster sustained professional development over one's career and lead to student benefits may be one of the few sources of revitalization and satisfaction left for teachers. And as Sarason (1971, pp. 166–67) observes, "if teaching becomes neither terribly interesting nor exciting to many teachers can one expect them to make learning interesting and exciting to students?"

What can be done to increase the number of successes and decrease the number of failures? Indeed, what can be done to increase the teacher's and the school's capacity for managing change and bringing about improvements on a continuous basis? The general principles and factors related to success described in Chapters 5 and 6 represent the underlying guidelines for doing and coping with change, and the reader should refer to these suggestions as a foundation. The chapters in Part II are intended to extend and specify change guidelines for those who are in the roles being analyzed. That is, the guidelines are from the point of view of the person in the role. Thus, guidelines for teachers working with others are discussed in this section, while guidelines for principals working with teachers are contained in Chapter 8. In the wider view, an understanding of teachers will clearly generate ideas for those in any role who deal with teachers. The message to everyone outside the role under review is: *Understand the subjective world—the phenomenology—of the role incumbents as a necessary precondition for engaging in any change effort with them.*

In the remainder of this chapter, I consider what makes change work with or among teachers, and I make recommendations to help teachers cope with and manage change more effectively. In the concluding section, I reflect on teachers' interest or lack of interest in educational change in the context of teacher professionalism.

Teacher isolation and its opposite—collegiality—provide the best starting point for considering what works for the teacher. I shall first examine the positive side of teacher collaboration for that is where the power for change lies. As with most solutions, we must also identify the "dark side" and potential misuses of this powerful research finding.

Chapter 5 was devoted to an explanation of what makes change work and not work. It may be recalled that at the teacher level the degree of change was strongly related to the extent to which teachers *interact* with each other and others providing technical help. Within the school, collegiality among teachers, as measured by the frequency of communication,

mutual support, help, etc., was a strong indicator of implementation success. Virtually every research study on the topic has found this to be the
case. And it does make eminent sense in terms of the theory of change
espoused in this book. Significant educational change consists of changes
in beliefs, teaching style, and materials, which can come about *only*
through a process of personal development in a social context. As Werner
(1980) observes in explaining the failure of social studies curriculum in
Alberta,

> Ideally, implementation as a minimum includes shared understanding
> among participants concerning the implied presuppositions, values and as-
> sumptions which underlie a program, for if participants understand these,
> then they have a basis for rejecting, accepting or modifying a program in
> terms of their own school, community and class situations. To state the aim
> another way, implementation is an ongoing construction of a shared reality
> among group members through their interaction with one another within
> the program. (pp. 62–63)

There is no getting around the *primacy of personal contact*. Teachers
need to participate in skill-training workshops, but they also need to have
one-to-one and group opportunities to receive and give help and more
simply to *converse* about the meaning of change. Under these conditions
teachers learn how to use an innovation as well as to judge its desirability
on more information-based grounds; they are in a better position to know
whether they should accept, modify, or reject the change. Sometimes
teachers cannot answer this question until they have had a chance to try
out the new program and to discuss it. For example, as I will describe in
Chapter 15, in-service education pertaining to an innovation must take
this into account by moving from the concrete to the abstract, from the
practical procedures and activities to a discussion of underlying principles, rather than the other way around as is the more frequent order.

It is essential to recognize that I am not referring only to innovations
developed externally to the school. Innovations decided on or developed
by teachers within a school also require teacher–teacher interaction, if
they are to go anywhere. Whether innovations are external or internal, the more teachers can interact concerning their own practices, the
more they will be able to bring about improvements that they themselves
identify as necessary. It will be recalled from Chapter 3 that even wanted
changes have costs and create ambivalence. Social support is necessary
for reducing costs and resolving the ambivalence in terms of how much
change is needed and what can feasibly be accomplished. Thus, whether
the source of change is external or internal to the school (and either may
be good or bad, feasible or infeasible), it is teachers as interacting professionals who should be in a position to decide *finally* whether the change is
for them.

FIGURE 7.2.   Learning Enriched Schools

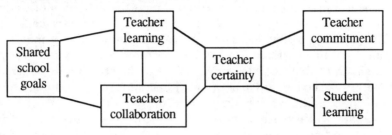

This is not to imply that teachers have the time to analyze every potential change. In many circumstances teachers may quite accurately conclude at the outset there is no need or time for interaction, and that no change is needed or possible. This outcome will occur in situations where teachers are satisfied with their current program and/or when they perceive that administrative support for change is low. We have seen that change is not necessarily progress. Not attempting to change may be the most appropriate response in some situations, if there is a disagreement about the innovation or if the minimal conditions for change do not exist; for example, there may be no resources to support implementation, or a major conflict may exist within the school or between the school and community, which must be resolved first.

Up to this point, we have been discussing the relationship between single innovations and teachers. When we shift our perspective to managing multiple innovations, we immediately confront the culture of the school. The school is the center of change because the norms, values, and structure of the school as an organization make a huge cumulative difference for individual teachers. Rosenholtz (1989) provides a thorough description of the collaborative work culture of the 13 "moving" or "learning-enriched" work environments in her study. Figure 7.2 contains an adapted summary of the main school-based elements associated with the successful schools in Rosenholtz' research. There are other factors influencing the six themes depicted in Figure 7.2, and the interactions among the themes are multifaceted, but the composite picture of how successful collaborative schools work is clear and convincing.

As Rosenholtz observes, teacher uncertainty (or low sense of efficacy) and threats to self-esteem are recurring themes in teaching (Ashton & Webb, 1986). In learning-enriched compared with learning-impoverished schools, Rosenholtz found that teachers and principals collaborated in goal-setting activities (or vision-building) that "accentuated those instructional objectives toward which teachers should aim their improvement efforts" (p. 6), and that shared goals served to focus efforts and mobilize resources in agreed upon directions. Principals and teacher-leaders actively fostered collegial involvement: "Collective commitment to student learning in collaborative settings directs the definition of leadership toward those colleagues who instruct as well as inspire awakening all sorts of teaching possibilities in others" (p. 68). In effective schools, collaboration is linked with norms and opportunities for continuous improvement and career-long learning: "It is assumed that improvement in teaching is a collective rather than individual enterprise, and that analysis, evaluation, and experimentation in concert with colleagues are conditions under which teachers improve" (p. 73). As a result teachers are more likely to trust, value, and legitimize sharing expertise, seeking advice, and giving help both inside and outside the school. They are more likely to become better and better teachers on the job: "All of this means that it is far easier to learn to teach, and to learn to teach better, in some schools than in others" (p. 104).

Becoming better teachers means greater confidence and certainty in deciding on instructional issues and in handling problems. Rosenholtz found that

> Where teachers request from and offer technical assistance to each other, and where school staff enforces consistent standards for student behavior, teachers tend to complain less about students and parents. Further, where teachers collaborate, where they keep parents involved and informed about their children's progress, where teachers and principal work together to consistently enforce standards for student behavior, and where teachers celebrate their achievements through positive feedback from students, parents, principal, colleagues, and their own sense, they collectively tend to believe in a technical culture and their instructional practice. (p. 137)

Teacher certainty and teacher commitment feed on each other, as Rosenholtz found, increasing teachers' motivation to do even better. All of these factors served to channel energy toward student achievement. Teachers in the learning-enriched schools were less likely to conform to new state or district policies that they judged ill conceived or as directing energies from classroom priorities, and more likely to assess innovations in terms of their actual impact on students.

I must caution the reader that the story up to this point is a little too smooth. Other factors feed into the equation, such as the quality of those entering teaching (Chapter 14). Moreover, the relationships among Rosenholtz' themes are not linear and hide an array of subvariables at work, which must be understood to avoid drawing superficial lessons from Rosenholtz' research. And to foreshadow a point we take up shortly, the relationship between collaboration and autonomy is not unproblematic. Nonetheless, the gist of Rosenholtz' main findings is backed up by a lot of other research. Most of Mortimore and associates' (1988) 12 key factors are related to Rosenholtz' themes—including the involvement of teachers, consistency among teachers, intellectually challenging teaching, work-centered environment, purposeful leadership, positive climate, and so on. Teacher and student commitment is heavily influenced by these school characteristics. Similar themes are found in recent studies of secondary school improvement (Firestone & Rosenblum, 1988; Louis & Miles, 1990; Wilson & Corcoran, 1988) as well as in all other major studies of collaboration at the school level (Goodlad, 1984; Little, 1982). As Nias (1989) concludes from her study of school cultures in England,

> [Teachers] are happiest in a social environment characterised by mutual dependence in which "sharing" is the norm and individuals do not feel ashamed to admit to failure or a sense of inadequacy . . . relationships between staff who can and do help each other, provide one another with oases of calm in a long and frenetic day, set one another high but attainable standards for professional performance and provide a mutually supportive social environment, are characterised by: personal accessibility; plenty of opportunity for discussion; laughter; praise and recognition. (pp. 152–53)

Before deriving implications for teachers, we must be careful not to assume that increasing interaction among teachers is automatically a good thing. Little (1990a) warns that there are many superficial examples of collaboration. She suggests that several forms of collegiality involving assistance, sharing, storytelling, etc., represent "weak ties" and are likely to be inconsequential and have little impact on the culture of the school. "Joint work" involves deeper forms of interaction, such as joint planning, observation, and experimentation, and is dependent on "the structural organization of task, time, and other resources in ways not characteristic of other forms of collegiality" (pp. 14–15).

Little does not assume that joint work is automatically more appropriate.

> The content of teachers' values and beliefs cannot be taken for granted in the study or pursuit of teachers' collegial norms of interaction and interpretation. Under some circumstances, greater contact among teachers can be expected to advance the prospects for students' success; in others, to promote increased teacher-to-teacher contact may be to intensify norms unfavorable to children. (1990a, p. 524)

And

> Bluntly put, do we have in teachers' collaborative work the creative development of well informed choices, or the mutual reinforcement of poorly informed habit? Does teachers' time together advance the understanding and imagination they bring to their work, or do teachers merely confirm one another in present practice? What subject philosophy and subject pedagogy

do teachers reflect as they work together, how explicit and accessible is their knowledge to one another? Are there collaborations that in fact erode teachers' moral commitments and intellectual merit? (p. 525)

Hargreaves (1991) goes further. He distinguishes between "contrived collegiality" and "collaborative cultures." Contrived collegiality

is characterized by a set of formal, specific bureaucratic procedures. . . . It can be seen in initiatives such as peer coaching, mentor teaching, joint planning in specially provided rooms, formally scheduled meetings and clear job descriptions and training programs for those in consultative roles. (p. 19)

Contrived collegiality can lead to the proliferation of unwanted contacts among teachers, which consume already scarce time. True collaborative cultures, according to Hargreaves, are "deep, personal and enduring." They are not "mounted just for specific projects or events. They are not strings of one-shot deals. Cultures of collaboration are constitutive of, absolutely central to, teachers' daily work" (p. 14).

In the same vein, Huberman (1990) observes:

Collegiality is not a fully legitimate end in itself, unless it can be shown to affect, directly or indirectly, the nature or degree of pupil development . . . by the same token, intensive collaboration—planning, exchanging materials, regulating pupil performance—does not automatically translate into observable changes in classroom practice and may, if pushed too hard, actually eat into time for ongoing instructional work in the class. (p. 2)

Further, we cannot assume that autonomy is bad and collaboration is good. One person's isolation is another person's autonomy; one person's collaboration is another person's conspiracy. We must not lose sight of the importance of solitude. Flinders (1988) claims that for many teachers isolation is a strategy for getting work done because "it protects time and energy required to meet immediate instructional demands" (p. 25). Flinders observes that most of us seek periods of independent work in order to meet obligations.

It is not uncommon to respond to increased job demands by closing the office door, cancelling luncheon appointments, and "hiding out" in whatever ways we can. We do not attribute our motives for such behavior to naturally conservative personality traits or to malevolent or unprofessional regard for our colleagues. On the contrary, it is professional norms that dissuade us from sacrificing our commitments to job responsibilities even when such a sacrifice can be made in the name of collegiality. (p. 25)

None of this is to deny that isolation can be a protection from scrutiny and a barrier to improvement, but it does say that we must put the question of autonomy and collaboration in a perspective conducive to assessing the conditions under which each might be appropriate.

This debate has practical implications. Striving for school-wide consensus and conformity among teachers is not where one would start or even end. Consensus seeking may inhibit creativity and may result in the wrong solution. Instead of seeking widespread involvement in the use of a particular innovation, it may be more appropriate, especially in larger schools, to stimulate multiple examples of collaboration among small groups of teachers inside and outside the school. Huberman (1990, 1991) draws such a conclusion from his study of the career cycle of teachers. In its basic form, according to Huberman, we need to increase the number and quality of colleagues or experts to which individual teachers could turn in the course of experimentation in their classrooms. The goal is to expand the network of people working on similar problems. Louis and Miles' (1990) observation that subthemes may eventually coalesce is probably a more apt image than the concept that school-wide goals guide everyone's action. Paradoxically, school-wide efforts to implement single innovations may have less of an impact on the professional culture of schools (and thereby on the basic capacity of schools to improve) than would multiple focused collaborative networks that become "deep, personal and enduring" in the service of improvement (see Hargreaves, 1989).

GUIDELINES FOR TEACHERS

Teachers, both individually and in small groups, need to consider several issues before deciding to throw their energies into a change effort (or before deciding to reject it).

First, and by no means self-evident, if the change is proposed from outside, does it address an important need? Is there evidence that the practice has worked elsewhere and achieved results? Being self-critical (analytic) is necessary in order to avoid the problem of false clarity, when a teacher superficially *assumes* that the goal is already being addressed but in reality is not employing teaching resources and behaviors that would maximize attainment. Related to this issue is the current tendency for many teachers to reject all external changes (particularly if they come from certain sources, such as governments). Rejecting *all* proposed changes out of hand may be just as regressive as accepting them all. However, even if the change is desired and needed, it will also be necessary to determine its *priority*. Since teachers are faced with too many changes at once, they individually or jointly must choose where to put their efforts. If everything is attempted (or rejected), nothing will succeed. In one sense, the best a teacher can do is work hard on one or two of the most important priorities at one time, and cope with the others as well as pos- sible. It helps if the teacher is part of a group or school that has a sense of direction or vision which serves to guide prioritizing.

Second, an attempt should be made to ascertain if the administration is endorsing the change and why, because some form of active commit- ment by administrators will be necessary for freeing up necessary re- sources (reducing the cost) for the innovation to succeed. It may be pos- sible to go it alone, if the specific change is highly valued by the teacher, but it will be difficult unless there is some support from the administra- tion. It is also important that teachers not automatically accept apparent lack of interest on the part of an administrator at face value. Administra- tors have their own worlds of pressure, which they frequently keep pri- vate. They are still learning how to cope with their roles as change man- agers (see Chapters 8 and 10). It may be that individual or group-based teacher initiative and negotiation with administration could lead to sig- nificant changes in support in some cases. Untested assumptions are fer- tile ground for false attribution of motives and intentions. Apparent lack of attention by the administrator may or may not mean lack of interest.

Third, the teacher should assess whether fellow teachers are likely to show an interest in the change. If collegiality among teachers in a school is already strong, the degree of teacher interest can usually be found out quite quickly. As before, one should not assume lack of interest. Because of the isolation of teachers from each other, there may be a lot of "plu- ralistic ignorance"—that is, each person assumes that no one else is inter- ested; everyone makes the same assumption, but no one bothers to test it. In any case, if peer interest exists or can be stimulated, it can represent one of the most satisfying (and necessary) aspects of the change process.

Fourth, regardless of outside pressures or opportunities, individual teachers have a responsibility to make some contribution to the develop- ment of collaborative work cultures—the cautions above notwithstanding (Fullan, 1990). Contributing ideas to others and seeking better ideas is the cornerstone of collaborative cultures. This need not be on a district- wide or school-wide basis; small-scale, focused, ongoing exchange and experimentation with a small number of colleagues to obtain better re- sults with students are perfectly fine.

Fifth, teacher-leaders, that is, those interested in playing a larger leadership role, face dilemmas as well as expanded opportunities in the form of coaching, mentoring, and the like (Chapters 14 and 15). Many teacher-leader roles end up distancing those in the roles from other teachers. In a study of those in teacher-leadership roles, Smylie and

Denny (1989) found that teacher-leaders consistently identified their roles in terms of helping and supporting fellow teachers in working with students and in improving practice, but actually spent most of their time attending meetings and "participating in various planning and decision-making activities at the district and building levels related to curricular, instructional, and staff development programs" (p. 8).

Similarly, teachers engaged in curriculum development or otherwise involved in content innovations must put their advocacy in perspective. If these teachers try to sell a product without recognizing that it may not be the most important thing on other teachers' minds, and without being sensitive to the need for other teachers to come to grips with the sense of the innovation, they will be doing exactly what most developers or advocates of change do—confusing the change with the change process. It is this tendency that led me to form the proposition that the more an advocate is committed to a particular innovation, the *less* likely he or she is to be effective in getting it implemented. The reverse is not true: Commitment is needed, but it must be balanced with the knowledge that people may be at different starting points, with different legitimate priorities, and that the change process may very well result in transformations or variations in the change. If the teacher as advocate can become skilled at integrating the change and the change process, he or she can become one of the most powerful forces of change. Teachers working with other teachers at the school and classroom levels is a necessary condition for improving practice. In situations mentioned earlier, where collegiality has developed, it has become a significant "practical" benefit of getting involved in an innovation or reform. According to House and Lapan (1978), "Satisfaction derived from cooperatively improving one's skills in the view of one's fellow teachers offers professional rewards, heretofore untapped" (p. 179). At least, such a development offers some potential for not only improving classroom practice but also remedying some of the burnout, alienation, and routine that blights the working day of many teachers.

Many so called teacher-leadership roles, as we have stated, do not easily lend themselves to the kind of collaborative work necessary for classroom and school improvement. Even when the role is designed to provide daily interaction with other teachers, the teacher-leader's task will not be easy because teachers have not been used to viewing and helping each other's work (Little, 1987; Smylie & Denny, 1989). The implication is that teacher-leaders should be working on improving the professional culture of the school—helping to make teaching more public, encouraging norms of improvement, helping teachers examine the consequences of instructional practices for students, etc. It will require confronting norms of isolation, while at the same time avoiding the imposition of solutions, premature forging of consensus, and failure to take into account the personal situations of those with whom the teacher-leaders wish to work (Fullan & Hargreaves, 1991).

Sixth, teacher unions and professional associations should and are taking a more active leadership role in helping to establish conditions for improvement and in following up to support implementation and to assess results. The general idea is that teachers formally (through collective bargaining) or less formally (in local teacher associations or subject associations) *negotiate* the conditions for innovation and improvement. House and Lapan (1978) anticipated this development more than a decade ago.

> In negotiated innovation those to be affected by the innovation would bargain with the innovators over the terms of implementation. How far would the innovation go? What would the teachers get out of it? What would be the rewards to innovators? What resources are available to implement? In this scheme both the costs and rewards are distributed by a deliberate bargaining process between the concerned parties. (p. 186)

McDonnell and Pascal (1988) trace the development of the relationship between teacher unions and districts in the United States relative to education reform over the past 20 years. They cite examples of "active reform leadership" at the national and local level. The American Federation of Teachers has laid out a platform for reform and was instrumental in establishing radical experiments through collective bargaining in Dade County, Florida and Rochester, New York (Shanker, 1988, 1990). The Rochester contract, for example, achieved a 40 percent raise in average salaries over three years in return for eliminating seniority as the most significant criterion in transfers, as well as set up school-based committees for decision making (McDonnell & Pascal, 1988). Albert Shanker, AFT's President, has written and spoken widely on the need to "redesign our schools and rethink the way we approach teaching and learning" (1988, p. 14). The other national union, the National Education Association, has developed its own strategy through policy statements such as *The Learning Workplace* (NEA, 1986) and by sponsoring innovative projects such as the Mastery in Learning Project Schools (NEA, 1988).

McDonnell and Pascal (1988) concluded that while teacher unions were often not a source of innovation, "despite charges to the contrary, teacher unions have not been a major obstacle to educational reform" (p. 51). They caution that particular outcomes depend on several local factors, such as the degree of perceived mutual interest, the nature of the relationship between district and union leaders, membership preferences, and the internal relationships within the union locally and between local and state or national level leaders.

We should not underestimate the *personal* responsibility that individual teachers have to make schools better, if for no other reason than that this might represent one of the few routes to improving their own working conditions. There is more at stake than the individual classroom (Fullan & Hargreaves, 1991). Barth states it best:

> To assert one's leadership as a teacher, often against forces of administrative resistance, takes commitment to an educational ideal. It also requires the energy to combat one's own inertia caused by habit and overwork. And it requires a certain kind of courage to step outside of the small prescribed circle of traditional "teacher tasks," to declare through our actions that we care about and take responsibility for more than the minimum, more than what goes on within the four walls of our classrooms. (1990, p. 131)

Individual and collegial action are not mutually exclusive.

PROFESSIONALISM AT THE CROSSROADS

Are teachers interested in change? Of course, some are and some aren't, but let us examine the question more closely. Most, not all, teachers see the need for and want to make improvements. In a U.S. nationwide poll of teachers (NEA, 1979), 65 percent of the respondents said that "to try more innovations" was needed in schools where they taught; 85 percent said that teachers and administrators should be required to update their skills periodically through training. Three-quarters of Goodlad's (1984) sample stated that they would like to observe other teachers at work (p. 188). The majority of teachers in Nias' (1989) study wanted more work collaboration with other teachers.

Teachers do not get more involved in improvement for a variety of reasons, which we have identified: Norms or expectations to collaborate are not well developed; organizational structures inhibit involvement; the type, design, and scale of particular innovations create far more costs than benefits in the eyes of teachers. And yes, the "psychological state" of some teachers leads them to resist change. Ashton and Webb (1986), Hopkins (1990), Huberman (1991), McKibbin and Joyce (1980), Rosenholtz (1989), and others have all found that teachers' sense of efficacy, self-actualization, control, motivation, and desire for change varies dramatically among teachers. Without question some of this can be traced to the quality of those entering the profession (Chapter 14). Beyond this, psychological states are shaped in told and untold ways over the course of one's career *depending on the particular schools in which one has taught and the image of teachers held by society.*

The conception of the teaching profession is at a crossroads. There are two dominant contradictory images evident. Cuban (1988c) describes these in terms of the teacher as technical actor vs. moral actor. The technocrat or bureaucratic image conceives of teachers as giving knowledge and following and applying rules. The moral actor as artisan and craftsperson sees teaching as transforming students. These are ideal types, of course, and it is likely, as we indicated below, that a mixture of the two is required. There is no denying, however, that in the quest for solutions the teaching profession may find itself being led or going down one road or the other.

We also see the struggle in how collegiality is being pursued. Hargreaves and Dawe (1989) identify two different, contradictory forms of collaboration.

> In the one, it is a tool of teacher empowerment and professional enhancement, bringing colleagues and their expertise together to generate critical yet also practically-grounded reflection on what they do as a basis for wiser, more skilled action. In the other, the breakdown of teacher isolation is a mechanism designed to facilitate the smooth and uncritical adoption of preferred forms of action (new teaching styles) introduced and imposed by experts from elsewhere, in which teachers become technicians rather than professionals exercising discretionary judgment. (p. 7)

We see this tension in "intensification"-based reforms prescribing and assessing teacher competencies vs. "restructuring" efforts to alter the workplace (see Chapter 1). My own image is that technical skills and inquiry-based judgment can be combined (Fullan, Bennett, & Rolheiser-Bennett, 1990).

The implications of our analysis are that, as with any complex profession, the science and technology of teaching are continually developing, and the job of teaching is an art and science that teachers study, reflect on, and refine throughout their careers (Fullan & Connelly, 1990). I reject the notion, underlying many intensification schemes, of the passive professional, but I also rule out the isolated, autonomous professional. *Interactive professionalism* is the notion arising from the analysis in this chapter. I see teachers and others working in small groups interacting frequently in the course of planning, testing new ideas, attempting to solve different problems, assessing effectiveness, etc. It is interactive in the sense that giving and receiving advice and help would be the natural order of things. Teachers would be continuous learners in a community of interactive professionals (see Chapters 14 & 15, and Barth, 1990).

Thus the meaning of change for the future does not simply involve implementing single innovations effectively. It means a radical change in the culture of schools and the conception of teaching as a profession. We have seen glimpses of that future in Rosenholtz' "learning-enriched" schools, but we have reason to believe that these types of highly energized collaborative schools do not last beyond the tenure of key individuals

(Little, 1989). By far, the main problem in teaching is not how to get rid of the deadwood, but rather how to motivate good teachers throughout their careers. Changes in the culture of teaching and the culture of schools are required. Cultural change requires strong, persistent efforts because much of current practice is embedded in structures and routines and internalized in individuals, including teachers (see the discussion of "programmed regularities" in Sarason, 1982). *Yet, cultural change is the agenda.* There appear to be many people willing to work on it, but they should realize how deep a change they are getting into.

The final conclusion that should be crystal clear from the descriptions of this chapter is that school improvement is related not just to what the teachers do and think. Equally important is what those around them at the school, district, provincial/state, and federal levels do. Too often we think of the need for change only in terms of the teacher. If there is any changing to be done, *everyone is implicated* and must face it in relation to his or her own role. In this network, because of closeness to the classroom situation and opportunity to alter workplace conditions, probably the most powerful potential source of help or hindrance to the teacher is the school principal.

CHAPTER 8

The Principal

Mother (calling upstairs in the morning):
It's time to get up for school.
Chris: *I'm not going to school!*
Mother: *Why not?*
Chris: *Because everybody at the school hates me—the teachers,
the kids, the janitor—they all hate me!*
Mother: *You have to go. You're the principal.*

Forget about the principal as head of the school for a moment and think of her or him as someone just as buffeted as the teacher is by wanted or unwanted and often incomprehensible changes—and, what is more, *expected to lead these very changes*. Change is only one small part of the forces competing for the principal's attention, and usually not the most compelling one. Yet some principals are actively engaged as initiators or facilitators of continuous improvements in their schools. The principal is in the middle of the relationship between teachers and external ideas and people. As in most human triangles there are constant conflicts and dilemmas. How the principal approaches (or avoids) these issues determines to a large extent whether these relationships constitute a Bermuda triangle of innovations.

An understanding of what reality is *from the point of view of people* within the role is an essential starting point for constructing a practical theory of the meaning and results of change attempts. This phenomenology is social science's contribution to addressing the frequent lament, "No one understands me." In the field of educational change, everyone feels misunderstood. One of the most revealing and frustrating indicators of the difficulties in educational change is the participants' frequent experience of having their intentions not only misunderstood but interpreted exactly opposite to what they meant. Principals should have no problem claiming their fair share of frustration, since the role of the principal has in fact become dramatically more complex, overloaded, and unclear over the past decade. On the optimistic side, very recent research has identified some specific change-related behaviors of principals who deal effectively with educational change. It is time to go beyond the empty phrase "the principal is the gatekeeper of change."

While research on school improvement is now into its second decade,

systematic research on what the principal actually does and its relationship to stability and change is quite recent. Some of the earlier implementation research identified the role of the principal as central to promoting
or inhibiting change, but it did not examine the principal's role in any
depth or perspective (e.g., Berman & McLaughlin, 1978a). During the
1980s research and practice focusing on the role of the principalship,
vice-principalship, and other school leaders mounted, resulting in greater
clarity, but also greater appreciation of the complexities and different
paths to success. Direct, firsthand programmatic research over the last
decade has uncovered more and more issues related to the principalship
(Barth, 1990; Bossert et al., 1982; Fullan, 1988; Hall & Hord, 1987;
Hord, Stiegelbauer, & Hall, 1984; Leithwood & Jantzi, 1990; Leithwood
& Montgomery, 1982, 1986; Leithwood & Steinbach, 1989a,b; Manasse,
1985; Smith & Andrews, 1989). The role is not as straightforward as we
are led to believe in statements constantly referring to principals as the
key to change. But the principal is central, especially to changes in the
culture of the school.

I start with a description of where principals are. I then turn to the
part of their role that interests us the most—what principals do and don't
do in relation to change. In the last section of the chapter, I discuss the
dilemmas of change faced by principals and outline some guidelines for
how they might manage change more effectively. Along the way I consider possible differences between elementary and secondary principals,
and in women compared with men.

WHERE PRINCIPALS ARE

If change is everywhere in the air, we would think that the greatest
pressure a principal feels is to bring about some major transformation of
the school. But the air is not the ground, and on the ground many principals experience (and some people may say too easily accept) precisely
the opposite—pressures to *maintain stability*. As we shall see in the next
section, this does not say that all principals work to maintain stability. But
there is often great pressure on them to do so. How this pressure is
handled depends on the conception that the principal has of his or her
role and on the expectations that the school district administrators have—
that is, what they *really* want principals to do. Nearly all school district
role descriptions (and courses in educational administration theory,
which nearly all principals take) stress the instructional leadership responsibilities of the principal—facilitating change, helping teachers work
together, assessing and furthering school improvement, and so on. However, how principals actually spend their time is obviously a better indicator of their impact on the school. If we were to follow principals around

on a typical day, what would we find out? The anthropologist Harry Wolcott (1973) did just that for an entire school year with one elementary school principal. He found that virtually all the principal's time was taken up in one-to-one personal encounters, meetings, and telephone calls.

Martin and Willower's (1981) and Peterson's (1981) observations of principals also found that principals' workdays were sporadic, characterized simultaneously by brevity, variety, and fragmentation. For example, Martin and Willower report that secondary school principals perform an average of 149 tasks a day, with constant interruptions—over 59 percent of their observed activities were interrupted. Most (84%) of the activities were brief (one to four minutes). Principals "demonstrated a tendency to engage themselves in the most current and pressing situation. They invested little time in reflective planning" (p. 80). Instruction-related activities took up 17 percent of their time.

Sarason (1982, Ch. 9) observes that most of the principal's time is spent on administrative housekeeping matters and maintaining order. Many principals expect or feel that they are expected to keep everyone happy by running an orderly school, and this becomes the major criterion of the principals' ability to manage—no news is good news, as long as everything is relatively quiet. House and Lapan (1978) summarize the problem.

> Another facet of trying to please everyone and to avoid any trouble that might reach central office is to deal with any problem that arises. The principal has no set of priorities except to keep small problems from becoming big ones. His is a continuous task of crisis management. He responds to emergencies daily. He is always on call. All problems are seen as important. This global response to any and all concerns means he never has the time, energy, or inclination to develop or carry out a set of premediated plans of his own. Containment of all problems is his theme. The principal cannot be a change agent or leader under these conditions. (p. 145)

A study of 137 principals and vice-principals in Toronto describes some of the overload principals feel (Edu-con, 1984): 90% reported an increase over the previous five years in the demands made on their time and responsibilities, including new program demands, the number of board priorities and directives, the number of directives from the Ministry of Education, etc. Time demands were listed as having increased in dealing with parent and community groups (92% said there was an increase), trustee requests (91% reported an increase), administration activities (88%), staff involvement and student services (81%), social services (81%), and board initiatives (69%).

Principals and vice-principals were also asked about their perceptions of effectiveness: 61% reported a *decrease in principal effectiveness,* with only 13% saying it was about the same, and 26% reporting an increase.

The same percentage, 61%, reported decreases in "the effectiveness of assistance . . . from immediate superiors and from administration." Further: 84% reported a decrease in the authority of the principal, 72% a decrease in trust in leadership of the principal, and 76% a decrease in principal involvement in decision making at the system level; 91% responded "no" to the question, "Do you think the principal can effectively fulfill all the responsibilities assigned to him/her?"

This is not to say that principals are not trying. The Edu-con study indicated that principals did not object to many of the new responsibilities per se, but rather that they were concerned more with the complexity and time demands involved in implementing the new programs than with the programs themselves. The amount and number of areas of expertise expected of the principal—school law, curriculum planning, supervision of instruction, community relations, human resource development, student relations, administration—are ever increasing.

The discouragement felt by principals in attempting to cover all the bases is aptly described in the following three responses from interviews conducted by Duke (1988) with principals who were considering quitting:

> The conflict for me comes from going home every night acutely aware of what didn't get done and feeling after six years that I ought to have a better batting average than I have.
>
> If you leave the principalship, think of all the "heart-work" you're going to miss. I fear I'm addicted to it and to the pace of the principalship—those 2,000 interactions a day. I get fidgety in meetings because they're too slow, and I'm not out there interacting with people.
>
> The principalship is the kind of job where you're expected to be all things to all people. Early on, if you're successful, you have gotten feedback that you are able to be all things to all people. And then you feel an obligation to continue to do that which in your own mind you're not capable of doing. And that causes some guilt. (p. 309)

Duke was intrigued by the "dropout rate" of principals after encountering an article stating that 22 percent of Vermont administrators employed in the fall of 1984 had left the state's school systems by the fall of 1985. In interviewing principals about why they considered quitting, he found that sources of dissatisfaction included policy and administration, lack of achievement, sacrifices in personal life, lack of growth opportunities, lack of recognition and too little responsibility, relations with subordinates, and lack of support from superiors. They expressed a number of concerns about the job itself: the challenge of doing all the things that principals are expected to do, the mundane or boring nature of much of the work, the debilitating array of personal interactions, the politics of dealing with various constituencies, and the tendency for managerial concerns to supersede leadership functions (Duke, 1988, p. 310).

While Duke's findings are from a small sample (four principals), they are by no means atypical. Duke suggested that the reasons principals were considering quitting were related to fatigue, awareness of personal limitations, and awareness of the limitation of career choices. All four principals experienced reality shock: "the shock-like reactions of new workers when they find themselves in a work situation for which they have spent several years preparing and for which they thought they were going to be prepared, and then suddenly find that they are not." Duke (1988) concludes

> A number of frustrations expressed by these principals derived from the contexts in which they worked. Their comments send a clear message to those who supervised them: principals need autonomy *and* support. The need for autonomy may require supervisors to treat each principal differently; the need for support may require supervisors to be sensitive to each principal's view of what he or she finds meaningful or trivial about the work. (p. 312)

Other studies confirm conditions of overload and fragmentation in the principal's role. Crowson and Porter-Gehrie (1980) carried out a detailed observation study over a period of time of 26 urban school principals in the Chicago area. The overwhelming emphasis in their daily work was oriented toward maintenance, specifically (1) student disciplinary control, (2) keeping outside influences (central office, parents, etc.) under control and satisfied, (3) keeping staff conflicts at bay, and (4) keeping the school supplied with adequate materials, staffing, and so forth. It is noteworthy that this "natural" description of what principals do rarely mentions attention to program changes.

Sarason (1982) and Lortie (1987) claim that the conservative tendencies in the principalship have historical roots. Sarason starts with the observation that being a classroom teacher by itself is not very good preparation for being an effective principal. In their interaction with principals, says Sarason, teachers (as future principals) obtain an idea of only a very narrow slice of what it means to be a principal. This is all the more the case where a teacher's experience is limited to one or two schools. The newly appointed vice-principal or principal is often faced with teachers who emphasize maintenance and stability. Despite the fact that the principal views his or her role as implying leadership, when resistance to recommendations or ideas for change are encountered, principals often respond in one of two ways. According to Sarason (1982), they "assert authority or withdraw from the fray" (p. 160). This is, no doubt, an oversimplification, but Sarason's overall conclusion is that the narrowness of preparation and the demands for maintaining or restoring stability encourage principals to play it safe.

Lortie (1987) draws specifically on his study of suburban elementary school principals in Chicago and more generally on his observations of American education. Lortie claims that there are four powerful "built-in tendencies toward stabilizing the principal's role," related to (1) recruitment and induction, (2) role constraints and psychic rewards, (3) the constraint of system standardization, and (4) career contingencies.

Concerning recruitment and induction, Lortie comments on the narrowness of experience and limited exposure to new ideas: "Persons who have been exposed to a wide range of educational ideas and practices, and have seen those in actual use, are more likely to favor and, when influential, push for change." But, Lortie says that principals he studied were not cosmopolitans who had witnessed considerable variety in their work lives: "There is little to encourage us to so classify them, at least on the basis of the typical work experience and study found in our sample; the large majority have worked in a small number of distinct settings" (p. 4).

The second major conservative tendency Lortie identifies is "role constraints and psychic rewards." Elaborating on Sarason's point, Lortie states that principals consider the relationship with teachers to be the most salient within their role, and that when it comes to change, the relationship is problematic.

> If change can be costly for those who are asked to undertake it, it follows that subordinates will be most ready to change when the superordinate can argue, with some degree of plausibility, that there will be gains to offset any losses. This is particularly difficult to demonstrate in education as technical knowledge in the field is insufficiently well developed to provide a strong rationale for innovation, to convince teachers that the change will produce the increased learning which could serve as a source of additional work satisfaction. (p. 7)

Third, Lortie talks about system standardization. He notes that three factors normally constrain the emergence of school individuality. The rationale of curricular integration, formal authority arrangements, and pressures toward system-wide equity, all "inhibit the impulse to innovate in individual elementary schools" (p. 11).

Career contingencies and system context is the last theme taken up by Lortie. When asked what criteria superordinates were most likely to use in evaluating their performance, many principals placed emphasis on the opinions of parents and teachers. Lortie asks

> What is the relationship between the introduction of change and the evocation of discontent? Is it not more likely that principals who challenge the

status quo are more likely to agitate conservative parents and/or resistant teachers? Are persons who are pleased by a particular change, or indifferent to it, as likely to register their views with central office? When can a principal have confidence that his superordinates will make a clear distinction between justified complaints and the noise made by those who are simply irritated by the new? (pp. 12–13)

Lortie concludes that successful innovation, in the circumstances he describes, requires "highly sophisticated managerial behavior" at both the system (superintendent) and school (principal) levels; and that "such talents are scarce in any organizational setting" (p. 15).

Before we conclude that the "big bad system" causes all evil let us return to Sarason. He takes up the additional theme that people's conception of "the system" governs what they do, regardless of whether it is a correct or faulty conception. He states the problem bluntly.

> While I do not in any way question that characteristics of the system can and do have interfering effects on an individual's performance, . . . "the system" is frequently conceived by the individual in a way that obscures, many times unwittingly, the range of possibilities available to him or her. Too frequently the individual's conception of the system serves as a basis for inaction and rigidity, or as a convenient target onto which one can direct blame for most anything. The principal illustrates this point as well or better than anyone else in the school system. (Sarason, 1982, p. 164)

Sarason then gives several examples of principals who used atypical procedures (for example, using older students to work with younger ones) in a school system, which other principals in the same system claimed would not work successfully because the system would not allow it, it was counter to policy, one would be asking for trouble, etc. Sarason suggests that the tendency for principals to anticipate trouble from the system is one of the most frequent and strongest obstacles to trying new procedures. Says Sarason, "The range of practices among principals within the same system is sufficiently great to suggest that the system permits and tolerates passivity and activity, conformity and boldness, dullness and excitement, incompetency and competency" (p. 171).

Some principals, then, do act differently from the norm. In a subsample of the 60 most "effective" principals as identified through reputational criteria, Gorton and McIntyre (1978) found that these principals focused on program development more than did the sample as a whole. They ranked program development first out of nine tasks in terms of time actually spent during the previous two weeks, compared with fifth out of nine among the larger sample.

In a study involving over 2,500 teachers and 1,200 school principals, Smith and Andrews (1989) found that effective principals were engaged in four areas of strategic interaction with teachers: (1) as "resource provider," (2) as "instructional resource," (3) as "communicator," and (4) as "visible presence." They identified 21 principals who were named as strong instructional leaders both by superintendents and by a group of principals who were peers. While both "strong" and "average" principals in the Smith and Andrews (1989) study rated "program improvement" equally highly, a much higher percentage of strong principals *actually* spent more time working with others on program improvement.

Furthermore, using teacher perceptions of principals' behavior Smith and Andrews found that "strong" instructional leaders, as compared with "average" and "weak" instructional leaders, were rated substantially higher time and again across the four dimensions mentioned above. For example, a typical item to measure "resource provision" was stated as follows: "My principal mobilizes resources and district support to help achieve academic achievement goals." The percentage of positive ratings from teachers on staff was 90% for strong leaders, 52% for average leaders, and 33% for weak leaders (p. 32). Results were similar for nearly all of the 18 questions used to measure the four dimensions of leadership. Essentially the same types of differences were found by Leithwood and Montgomery (1982) in a major review of research in which they compared the behavior of "effective" and "typical" principals.

Effective instructional leaders are distinctly in the minority. In case studies of four school districts in Ontario known for their focus on curriculum, the district with the best track record estimated that only about 10 percent of the principals were functioning as highly effective curriculum leaders. In more extensive work, Leithwood and Montgomery (1986) also estimate that less than 10 percent of principals they have studied could be classified as "systematic problem-solvers" (the highest level of their four-level profile of effectiveness). Cuban (1988c) conducted a historical review of the role of the principal, locating the earliest empirical studies around 1910. In examining research studies over a 70-year period, he concluded that "while styles differ, the managerial role not instructional leadership, has dominated principals' behavior" (p. 84).

I will make the claim later that some districts have higher proportions of effective instructional school leaders, and that the sheer number of principals actively involved in leading change seems to be on the rise, but as a group there is no doubt that the majority of principals have not been able to overcome the built-in obstacles described by Lortie, Sarason, and others.

Understanding the forces stalling improvement is only half the battle. We must also know how effective principals have managed to transcend the problems of overload. What do they do and with what consequences? The answer to this question is especially important since most principals say that they would like to spend more time on school improvement than they do. The skeptical reader may question the sincerity of some principals making this claim, but there should be no doubt that unless special steps are taken (by the principal and others), the principal will have little time for change.

Interestingly, as we shall see, effective principals do not neglect stability in favor of change. Since change is not always progress, the effective principal helps to protect the school from ill-conceived or unwanted change. The importance of the principal is highlighted when we realize that many things must be done even when he or she and the majority of teachers are in favor of a particular change. The school is the center of change. The school is an organization, and organizations change more effectively when their heads play active roles in helping to lead improvement.

THE PRINCIPAL AND CHANGE

Principals are middle managers. As such, they face a classical organizational dilemma. Rapport with teachers is critical as is keeping supervisors happy. The endless supply of new policies, programs, and procedures ensures that the dilemma remains active. The expectation that principals should be leaders in the implementation of changes that they had no hand in developing and may not understand is especially troublesome. Amidst the conflicting demands and problems described by principals and researchers, taking on a change agent's role seems most problematic, especially as it is not clear exactly what that means. Generalities, such as "the principal is the gatekeeper of change" or "the principal and the school is the unit of change," provide no practical clarity about what the principal could or should do. Given the other demands on the role, it is no wonder that most principals do not approach their change responsibilities with enthusiasm. In the best of times very few of us go out of our way to do something that is both complex and unclear. Stated another way, principals are being asked *to change their role* and become active in curricular leadership in the school (and many of them have tried to do so without notable success). The role change is a far more important innovation to the principal than any specific program innovation. Role changes, as we have seen with the teacher, have their costs and presumed benefits, which create ambivalence even among those who are willing to try. The principal has had little preparation for managing these dilemmas, and even less time to reflect on this aspect while on the job (see Chapter 15 for discussions of the preparation and continuing professional development of principals).

Despite these constraints, the principal's change agent role has come front and center. Over the last decade research has progressed from examining the principal's role in implementing specific innovations to her or his role in changing the very culture of the school. Let us start with the former.

In the first major study of innovation involving almost 300 school districts, Berman and McLaughlin found that "projects having the *active* support of the principal were most likely to fare well" (1977, p. 124, their emphasis). They claim that the principal's actions (not what he or she says) carry the message as to whether a change is to be taken seriously and serve to support teachers. Hall and his colleagues (1980) state it flatly: "The degree of implementation of the innovation is different in different schools because of the actions and concerns of the principal" (p. 26).

Research in the 1980s has identified the specific ways in which active principals support innovation. In a series of interviews I carried out in Ontario a number of years ago on what principals were doing with provincial curriculum guidelines (policy), one of the secondary school principals provided a good description of what active involvement means to him:

> The principal has to become directly involved. He may not know mathematics per se or science or history; but he can [be] and the teachers can see him as an expert in curriculum planning. That's one thing he has to do is develop and acquire some expertise in this area. I think he has to work with the departments in helping them plan what they are going to do with that guideline. He has to meet with them, he has to sit down with them, he's got to be familiar enough with the document that he can discuss it. He has to be prepared to give some of his time to that particular group of teachers, let's say the English department, and be involved in not all of their meetings, but some of them, keeping informed, being knowledgeable about what they are doing. I think he's got to help them plan what they are going to do and then help them measure whether they're doing it or not. *But if the principal detaches himself from it, and says, "Go ahead fellows," and that's what happens too often, then I don't think it will happen effectively.* (interview, June 1980, my emphasis)

The Principal–Teacher Interaction (PTI) Study conducted by Hall and associates in three school districts in three states (California, Colorado, Florida) provides detailed observation data on the number and nature of interactions principals undertake in relation to specific innovations (Hall & Hord, 1987). The PTI study involved observation and interviews with nine principals from the three districts over a year to analyze what they do related to the implementation of curriculum innovations in their schools. Research staff recorded 1,855 "incident interventions," or actions taken, across those schools. Incident interventions include such things as talking to individual staff members, consulting with resource staff, telephone calls, developing budgets, workshops, short meetings—all of the kinds of things that make up the normal running of the school. The total number is limited to what principals themselves described as applicable to one particular program, and as they recalled specific events. As such, it represents only the tip of the iceberg for the total school program.

The PTI study identified three different styles of leadership among the nine principals—responder, manager, and initiator. Hall and Hord (1987) define the styles illustratively as follows:

Responder
Herbert Johnson is a principal who is very pleasant. He speaks to students by name and inquires about family members of various faculty. He went to the first social studies inservice with the teachers but since that time he has not been engaged with the program. He tells his teachers that he doesn't know as much as they do and he trusts their judgement, but if they need anything to come to him and he will order it. He is interested in attending to their requests and keeping them satisfied. The district social studies coordinator has the "run" of the school and works a great deal with teachers to implement the social studies curriculum.

Manager
Helen James keeps the management systems and instructional programs of a well-oiled school humming smoothly. She is at school early and stays late seeing that all aspects of the newly adopted social studies curriculum are in place. She has put the resource teacher in charge of inventorying and managing the social studies materials and supplies for teachers. James telephoned the district coordinator and arranged for training for the teachers in the new curriculum. At a weekly meeting of her school's administrators James checks on progress of the implementation effort, solves problems with the other two administrators and plans for how to meet teacher needs. She stays in touch with teachers' efforts to change by reading their weekly lesson plans and having a conference when necessary. Teachers report that James is helpful, responsive and understanding in that she does not impose too much on them at once.

Initiator
Aramintha Smith's teachers call her a "go-getter." They elaborate by saying that Smith will get anything they need in terms of resources, staff development or policy changes that will improve the school's new social studies program for students. Teachers also say that Smith will "get after" teachers herself if she thinks they are not delivering the social studies curriculum in ways that increase student learning. Smith wants students to be motivated and she wants teachers to do everything possible to infuse the social studies activities and lessons with excitement and stimulation. She visits classrooms to see if this is happening and to lend her own energy and enthusiasm to a lesson if it appears to be lacking. (pp. 215–16)

Of the nine principals, two were classified as initiators, three as managers, and four as responders. Principal's style as change facilitator was correlated .76 with overall implementation success, with schools with initiator-style principals being most successful, manager-led schools next, and responder-led schools least successful (Hall & Hord, 1987, pp. 252–53).

The 1,855 interventions in the PTI study were classified according to major functions:

1. developing supportive organizational arrangements (36%);
2. training and ongoing information support (7%);
3. consultations and reinforcement (24%);
4. monitoring and evaluation (22%); and
5. other (11%).

Initiator principals worked more with staff to clarify and support the use of the innovation (consultation and reinforcement), with 40 percent of their interventions in this category compared with 20 percent for responders and managers. How principals worked with other change facilitators (a vice-principal, lead teacher) was noteworthy. Hall and his colleagues examined the intervention behaviors of these "second change facilitators" (CF's) as well. The manager principal actually made more interventions in absolute number than the initiator principal, but the average total number of interventions in initiator-led schools was higher; that is, the combined number of interventions of principals and second CF's was greater. In particular, the responder principals made 50 percent fewer interventions than the second CF's; the manager principals made twice as many interventions as the second CF's; the distribution between the initiator principals and the second CF's was about equal (Hall & Hord, 1987; Hall, 1988).

Initiator principals worked in collaborative ways with other change facilitators. These collaboratively led schools experienced more interventions (notes to staff, small meetings, conversations about progress) and more multiple target interventions (actions taken with a group or more than one person), more actions taken to consult with teachers, more direction by the principal, more action taken by teachers, and more focus on students and learning. The functions performed by effective principals—developing supportive organizational arrangements, consulting, reinforcing, monitoring, etc.—are those found in other major studies of reform (see Marsh, 1988; Louis & Miles, 1990). Hall (1988) concludes that

Principals do not lead change efforts single-handedly. Rather, principals work with other change facilitators, who, in most cases, are making a large number of interventions also. It was discovered in earlier studies that the key is not merely having other change facilitators active at the school site; the important difference seems to be related to how well the principal and these other change facilitators work together as a *change facilitating team*. It is this team of facilitators, under the lead of the principal, that makes successful change happen in schools. (p. 49)

Research on effective schools corroborates the findings of Hall and his colleagues and has proven rather conclusively that the principal is crucial to success. In a careful study of school effectiveness, Teddlie, Kirby, and Stringfield (1989) paired eight schools in Louisiana in terms of consistent superior or inferior academic performance over a two-year period, matching the schools according to socioeconomic status of the community. They found that the paired schools differed significantly in 9 out of 10 measures of teaching effectiveness drawn from the research literature (time on task, presentation of new material, high expectations, positive reinforcements, discipline, etc.). They illustrate differences in the role of the principal in one of the pairs that were identical (both had 50% white and 50% black students and were a few blocks from each other).

The principal at school 1 (the effective school) was described by one observer as "having her finger on the pulse of the school." She was frequently seen in the hallways and the classrooms; she was observed in her not infrequent role of teaching a class. She appeared knowledgeable regarding every significant innovation in every classroom and saw to it that teachers were exposed to new and creative ideas. (Teddlie et al., 1989, p. 231)

By contrast,

The principal at school 2 (the ineffective school) has had a teaching career marked with honors. This principal . . . stated that she had excellent dedicated teachers. Although never observed in the classroom, she was visible in the hallways. She welcomed visitors, conveying a "nothing-to-hide" attitude . . . she praised her school and staff, saying that everything was "just great." "Everything was just great," noted one observer, "until we went into the classrooms." (p. 232)

The authors conclude, "If the amount of time spent on academics was the most impressive feature of school 1, the lack thereof was the unifying characteristic of school 2" (p. 232).

Returning to Smith and Andrews' (1989) study of 1,200 principals, "schools operated by principals who were perceived by their teachers to be strong instructional leaders exhibited significantly greater gain scores in achievement in reading and mathematics than did schools operated by average and weak instructional leaders" (p. 9). Similarly, Mortimore and associates' (1988) impressive longitudinal study of 50 schools singled out "purposeful leadership of the staff by the headteacher" as key in schools found to be effective on a variety of academic and nonacademic criteria. They describe some of the subtlety in what these effective heads did.

> Purposeful leadership occurred where the headteacher understood the needs of the school and was involved actively in the school's work, without exerting total control over the rest of the staff. In effective schools, head-teachers were involved in curriculum discussions and influenced the content of guidelines drawn up within the school, without taking complete control. They also influenced the teaching strategies of teachers, but only selectively, where they judged it necessary. This leadership was demonstrated by an emphasis on the monitoring of pupils' progress, through teachers keeping individual records. Approaches varied—some schools kept written records; others passed on folders of pupils' work to their next teacher; some did both—but a systematic policy of record keeping was important. With regard to in-service training, those heads exhibiting purposeful leadership did not allow teachers total freedom to attend any course; attendance was encouraged for a good reason. (Mortimore et al., 1988, pp. 250–51)

Mortimore and associates also found that active involvement of the deputy head and the teachers in program planning and other policy decisions was a feature of the more effective schools, reflecting both a degree of collaboration with the head and delegated responsibilities from the head.

NEW DIMENSIONS OF LEADERSHIP

We have begun to make the transition from the principal's role in influencing the implementation of specific innovations to the principal's role in leading changes in the school as an organization. Let us make this transition more explicit. As Hall and others have found, principals can have a major impact on the degree of implementation of particular innovations. However, as others have rightly pointed out, successful implementation of innovations by teachers often occurs without the involvement of principals (Crandall et al., 1982). Further, Trider and Leithwood (1988) found that many principals favored innovations related to their background interests while not favoring other innovations that were unrelated. In other words, it was misleading to generalize from how a principal reacted to a given innovation. And, as I have said in earlier chapters, implementing single innovations is not a very accurate measure of long-term school improvement.

The implication is that we have to look deeper and more wholistically at the principal and the school as an organization. Louis and Miles (1990) make the distinction between *leadership* and *management* and emphasize that both are essential. Leadership relates to mission, direction, inspiration. Management involves designing and carrying out plans, getting things done, working effectively with people.

This distinction has been made before, as in Leavitt's (1986) pathfinder vs. implementer, but the two functions are often compared invidiously (leaders do the right thing; managers do things right) or in linear relationship (leaders set the course; managers follow it). There are two problems with this image. First, it casts the management function as dull and less important. Second, it implies that the functions are sequential and carried out by different people. Successful principals and other organizational heads do *both* functions simultaneously and iteratively. It is also important to note that when we refer to management we are not talking just about management for stability, but also management for change.

Louis and Miles list the main "action motifs" for "leadership" and "management" for change. The leadership aspects involve (1) articulating a vision, (2) getting shared ownership, and (3) evolutionary planning. The management function concerns (1) negotiating demands and resource issues with the environment, and (2) coordinated and persistent problem-coping (Louis & Miles, 1990, Ch. 2). Louis and Miles claim that management for change has been underestimated, must be conceived more broadly, and requires skills and abilities just as sophisticated as those for leadership. The main point is that both sets of characteristics are essential and must be blended or otherwise attended to within the same person or team.

We are beginning to obtain more clarity and more precision about the complex role of school leadership. Smith and Andrews (1989) corroborate Louis and Miles' findings. In comparing "average principals" with "strong instructional leaders," Smith and Andrews found that instructional leaders spent more time than average principals on "program improvement" (41% vs. 27%) and about equal time on "building management, operations, and district relations" (34% vs. 39%). They observe: "These data . . . suggest that it is a false dichotomy to draw the distinction between being a strong building manager and being a strong instructional leader. These 21 principals are both strong building managers and strong instructional leaders" (p. 29).

Being a strong building manager relates both to change such as mobilizing resources and to stability such as discipline, personnel, facilities, and budget management (Smith & Andrews, 1989, p. 10). Parenthetically, it is interesting to draw the analogy between school-wide discipline and classroom management: School-wide discipline is to school improvement what classroom management is to teaching effectiveness.

The elaboration of the importance and the complementarity of leadership and management functions helps us interpret the most recent findings that principals with very different personalities can be equally effective. Wilson and Corcoran's (1989) study of a large number of effective secondary schools is a case in point.

> What is most striking about this collection of schools is the diversity of leadership styles. No one leadership style appears to be dominant. What seems to matter most is the fit between the style of the principal and the various subcultures in the school community. In some cases, there are dynamic powerful principals who seem to be everywhere and orchestrating everything. . . . In other cases, the principals are collegial and low-key relying on persuasion, delegation, and their ability to select and develop strong faculty members. (pp. 80–81)

Different styles were evident, but effective principals in Wilson and Corcoran's research all focused on active leadership, motivating staff, motivating students, reaching the community, and continually improving the school.

In comparing these findings to those of Hall and Hord (1987), two observations can be made. First, while personal styles differed in the various studies, all effective principals were *actively* involved in bringing about change. Second, in examining implementation of specific innovations (as Hall and Hord did) more overt action by principals affects implementation of those changes, but when more wholistic reforms are involved a myriad of actions create patterns that affect success in a variety of indirect and direct ways.

Smith and Andrews' (1989) portrayal of seven effective instructional leaders provides similar insights. Some were strong, aggressive, fearless; others quiet, nurturing, supportive. All, however, paid attention to the four main task areas examined by Smith and Andrews (resource provider, instructional resource, communicator, visible presence), but they did it with different methods and styles depending on their personality and setting.

This research also warns us not to judge a principal superficially or by a single stereotype (for example, the flamboyant visionary). Research that lumps together all principals who are involved in innovations may result in misleading or inconsistent findings. Moorhead and Nediger (1989), for example, are conducting a multifaceted up-close study of the behavior of four secondary school principals in Ontario, all of whom have an established reputation as effective leaders. Based on observational data, Moorehead and Nediger labeled the four principals as "the committed maverick," "determined and friendly," "the innovator," and "the administrator."

Expecting to find innovativeness to be related to effectiveness, the authors report

> The results, which were supported by both teacher and student data, did not correspond as expected. . . . The data indicated that there was not a simple

correspondence between the principals' innovative behavior or affiliative/humanistic behaviors, and the principals' perceived effectiveness. Principal 1 (committed maverick) and 4 (the administrator) were perceived to be the most effective; Principals 2 (determined and friendly) and 3 (the innovator) were less so. (Moorehead & Nediger, 1989, p. 7)

Consistent with the findings discussed earlier in this section, it was the underlying orientations and behaviors that made the difference: encouraging high performance goals, providing a high level of support both emotionally and in terms of task, open and honest communication between the staff and the principal, and firmly held values that were enacted behaviorally (such as not just emphasizing visibility, but developing techniques and actions to demonstrate it).

The understanding of the principalship has been further advanced by the programmatic work of Leithwood and his colleagues. In earlier work they developed the "principal's profile," which contained four levels of effectiveness (Leithwood & Montgomery, 1986). The highest level was "the problem-solver." In their most recent work Leithwood and others have been attempting to unravel the meaning of problem solving by examining how "expert" vs. "typical" principals go about solving actual problems.

Leithwood and Steinbach (1989a) found that experts differed (1) in the extent to which they explicitly took into account the interpretation others (teachers, for example) had of the problem, (2) in viewing the problem in the context of the larger mission and problems in the school, and (3) in the degree of clarity they had about the problem and their ability to describe both their interpretation and the reasons they had for such interpretation. They also found differences in how experts thought about goals (getting agreement with staff), values (being more cognizant and explicit about values), constraints (anticipating and identifying deeper problems), solution processes (using collaborative problem solving), and affect (not letting frustration get to them). Leithwood and Steinbach suggest that "principals' impact may be felt through their actions (a) in generating better solutions to school problems, (b) in developing teachers' commitment to implementing such solutions and (c) in fostering long term staff development" (p. 27).

In further work, Leithwood and Jantzi (1990) compared principals who were particularly effective at transforming the culture of the school toward a stronger improvement orientation, with those principals who were less effective at school improvement. They found that the successful principals used six broad strategies. They took actions that:

- Strengthened the school's [improvement] culture;
- Used a variety of bureaucratic mechanisms to stimulate and reinforce cultural change;

- Fostered staff development;
- Engaged in direct and frequent communication about cultural norms, values and belief;
- Shared power and responsibility with others; and
- Used symbols to express cultural values (p. 22).

To summarize, the personal styles of effective principals differ. They are more or less directive, more or less flamboyant. We are beginning to obtain a more complex but clearer appreciation of the effective principal as a collaborative leader of continuous improvements in the school as an organization. The framework used by Rosenholtz (1989), described in Chapter 7 (Figure 7.2), reflects the big agenda for school leadership. It points to the centrality of the principal in working with teachers to shape the school as a workplace in relation to shared goals, teacher collaboration, teacher learning opportunities, teacher certainty, teacher commitment, and student learning. To take but one example, Rosenholtz found that in collaborative settings 87 percent of the teachers answered "yes" to the question that asked whether their principal was a good problemsolver, compared with about 30 percent in moderately or low-collaborative schools (p. 55). Rosenholtz concludes

> Great principals do not pluck their acumen and resourcefulness straight out of the air. In our data, successful schools weren't led by philosopher kings with supreme character and unerring method, but by a steady accumulation of common wisdom and hope distilled from vibrant, shared experience both with teacher leaders in schools and colleagues district wide. (p. 219)

The role of the principal is not in implementing innovations or even in instructional leadership for specific classrooms. There is a limit to how much time principals can spend in individual classrooms. The larger goal is in transforming the culture of the school. If successful, it is likely that some advanced models of the future will show collaborative groups of teachers organizing and conducting learning, perhaps without the presence of a principal as we now know the role. The principal as the collaborative leader portrayed above is the key to this future.

Before turning to some general guidelines for action, it is necessary to comment on possible differences among principals. I have already noted that personality and style among effective principals vary. But what about other structural differences, especially elementary vs. secondary principals, and the situations of women principals as compared with men? (For differences in relation to type of community see Chapter 12.)

We should observe first that the examples and research reported in this chapter come equally from elementary and secondary schools. The kinds of things that effective principals pay attention to are similar to all levels of schooling and sizes of schools. Leithwood (1987) carried out a systematic review of research comparing characteristics of effective elementary and secondary schools. Of the 34 characteristics he examined, 23 were common to both levels. There were some important differences, namely, that secondary schools: pursued a more complex and broader range of goals; require principals to consider more factors in order to exercise influence; have less need for close parent involvement, but more need for working with business and social institutions in the community; and are more concerned with developing a sense of community and affiliation among staff and students.

Smith and Andrews (1989) found similar differences. While "strong" high school principals spent more time on educational program improvements than did "average" high school principals, they spent less time on improvement than did middle/junior high and elementary principals. Strong high school principals also spent more time on "building management, operations, and district relations" than did their counterparts at earlier grade levels. Principals at elementary schools have more of an opportunity to influence instruction directly through classroom observation and working with teachers.

Taking into account the evidence as a whole, I believe that the difference is a matter of degree, not of kind. The up-close descriptions of effective high school principals (see Louis & Miles, 1990; Wilson & Corcoran, 1988) show an active leader working continuously on program and instructional issues, collaborative and professional work cultures, resource acquisition, stable work environments, engagement of staff and students, and monitoring for results. As a group, secondary school principals historically have paid less attention to these matters. However, now that some secondary school principals are becoming involved as school improvement leaders, it may be that they are focusing on more comprehensive organizational issues than are elementary school principals. Stated another way, the long-term *institutional* development of schools requires that principals help shape the instructional and work climate of the school as an organization, not that they spend large amounts of time on direct classroom observations with individual teachers.

Dwyer (1984), Hallinger, Bickman, and Davis (1989), Hallinger and Richardson (1988), and many others cited in this chapter all found that principals exercised instructional leadership through shaping the organization, climate, and resources of the school rather than by intensive, direct involvement in instruction (see also Duke, 1986, on "the aesthetics of leadership"). This is not to say that principals should avoid direct classroom observation; only that it is not the main route to organization-wide improvements.

As we consider men compared with women principals two observations stand out. First, in terms of statistics the principalship is dominated by men, although considerable gains have been made by women recently. In overall terms, women constitute about 69% of the teaching force and about 25% of the principalships/vice-principalships. Subpatterns vary according to jurisdiction and level (elementary vs. secondary). At the elementary level, the percent of women principals for most districts is in the 20%–50% range; for secondary schools, it is 5%–20%—vastly underrepresenting their numbers in teaching (Marshall & Mitchell, 1989; Mertz, McNeely, & Venditti, 1989; Schneider, 1988).

In a study of 44 large school districts in the United States comparing 1972, 1982, 1986, Mertz and associates found that the percentage of female incumbents increased in all categories: for high school the percentages in the three time periods were 5%, 14%, 23%; for elementary, 36%, 42%, 47%. The rate of increase was greatest in the 1982–1986 period, and was even stronger among those appointed to assistant principalships. Mertz and associates observe that the increase in percentage of women in administration is a continuing phenomenon, and that there is a broadening of the opportunity base for women in positions traditionally associated with men. (The disappearance of men at the elementary level in both teaching and the principalship represents a serious problem for the future, but that is another matter.)

While the trend is widespread, the figures in the Mertz and associates' study are from large school districts (where the number of openings is greater and where more women are appointed). If we examine the broader range of districts the percentages are much smaller. Schneider (1988), for example, reports that for the 1986–87 year in Wisconsin, women occupied only 19% of the elementary principalships and 4% of the secondary principalships. Marshall and Mitchell (1989) quote national figures of 25% and 8%, respectively. In Ontario percentages are 18% elementary and 11% secondary for 1988–89 (Ontario Ministry of Education, 1990; see also Chapter 15 where I discuss issues related to motivation, selection procedures, and the preparation of women relative to administrative positions).

Second, as a group women are more likely to evidence behavior associated with effective leadership. Smith and Andrews (1989, p. 30) found that female principals spent more.time in educational program improvement activities than did males. Marshall and Mitchell (1989) report studies that show that women are more attuned to curriculum issues, instructional leadership, teachers concerns, parent involvement, staff development, collaborative planning strategies, community building, and the like. In short, women are more likely to possess characteristics associated with effective leadership and effective schooling (Shakeshaft, 1987). However, these findings refer to women "as a group" or on the average. There are plenty of examples in the research cited in this chapter of male principals performing as highly effective school leaders (and there are examples of women principals performing poorly). The main implication is that the characteristics associated with effective leadership of schools should be continually fostered in both men and women teachers and principals.

WHAT TO DO?

Educational changes of various sorts are constantly before the principal as reformers or reactors try to right the educational system. Whether a particular change is seen as a backward or forward step depends on our point of view, but all reforms are proposals for change. The principal is constantly being admonished to ensure or support implementation of this or that new policy or project. In Canada, revised provincial curriculum guidelines are always on the doorstep as the cyclical revision process continues ad infinitum. Legislation for special education, community-based programs, and school-work options are added to the list along with any other project deemed important by school trustees or central district administrators. In the United States, it is all the more chaotic because more levels are involved. In addition to the local and state demands, the federal government, unlike in Canada, has had a strong indirect presence in local innovation. Categorical grants, federal legislation, Supreme Court rulings, and voluntary projects on every conceivable topic are being perpetrated on the educational system. It would not be unusual for a school district to be participating in 50 or more state or federally sponsored programs at any one time, all of which have implications for the principal.

What do school principals think of all this ferment? If we were able to get inside their minds, the following script would probably come close to the truth.

Here is another change that is politically and not educationally motivated, and which will probably be reversed in two years anyway. The teachers are not interested in it, or don't have the time to deal with it. They will groan and bitch about it. I hate to even present it to them. I really don't understand the program. It seems so abstract and full of nice generalities. The one-half-hour orientation we received at the last principals' meeting only confused me further. I doubt if the superintendent or the board members know what it means either, judging by their comments. The superintendent wants it in order to look good. I will put it on the agenda of the next staff meeting and get it over with. I worry about any future meetings we might have to have on it. I hope nobody follows up on it. My annual principal report will describe that the new program has been introduced.

Of course, a single fragment cannot capture the variety of change projects and reactions. Some projects have new staff positions, district project directors, and specified resources, which will require the principal to make certain decisions and to hold meetings and workshops to monitor how the change is going. If the project is not a sound one or the principal for whatever reason is not confident about the change and his or her role in it, these meetings (even if the principal does not have to participate) will be a painful, visible reminder of an undesirable anxiety-producing side of the job. Many principals will also have strong pangs of guilt and questions about their own adequacy and competence. They will know that many new policies are attempting to address important educational goals that are currently not being met, and that some students and their parents are not getting a fair deal. When they do make a sincere effort to bring the issues to the attention of teachers, countless more questions will emerge about how to address the problem. Each proposed solution seems to raise more new problems than it remedies. The veteran principal eventually learns to take all this with a grain of salt.

A number of things are implicit in the above descriptions.

First, the principal is usually not helped by central administrators in ways of dealing with the change. On the contrary, he or she is given a brief description in a meeting where it is difficult to say in front of peers or superiors, "I don't understand it," or "I have serious concerns about whether we ought to be doing this," without feeling stupid or being seen as reactionary.

Second, the principal will experience all these feelings and concerns *privately.* Principals do not have or create much opportunity to interact professionally with other principals, although there is some desire to do so (see Blumberg & Greenfield, 1980, p. 168). As Sarason (1971) observes, the principal "escaped from one kind of role loneliness [as a teacher] to another" (p. 117).

Third, the principal does not share concerns with teachers either. The tradition among teachers (which the principal learned as a teacher) and the history of relationships between principals and teachers are more based on keeping a distance and respecting each other's professional autonomy. The principal's supervisory/evaluative role creates another barrier to confronting the problems of change openly.

> He quickly learns that telling a teacher what is wrong or insisting upon a change is a far from effective means for changing attitudes and practices. The power to legislate change is no guarantee that the change will occur—a principle the principal learned when as a teacher he was confronted with changing the behavior of children. From the standpoint of the principal there is little he feels he can do about what goes on in the classroom, particularly if the teacher has tenure or has been a teacher for a number of years. (Sarason, 1971, p. 120)

In situations where interaction is awkward or painful for one or both parties (or presumed to be so) most people do the obvious, if they have the choice—*they minimize contact*. Without personal contact there is no significant change.

We are talking about the existence of historical norms in schools, according to which it is assumed that people want to be left alone to carry out their professional responsibilities. For many this is no doubt true, but *many other teachers and principals desire more social contact concerning professional matters, if it can be done in a supportive climate*. Unless all teachers and principals are isolates, it could hardly be otherwise. The problem with norms is that people sometimes mistakenly assume that they are held by others. For example, the principal who talks infrequently with teachers about recent changes, because he or she sees the teachers as "professionals," may be perceived by some teachers as not interested in the change or in them—a perception that could be far from the truth.

Fourth, few things could be more uncomfortable or more undermining of our confidence than being expected by our superiors to lead the implementation of a change (1) that we do not understand, (2) in which subordinates are not interested, or (3) in which they are interested but it is unclear how they are to obtain necessary resources and assistance.

Fifth, the principal is the middle of a highly complicated personal and organizational change process. Knowledge, understanding, and skills in the change process are essential in sorting out the potentially good from the bad changes and in getting the good ones implemented. We can never know absolutely what the good changes are, but we do know a fair amount about how to set up a process of change that makes it more likely that better decisions will be made and that fewer negative change experiences will occur. There are two ways in which a social system changes: Either those in the system change their behavior for whatever reasons, or new system members with different characteristics are added and replace some existing members. In most social systems, both types of change go on simultaneously to different degrees. So it is with the principalship. Many principals, particularly in school districts that emphasize principal leadership and provide principals with professional development and support, are becoming more involved in instructional and school improvement. At the same time, some principals are retiring, and newer ones are being appointed, with (in many cases) explicit change-related attitudes and skills among the criteria for their selection. It is not an attack on aging per se to recognize that thousands of principals were promoted in the 1960s, with little thought given to their roles as implementers of change. Nor could it have been otherwise, with the need to rapidly staff hundreds of new schools and with the lack of knowledge at the time about what it means to implement changes. Be that as it may, even today it is not clear how principals are selected (Baltzell & Dentler, 1983). The selection process varies a great deal from district to district, uses unclear criteria, and applies unevenly those that are used. Knowledge and ability as managers or facilitators of organizational change should be primary criteria for selection.

In the meantime every principal has a conception of his or her role; and these conceptions vary, as we have seen, in that some principals are actively engaged in leading or facilitating change, while others are not. Certainly, different systems (school districts, states, provinces) limit or facilitate change in different ways, but the starting point from the individual principal's point of view should be a reflection on whether his or her own *conception* of the role of principal has built-in limitations regarding change.

Principals within the same system operating in almost identical circumstances will work with change or avoid it, depending on *their* conception of the role. Just as teachers' sense of efficacy is important in bringing about school improvement, so is the principal's—perhaps more significant, because it affects *the whole organization*. We could also speculate that many principals are diffident about their change leadership role because they do not feel prepared or clear about how to carry it out. Principals as much as anyone else need to develop meaning about change and the change process. Opportunities for interaction and professional development about the role of the principal in change are very much needed, and only recently are being established (see Chapter 15).

The starting point for improvement is not system change, not change in others around us, but change in ourselves. There is a tendency to externalize the problem and to look for blockages or solutions at other levels of the system. Whether this is true or not in a given situation is irrelevant to the main point: Waiting for others to act differently results in inaction and playing it safe. In a previous publication, I offered 10 guidelines for the individual principal formulated to contribute actions not words and to overcome system inertia by placing the responsibility for initiating action on the individual.

1. Avoid "if only" statements, externalizing the blame, and other forms of wishful thinking.
2. Start small, think big. Don't overplan or overmanage.
3. Focus on something concrete and important like curriculum and instruction.
4. Focus on something fundamental like the professional culture of the school.
5. Practice fearlessness and other forms of risk-taking.
6. Empower others below you.
7. Build a vision in relation to both goals and change processes.
8. Decide what you are *not* going to do.

    9. Build allies.
  10. Know when to be cautious (Fullan, 1988, p. 25).

These guidelines do not assume that the principal should passively implement system policies. We know enough about how changes get generated (Chapter 2) to know that the system is overloaded, and not all that coherent or coordinated (see Patterson, Purkey, & Parker, 1986). The school is the center of change, and that is where focus, coherence, and consistency must be forged. And that is why the principal is so central to reform.

The message for principals is that they should critically reflect on whether their own conceptions of the role are placing unnecessary limits on what can be done. This kind of reflection is difficult to undertake unaided, so that collaboration and feedback from teachers and other principals is needed. In assessing the need for change, principals should talk with teachers about their views. If many teachers recognize the need, or if the principal observes that there is a serious problem, he or she should set up a change process built on the assumptions in Chapter 6, the concerns of teachers described in Chapter 7, and the knowledge presented in this chapter of what effective principals do. Knowledge and conceptions of the change process and corresponding planning are a necessary foundation, to which must be added some knowledge or familiarity with the content of change and communication and interpersonal skills.

It would be repetitive to review all the things that effective principals were found to do, but two things stand out. They showed an active interest by spending time talking with teachers, planning, helping teachers get together, and being knowledgeable about what was happening. And they all figured out ways of reducing the amount of time spent on routine administrative matters; they made sure that change had an equal priority. It may take some time to overcome teachers' historical experiences with principals, but the evidence shows that many teachers want to interact with colleagues on improvements and want direct support from principals. The principal, in other words, is a key to creating the conditions for the continuous professional development of teachers (see Chapter 7 and Leithwood, 1990).

The burden on the principal is considerable as Barth (1990) observes:

> If the teacher–principal relationship can be characterized as helpful, supportive, trusting, revealing of craft knowledge, so too will others. To the extent that teacher–principal interactions are suspicious, guarded, distant, adversarial, acrimonious, or judgmental, we are likely to see these traits pervade the school. The relationship between teacher and principal seems to have an extraordinary amplifying effect. It models what *all* relationships will be. (p. 19, his emphasis)

It was not so long ago that those interested in reform used to figure out ways of bypassing the principal in an attempt to get changes implemented directly in the classroom. The assumption was that the principal was more of an obstacle than a help, and that anything that would neutralize his or her role would be a good thing. Many soon found that the principal still ended up being a powerful force in whether the change went anywhere— all the more powerful by dint of his or her reaction to being ignored in the process. If these innovators concluded (as many did) that principals were incorrigible blockers of progress or that innovations could be implemented without principals, they did not learn their lesson. There are no doubt principals who should not be in their positions or who cannot manage or tolerate change; but by far the more important lesson is that school improvement, as we have seen throughout the previous chapters, is an *organizational process,* with all that that entails both within the school and in relation to external contacts.

Serious reform, as we have seen, is not implementing single innovations. It is changing the culture and structure of the school. Once that is said, it should be self-evident that the principal as head of the organization is crucial. As long as we have schools and principals, if the principal does not lead changes in the culture of the school, or if he or she leaves it to others, it normally will not get done. That is, improvement will not happen.

CHAPTER 9

The Student

*Why in a democratic society, should an individual's first real contact with
a formal institution be so profoundly anti-democratic?*
                                                —Bowles and Gintis (1976), pp. 250–51

In the field of educational innovation it is surprising how many times a
teacher will finally shout out of desperation, "But what about the students?" Innovations and their inherent conflicts often become ends in
themselves, and students get thoroughly lost in the shuffle. When adults
do think of students, they think of them as the potential beneficiaries of
change. They think of achievement results, skills, attitudes, and jobs. *They
rarely think of students as participants in a process of change and organizational
life.* While research of the 1980s has begun to look at students as active
participants in their own education, and it has become clearer what
should be done, too little has actually happened to enhance the role of
students as members of the school as an organization.

In this chapter, I continue to pursue the main theme of the book.
Educational change, above all, is a people-related phenomenon for each
and every individual. Students, even little ones, are people too. Unless
they have some meaningful (to them) role in the enterprise, most educational change, indeed most education, will fail. I ask the reader not to
think of students as running the school, but to entertain the following
question: *What would happen if we treated the student as someone whose opinion
mattered in the introduction and implementation of reform in schools?*

I start with a look at where students are, followed by consideration
of students and change, and implications for coping with change.

WHERE STUDENTS ARE

Tremendous numbers and diversity of students, combined with minimal research from the students' point of view, make it impossible to do
justice to the question of where students are. Instead I will present a summary of some of the main issues that seem to concern students. This will
be used as a context for considering the students and change.

In 1970–77, I was involved in a large-scale and smaller-scale intensive research project on the role of students in Ontario schools (see Fullan & Eastabrook, 1973; Fullan, Eastabrook, & Biss, 1977). My colleagues and I started with a survey of students in 46 Ontario schools representing a range of large-city, medium-sized-city, suburban, and rural settings. Information was gathered from a random sample of students in grades 5 through 13 (Ontario high schools went to grade 13 at the time). The information was collected directly by us in classrooms using a questionnaire. The original sample was 3,972, from which we obtained 3,593 returns, or a 90 percent response rate. Questions included both fixed-choice formats and open-ended questions asking for comments. We categorized the responses according to three levels: elementary school (grades 5–6, or 5–8 in some schools), junior high (grades 7–9), and high school (grades 9–13, or 10–13 in some schools). The following summarizes our main findings:

1. A minority of students think that teachers understand their point of view, and the proportion decreases with educational level— 41%, 33%, and 25% from elementary, junior high, and high school, respectively.
2. Less than one-fifth of the students reported that teachers asked for their opinions and ideas in deciding what or how to teach (19%, 16%, 13%), a finding that we consistently replicated in subsequent work in a large number of classrooms in other schools.
3. Principals and vice-principals were not seen as listening to or being influenced by students.
4. Substantial percentages of students, including one out of every two high school students, reported that "most of my classes or lessons are boring" (29%, 26%, 50%).

Written comments on open-ended questions elaborate the meaning of the fixed-format responses. About 1,000 students (of the total of almost 3,600) wrote comments about the school. Of these about 30 percent reflected such positive attitudes as:

• Teachers are friendly. (elementary)
• This school is great. (junior high)
• I think the school I go to is good the way it is now. It doesn't need any changes. (junior high)
• I like my school because it has modern techniques, teaching methods, and facilities. It is a clean and up-to-date school. I think they should keep the school just the way it is. (high school)

The other 70 percent of the comments are indicative of what we labeled generally "the alienation theme."

- I think schools should make students feel comfortable, and not tense. (high school)
- I feel that teachers don't really care about what happens to students as long as they get paid. (elementary)
- I know that school is important to me and that I need it to get anywhere in life. But I'm beginning to realize that this reason is not good enough. I don't enjoy school at this point. It is the last place I want to be. If I wasn't so shy I imagine I could express these feelings to a teacher, but I've never spoken to one, not even about extra help. (high school)
- I'm only in school so I can go to university so as to make more money than if I quit school now. I do not particularly like school, in fact sometimes I hate it, but I don't particularly want to be poor. (high school)

Our questions on principals and vice-principals stimulated many comments from junior high and senior high students along the following lines:

- I have never spoken to the principal, and I don't even know who the vice-principal is.
- It's hard to say anything about the principal. He's always hiding.
- We never see him and I think the only kids he knows is the head boy and the head girl. He seems like a nice man, but who really knows, when he is always in his office.

Finally, we asked students an open-ended question about what they thought of the questionnaire and the project. This opened a floodgate. Over one-third of the students wrote responses, nearly all of which indicated that students were interested in the topics and had something to say. Typical of these 1,200 responses were the following:

- I think this project is very interesting in many ways. It asks many questions that I have never been asked before. (elementary)
- I think it's great the grown-ups want our opinion. I feel that they treat us like babies. (elementary)
- It brought me to thinking about things I had never thought much about, and is giving you at the institution, knowledge of what we students think about the school. (junior high)
- No comment. Only that this may help the teachers or planning board realize what lousy classes and subjects we are taking. (high school)
- I think this is an excellent project. It gives the man at the bottom

of the ladder a chance to unleash his feelings and say something about this damn school. (high school)

We followed up this research with some intensive work in two high schools in which we worked in over 40 classrooms over a three-year period (Eastabrook & Fullan, 1978; Fullan et al., 1977). With the classroom as the unit, we met with students and teachers, developed a new questionnaire based on their input, had the questionnaires filled out, and reported and discussed the results with students and with teachers and students together. In addition to their corroborating the earlier findings, a number of more specific issues emerged.

1. While we found that students did not think that teachers understood them, there was even more of a communication gap among students (except those who were close friends or part of the same group). While 41 percent of the students felt that teachers did not understand their point of view, 63 percent indicated that fellow students did not know or understand their point of view. Most students had two or three close friends in a class; some were isolates. There was virtually no communication inside or outside class with *the vast majority of other students* (i.e., outside one's own small friendship group).

2. Only a small number of students participated regularly in classroom discussions (typically 5–8 students out of a class of 25–30). In response to a fixed-choice question, 86 percent of the students said that most fellow students did not participate in class discussions or ask questions. Lack of familiarity with other students, combined with extreme sensitivity and self-consciousness in the presence of peers, strongly inhibited classroom participation.

3. Students who were not interested in going to college or university were impatiently waiting for the day when they could leave the school and get out and make money. They were not at all interested in the curriculum. Interaction with close friends provided the only satisfaction at school.

4. College- or university-bound students were interested in discussing curriculum participation and had many ideas to suggest. However, their predominant orientation was to "cover the course topics" and "get good grades." These students valued teachers who were fair in their grading practices, knowledgeable in their subject areas, and friendly and helpful.

Research and practice concerning students in the 1980s contain bad news and good news. The bad news is that if anything, the situation has worsened for students compared with 10 years ago. The good news is that we now have more complete explanations of the problem, and more effective solutions are being attempted.

The key theme in this recent research is *student engagement* (or dis-engagement). Webster defines to engage variously as "to attract and hold through interest," "to cause to participate," "to connect or interlock with." In short, are schools interesting, engaging places to be? The bad news is that by and large they are not.

Recent research continues to confirm many of the findings we re-ported above. King's (1986) study of over 44,000 students in 60 Ontario schools found that 50 percent of students felt "that teachers did not understand their point of view." This figure was higher (62%) for stu-dents in general-level (nonuniversity-bound) sources. Almost one-third of the students said that "some teachers make me feel that I am not impor-tant," one-quarter agreed that "teachers often make me feel foolish in front of the whole class," and less than 40 percent felt that "my teachers treat every student fairly" (King, 1986, p. 99).

Based on his nationwide study Goodlad (1984) states that "learning appears to be enhanced when students understand what is expected of them, get recognition for their work, learn quickly about their errors, and receive guidance in improving their performance" (p. 111). Yet, he found that "over half of the upper elementary students reported that many stu-dents did not know what they were supposed to do in class" (p. 112). At least 20 percent of high school students did not understand teachers' di-rections and comments.

Striking at the core of our theme in this book Goodlad observes

> Somewhere, I suspect, down in the elementary school, probably in the fifth and sixth grades, a subtle shift occurs. The curriculum—subjects, topics, textbooks, workbooks, and the rest—comes between the teacher and stu-dent. Young humans come to be viewed only as students, valued primarily for their academic aptitude and industry rather than as individual persons preoccupied with the physical, social, and personal needs unique to their circumstances and stage in life. (p. 80)

As students moved through the grades, Goodlad (1984) and his col-leagues found that "there was increasingly less use of teacher praise and support for learning, less corrective guidance, a narrowing range and variety of pedagogical techniques, and declining participation by students in determining the daily conduct of their education" (p. 125). We see, says Goodlad, "a decline from lower to upper guides in teachers' support of students as persons and learners" (p. 126).

In other more explicit research we are beginning to see a clear causal picture operating at the high school level. Firestone and Rosenblum (1988) present such a framework in their research (see Figure 9.1). They

FIGURE 9.1.   The Dynamics of Teacher and Student Commitment

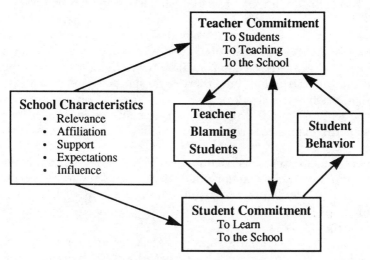

identify five major school context factors that affect teacher and student commitment: relevance, respect and affiliation, support, expectations, and influence. The first, relevance or sense of purpose, Firestone and Rosenblum claim, is especially difficult to achieve in urban high schools. Some teachers and students see relevance in relation to academic purpose, but most do not. The authors suggest that schools that are effective do a better job of developing relevant (meaningful) programs for low-achieving students, including work-study programs, and career-oriented and counseling programs.

The second factor, affiliation, is the sense of connectedness that students and teachers have to their surroundings. Its opposite—isolation— is more the norm in large high schools. Firestone and Rosenblum found that students were concerned with how adults in the school treated them:

> The teachers who blame students for difficult classroom situations are the most likely to display an "attitude" to students, to be abrupt with them, and not explain things in detail. Students receiving such treatment recognize that they are not respected which in turn reduces their commitment to the school. (p. 18)

At risk students are more likely to find themselves in such situations.

The third factor, support, concerns whether practices are fair for both teachers and students. Firestone and Rosenblum stress that *consistency* is the key: "A consistent environment is one where order is maintained, roles are clear, and rules are enforced fairly and rigorously, but not harshly" (p. 21).

Expectation—the fourth factor—is also a familiar theme in the literature. A certain amount of stress in the form of high expectations (combined with the other factors) serves to improve performance. Firestone and Rosenblum found three relatively distinct groups of schools. First, "in most schools there is little pressure for good teaching and student achievement" (p. 23). In a second, smaller group there is certain support for teachers for instruction, but "there is no special training or pressure for them to teach better" (p. 23). The third group (which appears to consist of one school) "combines strong management and incentives for students with an extensive program of teacher training and inservice" (p. 23).

The fifth factor described is influence. The authors found that teachers had limited interest in major policy decisions. They were concerned with more day-to-day matters pertaining to supplies, instructional leeway, etc. Student influence was not examined directly, but one can infer from other data that it is low.

Firestone and Rosenblum show how teacher and student commitment feed on each other in positive or negative ways. Students respond to the "respect" shown them by the teacher, the amount of interesting work, and the patience and caring of the teacher in explaining and re-explaining (Firestone & Rosenblum, 1988, p. 11). Similarly, teachers' commitment is heavily influenced by the response they get from students. Frustrated teachers begin to place the blame elsewhere—on students' family background, on lack of firm leadership at the school and district level. This cycle, in the absence of some intervention, is self-perpetuating and deepening.

> Students who do not understand their coursework withdraw from class and often become disruptive. Getting little positive response and a great deal of negative, teachers shift responsibility to others, both students and administrators. They become lethargic and impatient, stop explaining things to students and in extreme cases become verbally abusive. These behaviors in turn depress student commitment still further. . . . Once a student who has been in school for eight or more years meets a teacher with similar experience, both are well-primed to play out their parts of the cycle. (Firestone & Rosenblum, 1988, p. 14)

Wilson and Corcoran's (1988) analysis of 571 effective secondary schools contains almost identical conclusions, but they also show how some schools have intervened to reverse the cycle from negative to positive momentum. Certain factors (like sense of purpose and active leadership) create "conditions of teaching" that are more or less motivating for staff, which in turn influence "learning environments" that are more or less motivating for students. Wilson and Corcoran found that strong and focused "expectations, standards, and rewards" motivated students to become more involved in learning in effective schools compared with other schools. They make it clear that effective schools served "at risk youth" especially well. School after school is described in which new remedial and academic programs, new attendance and discipline policies, staff development, high expectations, praise and recognition, and overall collaboration among administrators, teachers, students, and community members resulted in dramatic improvements in academic achievement, lower absenteeism and dropout rates, and greater engagement and morale among students and staff (Wilson & Corcoran, 1988, Ch. 9).

In their comprehensive four-year longitudinal study of 2,000 elementary school students, Mortimore and associates (1988) also found that schools were differentially effective in motivating and engaging students. The factors that influenced student involvement and progress included: emphasis on positive reinforcement and rewards; challenging, interesting work; higher order inquiry; work-centered environment; focused curriculum; and maximum communication between teachers and students, as well as work-related interaction among students.

It is well known that teacher expectations influence student behavior, and that expectations vary for different types of students (Ashton & Webb, 1986; Rosenholtz, 1989, etc.). Teachers' social class and students' social class and behavior also influence teacher behavior (Metz, 1990). As Rutter, Maugham, Mortimore, Ouston, & Smith (1979) observe, "The initial teaching task is shaped by the attitudes, behaviors, interests and capabilities of the children in the class." Depending on how the teacher handles this it can lead, according to Rutter and associates, to "rising or falling spirals of expectations." Students, as Weinstein (1983) states, are aware of such cues.

> The research to date has pointed out that students are enormously sensitive to the differential behaviors that teachers might display toward various groups of students, such as high and low achievers, boys and girls. Students sense highly subtle differences in interaction patterns and are responsive as well to nonverbal messages conveyed. Through differential treatment, students can infer teachers' expectations for their academic performance. In classrooms where students were aware of the teachers' differential treatment of high and low expectations, the students' own expectations for themselves more closely matched the teachers' expectations, and the teachers' expectations for their students were powerful predictors of student performance. (p. 302)

The effects of this subtle interaction of teacher and student is one theme in understanding student behavior. Galton, Simon and Croll (1980) conducted one of the few projects that examined types of student behavior directly. The authors identified four types, which they labeled attention seekers (19.5% of the total), intermittent workers (35.7%), solitary workers (32.5%), and quiet collaborators (12.3%). The middle two groups of students had very little contact with the teacher.

Student behavior differed markedly with teaching style. Galton and associates had identified six main teaching styles (infrequent changers, class inquirers, group instructors, individual monitors, habitual changers, and rotating changers). Differences among pupil types is striking in some cases. For example, the percentage of intermittent workers ranged from 9.2% (in classrooms with teachers having a class-inquiry style) to 47.6% (with teachers who had an individual-mentor style). The other three student-to-teacher patterns showed similar ranges. Galton, Simon, and Croll (1980) also observed teacher and student behavior from one year to another. Every teacher observed in the second year displayed the same basic teaching style as in the previous year. However, 70% of the students changed their patterns of behavior on moving to a new teacher, in ways compatible with the style of the new teacher. Thus, individual students behave differently, and they do so in response to different teaching styles.

Sarason (1971, 1982) claims that students at the elementary level are not party to how classroom patterns are established. He conducted an informal observational study to see how the rules of the classroom were formed (what he calls the constitution of the classroom) and what assumptions about students were implicit in the process. In Sarason's words, "the results were quite clear": The rules were invariably determined by the teacher; teachers never solicited the opinions and feelings of students in developing rules. Sarason suggests several assumptions underlying the observed behavior.

1. Teacher knows best;
2. Children cannot participate constructively in the development of rules;
3. Children are not interested in such a discussion;
4. Rules are for children, and not for the teacher (rules state what children can and cannot do, but not what a teacher could or could not do), and so on (pp. 175–76).

Sarason also observed that teachers rarely, if ever, discussed their own thinking about planning and learning. Issues never came up pertaining to teachers' assumptions and theories of learning and thinking, whether children were interested in these matters, and whether they were able to talk about them. Rather, the task of the student was to get the right answer and know the facts. Sarason comments that teachers "unwittingly [created] those conditions that they would personally find boring" (p. 182).

The central issue, however, is contained in the following passage:

The point I wish to emphasize is that it appears that children know relatively little about how a teacher thinks about the classroom, that is, what he takes into account, the alternatives he thinks about, the things that puzzle him about children and about learning, what he does when he is not sure of what he should do, how he feels when he does something wrong. (Sarason, 1971, p. 185)

Sarason makes clear his own position:

If my experience with school children—in fact, with all levels of students, from elementary through graduate school—is any guide, that large part of a teacher's "thinking about thinking" which is never made public is precisely what children are interested in and excited about on those rare occasions when it becomes public. (p. 187)

These same issues could be stated in another more direct curricular way. When teachers plan a lesson or unit, do they discuss their ideas and concerns with students? Would it be helpful (regarding modification of the curriculum, achievement of objectives, etc.) if they did? The former question has been answered by our own research and that of others. Teachers do not discuss these issues with students. Clark and Yinger's (1980) close look at "the hidden world of teacher planning" confirms this finding and suggests an answer to the second question of whether it may be beneficial: "No matter how elaborate and complete a plan may be, it cannot be carried out successfully unless the students are brought rather fully into the knowledge of what to do and how to do it, and brought to a commitment to cooperation in the process . . . but communication of plans to students is almost never addressed" (pp. 21–22).

At the high school level, the patterns are more complex. Cusick (1973) carried out a participant observation study of students in one high school. He too found that students were relegated to the role of passive listeners in class and that student group-life rather than classroom interests dominated the school day.

For any single senior, the time spent actively engaged with some teacher over a matter of cognitive importance may not exceed twenty minutes a period for five periods a day. That is a high estimate. I would say that if an average student spent an hour to one and a half hours a day in school involved in subject matter, that was a good day. (Cusick, 1973, p. 56).

During the rest of the time the student is not paying attention (yawning, looking about, doodling, looking at pictures, chatting, etc.). Commenting on class discussion, Cusick (p. 180) notes that in one typical lesson he observed, only 5 of 22 students in the class participated (virtually identical to our finding). Regarding what interests students most, Cusick writes

> More and more, as I continued in the school, I saw that the students' most active and alive moments, and indeed the great majority of their school time, was spent not with teachers and subject-matter affairs, but in their own small-group interactions which they carried on simultaneously with their class work. (p. 58)

The consistent theme in Cusick's observations is that only a minority of students are really involved in basic educational processes, with the rest being passive watchers and waiters who pay a minimal amount of attention to formal classroom work while channeling their energy and enthusiasm into their groups of close friends (p. 222).

A number of researchers have shown that high school students are influential in negotiating a "live and let live" relationship with teachers (Cusick, 1983; Powell, Cohen, & Farrar, 1985; Willis, 1977). These implicit bargains allow some students to be left alone as long as they do not disrupt classroom life. Note that this form of bargaining protects the status quo, using power to form a negative pact that reduces pressure for reform.

Nowhere is the problem of engagement more obvious than in studies of retention and dropouts. Rumberger's (1987) review of research summarizes the evidence identifying personal, economic, and school-related reasons why students drop out (see also Wehlage, Rutter, Smith, Lesko, and Fernandez, 1990). Lawton, Leithwood, Batcher, Donaldson, and Stewart (1988) analyzed 20 empirical studies of high schools in order to develop a causal model of school-related factors influencing dropouts. They tested the model in 58 high schools in Ontario. They observe

> Research on school related factors has focused largely on student behaviors in school on the implicit assumption that it is the student who must change to fit the school. Hence, interventions to reduce dropout rates often take the form of counselling and the like. [But, future interventions] ought to assume that it is the school rather than or in addition to the student which needs to change. (Lawton et al., 1988, p. 27)

Lawton and colleagues' review generated 34 school-related characteristics concerning retention/dropout, which they grouped into seven categories.

1. goals shared (clarity and commitment about purpose);
2. teachers (dedication, expectations, collaboration, etc.);
3. school administrators (active leadership and support);
4. school organization and policies (academic achievement, resources, size, discretion, district support);
5. program and instruction (rigorous and focused curriculum, instructional time, etc.);

6. school culture (positive, orderly, shared, etc.);
7. school–community relationship (use of community resources, community support sought, etc.).

In applying the model to the 58 high schools, Lawton and colleagues found that the seven categories explained 55 percent of the variance in student dropout rate. What is most noteworthy about this research is that the set of factors influencing the specific problem of student dropouts is the *same* set that has been found to relate to school improvement and school effectiveness. Thus the tendency for students to drop out is not a separate issue, but is part and parcel of the basic improvement of schools, that is, making schools more engaging for all students and all teachers.

This conclusion has been confirmed in Bryk and Thum's (1989) analysis of a sample of 160 schools (4,450 students) from the "High School and Beyond" database. Using somewhat different language than Lawton and colleagues, but essentially the same types of measures, Bryk and Thum examined five clusters of factors.

1. perceived teacher quality and interest in students;
2. the academic press in the school environment (e.g., focus on academic subjects, student attitudes toward getting good grades, etc.);
3. the disciplinary climate of the school;
4. curricular differentiation and commonality; and
5. social and academic background composition of the school.

Bryk and Thum found that both absenteeism and dropping out are less prevalent where faculty are interested in and involved with students, where there is an emphasis on academic pursuits, where there is an orderly social environment, and where there is more commonality in program (i.e., less differentiation of curriculum for different groups). They emphasize that the effects of these factors "persist even after controlling for student level differences in social class, sex, academic background, and race/ethnicity" (Bryk & Thum, 1989, p. v).

Bryk and Thum also found that the effects of school size on absenteeism and dropout were substantial, "but mostly indirect, acting to either facilitate (in small schools) or inhibit (in larger schools) the development and maintenance of a social environment conducive to student and faculty engagement with the school" (p. 26).

The review in this section of where students are by no means captures all aspects of the students' thoughts and experiences. For many students, especially in urban areas, personal safety at school, hunger, discrimination, racial fights, and unhappy home lives are far more preponderant issues on their minds. It is also necessary to examine subcultural differences in how different ethnic groups experience schooling, and how the experience and orientation of males and females differ.

Despite the need to analyze in more detail the differences just mentioned, we can be fairly confident in our main conclusions of where students are. The percentage of students who drop out before graduating from high school ranges from 20% to 50% in some jurisdictions. In the province of Ontario the average dropout rate is 34%. Dropping out, as Bryk & Thum (1989, p. 3) state, is "an end-point of a process of increasing academic and social distance from the mainstream of school life." In addition, we have seen that many students who remain in school are hardly engaged in active learning. Taking a hypothetical cohort of students who enter grade 9, and using a conservative estimate, it seems likely that on the average one-third will leave school before graduation, and at least another one-third of the remaining group will lead school lives of uninspired passive learning. What is more, as students move through the grade levels from elementary to secondary, they become *increasingly bored and alienated from school.*

Does and could educational innovation have any relevance for the two out of three students currently finding little intrinsic meaning in school?

THE STUDENT AND CHANGE

As I have indicated, we hardly know anything about what students think about educational change because no one ever asks them. If we were to attempt to infer what some of the experiences with change meant to students, several images come to mind. Four such images that seem to have some basis in fact concern (1) indifference, (2) confusion, (3) temporary escape from boredom, and (4) heightened interest and engagement with learning and school.

Indifference is closely tied to the claim that the more things change in education, the more they remain the same. There is a great deal of evidence that indicates that many changes in curriculum materials have not resulted in any real change in how the classroom operates. To the extent that this is true, students would not notice any significant change. As they moved from one grade level to another, their experience in the classroom would be pretty much the same (a good teacher here, a bad teacher there, etc.). For many students the classroom is not the most interesting aspect of schooling anyway. For them the main benefit of the school is the opportunity it provides to interact with close friends on a daily basis. In short, a certain percentage of innovations adopted in schools are reacted to with indifference by students, simply because *the changes in fact do not make a difference to them.*

Nonchange is one form of failed implementation. But misdirected change resulting in *confusion* is something else, because "something" does change. If we consider the changes undergone by students over the past 20 years, it does not seem out of line to suggest that the extent to which new policies and programs were not clear in the minds of administrators and teachers would be closely related to *confusion on the part of students.* While somewhat dated, Smith and Keith's (1971) detailed case study of a new open-education elementary school illustrates the point.

> The possibility that students might not yet be able to work in a program that emphasized considerable pupil responsibility had not yet been fully taken into account. When the staff spoke of changing pupil roles, they seldom considered equipping the students with techniques that would insure facility in performing the new roles. (p. 140)

Students were described as "running around a lot" (p. 141), "wandering and milling" (p. 156), "restless" (p. 156), and not knowing how to work in small groups (p. 141). As with other research, no one (including Smith and Keith) asked students about their experiences, but the description strongly indicates massive confusion.

Some evidence from a project in Britain that directly *examines* the perceptions of pupils indicates that student expectations are a neglected yet crucial aspect in relation to the success of some innovations. Hull and Rudduck (1980) report on interviews with students involved in a new humanities curriculum project. The authors claim that pupils' interpretations of their traditional roles in the classroom "may well constitute a barrier to change [which] could be crucial" (p. 1). As one student expressed it, "You suddenly get dumped in the deep end. Suddenly they say they are going to teach us as adults after teaching us as babies for years" (p. 2).

Curriculum innovations vary according to how much change in student roles and activities might be involved, but all innovations by definition involve something new for students. The main argument is very simple. Any innovation that requires new activities on the part of students will succeed or fail according to whether students actually participate in these activities. Students will participate to the extent that they understand and are motivated to try what is expected. We have every reason to believe that, whatever the causes, students' experiences with innovations are not conducive to increasing their understanding and motivation. Nor could we expect it to be otherwise, if teachers, principals, and other administrators are having similar problems.

The *temporary escape* pattern of response concerns the possibility that some innovations provide a welcome change of pace in the routine and boredom of schooling. This response is seen most clearly in Farrar and associates' investigation of the large-scale Experience Based Career Education (EBCE) program at the high school level in the United States. The authors state

> Students tend to see EBCE as an alternative to the regular high school program, and so many use it as a way to get out of regular school. A large percentage of EBCE students seem to dislike or to be bored with school, or want to experience something more before graduation. So they join EBCE as a way to get out of regular classes. Although their motives vary widely, many students interpret EBCE as an escape from school. (Farrar et al., 1979, p. 50)

The final possible outcome for students—*heightened interest and engagement*—is obviously central to any solution, and as such is important to examine closely. At an overall level, we have cited a large amount of consistent evidence, especially from the 1980s, that shows that some schools, regardless of student background, do things that enhance student motivation, performance, and overall engagement in learning and the life of the school. Students in such schools are more likely to find school meaningful. While the dynamics are complex, the causal network seems fairly clear.

We can also make the direction of the solution for students even more explicit, at least through illustration. Changes have to be made in concert, at two levels. Improvements are required at the instruction and classroom level, and at the level of the school as an organization (Fullan, Bennett, and Rolheiser-Bennett, 1990). Relative to the former, the question is what kinds of pedagogical or instructional changes will make learning intrinsically more engaging for students.

Recent instructional improvements in the use of "cooperative learning" and "cognitive psychology" provide excellent examples of the power of change in pedagogical practices. There are several cooperative learning techniques, but they all share an interest in developing teaching approaches that promote small-group and individual learning as alternatives to "frontal teaching" (whole-class instruction) and individual seatwork. Johnson and Johnson (1989) state that five conditions are necessary for group efforts to be more productive: positive interdependence, face-to-face interaction, personal responsibility (individual accountability), sound skills (interpersonal and small-group skills), and group processing. Five major cooperative learning techniques have been developed and go under the labels

1. Jigsaw
2. Teams-Games-Tournament
3. Student Teams Achievement Divisions

4. Learning Together
5. Group Investigation.

Unlike open education as we have seen in Smith and Keith (1971), cooperative learning helps students develop skills to work in groups. Cooperative learning is a remarkable innovation in that it has been heavily researched in terms of its effects, addresses both academic and personal development goals, and gets impressive results. Moreover, it is one of the very few innovations that both is powerful and actually makes the teacher's job easier once the skills have been mastered. I will not review the research in detail. Johnson and Johnson (1989, 1990) conducted a review of research findings, which showed that cooperative learning causes: higher achievement, increased retention, greater use of higher level reasoning, increased perspective taking, greater intrinsic motivation, more positive heterogeneous relationships, better attitudes toward teachers, higher self-esteem, greater social support, more positive psychological adjustment, more on-task behavior, and greater collaborative skills.

In a review focusing on grades 7–12 (where cooperative learning has been less used), Newmann and Thompson (1987) examined 27 reports of high-quality research studies involving 37 comparisons of cooperative vs. control groups. They found that 68 percent of the comparisons favored a cooperative learning method in terms of student achievement, although some methods had more success than others, and the rate of use and success was lower in grades 10–12 compared with grades 7–9.

Sharan and Shaulov (1989) carried out a detailed experimental study of the Group Investigation (GI) method in which they examined the effect of GI on both student motivation to learn and academic achievement. They compared 10 classes being taught with the Group Investigation method with 7 control classes. Motivation to learn was measured behaviorally as a combination of (1) task perseverance, (2) involvement in classroom learning, and (3) investment of effort in homework. Achievement was measured in relation to progress in three subject areas—mathematics, Bible, and reading comprehension.

Their study found that students in classrooms using Group Investigation as compared with the control group were substantially more motivated to learn on all three measures and achieved higher scores on all three subjects. For example, in the control classes the proportion of high, medium, and low achievers did not change from pre- to posttest, but in the GI classes the proportion of high achievers increased dramatically (35% to 50% in Bible; 22% to 50% in reading; and 18% to 28% in mathematics). Sharon & Shaulov (1989) provide clear evidence that cooperative learning (GI) "promoted students' intrinsic interest in learning tasks by comparison with students in classrooms taught with the whole-class method" (p. 27). To take but one measure—participation in class discussion—student participation in the control class changed little from pre- to posttest, while in the Group Investigation class it went from 20% in the pretest in the high category to almost 60% in the posttest.

Cooperative learning is not a panacea. Even its proponents caution against overuse. In the Sharon and Shaulov study, Group Investigation teachers still lectured 28% of the observed time (compared with 48% for the control group; the authors note that this 20% decrease in lecture time is a very substantial change in how time is used in the classroom). Sharon and Shaulov also stress that student preference for individual and group work must be taken into account. The norm, however, is that students are rarely treated as if their opinion mattered.

As one set of teaching methods, however, cooperative learning provides a clear and convincing example of changes that are within the control of individual teachers and that engage and empower students. Johnson and Johnson (1989) summarize

> Students often feel helpless and discouraged. Giving them cooperative learning partners provides hope and opportunity. Cooperative learning groups empower their members to act by making them feel strong, capable and committed. It is social support from and accountability to valued peers that motivates committed efforts to achieve and succeed. (p. 4:1)

And

> Students who are "at-risk" for dropping out of and/or failing in school are typically in need of caring and committed peer relationships, social support, and positive self-images, as well as higher achievement. These are obtained from cooperative learning experiences. In order to work cooperatively, at-risk students need the social skills required to work effectively with others. Within most classrooms, however, the status quo is either competitive or individualistic instruction within which students are expected to listen to lectures, participate in whole-class discussions, individually complete worksheets without interacting with their classmates, study by themselves, and take the test. (Ch. 4, p. 25)

Other recent pedagogical developments in cognitive psychology, while more complex, provide potentially powerful strategies for putting students more in control. Prawat (1989) sees empowerment as best viewed from an outcome perspective emphasizing "access," or the extent to which students are able to utilize their intellectual resources. Teachers can empower students by providing them with cognitive strategies that allow them to regulate their own learning. Prawat's model involves three interactive levels: motivational dispositions, learning strategies, and factual or conceptual knowledge. Each level is mediated by organization (of knowledge or strategies) and reflection (the ability of students to reflect on what they know and use it in a different way). It is Prawat's thesis that teaching strategies are available (involving verbalization, writing about content, classroom dialogue, etc.) that help students develop, organize, become aware of, and, in short, access their own and others' knowledge. Access involves helping students develop networks of knowledge and reflective awareness of these networks: "In short, it involves thinking of the child as a total cognitive being, one who, when empowered, has access to a full range of intellectual resources and thus can respond proactively as opposed to reactively in various in-school and out-of-school contexts" (Prawat, 1989, p. 34).

Much more development is needed in this area to generate specific teaching approaches and practices that are practically usable. One particularly powerful example is evident in Bereiter and Scardamalia's work on "intentional learning" (Bereiter & Scardamalia, 1987; Scardamalia & Bereiter, 1989). Developing computer-based systems in regular classrooms, Bereiter and Scardamalia have been able to develop procedures through which students can access knowledge and use certain learning techniques such as writing, thereby gaining greater "executive control" over their own learning.

In discussions with young students (9–12 years old) about how they come to learn and understand, Scardamalia and Bereiter (1989) found the average classroom situation wanting.

> These discussions have impressed us with how far removed the normal run of educational activity is from engaging children in the identification and discussion of advances in understanding. Educational tasks have, as an underlying goal, the advancement of understanding. But their structure, as explicitly conveyed, highlights the superficial structure of school activities. The explicit goal is to complete a task—to finish a reading or writing assignment, to engage in some activity, to turn in a report, to answer questions, etc. The theory of learning that is conveyed via this more superficial structure is that involvement in activity or exercise of skill is sufficient for advancing knowledge [and, as we have seen, many students are not involved even at this level]. . . . Trying to come to terms with questions such as "But how did that advance your understanding? What do you understand now that you didn't understand before?" requires an additional level of involvement with the educational material. (pp. 2–3)

To advance this additional level of involvement Scardamalia and Bereiter have been developing in two regular grade 5–6 classrooms a model that they call CSILE—Computer-Supported Intentional Learning Environments. CSILE is designed to support students in collaborative knowledge-building activities.

> CSILE is central to classroom activities in all subject areas. It is designed with a communal database at its core. Students contribute information, search for

misconceptions and publish their discoveries. They are assessed on their contributions. CSILE is, at its core, a knowledge exploration . . . rather than
knowledge delivery . . . system. Knowledge-structuring environments allow
students to take pride in increasingly broad and complex arrays of knowledge to which they have contributed. (Scardamalia & Bereiter, 1989, p. 11)

In the CSILE classrooms the students interact with outreach databases
to pursue and pose questions, construct plans for gathering information,
elaborate what they know and wonder, and the like. Students identify
certain notes as "candidates for publication" (sharing) or as "candidates
for submission to our biology expert" (either the teacher or someone des-
ignated outside the classroom). Thus, "learning becomes exploration-
driven rather than task-driven" (p. 13), increasing students' abilities in
reading, writing, questioning, and higher order thinking via a variety of
subject areas. Scardamalia and Bereiter are currently extending CSILE toward "a common educational operating system, capable of operating at
all ages, and across all curricular" (p. 16). The goal is to make students
critical, collaborative learners engaged in focused inquiry using an array
of information and expertise (see Scardamalia, Bereiter, McLean, Swallow & Woodruff, 1989).

These two examples—from cooperative learning and from cognitive
science—are not mutually exclusive. One approach can be used in the
service of the other. And, they are not meant to capture all teaching approaches available that could activate the learning of all students equally.
They do illustrate powerful advances that are being made in teaching
practices that promise to provide students with the conditions and skills
needed to achieve their own control and meaning in classrooms.

Intimately related to improvements in instruction are changes at the
level of the school as an organization. Many of these changes, as described
in Chapters 7 and 8, will indirectly improve the lot of students. Some of
these changes combine new organizational arrangements and learning
experiences in work-study partnerships with business (MacDowell, 1989).
Other reforms foster collaborative work cultures, active leadership, continuous improvement, greater teacher skill and commitment, and so on,
which make the school a better place for learning for both adults and
children. Additional direct proof of this claim was offered in the studies
cited earlier in this chapter that identified the organizational characteristics of effective schools as they affected student engagement.

IMPLICATIONS

Fundamental to the argument in this chapter is that treating students
as *people* comes very close to "living" the academic, personal, and social

educational goals that are stated in the official policy documents and programs in most jurisdictions (see also Barth, 1990). Since the student is at
the bottom of the heap, he or she has only limited power to bring about
positive changes (students can, as we have seen, exercise great negative
power to reject what is being imposed).

Effective change in schools involves just as much cognitive and behavioral change on the part of students as it does for anyone else. Earlier
I said that implementation frequently involves role change by the teacher
in the classroom. The more sociologically accurate statement is that implementation actually comprises a change in the *role relationship* between
teachers and students. We could take any number of innovations (a new
social studies curriculum, mainstreaming, cooperative learning, intentional learning, microcomputers, parent involvement, work-study programs, etc.) and identify the kinds of student activities and teacher activities that make up the change. Critical to understanding educational
change is the recognition that these changes in students and teachers
must go together—that is, students themselves are also being asked to
change their thinking and behavior in the classroom. Most students will
not or cannot change simply by being lectured to or ordered to, any more
than the rest of us would. The reason that this issue is critical is that
student motivation and understanding regarding a change are directly
related to whether and how they engage in what we might call implementation activities, which are the *means* to achieving the learning outcomes
in question. If these assumptions are correct, we should stop thinking of
students just in terms of learning outcomes and start thinking of them as
people who are also being asked to become involved in new activities.

Another problem is that information is negligible as to what students
think of specific innovations that affect them. To say that students do not
have opinions and feelings about these matters is to say that they are
objects, not humans. Those responsible for innovations (whether teachers, principals, or others) would be well advised to consider explicitly how
innovations will be *introduced* to students and how student reactions will
be obtained at that point and periodically *throughout implementation.* Hull
and Rudduck (1980) conducted a project in four schools in England to
experiment with and develop ways in which curriculum innovation might
be introduced.

> In each case our aim will be to assist in mounting induction courses for pupils
> who will be involved in the planned change. The courses will centre on
> audio-visual representation of the new form of working, which will provide
> the starting point for group discussion. (p. 6)

The more complex the change, the more that student involvement is
required. A study of "Project Excellence," an alternative high school pro-

gram in Ontario, is a case in point (Anderson, Stiegelbauer, Gerin-LaJoie, Partlow, & Cummins, 1990). Project Excellence is a student-centered, individualized learning program that includes teachers as advisers and learning center resource supports rather than classroom instructors. Students were consulted frequently during implementation about their response to what was unfolding, and adjustments were made based on their input. The administration continues to invoke students in evaluating program refinements, seeing them as part of the school team with teachers and administration. Restructuring reforms can involve students in small (each classroom or teacher) and big (school-wide) ways, but it is going to be the accumulation of a multitude of small ways that counts for the individual student, not the participation of a few student leaders.

This chapter can be more fundamentally summarized in other words. *Effective educational change and effective education overlap in significant ways.* Involving students in a consideration of the meaning and purpose of specific changes and in new forms of day-to-day learning directly addresses the knowledge, skills, and behaviors necessary for all students to become engaged in their own learning.

Teachers who blend education and change, periodically discuss the meaning of activities with students, work on the skills students need to participate in new educational reforms, and consider the relationship between old and new, will be going a long way in accomplishing some of the more complex cognitive and social educational objectives contained in the policy statements and curricula of most school districts.

CHAPTER 10

The District Administrator

To get the whole world out of bed,
and washed, and dressed, and warmed, and fed,
Believe me, Saul, costs worlds of pain . . .
        —John Masefield, "The Everlasting Mercy" (1911)

Chapter 5 described the factors that determine whether educational change gets implemented. The conclusion was that there are many different ways in which change can and does go wrong. The task of the district administrator is to lead the development and execution of a system-wide approach that explicitly addresses and takes into account *all* these causes of change at the district, school, and classroom levels.[1] In addition to doing this for specific policies, it is also the district administrator's task to increase the basic capacity of the system to manage change effectively. No wonder there is such a high turnover rate among superintendents! This is a great expectation, and failure to meet it in some cases may have more to do with the impossibility of the odds than with the skills of the administrator. As the quote above suggests, just getting the kids and teachers through a school day without incident costs worlds of pain and represents a major accomplishment. But some school districts do establish effective change processes, while others follow a disastrous pattern. The district administrator is the single most important individual for setting the expectations and tone of the pattern of change within the local district. (This statement, of course, does not deny that change can occur at the school level without central office involvement.)

I follow the standard sequence in this chapter: commencing with a discussion of where district administrators are, then reviewing what is known about the administration and change, and concluding with a set of guidelines for the district administrator interested in managing change more effectively.

WHERE DISTRICT ADMINISTRATORS ARE

Nearly all district administrators are men—upward of 95 percent in most jurisdictions (we will return to this matter later). They work in school systems ranging in size from fewer than 100 students to more than 200,000. As we could imagine, the conditions and tasks vary tremendously across these situations; but in one way or another all district administrators face big problems. In smaller districts they frequently carry out several functions with few resources, and in larger districts they are constantly dealing with conflicts and crises and large financial and personnel issues through an elaborate bureaucracy of specialists. The vast majority of superintendents are appointed (and fired) by locally elected school boards. In some smaller, rural districts in the southern United States, chief superintendents are locally elected rather than appointed. Although there is a fair amount of evidence about the role of the administrator and change (which is the subject of the next section), there is little representative information on what administrators do and think in their total roles. Goldhammer (1977) reviewed the changing role of the American school superintendent from 1954 to 1974 and suggests that the major change over the 20-year period has been away from the role of educational spokesperson and executive manager of a relatively homogeneous system, toward one where negotiation and conflict management of diverse interests and groups predominate. School boards have become more politically active, as have teacher unions and community and other special-interest groups. Communities have become more heterogeneous. Federal and state government agencies and courts in the United States have become major participants in educational programming through financial and legislative means (see Chapter 13). The superintendent, says Goldhammer (1977, p. 162), has become more of a negotiator than a goal-setter, a reactor and coordinator of diverse interests, and a person who must learn to lead and involve teams of specialists.

Blumberg (1985) studied 25 school superintendents, interviewing them about their roles, responsibilities, and perceptions of impact. Overwhelmingly, his respondents described their role as one of "conflict" and ambiguity mediated by everyday tasks. Blumberg (1985) observes that superintendents face

> the necessity of having to live daily with conflictual or potentially conflictual situations in which the superintendent plays a focal role as decision maker, mediator, or simply as a human lightning rod who attracts controversy. Some of the conflicts take on major, systemic proportions, affecting the entire school district. Some are major but affect only individuals. Some are minor. Some relate to the superintendent as a person, some to his job and career, and some to his family. Regardless of the focus or substance, a seemingly absolute condition of the superintendency is that there are only rarely days when the superintendent is not called upon to make a decision that will create some conflict, or is not involved somehow in conflicts of his own making. All of this seems to occur irrespective of the person involved: "it comes with the territory." (p. 1)

In Blumberg's perception the role of the superintendent is different from that of other chief executive officers due to

> the public perception of the superintendent as guardian of a sacred public enterprise, the education of the community's children; the politicalness of the relationship between the superintendent and the school board; and the fact that superintendents once held the same job—that of a teacher—as the people over whom they are now expected to exercise authority; the huge number of community and governmental groups with one or another stake in the school; the superintendent's visibility and accessibility as public property. (p. 188)

As one superintendent described it,

> It's always a balancing act because there are so many pressure groups. More so than ever before, and the funny thing is that we have made it happen that way. We have really pushed the idea that everyone should be involved in schools. So now I have so many different constituencies out there with so many different interests that my problem is to try and keep them all appeased. (p. 67)

What is most revealing about Blumberg's extensive exploration of the working lives of chief superintendents is the infrequency with which curriculum and instruction matters "naturally" arise in the interviews. Superintendents talk about politics, school boards, teacher unions, stress, public exposure, conflict, and so on. Curriculum, instruction, staff or professional development rarely arise in a prominent way and do not appear at all in the index of Blumberg's book. This is not to say that these 25 superintendents had no impact on curriculum and student achievement in their districts, only that keeping conflict at bay preoccupies superintendents unless they take extraordinary steps to go beyond it.

Cuban (1988c) identifies three dominant themes in relation to the role of the superintendent as it has evolved since initial use of the title in 1830—instructional (teacher of teachers), management (administrative chief), and political (negotiator). He describes what seem to be common patterns.

> The superintendency is a constant stream of brief encounters, mostly with school board members and subordinates in the central office; constant interruptions; little time spent at the desk or in the schools; a decided concentration upon verbal exchanges with people . . . and a conflicting set of expectations based on a historic desire for an efficient technocrat/manager and a professional who will improve the district. (pp. 129, 131)

Cuban analyzes the historical trends and associated research, as well as provides portrayals of several outstanding superintendents over the years. Two conclusions stand out. First, like Blumberg, Cuban concludes that the managerial and political roles, not the instructional role, dominate superintendents' behavior. Second, all superintendents deal with all three themes, but some individuals, albeit a minority, have been able to elevate instructional leadership as the central focus, using politics and management in its service. The latter notwithstanding, both Cuban and Blumberg make it clear that political events and conflict frequently carry the day and often lead to the firing and resignation of superintendents.

There have been a few Canadian studies of superintendents. Duignan (1979) conducted an observation study of eight school superintendents in Alberta in which he found that

> The superintendent averaged 26 discussion sessions each day, and these talks accounted for approximately 70 percent of his daily working time. Specifically, 70 percent of this discussion time was spent with school trustees, central office staff members, and building-level administrators. *Less than 7 percent of the time he spent in conversation was with teachers and less than half of 1 percent with students.* (p. 34, emphasis in original)

Also in Canada, Leithwood and Steinbach (1989b) have embarked on an important study of the problem-solving orientation of chief superintendents. In a study of eight directors of education in Ontario, Leithwood and Steinbach found that, compared with principals, the chief executive officers (CEOs) "spend more time interpreting the problem, use more values or principles to direct their problem solving, have fewer explicit 'product' goals, and plan fewer steps in the solution process" (p. 22). Leithwood and Steinbach examined how CEOs classified problems in terms of clarity of solution. Chief executive officers frequently deal with complex problems whose solutions are unclear and fraught with dilemmas. Leithwood and Steinbach depict the solution process for unclear administrative problems as involving multiple paths toward solutions, which are not initially identifiable. Effective superintendents must embark on the right paths, sorting out solutions as they proceed.

Fullan and associates (1987) conducted an extensive study of "supervisory officers" in Ontario (those above the role of principal in line positions up to and including the director or chief superintendent). Over 200 supervisory officers were interviewed in 26 school districts (one-quarter of the total) in the province. Three summative style dimensions were developed: system driven vs. school driven, reflective vs. fire fighting, and generalist vs. specialist (Fullan et al., 1987). As might be expected, directors, compared with other central office superintendents, scored consistently higher on the system, reflective, and generalist dimensions.

Allison (1988) in further analysis of the Fullan and associates data and focusing on the 22 directors of education on whom there were data, found that the directors commonly perceived three distinct sectors with which they worked: board (trustees), system, and community. In comparing the situation of chief executive officers in the United States with those in Ontario, Allison suggests that the Ontario directorship evolved from a more stable tradition (see also Boich, Farquhar & Leithwood, 1989). By contrast, Allison states that the emergence of the superintendent's role in the United States is characterized by a culture of "conflict, insecurity and uncertainty" (p. 5).

Some specific features provide support for Allison's observation. Compared with their American counterparts, Ontarian and, more broadly, Canadian superintendents are more likely to head larger, more stable school systems, are less laterally mobile, are more likely to be appointed from within their own systems, and have longer tenure as chief executive officers (Allison, 1988; Fullan et al., 1987). For example, in the United States a typical term seems to be three years. Gaines (1978) states that the average tenure of a superintendent is "a short two years and three months." In Michigan, superintendents normally have two- or three-year contracts (Keidel, 1977). In West Virginia, Martin and Zichefoose (1979, p. 5) found that the superintendent "failure rate" (defined as superintendents who were fired, not rehired, or forced to resign) was 90 percent over a six-year period. In Louis and Miles' (1990) study of five urban secondary schools, four had witnessed a decade where the typical superintendent stayed for only two or three years before being forced out or moving on by choice. By contrast, in our Ontario sample, the average tenure of the directors was over seven years, and they were still in their positions.

We must be careful in drawing inferences. No Canadian superintendents would say that they are leading peaceful professional lives. Politics, crises, and conflict are common fare for all superintendents. In general, however, U.S. compared with Canadian superintendencies are more volatile. This presents one major and paradoxical implication for reform. In high turnover situations there are more occasions for reform, but less continuity for actually bringing it about. In low turnover situations, there is more inbrededness and complacency, but better conditions for follow-through when major reforms are initiated.

Before turning directly to the question of the district administrator and change, there are three other aspects of the situation of superintendents that should be taken up, namely, gender of administrator, size and type of district, and the relationship to other central office administrators.

I have already observed that in most jurisdictions the percent of male chief superintendents is above 95. That figure is changing for large districts. Mertz, McNeely, and Venditti (1989) analyzed historical statistics in 44 large school districts in the United States. The percent of female chief superintendents increased from 0 (1972) to 9.3 (1982) to 15.9 (1986). Not only is 15.9% still very low, but the figure is much lower for the range of school districts. Thierbach (1988) states that only 2% of the superintendencies in Wisconsin are held by women. Bell and Chase (1989) report that 2.8% of the 10,960 chief superintendencies were held by women in 1986–87. In Ontario the figure is 5%, with more than half accounted for in the past 12 months.

Because the numbers are small, there are few studies yet of women chief superintendents, especially those recently appointed (who are both more numerous and may differ in some key respects compared with women appointed in the past). Early studies by Bell and Chase (1988, 1989) and others are beginning to map out the research and policy issues. In their first project, Bell and Chase (1988) studied three districts with women superintendents. They found that many board members were concerned about the hiring of women and worried about whether women could handle the job (assert authority, etc.). In their later research Bell and Chase (1989) conducted in-depth interviews with 17 women superintendents. Bell and Chase, as others, suggest that women have a greater preference than men for activities related to curriculum, instruction, and staff involvement and development, and for less bureaucratic, hierarchical forms of management, although as superintendents they certainly engage in the latter (Bell & Chase, 1989; see also Marshall & Mitchell, 1989). The cases are too small in number to draw conclusions, but the orientations, actions, and strategies employed by women as well as men superintendents should be investigated carefully in future research.

Differences in size and type of district appear to be ones of degree rather than of kind. In our own study we found no differences in the skills required of directors of smaller as compared with larger systems, although directors in smaller systems tended to be involved more directly in managing some specific operational aspects of the system (Fullan et al., 1987). Louis (1989) indicates that superintendents in rural and small districts are often more critical in decisions to adopt specific policies and innovations. In studies of five effective rural districts, Hord (1988) states: "It is clear in the five sites in this sample, that the key leader and decision maker for the system is the superintendent" (p. 13). In cases where the superintendent actively sought change (2 of the 5), he or she "recognizes the needs of the system and assumes that the system can change and act differently; . . . opportunities for assistance are recognized, and/or vigorously sought" (p. 13). Smaller, especially rural districts also face more difficult problems of fewer resources, geographical spread, difficulty in recruitment of teachers and administrators, and so on (Louis, 1989; Rosenholtz, 1989).

Finally, we have been concentrating only on the *chief* district administrator. Other district administrators (assistant superintendents, area superintendents, directors and superintendents of curriculum, etc.) are directly responsible for program development and improvement. Research studies of these roles is extremely limited, perhaps because of diversity of roles and organizational arrangements. Hall, Putman, & Hord (1985) in studying the roles of district office personnel in 11 districts found great variation and lack of clarity, leading them to subtitle their study "what we don't know." Recognizing this deficiency, Research for Better Schools recently launched a three-year study of the role of the district in school improvement involving ten sites—five small and five medium-sized districts (D'Amico & Corbett, 1988). The intent is to assess the extent to which districts have an "improvement focus" in their central operations and activities, and to link this to the degree of building-level school improvement activity. In the meantime we know that central office staff are often responsible for the initiation and follow-through of specific innovations that get implemented in schools (Huberman & Miles, 1984). Instead of considering the roles of chief superintendent and other central administrators separately, it is best to examine the district administration as an entity, especially with respect to its complex role of managing district–school relationships for the purpose of bringing about improvements.

THE DISTRICT ADMINISTRATION AND CHANGE

The greatest problem faced by school districts and schools is not resistance to innovation, but the fragmentation, overload, and incoherence resulting from the uncritical and uncoordinated acceptance of too many different innovations. Changes abound in the schools of today. The role of the district is to help schools sort out and implement the right choices. I pursue this problem by starting with the relatively simple notion of implementing single innovations, then turn to the more complex matter of district–school relationships in the context of managing multiple innovations simultaneously—labeled more simply the problem of sustained improvement.

Implementing Innovations

We have seen in Chapter 4 that district administrators are usually the critical source of initiating specific innovations (Berman & McLaughlin, 1977; Crandall et al., 1982; Huberman & Miles, 1984). Using the familiar paradigm of initiation-implementation-continuation, we know that district staff are typically the ones to introduce new district programs. Even when the source of change is elsewhere in the system, a powerful determining factor is how central office administrators take to the change. If they take it seriously, the change stands a chance of being implemented.

If they do not, it has little chance of going beyond the odd classroom or school.

The crunch of whether a change has been taken seriously by the district administration comes forcefully at the implementation stage. Adopted changes will not go anywhere on any scale unless central staff *provide specific implementation pressure and support* (Huberman & Miles, 1984). As I have said of the principal, being neutral or offering general verbal support does not amount to much. For multiple-school innovations, district staff must lead a process that

1. tests out the need and priority of the change;
2. determines the potential appropriateness of the particular innovation for addressing the need;
3. clarifies, supports, and insists on the role of principals and other administrators as central to implementation;
4. ensures that direct implementation support is provided in the form of available quality materials, in-service training, one-to-one technical help, and opportunity for peer interaction;
5. allows for certain redefinition and adaptation of the innovation;
6. communicates with and maintains the support of parents and the school board;
7. sets up an information-gathering system to monitor and correct implementation problems; and
8. has a realistic time perspective.

This is no doubt a tall and impossible order in some situations. But it is precisely what effective districts do.

The above set of factors does not occur by accident. Someone at the district level must know what he or she is doing, and plan for them to happen. The leader's *conceptual understanding of the dynamics of organization, the processes of change, and the people in his or her jurisdiction* represents the most generative (or degenerative, if it is missing) source of ideas about what goes into a plan and what steps have to be taken when things go wrong. Successful administrators operate implicitly or explicitly from a basic set of principles—a theory of change. A theory of change, as stated in Chapter 6, combines knowledge about factors that inhibit or facilitate change and knowledge about how to influence or alter these factors in more favorable directions. No technical checklist, even if religiously followed, can come close to matching the power of knowing the dynamics of social change. Dealing effectively with the implementation of educational change involves more than anything else a way of thinking—a feel for the change process.

No amount of good thinking by itself will address the ubiquitous problem of *faulty communication* (Sarason, 1972, p. 206). Because change is a highly personal experience, and because school districts consist of numerous individuals and groups undergoing different (to them) experiences, no simple communication is going to reassure or clarify the meaning of change for people. A cardinal fact of social change is that people will always misinterpret and misunderstand some aspect of the purpose or practice of something that is new to them. Of course, the administrator who has adopted an innovation without being aware of or interested in implementation needs aggravates the problem; that is, the worst suspicions of subordinates may be correct. But even the administrator who thinks of "everything" will still face the problem of communication. The effective district administrator is one who constantly works at communication, not because he or she thinks that people are resistant or dense, but because he or she realizes that difficulties of communication are natural and inevitable. The administrator's theory of change will have told him or her that frequent, personal interaction is the key to implementation, and his or her interpersonal skills as a communicator (communicating concisely and clearly, and listening perceptively) will determine the effectiveness of confronting this perennial problem.

Two-way communication about specific innovations that are being attempted is a requirement of success. To the extent that the information flow is accurate, the problems of implementation get identified. This means that each individual's personal perceptions and concerns—the core of change—get aired. The district administrator more than any other individual in the district sets the pace and tone concerning the climate of communication. Sarason's (1972) comment about the leader is on target: "There can be no question that the leader plays the most crucial role. He is the most visible and influential model of how one should think and talk, what one should talk about, how one deals with reality, and how one anticipates and deals with problems" (p. 206).

Schlechty (1990) argues that such leadership is essential for improvement:

> Intellectual leadership emerges in school systems when top leaders are viewed as valuing ideas, valuing the reading of books, and valuing the interchange of ideas that lead to creative formulations and innovative solutions. To establish such values, those in authority—in the superintendent's office, the union office, and the principal's office—must model what they value. (p. 101)

The continuation or institutionalization stage does not require extensive discussion, except for three points. First, if implementation has been well established in terms of teacher mastery and commitment, an innovation has more of a basis for continuation (Huberman & Miles, 1984). Second, if the change project depends on external or other special funds (as many do), what the administrator does and does not do to plan for continuation is crucial. Berman and McLaughlin (1978a) found that only a small proportion of projects were effectively institutionalized in the 293 districts they studied. In those projects that did become institutionalized, district officials paid early and continuing attention to how the program could be incorporated into the budget with respect to personnel and other support needs.

Third, in addition to the question of incorporation in the budget, *turnover*, a longer-term phenomenon, takes a heavy toll on change. It is so difficult to get change started and so easy to get it stopped. Turnover can facilitate change, if it is used to bring in administrators and others favorable to and skilled in the change, and many districts do just that. It can also be positive when career-related motives generate energy and enthusiasm for the extra work required at the early stages of a change effort (Huberman & Miles, 1984). But the unseen hand of destruction of enthusiastic or heavily promoted change efforts over time is the changeover of personnel. Change is a continuous process, and district administrators or school administrators who know change will also know that systematic provisions for orientation and follow-up with new members must be part of the plan. When there is turnover of administrators, this need applies in spades. When a school district experiences frequent changes in its chief executive officer, it is virtually impossible to establish an effective change process.

All of this—persistent support of chosen innovations—seems complicated enough. We do know quite a lot about how particular innovations, including major ones, get implemented. The role of district staff in promoting and sustaining district-wide or multiple-school innovations is becoming increasingly clear (Fullan, 1985). But there is a limit to this paradigm. Districts are not in the business of implementing one innovation at a time. Rather they must contend with ever evolving *multiple innovations* simultaneously. While many of the "lessons of implementation" are applicable, new more complex (but more powerful) formulations are emerging in recent research on sustained improvement.

The Problem of Sustained Improvement

To start with a discouraging note, neither centralized nor decentralized approaches work. Centralization—intensification being the extreme example (Chapter 1)—does not work because it attempts to standardize curriculum and performance in a way that is inappropriate and ineffective except for the narrowest goals (Corbett and Wilson, 1990; Wise, 1988). Decentralization—such as school- or site-based management—is problematic either because individual schools lack the capacity to manage change or because assessment of attempted changes cannot be tracked. I will start with the problem of school-based models because it is closer to the required solution. After providing a critique and discussion of the dilemmas of school-based approaches, I will reiterate the basic purpose of improvement and examine selected recent research that shows how successful districts pursue this purpose using what amounts to simultaneous top-down/bottom-up approaches.

Levine and Eubanks' (1989) research contains an excellent analysis of the problems of local school reform that uses school-based models and empowerment assumptions. They identify six major obstacles.

1. inadequate time, training, and technical assistance;
2. difficulties of stimulating consideration and adaptation of inconvenient changes;
3. unresolved issues involving administrative leadership on the one hand and enhanced power among other participants on the other;
4. constraints on teacher participation in decision-making;
5. reluctance of administrators at all levels to give up traditional prerogatives; and
6. restrictions imposed by school board, state, and federal regulations and by contracts and agreements with teacher organizations (see Levine & Eubanks, 1989, pp. 4–8).

In terms of the analyses in this book, school-based councils and the like do not work any better than parent councils do, because they do not get at the problem of meaning for the everyday teacher. Levine and Eubanks turn to the research findings.

> As the empowerment movement has coalesced and spread rapidly during the past few years, researchers have begun to assess outcomes in districts which have been early adopters of one or another approach to site-based management and/or enhanced faculty collaboration in decision making. Given the many difficult problems and obstacles such as those enumerated above, perhaps it is no surprise that research-to-date generally has reported conclusions that appear to be more neutral and disappointing than positive and encouraging. (p. 8)

Citing several studies, Levine and Eubanks report that school-based management projects encountered numerous problems over delegation, training and skill requirements, and taking action (see also Lindquist & Mauriel, 1989). Ogawa and Malen (1989, pp. 2–3), in fact, claimed that "shared governance [in the eight schools they examined] had done more than simply fail to alter traditional decision making relationships; it has actually worked to reaffirm them" by defusing important issues and by developing loyalties without targeted action. When positive results were found they tended to be more superficial. David's (1989a, 1989b) study and synthesis of research on school-based management makes this point rather clearly.

> In districts that practice school-based management essentials, research studies find a range of positive effects, from increased teacher satisfaction and professionalism to new arrangements and practices within schools. . . . There are [only] a few examples of second-order change, schools that have altered the daily schedule to allow more time for teachers to work together or to increase time devoted to reading. . . . This is not surprising, since studies of school improvement find that school councils rarely tackle even instructional issues, let alone second-order change. (quoted in Levine & Eubanks, 1989, p. 9)

Levine and Eubanks warn us of three dangers. The first problem is "the confusion between satisfaction and performance."

> There are few if any indications, that early movement toward site-based management has been associated with substantial change in instructional delivery or student performance. To a significant degree, satisfaction may have been attained precisely through neglecting requirements for inconvenient institutional reform [in favor of more superficial easier to implement changes]. (p. 20)

The second danger is the "substitution of site-based management approaches for central responsibilities involving initiation and support of comprehensive school reform efforts" (p. 20).

> If power and resources can be shifted to the school level, central authorities may also be able to shift most or all of the responsibility for failure to improve student performance to teachers and administrators in the schools. . . . It is but one additional small step to treat site-based management as a substitute for district wide reform initiatives. (p. 21)

And the third is "the confusion between site-based management and effective schools' approaches" (p. 24). In particular, Levine and Eubanks emphasize that improvement must focus on instruction: instructional leadership, organization and implementation of instructional services, teacher development, and expectations and monitoring of student performance, which is not necessarily front and center in school-based management. In other words, restructuring efforts such as site-based management have not yet demonstrated that they focus on, let alone alter, the deeper second-order changes required for reform. The point is not to throw out the baby with the bath water. Some very significant restructuring efforts involving site-based management are going on, and many more are being developed (David, 1989b). The school is still "the unit of change," but that concept remains one of the most misunderstood in the field of school improvement. Sirotnik (1987) provides a very helpful clarification in his claim that the school should be conceptualized as the *center* of change. As he states, "To say that something is at the center implies a good deal around it" (p. 21). In his words,

> We are led to the organization, e.g., the school as the center of change. We are not lead naively to see the school as isolated from its sociopolitical context, able to engage in miraculous self-renewing activities without district, community, state, and federal support. But we are led to where the day-to-day action is, to where with the proper motivation and support, the prevailing conditions and circumstances of schools can be challenged constructively within the context of competing values and human interests. . . . In short, . . . people who live and work in complex organizations like schools need to be thoroughly involved in their own improvement efforts, assuming significant and enduring organizational change is the purpose we have in mind. (Sirotnik, 1987, pp. 25–26)

A more subtle conclusion is that the school will never become the center of change if left to its own devices.

In order to work out of the apparent dilemma of centralization vs. decentralization we need to return to the basic question asked in Chapter 1—what is school reform for? Basically the purpose of reform should be to help schools accomplish their educational goals more efficiently and effectively for all students. In the chapters in Part II, we have begun to see deeply what the basic problem is. In a nutshell, *the core problem is that education as it is now practiced does not engage students, teachers, parents, and administrators.* The next generation of reform, according to Elmore (1988), must face this central problem: "how to change dominant modes of instruction that discourage engagement and how to change a bureaucratic structure that discourages people with a strong professional interest in teaching and learning" (p. 11). Elmore says that there are three themes at stake in this reform effort: "an increasing proportion of hard-to-reach students, increasing attention to problems of engagement in teaching and learning, and increasing attention to problems of attracting and retaining educators with a serious interest in teaching and learning" (p. 11).

Elmore (1988) suggests that reforms, if they are to be successful, will have to be played out in what he calls four "contested terrains."

1. The classroom (Can adults sustain enough authority and interest with students to produce engagement in learning?)
2. The school (Can we create forms of school organization that reward competence in teaching and learning?)

3. Schools with school systems (Can school systems help establish schools that place primacy on engagement in teaching and learning rather than resistance to or compliance with central directives?)
4. School systems and communities (Can clients, constituents, and other policy-makers grant schools the discretion necessary to create forms of organization that foster commitment to learning?)

It seems to me that this leads us inevitably to two paramount conclusions. First, we are talking about changes in the culture of schools, not the implementation of particular reforms. Second, it is no longer a matter of centralization vs. decentralization, since it is clear that all levels are profoundly implicated—the classroom, the school, the school district, and beyond.

How can schools and districts interact, avoiding center dominance on the one hand, or disregard of the center on the other? I cite four among many recent examples to show how this new model of collaboration works, although none of them yet evidences the degree of cultural change envisioned by Elmore (Fullan, Bennett, & Rolheiser-Bennett, 1990; LaRocque & Coleman, 1989a; Louis, 1989; Rosenholtz, 1989).

Louis (1989) analyzed the nature of the relationship between particular schools and their districts. She and her colleagues conducted case studies of five reportedly effective secondary schools and found that two were indeed quite successful, while the other three had mixed or limited success.

Louis then examined the school–district relationships, which involved drawing on other research as well. She found that there were two separate dimensions that affected the quality of the relationship. One she called the degree of "engagement" (frequent interaction and communication, mutual coordination and influence, some shared goals and objectives); the other she classified as the level of "bureaucratization" (the presence of extensive rules and regulations governing the relationship). To oversimplify, in situations of low engagement and high bureaucracy, Louis observes that there is frequent reference to rules but limited enforcement, because the schools and districts operate in isolation from each other. The principal, for example, often operates as a buffer to central rules. In the case of high engagement and high bureaucracy, Louis found conflict, interference, resistance, and ultimately failure. (This scenario, of course, is the intensification theme, which can be successful for narrow goals for short periods of time.)

The third situation—low engagement and low bureaucracy—is one of loose federation, informality, and laissez-faire, in which people essentially did not try to engage in comprehensive change. The fourth scenario—high engagement and low bureaucracy—presented "the only clearly positive district contexts" (p. 161). Louis (1989) summarizes: "Essentially, the picture is one of co-management, with coordination and joint planning enhanced through the development of consensus between staff members at all levels about desired goals for education" (p. 161). It was only the schools with this district profile that experienced successful school improvement projects.

Similar findings, independently and more systematically arrived at, are contained in LaRocque and Coleman's (1989a) analysis of "district ethos" and quality in school districts in British Columbia. The authors compiled performance data by aggregating school results on province-wide achievement tests. They rated the districts according to high, medium, and low performance. They selected 10 districts for more detailed analysis taking into account size and type of school community. LaRocque and Coleman (1989a, p. 169) hypothesized that positive district ethos would be characterized by a high degree of interest and concern relative to six sets of activity and attitude "focuses."

1. taking care of business (a learning focus);
2. monitoring performance (an accountability focus);
3. changing policies/practices (a change focus);
4. consideration and caring for stakeholders (a caring focus);
5. creating shared values (a commitment focus); and
6. creating community support (a community focus).

Three of the ten districts were classified as having a strong district presence in the schools, which is described in the following terms:

> The district administrators provided the principals with a variety of school-specific performance data; they discussed these data with the principals and set expectations for their use; and they monitored through recognized procedures, how and with what success the schools used the performance data. . . .
>
> The district administrators used their time in the schools purposefully to engage the principals in discussion on specific topics: school performance data, improvement plans, and the implementation of these plans. . . .
>
> In spite of the emphasis on school test results, the nature of the discussions was collaborative rather than prescriptive. The district administrators acknowledged good performance. They helped the principals interpret the data and identify strengths and weaknesses, and they offered advice and support when necessary. Ultimately, however, plans for improvement were left up to the principal and staff of each school—this point was stressed by the principals—although their progress in developing and implementing the plans was monitored. The features of collaboration and relative school autonomy probably reinforced the perception of respect for the role of the principal and recognition of the importance of treating each school as a unique entity. (LaRocque & Coleman, 1989a, p. 181)

All three of these districts had a high performance rating on the achievement tests.

At the other end of the continuum, three districts were characterized by an absence of press for accountability: Little or no data were provided to the schools, and no structures or processes were established to monitor or discuss progress. All three of these districts were found to be low on achievement results.

LaRocque and Coleman (1989a, p. 190) concluded that effective districts have an active and evolving accountability ethos that combines interactive monitoring with a respect for school autonomy.

A third example is provided in the Learning Consortium arrangement, which we have established in Ontario (Fullan, Bennett, & Rolheiser-Bennett, 1990). In a partnership of four large school districts and two higher education institutions, for the past two years we have been attempting to bring about and link classroom improvement and school improvement through collaborative university/district and school activities. The focus is on instruction and learning in the classroom and continuous teacher development. We use cooperative learning, classroom management, and other approaches. At the same time, we work on the development of coaching, mentoring, school leadership, and collaborative work cultures. The hallmark of the Learning Consortium is the opening up of relationships across classrooms, schools, and systems by developing and implementing new norms and practices for continuous improvement. The Learning Consortium has been successful in mobilizing large numbers of school and district personnel in voluntary, cooperative action to improve the learning environments of both teachers and students (see also Sirotnik & Goodlad, 1988, for the nature and power of school–university partnerships).

As might be recalled from Chapter 7, Rosenholtz (1989) studied 78 elementary schools in 8 school districts characterizing some schools as "stuck" and others as "moving," with the rest in between. Rosenholtz also found that "districts" could be classified in the same terms. Two districts scored consistently high on teacher commitment, teacher learning opportunities, task autonomy, and school rewards; three scored consistently low, while three were in between (p. 169). For example, the two higher performing districts had a disproportionately high percentage of moving schools (67% and 60%) compared with a low percentage of stuck schools (17% and 0%), while stuck districts showed the reverse pattern (0% to 9% moving schools, and 45% to 63% stuck schools). Rosenholtz notes that stuck districts in her sample were rural and had elected superintendents; moving districts had higher per pupil expenditures, higher educational attainment of teachers, and were smaller in size than the others, although district socioeconomic status did not make a difference.

At the operational level, Rosenholtz discovered three major differences between moving and stuck school districts in relation to

1. school goal-setting and district monitoring (including superintendent learning);
2. principal selection and learning opportunities; and
3. teacher selection and learning opportunities.

We see familiar patterns, but more comprehensively treated. Concerning
goal-setting, Rosenholtz states

> In both moving districts, superintendents involve principals in setting district
> goals or policy, in determining their school's technical needs, and in specific
> problem-solving, forging a shared reality about district and school-level prac-
> tice. More than that, ties between schools and districts indicated strong mu-
> tual influence; it went both ways. Reviewing, revising, and reconstituting
> goals over time required frequent task-focused interaction. . . .
>   . . . Of equal if not greater importance, moving superintendents estab-
> lish through their goals that district policy relates integrally to teachers' prac-
> tice and that there are also corresponding linkages between the behaviors of
> principals and teachers and student learning outcomes. (p. 173)

Goal-setting in stuck districts, by contrast, was vague and unfocused.
Goal-setting orientations for both moving and stuck districts carried over
into performance monitoring. In moving districts, superintendents required principals and teachers to set school learning goals relevant to the
students they served, and monitored and stimulated progress by linking
activities and performance data to improvement criteria, reinforced by
frequent visits to schools by superintendents and other district staff (see
also LaRocque & Coleman, 1989a). Moreover, the two superintendents in
moving districts constantly availed themselves of opportunities to learn
about new ideas and practices from research and programs outside their
own jurisdictions, exemplifying at the system level the norms of collegiality and continuous improvement we discussed in Chapter 7. By contrast, "stuck superintendents, wholly analogous to the isolated teacher,
appear to make no attempt to weave new technical knowledge into the
old" (Rosenholtz, 1989, p. 184).

These features carried over into the second major domain—principal selection and learning opportunities. Principals, as we know, can be
powerful forces for improvement or giant obstacles to reform (see Chapter 8). Moving districts explicitly cultivate and select principals whose
foremost concern is student learning and who are skilled at the instructional leadership necessary for attending to continuous improvement
(Rosenholtz, 1989, p. 185). Both through selection criteria and procedures, and through preservice and on-the-job training, the two moving
districts constantly generated a pool of tested candidates and incumbents.

> The contrast between stuck and moving districts, nowhere more apparent
> than here, underscores how principals become helpful instructional advisors

or maladroit managers of their schools. It is also clear that stuck superintendents attribute poor performance to principals themselves, rather than accepting any responsibility to help them learn and improve. This again may indicate their lack of technical knowledge and subsequent threats to their self-esteem. If districts take no responsibility for the inservice needs of principals, of course, principals become less able colleagues, less effective problem-solvers, more reluctant to refer school problems to the central office for outside assistance, more threatened by their lack of technical knowledge, and, most essential, of substantially less help to teachers. Of equal importance, with little helpful assistance, stuck superintendents symbolically communicate the norm of self-reliance and subsequently professional isolation— that improvement may not be possible, or worthy of their time and effort, or that principals should solve their school problems by themselves—lugubrious lessons principals may unwittingly hand down to poorly performing teachers, and thus teachers to students. (Rosenholtz, 1989, p. 189)

Superintendents in the moving districts made it clear that principals must be continuous learners and through their leadership help create conditions for teachers to be learners.

Finally, teacher selection and learning, as we have seen in Chapter 7, is a critical feature of effective schools. In the moving districts, teacher selection followed from the goals of student learning and continuous improvement, whereas stuck districts had no coherent plan and relied on local availability. Teachers' opportunities to learn once on the job were built into school and system practices in the moving districts.

In Sunnyview and Richland [the two moving districts], superintendents' perceptions that teachers can improve if only provided with the proper resources to do so leads to actions that mobilize those critical district resources. . . . In Hillcrest, Eastside and Jefferson [the stuck districts], superintendents' perceptions that improvement depends entirely on teachers' personal initiative leads them to abandon ship at the first bit of stormy weather. (p. 199)

Stuck districts tended to transfer problematic teachers and principals rather than confront the issue. Moving districts helped teachers improve through specific supportive practices, considering firing or counseling out as a last resort. Paradoxically, stuck districts, because of their internal isolationism, are *less* likely to take action against ineffective teachers (McLaughlin & Pfeiffer, 1988; Rosenholtz, 1989). In short, Rosenholtz says: "Successful superintendents seek out and satisfy teachers' professional needs while stuck superintendents conspicuously ignore them" (p. 204).

Rosenholtz' districts, especially the three rural stuck districts with elected superintendents, are not typical, but the patterns of district effectiveness and ineffectiveness are becoming recognizable. We have seen them in the other studies cited earlier in this section. We see the same general findings in our case studies of four school boards in Ontario (Fullan, Anderson, & Newton, 1986). We see the same trend in David's (1989b) analysis of the "pioneering" restructuring efforts in nine school districts in the United States: new goals, visions, and attitudes; new roles and relationships; new coalitions and accountability. According to David, these major experiments are providing new leadership, new structures, and new support and assistance to target continuous school improvement at the school level (David, 1989b, pp. 42–43). We see these issues in Joyce, Murphy, Showers, and Murphy's (1989) major initiative in one southern school district, and in several other major restructuring efforts currently being attempted (Anderson, 1989; Harvey & Crandall, 1988). We see the same focus in Murphy and Hallinger's (1986) interviews with superintendents from 12 of the most instructionally effective districts in California (measured as school districts whose student achievement scores consistently exceeded the scores of other districts, controlling for type of community). These superintendents actively and systematically worked on the familiar ingredients for success: setting goals and expectations, selecting staff, supervising and supporting professional development, focusing on instruction and curriculum, ensuring consistency, and monitoring instructional progress. They were, in a phrase, preoccupied with instructional issues. We see these same trends in government attempts to restructure entire states and provinces (see Chapter 13). Comprehensive change in education is definitely in the air.

There are two broad conclusions that we can draw from this analysis. First, sustained improvement requires serious restructuring of the school, the district, and their interrelationships. The roles of students, teachers, principals, parents, and district staff are all implicated, as is the structure, governance, and design of work and learning (Elmore, 1989; Harvey & Crandall, 1988; Murphy, in press). Schools and districts cannot now manage innovation, and never will be able to without radically redesigning their approach to learning and sustained improvement. Second, and less obvious but equally important, is that schools cannot redesign themselves. The role of the district is crucial. Individual schools can become highly innovative for short periods of time without the district, but they cannot *stay* innovative without district action to establish the conditions for continuous and long term improvement.

CAUTIONS AND GUIDELINES

The overarching caution and guideline is the recognition of how very fundamental the task of reform is. We are talking about changes in the culture and programmatic regularities of schools, through multilevel reform from the classroom to the state. The agenda is to focus on the right things and to stay on course despite ubiquitous obstacles. At the district level, we have seen in this chapter what many of the right things are: focusing on instruction, teaching, and learning; creating the conditions at the classroom and school level for collaborative teacher and principal professionalism; mobilizing parents and communities; using district resources to hire, promote, and support the right people and to orchestrate the pressure and support necessary for continuous classroom and school improvement.

It is a discouraging agenda. Collaborative work cultures in schools take a long time to develop, yet can disappear overnight when a few key people leave (Little, 1987). Introducing specific innovations and bringing about formal restructuring can give us a false sense of progress because they are on the right track, but only mimic more fundamental change. And the changes we are talking about take up to 10 years in a given jurisdiction—10 years of doing the right things consistently and persistently.

If there is constant, conflictful turnover of chief superintendents, as we have seen in some jurisdictions, the task will be impossible. We are seeing more situations where there is continuity. What it takes is a leading superintendent with a term of five to seven years, followed by another successful superintendent for a further five to seven years, deliberately selected to complement and extend the work of the district (Fullan & Watson, 1991). Under the best of circumstances, then, it is going to take two or three successive superintendencies all working on fundamental matters, and more superintendencies to consolidate and build on achievements.

Chief executive officers, as many have observed, frequently feel just as powerless as the rest of us (Block 1987; Blumberg, 1985). Over the long run, however, they have potentially more power to do good (or bad). The first task for superintendents is to recognize and unleash the power they have to do good. Block (1987) in *The Empowered Manager* states it best.

> At the deepest level, the enemy of high performing systems is the feeling of helplessness that so many of us in organizations seem to experience. . . .
>
> The core of the bureaucratic mind-set is not to take responsibility for what is happening. Other people are the problem. . . . Reawakening the original spirit means we have to confront the issue of our own autonomy. To pursue autonomy in the midst of a dependency-creating culture is an entrepreneurial act. (pp. 1, 6)

Block suggests that maintenance means being preoccupied with playing it safe. He acknowledges that maintenance and caution are often necessary (and the superintendent more than most is frequently in such a situation). However, Block argues that to break the mold we must practice "enlightened self-interest" by engaging in activities that have as their basis: *meaning* (activities that are genuinely needed); *contribution and service* (the decision to do things that seriously contribute to the organization and its purpose); *integrity* (putting into words what we really see is happening, making only those promises we can deliver on, feeling that the authentic act is always the best for business); *positive impact on others' lives* (in the long run it is in our self-interest to treat other people well); and *mastery* (simply learning as much as we can about the activity that we are engaged in).

As I noted in Chapter 6, the goal is "to produce a stream of wise decisions designed to achieve the mission of the organization," accepting that "the final product may not resemble what was initially intended" (Patterson, Purkey, & Parker, 1986, p. 61).

Purkey and Smith (1985) make a number of policy recommendations for districts committed to school reform. They observe that "efforts to change schools have been productive and most enduring when directed toward influencing the entire school culture via a strategy involving collaborative planning, shared decision making, and collegial work in an atmosphere friendly to experimentation and evaluation" (p. 357). The school may be the center of change, but it cannot do it alone. Purkey and Smith advocate that change itself must be conducted with "top-down policy and bottom-up planning and implementation" (p. 364). The district has in its power the potential of offering policy incentives (extra funds, release time, developing pilot schools) that encourage individual schools to participate and/or that respond to school initiatives. Purkey and Smith suggest that balance "between an incentive-based and a mandated school change project seems most workable" (p. 367).

This "balance" represents a major theme of this book. We have said that empowerment is necessary for both upper administration and school members. *Neither centralization nor decentralization really works.* Mandates make people resist change. Leaving it to the school denies the benefits of coordinated support and problem solving. What does work is interactive pressure and support, initiative-taking, and empowerment through coordinated action based on individual realms of activity. Change should be a *negotiated* process. The board and the superintendent would help "create the conditions for the process of change, specify district goals, ensure accountability, and set reasonable timelines" (Purkey & Smith, 1985, p. 376). Individual schools would have "building level responsibility for implementation and staff flexibility to respond to their particular environment, though not at the expense of district goals" (Purkey & Smith, 1985, p. 376; see also Leithwood, 1989). The problem, of course, is that the matter of school/district balance is not solvable, precisely because it represents an inherently complex dilemma between autonomy and accountability, variation and consistency, and the like. Effective superintendents continually negotiate and monitor this relationship with school staff, attempting to stay within an acceptable corridor of mutual influence.

It is important to reiterate that becoming involved in innovations, even major restructuring experiments, is not the answer in and of itself. The wrong reforms, or the right reforms wrongly implemented, can make matters worse. Districts vary quite fundamentally in how they work with the same reforms—some achieving considerable success, others badly losing ground (see Firestone & Bader, 1990). There is tremendous pressure on districts to innovate, and this frequently leads to faddism, superficial change, and misdirected efforts despite the best of intentions. Thus, the problem is not merely to increase the level of innovative activity. Districts are innovating all the time. The trick is to get better at working through and thinking through a process of change that really *works!*

The most important guidelines are grounded in the values and orientations just described (see also Schlechty, 1990, Chapter 9). A highly condensed version of other guidelines that the administrator should consider can be set forth as follows:

1. *Choose a district in which change has a chance of occurring or do not expect much change.* Some communities are dominated by a power structure that is more interested in the status quo; other communities are so fractious that the superintendent is the inevitable victim; others expect administrators to lead change. Although the classification is greatly oversimplified, the main message is sound—the interest in change, or leverage for change, in a district must be minimally present. Without that the chief executive officer is as powerless as anyone else, and in fact will likely become the convenient scapegoat.

Other district administrators (below the level of the chief executive officer) will have to make similar choices, and will also have to determine whether the superintendent with whom they will be or are working is knowledgeable and actively supportive of change—ideally, someone who can teach them something about how to implement change effectively.

2. Once in a district, *develop the management capabilities of administrators—other district administrators and principals—to lead change.* Using a combination of promotion criteria, in-service training emphasizing development and growth, and replacement of administrators through attrition or forced resignation (in extreme cases), the goal is to develop incrementally the district's administrative capability to lead and facilitate improvement. Among other things, the administrator must require and help principals to work with teachers, which means that he or she, as district administrator, must have the ability and willingness to work closely with principals.

3. *Directly and indirectly (e.g., through principals) provide resources, training, and the clear expectation that schools (teacher, principals, etc.) are the main centers of change.* District administrators, at the early stages of their ap-

pointments, will have to convince and prove to teachers and principals that "this time it will be different." That is, they will have to understand the local history of innovation experiences and overcome the barriers by their actions in helping to determine the specific need for change and in supporting improvement efforts at the school level for those initiatives that are undertaken. The district approach must address the practicality concerns of teachers and the role concerns of principals, described in Chapters 7 and 8. Helping to provide more positive experiences with change would be a fundamental accomplishment.

4. *Focus on instruction, teaching, and learning, and changes in the culture of schools.* Both short-term and long-term strategies should be used consistently and persistently to establish norms and the capacity for collaboration and continuous improvement in the learning environments of students and educators.

5. *Recognize that implementing any strategy for improvement is itself a fundamental implementation problem.* The ultimate irony would be for a district administrator to formulate a plan for change and to introduce it into the system in exactly the same self-defeating way as most curricular innovations have been introduced (that is, in a top-down manner, having foreign meaning to participants, and providing little opportunity to develop skills in the change process). Developing new procedures for improvement means working with system members over a period of time in which they increasingly come to understand, modify, become skilled in, and believe in the effectiveness of the approach to change being used.

6. *Monitor the improvement process.* The need for monitoring is never ending. The information-gathering system to assess and address problems of implementation must be institutionalized. The more horizontal and vertical two-way communication that exists, the more knowledge there will be about the status of change. Williams (1980, pp. 90–91) claims that the need is not for formal research methodologies but for "competent, reasonable people" in the system to be concerned about improvement through careful observation, questioning, and discussions. This is none other than the systematic social interaction referred to so frequently as the core ingredient of developing knowledge and meaning about change. More formal information-gathering systems can also be very effective, if they are integrated with procedures for instructional improvement.

7. *Above all, work on becoming an expert in the change process.* Vision-building—working with others "to think through problems and conceive alternative futures" (Schlechty, 1990, p. 98)—is part of it. But so is con-

ceptualizing and acting on a process of change that combines short and long-term strategies designed to create second order changes at the school level, that is, fundamental instructional and structural changes that motivate and engage students and the adults working with them. Becoming an expert in the change process means increasing the number of people in the district—at both central and school levels—who themselves become experts in change. Capacity for improvement must permeate all aspects of the system. If it is to be effective, capacity for change cannot reside only at central leadership level.

There can be no one recipe for change, because unlike ingredients for a cake, people are not standard to begin with, and the damned thing is that they change as you work with them in response to their experiences and their perceptions. The paramount task of the district administrator is not to get this or that innovation put into practice, but to *build the capacity of the district and the schools to handle any and all innovations* (which is not to say to implement them all). The administrator who tries to deal with innovations one at time will soon despair or be victimized. The one who works over a five- or six-year period to develop the district's and schools' core capacity (that is, teachers', principals', other administrators', and the school board's capacity) to process the demands of change, whether they arise internally or externally to the district, *may find change easier as time goes by.* More important, people in the district may find innovation and improvement more engaging and deeply satisfying. If anyone has the opportunity to lead the way, for larger numbers of schools, it is the district administrator.

CHAPTER 11

The Consultant

. . . the omnibus portfolio . . .

Subject consultant, curriculum coordinator, program adviser, resource teacher, organization development specialist, change agent, project director, linkage agent—the educational consultant comes (and goes) in many different shapes and sizes. In Canada, school district consultants primarily work on subject or grade-level curricula arising from provincial and local policies and programs. In the United States, district curriculum staff also exist, but layered in are a host of other consultants and program directors paid for through federal and state special project grants.

In addition to these local or internal district consultants, there are numerous types of external consultants. Some work in provincial/state or federal education departments, others in regional educational laboratories or centers (in the United States), and still others in universities and private consultancy firms. Within those various agencies, some are on permanent staff, while others' positions are due to major special projects that frequently last for only two or three years. In one survey focusing only on "effective schools" programs, Miles and Kaufman (1985) found 2,500 "assisters" involved as facilitators.

As the kinds of changes introduced to schools have increased in complexity over the last decade—from curriculum- and classroom-based innovations to "restructuring" whole systems—the skills required of schools to implement them have also become more complex. The goals of change are becoming more comprehensive and require greater assistance to achieve. More frequently, schools are turning to internal and external "helpers" to fill gaps in expertise and to assist in charting and implementing courses of action. This in itself has lent some focus to the role of the consultant, though there is still much to learn. The interaction of consultant roles and skills with a diversity of individual contexts makes it difficult to generalize. As needs for help accelerate, so do needs for the preparation of helpers and efficient utilization of help.

Because my primary interest at this point is on what happens at the local level, I will start with school district consultants. In the subsequent section the discussion will expand to include external consultants. In the last section of the chapter, some conclusions will be drawn about the role of internal and external consultants.

INTERNAL AND DISTRICT CONSULTANTS

In keeping with the theme of this book, we should like to know how effective district consultants are in introducing and responding to new ideas and, more important, in following through with new programs to support implementation and continuation. The truth of the matter is that very little is known specifically about the role of district support staff. School districts, even those of the same size and with similar total budgets, are organized very differently in terms of the extent, nature, and duties of support staff. Districts focus on different parts of the change process: Some are preoccupied with adopting externally produced programs, while others work more at facilitating exchanges or development internal to the district. In addition to (or because of) this confusing variety, there has not been much thorough research on the topic, although Cox (1983a, 1983b); Miles, Saxl, and Lieberman (1988); and Ross and Reagan (1990) have made significant recent contributions to research on the role. As so many of the settings in which consultants work are unique, commonalities are hard to arrive at. What we can do is to examine some findings and attempt to understand them in terms of what we know about the theory and practice of change described in previous chapters. Out of this we begin to obtain a clearer picture of the roles and skills required of change facilitators and how these relate to the processes and meaning of change. (See also Chapter 15 on professional development.)

In examining recent research on the role of local facilitators, we focus here on district and school staff in consultative or resource support roles. It will be necessary to refer to their relationship to line administrators, but the role of the latter group is taken up in Chapters 8 and 10.

Hall, Putnam, and Hord (1985) provide one of the few empirical studies that reveal the problems in sorting out the roles of local change facilitators. They conducted an analysis of the roles of district office staff in 11 school districts. Their observations indicate the scope of the problem:

- A wide range of titles is used for district office positions.
- Personnel in the district office often seem to have relatively little clarity about the scope and primary purposes of their roles.
- There is tremendous variation in how much time district-office personnel spend in schools.
- There is a dramatic difference in the amount of real authority and

power individual district personnel have; this difference is related to whether they are in line or staff positions.

- There is little congruence between what district-office personnel in staff positions say they do and what others perceive they do.
- Teachers view district-office people in line positions as remote from the classroom.
- Teachers have very little understanding of what persons in the district office really do.
- District-office personnel provide the impetus for, as well as being the source of, many innovations that are implemented in schools.
- District-office personnel are consistently in a crossfire of demands and expectations.
- District-office personnel do not have specialized training for their positions.
- Describing what district-office personnel do is difficult.

While the role and organization of district personnel are unclear, we have a better picture of the strategies and skills used by effective local facilitators. The DESSI study, especially the 12 case studies, describes the important role of ongoing internal district assistance by local facilitators (Huberman & Miles, 1984). In the short run, assistance contributed to the development of support, technical help, and clarity about the innovations being implemented. In the longer run, assistance contributed to greater mastery, confidence, and ownership.

Cox (1983a, 1983b) analyzed the data from the larger DESSI sample of 146 schools involved in 61 innovative practices. In this study 80 facilitators external to the district (see next section) and 78 local (within-district) facilitators were interviewed. A large number of specific facilitator activities were identified, which were factor analyzed to produce nine clusters of activities. Internal facilitators did the following:

- become familiar with the needs of students in individual schools in their district;
- located and helped select the new practice;
- knew the content of the new practice, its purpose, and the benefits that were to result from its use;
- helped arrange and conduct training in the new practice, working with external assisters;
- arranged funding and other support from the district or other sources;
- obtained endorsements for the new practice from the superintendent, school board, principal, and teachers;
- worked with teachers using the practice in the classroom, working out "bugs" and overcoming obstacles;
- assisted in evaluation; and

• helped plan how to continue and institutionalize the new practice (Cox, 1983a, p.12).

The local facilitators spent more time on nearly every aspect of the effort than did external facilitators (although the latter role, as we shall see, was important).

It is important to emphasize that the DESSI researchers were examining, by design, local facilitators who were nominated as being active and effective in working with schools. Thus, we get a clear picture of the multiple and ongoing ways in which facilitators provide effective assistance, that is, we are seeing what it looks like when it works. By contrast, in the earlier Rand Change Agent study, which investigated the adoption of a wide range of innovations, Berman & McLaughlin (1977) found that the sheer *amount* of assistance by district resource staff was not related to achievement of project goals but that specific kinds of assistance were helpful. When district resource staff helped with demonstrating or making suggestions for classroom implementation they were very effective. When they offered only general or abstract advice they were not; in fact, "numerous visits to the classroom by district or project staff do more harm than good when teachers do not feel they are being helped" (Berman & McLaughlin, 1977, p. 109).

Ross and Reagan (1990) studied 12 district curriculum consultants in two school boards in Ontario, selecting them into two groups—experienced effective consultants and inexperienced consultants. They wanted to find out if effective or "expert" consultants carried out their work differently from "novice" consultants across various phases of the change process, which they identified as initiation, planning, delivery, and follow-up. They found that expert consultants derived their initiative from a system plan, worked with teams and organizations as compared with working alone or only with individual teachers, conducted wider searches for information, planned workshops in a series vs. one-shot events, used a variety of strategies tailored to the range of individuals and situations, focused on practice and feedback, and gathered ongoing data that were used to make adjustments; novices, on the other hand, gathered little implementation data and made no or minimal adjustments. In short, expert consultants were more likely than novices to conceptualize their roles as working with systems as well as with individuals, and were more focused and persistent in pursuing and documenting changes in practice. Ross and Reagan (1990) conclude:

> The experienced consultants in our sample knew more about the degree of effort required to bring about change and the specific strategies for doing so. In contrast to their inexperienced peers, the experienced consultants arranged for a series of interactions with individuals and groups. . . . System

plans, networking with teams of consultants, and coordinating support between line and staff positions were key elements in the strategic planning of experienced consultants. (p. 176)

In case studies of curriculum procedures in four Ontario school boards, we also found that district curriculum consultants were moving away from focusing mainly on curriculum development toward setting up field-based processes to support implementation (Fullan, Anderson, & Newton, 1986). Consultants reported that they needed skills in both the content and the process of change; 88 percent indicated that "on-the-job experience" was their main source of learning to be a consultant, while only 13 percent indicated that they had received "board-sponsored training" (p. 332). We, as others, found that district consultants learn their skills incidentally through trial and error.

Hall and Hord (1984), in a study of principals, discovered the critical role of several change facilitators (CF's) who were district-level consultants, resource teachers, and sometimes assistant principals. We know that the role of the principal is crucial, but in addition Hall and Hord found that these second change facilitators actually played a more intensive role.

A larger percentage of principal interventions are of the simple type— briefer and less involved substantively. By contrast, the second CFs' interventions are more likely to be of the complex, chain, or repeated type, that is, interventions involving more than a single action. Consequently, the second CFs' interventions with teachers are longer and contain multiactions. An additional tendency is for the second CF interventions to be more frequently of an interactive nature, unlike the principal who is more often direct and one way. This finding relates to the one above; that is, the principal intervenes quickly, simply, and in a direct manner; the second CF intervenes more interactively with more complex and involved interventions. (p. 280)

Another advance has been made in zeroing in on the skills of effective change facilitators. Miles, Saxl, and Lieberman (1988) conducted an intensive interview and observation study of 17 "assisters" in New York City. All 17 were working as within-district facilitators on particular programs helping individual schools. Miles and associates identified 18 key clusters of skills used by a majority of the assisters (e.g., initiative-taking, conflict mediation, diagnosing problems, training, educational content, etc.). They describe and emphasize the complexity of the change agent's role not only in terms of the 18 skills but also by noting that such skill clusters contain a number of subskills. Miles and associates observe, as others have done before, that district consultants frequently receive little training in these key skill areas prior to being appointed, and little or no on-the-job training, a point to which we will return in the final section of this chapter.

Miles and associates also make the important observation that change facilitators address multiple outcomes and that some are more difficult to achieve than others. They ordered their outcome data from easiest to hardest to achieve starting with short-term or single-event success, through the use of specific products and program implementation, to impact on student achievement and improved capacity of teachers and the organization (p. 171). They hypothesize that outstanding facilitators work on multiple outcomes simultaneously and are more likely to address more fundamental and harder to achieve outcomes.

Local facilitators also frequently face a dilemma between district-sponsored activities and school- and teacher-based needs. In a comprehensive study of staff development in 30 school districts in California, Little (1989) found that staff development was highly centralized. Little found that one-half of the districts' expenditures for staff development went to the salaries of staff development leaders. Additionally, central-office specialists accounted for the design and delivery of over 90 percent of all activities, and relatively few resources were devoted to teacher time and follow-through. On the positive side, Little found fewer instances of one-shot workshops than anticipated; 76 percent of the activities were 12 or more hours in duration, although Little also noted that there were few examples of follow-up support into implementation.

Little characterized the local orientation as one of "service deliverer" with an emphasis on packaged programs, uniformity, and standardization of content. Only a minority of districts focused staff development activities on a few priorities and attempted to interrelate what they did. District-wide and school-based priorities are not necessarily incompatible, as we have seen in Chapter 10, but it requires great sophistication to negotiate and coordinate them. District facilitators in staff positions have little leverage and training to influence the complexity of district-school relationships.

A number of conclusions can be derived from this research on the role of local facilitators, given the perspective of the practical theory of change being developed in this book. First, if local facilitators work just on a one-to-one basis, they will have limited impact because they will reach only a minuscule percentage of teachers. Second, if they are in a district that does not have a coordinated plan for managing change, it will be extremely difficult for them to set up activities involving the continuous assistance and follow-up so necessary to support change in practice. Put positively, the more that conditions conducive to improvement exist at the school and district level, as described in previous chapters, the more impact that effective consultants can have. Third, local facilitators have to access and balance expertise in both the content of change and the process of change. Fourth, and central to the meaning of educational change, local facilitators must take into account each school and classroom context with which they wish to work. Finally, local facilitators must develop ongoing complementary working relationships with other change leaders—principals, vice-principals, department heads, resource and other lead teachers, central office administrators, and other district consultants. Depending on how these relationships develop they may represent a constant source of aggravation, or a valuable set of resources and alliances. One such alliance is the external consultant.

EXTERNAL CONSULTANTS

In Canada the structure of external assistance is fairly simple. There are provincial ministry of education personnel (sometimes including those in regional offices) whose main job is to disseminate new policies and programs, and monitor and get feedback on the quality and impact of programs. In addition to these "official agents," the other main external consultants come from professional development activities of university faculties of education and teacher unions or associations. There is little national presence in the forms of external change facilitators focusing on education.

There are few studies in Canada that examine closely the impact of these external forces on educational change. The general-survey type studies have placed these external agencies near the bottom of any list of helpful or influential resources. For example, Aoki and associates (1977) surveyed 1,488 teachers in British Columbia regarding their teaching of social studies. Teachers placed teacher federation professional development staff, university faculty of education personnel, and ministry of education consultants at the very bottom of a list of 13 support services (school librarians, fellow teachers, and district resource centers were at the top). The researchers state: "Although the services of Faculty of Education personnel and Ministry of Education consultants are unavailable to 68 to 80 percent of teachers, respectively, assistance from these two groups is rated as 'inadequate' by teachers for whom these services *are* available" (Aoki et al., 1977, p. 41, their emphasis).

The situation in the United States is considerably more complicated. There have been numerous federally sponsored programs involving "linkage agents": the Pilot State Dissemination Program, the National Diffusion Network, the R&D Utilization Project, the State Capacity Building Project, the R&D Exchange, the Documentation and Technical Assistance Project, and Technical Assistance Groups, as well as several large-scale research studies on these and other programs. There are also state departments of education, regional educational laboratories or R&D centers, and intermediate agencies in which several school districts band together to create a regional unit that provides certain types of resource services.

In evaluating the R&D Utilization Project, for example, Louis and Rosenblum (1981) found that external "linkers" associated with the projects were seen by schools as valuable in identifying needs, selecting solutions, and facilitating the implementation of validated R&D projects. Louis and Rosenblum report

> The *amount of training* received by the site staff prior to implementation has a strong positive effect, and this impact is augmented by having *training provided by a variety of types of people.*
>
> The *time that the linking agent* spends with local site committees or "problem solving teams" is predictive of several dependent measures. Our site visits revealed that much of the importance of the agents can be attributed to the role that they played on-site in both stimulating committee members to stay active and to reach decision points, and also of providing logistical support to ensure that the meetings were scheduled regularly, that suggestions for consultants were obtained etc. Thus, the actual presence of the agent on-site was important. (p. 7, their emphasis)

The DESSI large-scale study found that external facilitators were especially helpful in making school people aware of new practices, helping them choose among a range of alternatives that matched local needs, working with local administrators to arrange for and conduct training, ensuring that resources and facilities were available, and helping to plan implementation and continuation support (Cox, 1983a, 1983b). Cox also reports that *local* facilitators spent more time on teacher support and implementation activities when external facilitators were involved than when they worked without outside help. And, in sites with both external and internal facilitators present the impact on change in teacher practice was greatest.

The DESSI findings clarify the earlier Rand Change Agent analysis of the role of external consultants. Berman and McLaughlin (1977) concluded that the use of external consultants was not related to achievement of project goals, and that by and large external consultants were superficially or poorly used. As Datta (1981) observes about the Change Agent study, one-shot or general assistance is a far cry from "extensive technical assistance from a recognized authority in the subject area who had experience in the program development, implementation and dissemination" (p. 109). The DESSI study found that external facilitators working collaboratively with internal facilitators can achieve a great deal. Corbett, Dawson, and Firestone (1984) in their study of external field agents emphasize that *the* major requirement for external assisters is to figure out how to work with local context and school conditions, in relation to four categories of problems.

1. the availability of resources to support project activities, primarily staff time, staff knowledge of the program's content area, and clerical resources;
2. the extent of tension among staff factions;
3. the amount of staff turnover and disruptions to the schools' daily routines; and
4. staff expectations about the usefulness of external assistance, based largely on their experiences in previous projects. (p. 32)

Thus, the issue is how external and internal factors interact. The Renfrew Quality Education Project in Ontario provides a clear example of how this works (Sharon, 1988). The project was developed cooperatively between TVOntario and the Renfrew school district. The purpose was to train teachers (N–8) in using television as an educational tool to support the child-centered teaching strategies of the district. The external facilitator from TVOntario worked with the superintendent of curriculum to design a training series explicitly using the ideas from research on implementation—having a proven "product" in the form of television programs geared to the curriculum, using an incremental process over two or three years, obtaining resources and support from the superintendent and principals, providing opportunities to try ideas and get feedback, establishing ongoing collegial interaction among teachers, monitoring progress through personal performance contracts between the external assister and teachers, and serving as trainers for other teachers. Despite the fact that half of the eight teachers were skeptical at the outset, the project was a success in terms of increasing teachers' skills and commitment to use television as an educational tool, and in its impact on students and their learning (Sharon, 1988). Six of the eight teachers proceeded to work with other teachers as lead teachers, although, predictably, new concerns arose at this stage as they faced the prospect of being change facilitators themselves.

IMPLICATIONS

In drawing together the main implications about the role of consultants, it is useful to consider two issues: what resources are available to help clarify and develop the skills of consultants, and what advice can be offered about the selection and use of consultants.

Skills of Consultants

One of the most valuable and pertinent resources now available concerns the materials developed from the Miles and associates (1988)

Change Agent study in New York City. Saxl, Miles, and Lieberman (1990) created training modules based on the skills and aspects of effective assistance that they researched. Modules have been developed to address six skill clusters: (1) trust/rapport building, (2) organizational diagnosis, (3) dealing with the process, (4) resource utilization, (5) managing the work, and (6) building skill and confidence in people to continue. All modules are structured to include a statement of objectives, definition of the skill cluster, examples of the skills, conceptual materials, a range of activities to assess and practice the skills (assessment instruments, simulations, case studies, etc.), evaluation and feedback, and a list of references.

There are also some excellent resources from the larger organizational literature. Lippitt and Lippitt (1986) outline six major strategies for the change facilitator: (1) involving the work force, (2) dealing with ambivalence, (3) assembling task forces, (4) establishing steps toward progress, (5) supporting quality action, and (6) maintaining change momentum and achieving changeability. Similarly, Block (1981) has a range of advice for establishing relationships and contracts, handling resistance, diagnoses, action, and follow-through.

The Use of Consultants

When all is said and done it is the selection and use of internal and external consultants that counts. To start with the change process, let us recall that we are interested in the entire process defined as encompassing initiation, implementation, and continuation. Thus, the consultant, whether internal or external, who gets a new program "adopted" may do more harm than good if little effective implementation follows. Put differently, in deciding on or in assessing the role of consultants, we should have in mind not only whether they obtain or provide good information on given occasions (e.g., a workshop), but also whether they or someone else follows through to provide support for the use of that information. Effective implementation involves the development of individual and organizational meaning vis-à-vis a particular change. Consultants, if they are to be effective, must facilitate the development of that meaning as they interact with school and district personnel.

It is also clear that as systems have become more complex, and as the change agenda has become more fundamental (that is, addressing more basic, difficult to achieve improvement goals), the role of change facilitator has become as crucial as it is demanding. Yet external consultants appear to be unused or misused, and internal consultants often have limited clout. Relative to the former, Lyon, Doscher, McGrahanan, and Williams (1978) found that 50 percent of the 750 school districts in their survey did not spend *any* money on external consultants. Miles (1987), in studying the planning and implementation of new schools, identifies the dilemma of "expertise-seeking vs. self-reliance" (p. 15). He found that school districts did not seek much external knowledge. Even when confronted with the opportunity to take advantage of matching funds from the project to bring in external consultant help, districts refused on the grounds that "district resource staff would provide all the help that was needed" (p. 15). Yet, in analyzing the planning and implementation process, Miles found that internal help was not used or was not adequate to the tasks.

In order to make some sense of all this, let us consider two perspectives—that of the district looking out (including assessing its own capacity) and that of the external consultant looking in. The district faces a dilemma, as Miles has identified. Some external consultants are not good; others offer packaged "solutions," which even when appropriate do not go very far; and still others are inspiring, but nothing comes of the ideas once they leave. But not to seek any outside help is to be more self-sufficient than the demands of educational change would allow. The primary task of the school district should be to develop its own internal capacity to assist and manage both the content and the process of change, relying selectively on external assistance to train insiders and to provide specific program expertise in combination with internal follow-through. We have seen rather clearly that the internal consultant, to be effective, must become a master of the change process, setting up a system of initiation and follow-through in working with teachers, administrators, and external resource people.

Miles and associates (1988, p. 188) recommend that districts can increase the effectiveness of internal facilitators by concentrating on selection criteria, and pre- and post-job skill and experience training. They suggest that selection criteria should include: interpersonal ease, previous educational background (broad-based), educational content expertise, previous experience in training or teaching adults, a personal style that emphasizes both initiative-taking and energy, and prior administrative or organizational experience. Regardless of selection, we also know that district consultants rarely receive preparation and in-service professional development for their roles as change agents.

Of course, it may not be possible for the individual consultant to have a great influence on the district's approach to educational change. As I stated in Chapter 10, the district administration can go a long way in making it more likely or less likely that district consultants will operate as effective change agents; but even with this constraint, the individual consultant has some leeway in how he or she works with teachers and principals.

The perspective of the external looking in is the other side of the same coin. As we have seen, most research shows that external consultants are effective only when there is an internal consultant or team that supports their activities. External change agents who are interested in facilitating real educational change, therefore, should establish some ongoing relationship with internal district administrators, consultants, and teachers who will act collectively to follow through on the change. External agents, like other change facilitators, need both technical and change process expertise.

In some cases (e.g., in provincial/state or federal agencies), external agents have mandates to ensure the implementation of "official policy." What does an external agent do when a district shows no interest in policies or programs that are required to be implemented? I take up the question of compliance with government policies in Chapter 13. At this point, it is sufficient to say that there may be cases in which districts can be forced to comply with certain categorical requirements, but that effective implementation of most programs needs the kind of external-internal relationships referred to above (see Elmore, 1980). To put it more positively, external agents probably have more willing school districts with which to work than they can currently handle.

Indeed, the dilemma faced by both internal and external consultants is one of scope vs. intensity. Although effective change requires intensive, ongoing contact, the number of clients is far beyond the available time and energy of consultants. Like most dilemmas, it is not solvable; but by employing principles of social change, including the setting up of peer support systems, consultants (whether internal or external) can reach and respond to more people more effectively than they currently do.

As norms of collaboration and continuous improvement become embedded in more schools, seeking assistance to solve complex problems is perceived as a source of strength and wisdom rather than as a sign of weakness. Part and parcel of the same development is the presence of more and more effective facilitators among all groups—administrators, teachers, and consultants themselves. District curriculum consultants, staff developers, and other local facilitators have an opportunity to be more influential than ever before. They have an opportunity not only to assist in the implementation of specific programs, but more important to help establish the district- and school-level conditions necessary for continuous improvements (see Fullan, 1990).

CHAPTER 12

The Parent and the Community

Whose school is it, anyway?
—Gold and Miles (1981)

If teachers and administrators who spend 40 to 60 hours a week immersed in the educational world have trouble comprehending the meaning of educational change, imagine what it is like for the parent. Highly educated parents are bewildered; what of the less educated ones who have always felt uncomfortable in dealing with the school?

The question of parent and community involvement in schools has been the subject of hundreds of books and articles over the past 30 years. At first glance this literature appears to be a mass of contradictions, confusion, and hopelessness for understanding—let alone coping with—the relationship between communities and schools. Yet, emerging from this research is a message that is remarkable in its consistency: *The closer the parent is to the education of the child, the greater the impact on child development and educational achievement.* Of course, it is not quite that simple, because such a statement encompasses a multitude of variables that make it more or less probable that closeness will occur. And certainly we can imagine situations in which closeness per se could be harmful to the growth of the child. Moreover, decisions about the precise nature of parent involvement must take into account cultural, ethnic, and class differences as well as variations related to the age and gender of students. Most of the research has been on elementary schools, although many of the principles I will identify are also applicable at the secondary school level.

In determining under what conditions parent and community involvement is most beneficial, we have to understand the different forms of parent participation and their consequences for the student and other school personnel. Stated another way, why do certain forms of involvement produce positive results while others seem wasteful or counterproductive?

I start with the role of parents and the local classroom and school because this is where the most powerful instrument for improvement resides. Second, I consider the role of school boards and communities as they influence the initiation or rejection of new policies and reforms. In the final section, as with preceding chapters, I formulate some general guidelines as to how parents and school people might better cope with educational change together.

PARENT INVOLVEMENT IN SCHOOLS

Studies conducted in the United States, the United Kingdom, and Canada over the last decade increasingly point to the necessity of parent and community involvement for classroom and school improvement (e.g., Dauber & Epstein, 1989; Epstein, 1988; Epstein & Dauber, 1988; Fantini, 1980; Mortimore et al., 1988; Rosenholtz, 1989; Wilson & Corcoran, 1988; Ziegler, 1987). The evidence that these and other authors present is as convincing and as impressive as any in the field of educational change.

One of the reasons that the role of parents is so confusing is that what is meant by involvement is often not specifically defined, nor is it linked to particular outcomes. As with other research on school improvement, research on parents and schools has become increasingly focused. There is no question that family background and home situation make a difference. Students from more privileged families (in terms of home conditions that support learning) do better at school. The educational change question is whether certain parent-related classroom and school practices make additional substantial differences in the performance of students, especially in helping at risk children.

Epstein (1986, 1988), who has conducted systematic research throughout the past decade on parent and school interaction, leaves no doubt in answering the question just posed.

> There is consistent evidence that parents' encouragement, activities, interest at home and their participation at school affect their children's achievement, even after the students' ability and family socioeconomic status is taken into account. Students gain in personal and academic development if their families emphasize schooling, let their children know they do, and do so continually over the years. (Epstein, 1988, Ch. 1)

The main forms of parent involvement include

1. parent involvement at school (e.g., volunteers, assistants);
2. parent involvement in learning activities at home (e.g., assisting children at home, home tutors);
3. home/community–school relations (e.g., communication);
4. governance (e.g., advisory councils) (Epstein & Dauber, 1988).[1]

The first two forms of involvement have a more direct impact on *instruction* than do the other forms, and as such have a much greater influence on student learning. For this reason I will divide the discussion into instructional and noninstructional forms of parent involvement. In general, instructionally related forms of parent involvement have occurred more at the elementary and middle grades compared with the secondary grades, while noninstructional forms occur across all grade levels. Later in the chapter, I will compare elementary and secondary schools in relation to the question of parent and community involvement.

Instructionally Related Involvement

Clark, Lotto, and MacCarthy (1980) carried out a literature search to identify studies that presented evidence on "exceptional performance in urban elementary schools." Their purpose was to discover the main school-related factors that seemed to account for educational success. After a thorough search, 40 reports were retained for analysis. Of the 40 studies, 13 involved the relationship between parent involvement and achievement, and 11 of the 13 reported a positive relationship. Clark and associates (1980, pp. 468–69) include excerpts from some of the studies.

> Among the characteristics common to the more successful programs in the basic skills is the active involvement of parents in instruction.
> Successful schools were more likely to have parents in the classroom as aides, visitors, and as volunteers . . . involvement in the *classroom* rather than in the school in general, is related to academic success . . . that *parent* involvement specifically, and not the use of instructional aides in general, is associated with school success.

Similarly, Fantini (1980) cites several other studies that draw the same conclusions. Among many examples,

> Masoner reports that educators in St. Paul, Minnesota have developed an ongoing home-based program involving parents as tutors for their own children. Mothers, fathers and grandparents of over 50% of the students in participating schools have been trained to assist their youngsters in mathematics as a supplement to the normal school curriculum. As a result, student achievement has jumped significantly. (p. 14)

Berlin and Berlin found that Head Start remedial programs showed no lasting effect "except for children whose mothers became directly involved in the classroom process" (Fantini, 1980, p. 14). Armour and associates (1976) investigated the impact of a reading program on the reading gains of students in 10 minority (black and Mexican-American) Los Angeles schools; they found that "greater number of parent visits to the classroom . . . were associated with higher levels of reading progress" (p. 25). They also found that in the black communities, overall levels of in-

Table 12.1.   Patterns in Four Federal Parent Involvement Programs

	Title I	ESAA	Title VII	Follow Through	Total
Sites with parents as paid aides	12	5	3	14	34
Sites with parents as home tutors	2	0	3	12	17
No. of sites	16	12	13	16	57

Source: The four site reports respectively: Melaragno et al. (1981); Robbins and Dingler (1981); Cadena-Munoz and Keesling (1981); Smith and Nerenberg (1981).

volvement by parents in the school (e.g., being in the school in space provided for parents) were related to reading gains (but no such relationship was found in the Mexican-American communities).

Barth (1979) carried out a review of programs using "home-based reinforcement of school behavior." In a review of 24 studies using the approach (i.e., parents and teachers together targeting specific academic skills and scheduling specific reinforcement practices for the home and the classroom), Barth found significant improvement on even the most difficult learning problems.

Most compensatory programs in the United States mandate parent participation in decisions, although very few require parent involvement in instruction. The System Development Corporation (SDC) conducted a major evaluation of parent involvement programs for the Office of Program Evaluation of the U.S. Education Department (see Keesling, 1980; Melaragno, Lyons, & Sparks, 1981). Four major federal programs were evaluated: Title I, Title VII bilingual, Follow Through, and the Emergency School Aid Act (ESAA). The study consisted of two parts: one a survey of 369 districts and 869 schools participating in the four programs; the other a detailed on-site investigation of 57 projects (selected approximately equally from the four programs). Five forms of parent participation were investigated: governance, instruction, parent education, school support, and home–school relations. In this section I take up the question of parent participation in instructional activities—as paid aides and as home tutors. Table 12.1 shows the patterns found by the researchers across the four programs.

Most Title I and Follow Through sites had parent aides (while most of the other two did not). The majority of Follow Through sites had formal parent home tutoring activities, compared with only a total of 5 of the 41 sites in the other three programs. Keesling (1980) suggests that the reason for such high involvement in Follow Through is related to two main factors: federal regulations that require hiring of parents where possible and that tie refunding to proof of implementation; and the more comprehensive philosophy of parent participation in Follow Through (see also Rhine, 1981; Hodges and associates, 1980). In those cases where there was parent involvement, positive outcomes were found regarding student learning, student attitudes, and parent attitudes. Smith & Nerenberg also note that where home tutoring programs were used, they involved many more parents in an active, ongoing way than did any other form of parent activity in their study. The successful "parent as tutor" programs had four common features: "They were centrally coordinated by project staff; they included procedures for developing instructional plans for children; they provided individualized training to parents in those plans; and they included mechanisms for monitoring parents' and children's progress in the home instruction" (Smith & Nerenberg, 1981, pp. 9–11). It is no accident that these factors correspond to the principles of effective implementation described in Chapter 5.

The use of parents as paid aides was also related to positive outcomes. Parents who served as aides report many positive personal benefits (as other studies have found). Melaragno and associates (on Title I) emphasize: "Undoubtedly the most striking outcome of an institutional nature was that students developed better attitudes toward their work when their parents were involved with the school's instructional program" (p. 7).

This carry-over effect on students occurred as a result of parents' familiarity with the school and the instructional program, and was not confined to the situation where parents were working in their own children's classroom. In the site studies, the sDc researchers also found some negative outcomes of a logistical nature: teachers' needing extra time to coordinate the work of aides; doubts in some cases about the skill and commitment of parent aides; and some parents' reporting that some teachers were intimidating. These negative cases, according to the researchers, were "exceedingly rare." In three of the four programs, the researchers concluded unequivocally that the programs affected the quality of education positively in the several sites in which parents were active. The ESAA program was the exception; the researchers felt that they could not make such an overall statement. The size of the financial grant was unrelated to the proportion of parents involved in any of the four programs.

Ziegler (1987) conducted a review of research on the effects of parent involvement, drawing on both Canadian and U.S. studies. Her conclusions confirm the central finding of this section that parent involvement in instructionally related activities at home and/or at school benefits children.

The real issue, however, is the fact that not all parents show an interest in their children's school work, and not all teachers and schools seek active parent involvement. In Mortimore and colleagues' (1988) big study of school effectiveness, parental involvement practices represented one of 12 key factors that differentiated effective from less effective schools.

> Our findings show parent involvement in the life of the school to be a positive influence upon pupils' progress and development. This included help in classrooms and on educational visits, and attendance at meetings to discuss children's progress. The headteacher's accessibility to parents was also important; schools operating an informal, open-door policy being more effective. Parent involvement in pupils' educational development within the home was also clearly beneficial. Parents who read to their children, heard them read, and provided them with access to books at home, had a positive effect upon their children's learning. (p. 255)

Rosenholtz' (1989) study, with which we are familiar, found important differences in how teachers in "moving" vs. "stuck" schools related to parents. Teachers from stuck schools "held no goals for parent participation" (p. 152), while teachers from moving schools "focussed their efforts on involving parents with academic content, thereby bridging the learning chasm between home and school" (p. 152). Teachers in stuck schools were far more likely to assume that nothing could be done with parents, while teachers in moving schools saw parents as part of the solution.

Only a minority of teachers attempt to involve parents systematically. Becker (1981) surveyed 3,700 elementary school teachers and 600 principals. Becker asked about the use of 14 specific techniques of involving parents and found that despite a general endorsement by teachers of parent involvement at home, "very few appear to devote any systematic effort to making sure that parental involvement at home accomplishes particular learning goals in a particular way" (p. 22). Only 9 percent of the sample "required" parental cooperation; the rest made various "suggestions." Those teachers who were more active users of parent-involvement-at-home techniques were also more likely to involve parents in the classroom as volunteers, aides, or observers. Apparently the other teachers, despite a general endorsement of parent involvement, did not know how to go about it, perceived parents as not interested in becoming involved, or did not take the time to develop a program of participation. Or perhaps many teachers felt that parents could not make a worthwhile contribution to their child's education.

Some teachers "believe that they can be effective only if they obtain parental assistance on learning activities at home" (Epstein, 1986, p. 277); other teachers believe that their professional responsibilities are in jeopardy if parents are involved. Epstein (1986) conducted a statewide survey in Maryland involving 82 grades 3 and 5 classrooms and 1,269 parents. The sample was purposely selected to include "36 'case' teachers who were identified in an earlier survey as strong supporters and users of parent involvement in learning activities at home, and 46 'control' teachers who, by their own report, did not emphasize parent involvement" (p. 278). Parent involvement was measured in terms of the frequency of participation by parents in 12 types of learning activities that teachers ask parents to participate in at home or in the school (e.g., read to child, give spelling or math drills, visit classroom, etc.).

In the statewide survey Epstein found that 58 percent of the parents reported rarely or never having received requests from the teacher to become involved in learning activities at home, while over 80 percent said they could spend more time helping children at home if they were shown how to do specific learning activities (Epstein, 1986, p. 280).

There were significant differences between the teacher-leaders in parent involvement and the comparison teachers, even though the two groups were matched on characteristics and type of community. For example, teacher-leaders involved parents from differing educational backgrounds compared with the control groups, which reported that parents with little education "could not or would not help at home." Parents of children in the classes of teacher-leaders reported significantly more frequent use of 9 of the 12 parent involvement practices. The effect on parents was positive and multifaceted. Parents increased their understanding about school most when the teacher frequently used parent involvement practices. Epstein (1986) states

> What is important in our findings is that teachers' frequent use of parent involvement practices improved parents' knowledge about their child's instructional program, after the grade level, racial composition, and parent education composition of the classroom were taken into account. (pp. 288–89)

Epstein concludes

> Parents were aware of and responded positively to teachers' efforts to involve them in learning activities at home. Parents with children in the classrooms of teachers who built parent involvement into their regular teaching practice were more aware of teachers' efforts, received more ideas from teachers, knew more about their child's instructional program, and rated the teachers higher in interpersonal skills and overall teaching quality. Teachers' practices had consistently strong and positive effects on parent reactions to the school program and on parent evaluations of teachers' merits for parents at all educational levels. . . . Teacher practices of parent involvement had more dramatic positive links to parents' reactions than general school-to-home communication or parent assistance at the school. (p. 291)

And most parents said that they could do more if teachers would tell them what to do.

In further work, Epstein and Dauber concentrated, respectively, on *teacher attitudes and practices of parent involvement* (Epstein & Dauber, 1988) and *parents' attitudes and practices* (Dauber & Epstein, 1989) in eight inner-city schools in Baltimore (five elementary and three middle schools). In examining teacher attitudes and practices of the 171 teachers, Epstein and Dauber (1988) found

- Almost all teachers express strong, positive attitudes about parent involvement in general. But the strength of school programs and teachers' actual practice vary considerably, with elementary school programs stronger, more positive, and more comprehensive than those in middle grades.
- The individual practices of each teacher at particular grade levels and in particular subject areas are the keystone for strong programs of parent involvement.
- The individual teacher is not, however, the only factor in building stronger programs. Analyses of "discrepancy scores" showed that differences between self and principal, self and teacher colleagues, and self and parents were significantly associated with the strength of schools' parent involvement programs. Programs and practices were stronger in schools where teachers saw that they, their colleagues, and the parents all felt strongly about the importance of parent involvement.
- Without the schools' assistance, parents' knowledge and actions to help their children are heavily dependent on the parents' social class or education. But schools—even inner city schools—can develop strong programs of parent involvement to help more families become knowledgeable partners in their children's education. (pp. 11–12)

Epstein and Dauber also report that teachers with more positive attitudes toward parent involvement report more success in involving "hard-to-reach parents including working parents, less educated parents, single parents, parents of older students, young parents, parents new to the school, and other adults with whom children live" (p. 5).

In the comparison study focusing on *parents'* attitudes and activities, Dauber and Epstein (1989) found

- Parents report little involvement at the school itself. Many parents work full or part-time and cannot come to the school building during the school day.
- Parents in all of the schools in this sample are emphatic about wanting the schools and teachers to advise them about *how to help their own children at home* at each grade level.
- Parents believe that the schools need to strengthen practices such as

giving parents specific information on their children's major academic subjects and what their children are expected to learn each year.

- Parents of young children and better-educated parents conduct more activities at home that support their children's schooling.
- Parents who were guided by teachers on how to help at home spent more minutes helping their children with homework than other parents.
- Most important for policy and practice, parents' level of involvement is directly linked to the specific practices of the school that encourage involvement at school and guide parents in how to help at home. The data are clear that the *school's practices* to inform and to involve parents are more important than parent education, family size, marital status, and, even grade level in determining whether inner city parents stay involved with their children's education through the middle grades. (pp. 15–16, their emphasis)

It is especially important to note that parent involvement practices succeed with less-educated parents and disadvantaged students, where it is crucial that the school make a difference. Johnson, Brookover, and Farrell (1989) investigated the link between principals', teachers', and students' perceptions of parent expectations and parent involvement, and the students' "academic sense of futility," which was defined as "the students' feeling that they were unable to succeed in the school's social system, or a feeling of hopelessness" (p. 2). They examined three groups—a statewide sample, a majority white sample, and a majority black sample—of fourth- and fifth-grade students in Michigan.

Johnson and associates found, as expected, that perceived low expectations on the part of parents for their children were strongly correlated with students' academic sense of futility (these are fourth- and fifth-grade students). However, they also discovered an important difference among the groups. For the statewide and majority white samples, "school personnels' [principals and teachers] perceptions of parents' interest and expectations for their children had little impact on students' feelings of hopelessness" (p. 14); while "in the predominantly black school sample, school personnels' perceptions of parents' interest and expectations for their children explained most of the variance" in students' sense of futility (p. 15). In other words, for statewide and white students, children's perception of parents' expectations was the key influence, but for black students school expectations were the determining factor. Johnson and associates state: "Students in predominantly black schools believed that the school social system functioned in such a way as to limit their opportunity to succeed there" (p. 15).

And, a sense of futility explained 69 percent of the variance in student academic achievement for black students. Johnson and associates

conclude: A "high sense of futility impeded children's achievement motivation which ultimately affected mean students' academic achievement
in the school" (p. 16). The main point, as we have seen, is that teachers
vary in whether and how they involve parents even when they face the
same communities. One more example, this time from white middle-class
communities in two suburban public elementary districts: Hulsebosch
(1989) surveyed teachers in six schools, three from each district, about
parent involvement practices. From the survey, Hulsebosch selected nine
teachers for in-depth interviews—five high parent involvement teachers
(called "case" teachers) and four low involvement ("contrast") teachers.
Her findings are most revealing. High involvement teachers differed in
the frequency and variety of contacts with parents. Most important, case
teachers "conceptualized" their relationship to parents in radically different ways. Case teachers had a greater plurality of goals: instilling confidence in children, developing their personality, and making them feel
cared for. Contrast teachers defined their role more narrowly: to help
children to be good citizens, to help them develop academically.

Correspondingly, high involvement teachers conceived of the solution in more wholistic collaborative terms: "Instead of seeing themselves
as the sole conductor of these complex objectives they seem to see themselves as one among several important influences in the child's life" (p.
10). Hulsebosch found several themes that derived from this view of
teaching. High involvement teachers described parents as assets, while
low involvement teachers perceived parents as problems or liabilities.
Compared with low involvement teachers, high involvement teachers saw
parents as providing important input (vs. infringing), as basic (vs. add on)
to teaching, as intrinsic (vs. distractions) to learning. Hulsebosch describes
the multifaceted ways that high involvement teachers think and act to
incorporate parents into the basic work of teaching.

> Thus we have the high involvement teachers who view parents as significant,
> ongoing, and, for the most part, positive influences in the educative life of
> the child. In contrast there is the low involvement teacher who sees the influ-
> ence of parents as tangential and neutral, at best, or, more often, as problem-
> atic. (p. 28)

The concept of teacher is defined differently by the two groups. High
involvement teachers value professional autonomy, but they do so in a
way that promotes reciprocity, openness, closeness, and collaboration with
students as well as with parents. Low involvement teachers define their
autonomy in ways that maintain separation and distance (Hulsebosch,
1989, p. 45).

There is no need to go into details of other research except to note
that an ironic and frustrating picture emerges. On the one hand, most

teachers say that they want more contact with parents, but seem to feel that many parents are unavailable or uninterested. On the other hand, most parents say that they want to find out more about what their children are supposed to learn and what they can do at home to help, although they need specific direction and support to carry out this role. As most schools go, these interests get expressed, if at all, in negative episodic ways—"parents interfere," or "teachers blame the parents for not being interested or for providing a poor home environment." Yet, as the evidence shows, once teachers and parents interact on some regular basis around specific activities, mutual reservations and fear become transformed, with positive results for the personal and academic development of students and for parent and teacher attitudes. One other fact should not escape us: Some teachers and schools incorporate parents in the education of their children in fundamental and multifaceted ways, in contrast to other teachers and schools *facing identical parents and communities.* The evidence is that individual teachers can establish effective parent involvement practices without strong school support, but the impact is greater if teachers and principals are working together.

Those familiar with the theory of change being developed in this book may have formed at least one major impression from the above findings that is consistent with that theory: It is intuitively if not theoretically obvious that direct involvement in instruction in relation to one's own child's education is one of the surest routes for parents to develop a sense of specific *meaning* vis-à-vis new programs designed to improve learning. Jobs as paid aides provide this opportunity for some parents. Experience as home tutors and other forms of involvement with teachers provide the opportunity for every parent at the elementary grade levels.

Noninstructional Forms of Parent Involvement

There are two main forms of noninstructional parent and community involvement. One concerns participation in governance and advisory councils, and associations. The other involves broader forms of community–school relations and collaboration.

As the following pages show there is little evidence to suggest that parent involvement in governance affects student learning in the school, although there may be other benefits and indirect effects. The School–Community Relations Group at the University of Wisconsin–Madison conducted a series of case studies in five very different settings (rural, urban, elementary, secondary, and varying in social class). In every case they found virtually no relationship between amount of parent participation on advisory councils and student achievement (Bowles, 1980). Mortimore and colleagues (1988, p. 255) found in their longitudinal study of 50 schools that the existence of formal Parent–Teacher Associations was not related to effective schooling.

Fantini (1980) in his review suggests that the research on governance forms of involvement clearly supports the generalization that for "parents as decision-makers, no direct evidence was found to confirm or reject the basic hypothesis about impacts on children, although there is evidence of benefits in participating adults" (p. 10). Another study of parents' participation as decision-makers on advisory councils found that school principals dominated information and decisions. The title of the paper tells it all: "The Myth of Parent Involvement Through Advisory Councils" (Paddock, 1979).

In the same vein, Lucas, Lusthaus, and Gibbs (1978–79) examined parent advisory councils in Quebec, which legislates such councils for every school. Lucas and colleagues investigated what was happening in 10 elementary and 5 secondary schools by doing a content analysis of committee minutes during the school year. These researchers found

1. pedagogical issues were infrequently discussed;
2. whatever was discussed was mainly of an informational nature (as distinct from a recommendation role, which occurred less than 4% of the time); and
3. topics of discussion were initiated mostly by administrators or teachers (67.2% at the elementary level and 78% at the secondary level) rather than by parents (27.6% at the elementary level and 17.9% at the secondary level).

The System Development Corporation (SDC) research contains the most comprehensive information on parent involvement in governance, since it covers four major programs. All four programs mandate district and/or school parent advisory committees. The site studies tend to confirm other research on parent participation in governance: namely, that when advisory committees are mandated, they work in a very small proportion of cases. For example, of the 16 Title I sites, only 3 district advisory committees were found to be actively involved. Of the other 13, 1 had no committee at all, 7 had committees but no involvement, and 5 had "token involvement" (Melaragno et al., 1981, pp. 5–38). Similarly, for school-level advisory committees, Melaragno and his colleagues found that only 3 of 31 school committees played an active role in project governance. Of the others, most played a token role; in fact, in 12 of the 31 schools the committees had never been formed, existed only on paper, or met so seldom that there was no opportunity for any involvement.

The site studies also provide information on factors associated with effective committees. The most active councils occurred

1. where federal or state legislation was precise and monitored regarding the specific forms of involvement;
2. where state departments were committed to parent involvement and actively pursued that goal through providing assistance, frequently visiting districts, etc.; and
3. where local districts specified parent roles, provided training for parents, and had active parent coordinators who facilitated the involvement of other parents.

As to outcomes, both personal benefits (e.g., personal growth, knowledge) and project benefits (e.g., better delivery of instruction) were reported by parents and district staff in the cases where councils were active. The main finding, however, remains: Very few councils at either the district or school level were implemented in a manner that resulted in more than token participation.

Nor do most parents seem to want to be involved in advisory committees or councils. A 1979 Canadian nationwide survey of over 2,000 parents asked such a question. Overall, 63.4 percent of the respondents indicated that they would not like to serve as a member of a home–school advisory committee (Canadian Education Association, 1979).

On the other hand, part of the problem may be that many advisory councils and other forms of parent participation in decision-making do not have a clear focus and are not well implemented—that is, they do not address the needs of parents, and are inefficient, unproductive, and the like. For example, Joyce (1978) in a study of councils in California presents convincing evidence that a large number of parent–school advisory councils can be very effective when they have a clear task and are carefully developed. Similarly, the Designs for Change organization in Chicago has demonstrated that parent groups can be very effective in influencing decisions and improving schools, *provided* that they are assisted in developing three major areas of skills.

1. the capacity to gather accurate information about the system they are trying to change;
2. mastery of a variety of techniques for intervening skillfully; and
3. the capacity to ensure that their own group functions effectively as a group (see Moore, Weitzman, Steinberg, & Manar, 1981).

Also, involving parents in the school can result in support for obtaining additional resources and in dealing with problems in relations with the district office and other agencies outside the local community.

In a further study Moore, Soltman, Steinberg, Manar, and Fogel (1983) stress the importance of parent and citizen groups in pressing for reforms in school-based "service quality" (1983, p. 46), that is, in monitoring and maintaining the structures necessary to ensure the quality of education for all students. Moore and associates caution, however, that groups need to be proactive rather than reactive in their analysis and solutions to problems. Their study suggests that most community groups lack this proactive stance. In line with the results of the 1981 study mentioned above, parent advocacy groups need training to organize their efforts under the model provided by nonschool-based advocacy groups.

It is important to be clear about what is and is not being said in this section. First, the focus is on parent involvement in educational matters. Thus, I have not wandered into the rather large separate literature on adult education, community use of school, and "community schools." Second, as I have indicated, the discovery that there is no relationship between parent participation in governance and student achievement leaves a number of unanswered questions. Is the lack of relationship due to poorly implemented governance councils? That is, if those councils worked as intended, would there be a positive impact? (The Designs for Change work and Joyce's research indicated that this might be the case.) Third, the findings do not lead to the conclusion that advisory or other forms of parent involvement in governance should be abandoned. The more accurate conclusion is that councils or associations by themselves do not make much of a difference. Epstein and Dauber (1988) found that schools involved in promoting parent involvement activities at home were more likely to be engaged in other types of parent involvement as well. Multiple forms of involvement have a mutually reinforcing, synergistic positive impact.

Indeed, the good news is that more comprehensive forms of parent/ community–classroom/school collaboration are developing and beginning to pay off for both elementary and secondary schools (Davies, 1989; Jackson & Cooper, 1989; Wilson & Corcoran, 1988; special issue of *Educational Leadership*, October 1989). In these developments we are beginning to see how high schools, to be effective, must form broad-based relationships with their communities. Community involvement was one of six major themes that characterized the effective schools in Wilson & Corcoran's (1988) analysis of 571 secondary schools. But the form of involvement is different and more complex than that in elementary schools. Wilson and Corcoran entitle their theme, public involvement: reaching the community. They found five interrelated components of successful reaching out.

1. human resources (recruitment of community members in the school);
2. public relations (aggressive marketing);
3. fiscal resources (additional monies);
4. community services (involvement of students in the community); and

5. building an identity (symbolic sense of identity with the community) (Wilson & Corcoran, 1988, Ch. 7).

Wilson and Corcoran conclude that

The establishment of more collaborative links with the community brings concrete benefits to schools and their staffs. First, collaborative links with the community strengthen the technical aspects of the school. Community people represent an enormous pool of expertise that creative people can tap. . . . Second, strong community involvement makes schools more accessible and attractive places and builds political support across constituencies. As people come to know the schools and to feel that they can contribute to their success, ignorant criticism diminishes. . . . Third, participation in school activities by adults other than school staff communicates an important message to students. If adults are willing to take time from their schedules to help schools, it must be an activity of some significance. . . . Finally, collaborative activities shape the school–community culture that encourages a sense of concern about the quality of life that is so often missing in today's harried, noisy world. . . . Fostering all kinds of involvement of school staff members in the community and of community members in the school sends a message to the school's neighbors. It says, "we care about you, we want to know you, and we want you to know us." (pp. 116–17).

More deliberate projects to train and support both parents and school staff are building on these research findings. Jackson and Cooper (1989) report on a major project in New York City involving groups of parents in three high schools in the Bronx and five in Staten Island.

The initial focus was on the needs and concerns of the parents as people, not on learning more about the school programs nor on emphasizing any failure on the part of their children. . . . The Support Group provided a forum for parents to learn about parental failure and successes; to teach parents how to deal with personal problems; and most importantly to help them realize that many other parents have the same failures, successes and problems. (pp. 4–5)

In a second phase the focus shifted to home and school interaction, examining topics such as the school's expectations, parents' expectations, home–school relationships, and the like.

The project is still in the early stages, but the first-year evaluation indicates some success and lessons for extending the project. According to Jackson and Cooper the important factors related to success include: visible, active involvement of the principals; open lines of communication between the principal and project staff; sufficient time to plan, recruit, and follow up; understanding and appreciation by project staff of the culture of both parents and the schools; involvement of teachers so that they can see parents in a different light; recognition in a visible way of parents and all others who participate; and involvement of outside groups to assist and help present the school to the larger community.

At the elementary level a similar example exists in "The Schools Reaching Out Project" coordinated by the Institute for Responsive Education (Davies, 1989). Two elementary schools are involved—the David A. Ellis School in Roxbury in Boston and P.S. 111 in New York. The schools are trying a wide variety of approaches "to involving families and the community in order to improve the effectiveness of the school" (Davies, 1989, p. 4). The project is backed up by a 19-member national commission of researchers and educators, which provides input, resources, and assistance in conducting research and disseminating results to focus national attention on the need for stronger links between schools, families, and communities. Davies puts it powerfully: "The connections between families, schools, and communities are not yet seen as vitally related to the premier social task of breaking the link between poverty and social and academic failure for so many poor children" (p. 13).

The power of parent–school partnerships can be seen in Tennessee's statewide effort in which 11 models of parent involvement in elementary schools were funded at 17 sites (Lueder, 1989a, 1989b). The models focused on such topics as "active parenting" (training sessions for parents), "new parents as teachers" (a program for teenage parents), "operation fail-safe" (parent-student-teacher conferences to raise student achievement), and "family math" (a program for parents and students to work together on math). Over 95% of the parents reported that they were more involved with their children's education; over 90% reported that their children's skills and overall attitudes had improved, and 81% perceived an improvement in their children's behavior (Lueder, 1989a, p. 17). In one project, for example, parent participation was considerable and resulted in significant increases in children's listening, reading, and math scores compared with two control groups of students (Lueder, 1989b).

The Annie E. Casey Foundation's New Futures Initiative for at risk youth provides an excellent example of school–community integration at the high school level (Wehlage & Lipman, 1989). Projects are funded in five cities—Dayton, OH, Lawrence, MA, Little Rock, AR, Pittsburgh, PA, and Savannah, GA—which are "embarking on a 5 year commitment to comprehensively address the causes of dropping out, low school achievement, teenage pregnancy, and youth unemployment" (Wehlage & Lipman, 1989, p. 1). Among the aims of the five-year effort, which commenced in 1989, are: to empower at-risk youth by providing them access to activities, experiences and knowledge that surpass the traditional boundaries of school, to include parents and community members in the decision-making process, to strengthen families and communities, to involve community members in carrying out a range of valuable learning activities inside and outside the school, and more broadly to establish councils that coordinate the involvement of agencies like the mayor and city council, chamber of commerce, business and industry, social services, labor unions, higher education, schools, parents and young people, and their neighborhoods. The New Futures Initiative involves accountability structures and a commitment to examine verifiable results. In each of five cities the projects are intended not only to integrate schools and communities, but also to develop the reforms "in the context of a city wide mandate to reshape the institutions and conditions that affect youth" (Wehlage & Lipman, 1989, p. 20). Such multi-agency partnerships, to be successful, must focus on specific problems and solutions (MacDowell, 1989).

Having examined rather thoroughly the role of parent involvement and improvement, there remains one final element to consider briefly before turning to guidelines for action—the role of school boards and communities vis-à-vis innovation and reform.

SCHOOL BOARDS, COMMUNITIES, AND CHANGE

Communities can either (1) put pressure on district administrators "to do something" about a problem, (2) oppose specific innovations that have been adopted, or (3) do nothing (passive support or apathy). Although there are several dramatic individual examples of the first two types of situations, by far the most prevalent case is that school boards and communities do not initiate or have any major role in deciding about innovative programs; that is, administrators and teachers develop or make recommendations about most new programs, or governments legislate new policies. That this is the case can be seen from the national large-scale DESSI study in the United States, in which a number of major categories of innovations adopted by school districts were investigated (Crandall et al., 1982). The study was comprehensive in its coverage. While the initial sampling design called for interviews with chairpersons of school boards about particular major innovations adopted in their districts, this part of the design soon had to be abandoned when interviewers found that the chairpersons knew virtually nothing about the innovations.

Boards and communities can be radically powerful in the smaller number of cases where, for whatever reasons, they become aroused. One of the more typical pressures for change over time comes as a result of population shifts. Berman, McLaughlin, and associates' (1979) study of five school districts undergoing change illustrates that major demographic changes (rapid growth or decline in population, changes in ethnic or class composition) lead to the development of community activism in a previously stagnant school system, election of new board members, hiring of an innovative superintendent, wholesale restructuring of central staff roles and activities, facilitation of school-level involvement in change on the part of principals and teachers, and so on. The districts became transformed in a short time, with many new programs successfully implemented. It would be easy to locate other case studies that show similar patterns of cumulative community pressure leading to successful change or to endless conflicts between the community and the central administration. My point is twofold. First, such cases do occur, are dramatic, and can lead to positive change (good new programs implemented) or to negative change (continual conflict). Second, these cases of community pressure leading to change are very much in the minority.

Boards and communities, if ignored, can also bring an end to innovations adopted without their informed consent. Gold and Miles (1981) describe the painful history of what happens when middle-class communities do not like the innovations they see in their schools. In this case study, the school attempted to implement open education (a notoriously undefined and ambiguous innovation) without involving the community. Parents became increasingly concerned about whether the innovation was appropriate, as teachers did not seem to be able to explain why they were doing what they were doing. The concern mounted, and before long the parents did not have any trouble putting the innovation to rout.

Schaffarzick's study of 34 San Francisco Bay Area districts provides additional evidence for the pattern we have been discussing. He found that in 62 percent of the major curriculum decisions he examined, there was no lay (community) participation (cited in Boyd, 1978, p. 613). However, in those cases that involved conflict and bargaining, the community groups nearly always prevailed. Similarly, the two case studies in the late 1960s that launched the focus on "failed implementation" are classic examples of disregarding the community, adopting progressive undefined innovations, and paying the price—failed and eventually abandoned innovation, poor morale, and attrition of administrations and teachers (Gross et al., 1971; Smith & Keith, 1971).

On the positive side, what these experiences say, in effect, is that communities can rise to the occasion to reject ill-conceived innovations—what some impolite observers refer to as the "crap detector" capacity of those on the receiving end of change. Unfortunately (and this gets us to the negative side), confidence, insight, and power to crap-detect are not evenly distributed. Communities in which parents are less educated are not as able to translate their doubts into concerted efforts to combat change for the sake of change. In other words, middle- and upper-class communities are more able to keep school districts honest. As Bridge (1976) says: "The unfortunate fact is that 'disadvantaged' families are usually the least informed about matters of schooling and the result is that advantaged clienteles will have the largest impact on school innovations unless extraordinary efforts are made to involve others" (p. 378).

Further, local school boards are often overlooked in reform initiatives. Danzberger, Carol, Cunningham, Kirst, McCloud, & Usdan (1987) call boards "the forgotten players on the education team." They undertook a national study of local school boards in the United States, in which they surveyed 450 board chairpersons of city districts and 50 in rural districts, and interviewed a variety of local leaders.

Danzberger and her colleagues found that state governments were becoming more and more directive, that the role of local boards was unclear, that board members received little preparation and training for their roles, and that only one-third of the boards surveyed had any process for evaluating or monitoring the board's role. They observe that boards are crucial agents for school improvement, and recommend that state reforms should be concerned with strengthening the capacity of local boards to bring about and monitor change, and that boards themselves should be engaged in self-improvement through in-service and by establishing systems to assess their own effectiveness.

School boards, depending on their activities, can make a difference. LaRocque and Coleman (1989b) investigated the role of school boards in relatively successful compared with less successful districts (as measured by student achievement) in 10 districts in British Columbia. On the surface, many of the policies and initiatives were similar across all boards. Through interviews and the examination of specific activities, LaRocque and Coleman found that school trustees in the more successful boards:

(a) were considerably more knowledgeable about district programs and practices;
(b) had a clearer sense of what they wanted to accomplish, based on a set of firmly held values and beliefs; and
(c) engaged in activities which provided them with opportunities to articulate these values and beliefs. (p. 15)

Successful boards also worked more actively and interactively with superintendents and the district administration. There were no demographic differences in the type of community or characteristics of the trustees in the successful compared with the less successful boards. But, as I have said, how to increase the effectiveness of school boards is an unstudied problem.

Given that boards and communities, whether lower or middle class, frequently do not have an influential role in determining change, one can ask, "How many inappropriate innovations have been perpetrated on the educational public over the past three decades?" The simple answer is "Far too many," which is another way of saying that the importance of the role of parents in educational reform has been both sadly neglected and underestimated. More broadly, those interested in effective educational reform will have to deal with school boards and with community members in a way that confronts the fact that these groups are essential for the eventual implementation of many reforms: the school board for its endorsements, provision of resources necessary to support implementation, and ability to ask the right questions about results; parents for their support, reinforcement, and influence at the family and classroom levels.

GUIDELINES FOR COPING

How would you feel if you were poor, had dropped out of school, were a single parent, had two or more children, were getting $160 a month . . . had trouble reading the notes your children bring home from school, couldn't write notes back to school, and lived in a dangerous community surrounded by violence and drugs?
—Brown and Lueder (1989)

This is not a book on how to fight city hall. Other people have written on citizens' rights and how to use power-based strategies (e.g., Huguenin et al., 1979; Moore et al., 1983). Parents need skills and opportunities for participating at home and/or at the school in improving education for their children. Guidelines are thus needed for school people about parents as well as for parents about schools. As we have seen, there is substantial evidence that parents make a major difference on children's development and education, and that parents can be involved and supported in a number of specific low-cost ways to play a greater role. Because parents are such a crucial force, and because only a minority of parents are currently successfully involved (Epstein, in Brandt, 1989, estimates 20% at most), strategies to involve parents represent one of the most powerful underutilized instruments for educational reform. Even a modest increase in the number of parents involved would bring substantial benefits. Wilson and Corcoran (1988, p. 118) found that while poor school–community relations was one of the five most pressing problems for schools, "it was also one of the problems most susceptible to solution, since twice as many schools reported converting school–community relations from a problem to a strength than was true of any other problem area."

Advice to Parents

General advice to parents about what they should know about schools is only marginally helpful. In fact, as outsiders, parents are at a very great disadvantage if the school wants to keep them at a distance, as most do.

The Designs for Change handbook, *Child Advocacy and the Schools* (Moore et al., 1983), would be a good place to start for parent and citizen groups interested in bringing about improvements in their local schools. The Designs for Change organization attempts to support parent groups through advice, training, and other forms of technical assistance, helping them define their concerns, gather accurate information to document problems, and carry out a variety of intervention activities designed to generate action to make improvements. Davies (1989) stresses that outside pressures and demands are essential.

> Without pressure from the outside—in the form of laws, mandates, and citizen organizations demanding change, and parent and citizen protests of inadequate school results—organizations like schools are not likely to be able to overcome the built-in inertia that defeats change. Without organized public dissatisfaction politicians are unlikely to make substantial shifts in the allocation of public resources. This points to the need for a pincer movement—work inside schools such as our Schools Reaching Out project and work outside the schools by grassroots parent and community organizations to press for school reforms and improved results. (p. 15)

Additional guidelines at the level of the individual parent can be suggested.

- If you have a choice of schools, check out the history and attitude of each school toward parent and community involvement. (More-educated parents are more likely to check out the school than are less-educated parents—see Wimpelberg, 1981.)
- If you are lucky enough to be in a community where the principal and teachers are doing something to involve parents in instructional matters, then be responsive and participate.
- Wherever you are, do not assume that teachers do not want you. Teachers have their own beleaguered world. They may be overwhelmed. They may be faced with an innovation adopted by the board or another level of government about which they are unsure, and consequently are reluctant to show their confusion to parents.
- Become familiar with some of the curriculum your child is using (through workbooks, discussions).
- Ask the teacher if there is anything you can do at home to help the child. The receptive teacher may be willing to develop a small workshop for parents.
- If you do not instantly understand the curriculum and other changes being used in the school, you are not alone. It takes time and interaction to develop some understanding.
- For most educational innovations, parents can learn in a relatively short time some activities to do with their children. Moreover, you know

things about the family environment and about your child that the teacher doesn't know (and the teacher probably knows things about your child that you don't know). The most powerful combination for learning is the family and school complementing each other.

• If you are in a desperate situation of apparent prejudice, lack of caring, and no interest on the part of the school, fight for your rights alone or with other parents. If you are really up against a stone wall these guidelines will only be minimally helpful. Put another way, get involved with other parents using power-based strategies. Even if the school is uncaring, you can do a number of home-based activities that can be very useful.

Parent involvement is not the only answer. Nor is it free from danger. Some situations of involvement may turn out to have harmful consequences if they result in endless conflict, lowered morale, and the like. As with other educational reforms the implementation of involvement programs should be carefully carried out and monitored as to problems and impact. Moreover, I do not delude myself that the ideas in this chapter can be used to accomplish widespread effective reform in the short run. The guidelines may seem naive and foolish in some situations in light of societal dominance, daily prejudices, poverty, and simply surviving physically and psychologically.

Nonetheless, individuals have to start somewhere. There are many, many more effective parent involvement programs in operation than was the case a few years ago. There has been a social movement beyond the rhetoric of general endorsement or rejection of community involvement, toward the development and use of specific programs involving parents in instructional activities in the classroom or at home. These forms of involvement have become purposeful and meaningful at the individual level. And, as we have seen in this chapter, they are making a difference for students, teachers, and parents. We know better what works and why it works. It is not easy to set up effective parent–school activities, but it can be done with success with the vast majority of parents. (Epstein, in Brandt, 1989, estimates that only about 2 to 5% of parents are unreachable.)

Advice to School People

In introducing new programs or initiating new parent involvement activities the advice is consistent with the principles of change espoused throughout this book. Start small. Hold a meeting with parents. Explain the objectives and methods being used. Establish a few small exercises taking 5 or 10 minutes that parents could do at home with students. Hold a workshop for parents. Link up with one or two other teachers. Use parents to involve or help other parents. Involve parents in the classroom where there is interest. Through interaction, attempt to understand the concerns of parents and the family learning environment. Involve students (the relative involvement of students and parents will vary by grade level). Discuss how performance and progress are to be measured. Do not expect 100 percent success, but do expect real improvement. In brief, have an explicit, even if small-scale, plan to involve parents. All of this will be facilitated if the school has an approach to and experience with involving parents, including materials, training, and other activities. Starting small and building incrementally can lead to multiple forms of community involvement that reinforce each other.

Taken as a whole, this chapter is replete with ideas and resources for school people to involve parents effectively in classroom and school improvement. To summarize the advice in general terms:

1. At the school and classroom level make parent involvement a fundamental part of the definition and mission of an effective school. It is not an add-on. It is not just nice. It is part and parcel of student development and engagement in education.
2. Establish specific programs and practices at the individual teacher level. Teachers need materials that are clear and easy to follow for parents.
3. Use the basic "implementation principles" in putting into practice any new activity or program: clear objectives, good materials, training, continuous follow-up, and monitoring that involve parents in suggesting activities and changes and in assessing results.
4. Principals should establish a (part-time) coordinator at the school level whose responsibility is to work with teachers and the principal to initiate, support, and coordinate school-wide parent involvement. Parent involvement represents an organizational change, not just an individual classroom change.
5. At the school and district levels develop policies and programs that include the several types of parent and community involvement discussed in this chapter.

The underlying consequence of the above set of activities is the development of *knowledge* on the part of parents, teachers, and students and of *skills* in relation to specific practices. It is, in other words, the development of the meaning of change at the level of individuals with some opportunity to achieve shared meanings.

As with most aspects of change the hardest thing is to get started. Many parents and teachers are overloaded with their own work-related and personal concerns. They also may feel discomfort in each other's presence due to lack of mutual familiarity and to the absence of a mechanism for solving the problems that arise. In examining the research presented in this chapter, it is encouraging to observe that parent participation was effective when someone or some group (parents, teachers, district staff, program developers) had the responsibility for organizing and conducting specific activities that brought parents and school people together for a particular purpose. Success did not happen by accident.

In the meantime, the simple conclusion of this chapter is twofold. First, the vast majority of parents find meaning in activities related to their own children rather than in school- or system-wide endeavors. Second, educational reform requires the conjoint efforts of families and schools. Parents and teachers should recognize the critical complementary importance of each other in the life of the student. Otherwise, we are placing limitations on the prospects for improvement that may be impossible to overcome.

Part III

EDUCATIONAL CHANGE AT THE REGIONAL AND NATIONAL LEVELS

CHAPTER 13

Governments

. . . his obsession with rationalism had isolated him. For four years [he]
talked about the big ideas he wanted to talk about. He never once listened
to what the public was trying to say to him, about its problems, its fears,
its dreams. Above all . . . he ignored rationalism's essential flaw. To be
systematic is sensible. To be systematic without common sense, without
humour, is to treat systems as more important than people.
— Richard Gwynn (on Prime Minister Trudeau),
in *The Northern Magus* (1980), p. 107

Now we get to the biggest culprit of them all—the government. But if we
are true to the phenomenological basis of our analysis, we will realize that
what government policy-makers and administrators do is perfectly
understandable—to themselves. If it is difficult to manage change in one
classroom, one school, one school district, imagine the scale of the problems faced by one state or province or country in which numerous agencies and levels and tens or hundreds of thousands of people are involved.
It is infinitely more difficult for that government if its personnel do not
venture out to attempt to understand the culture and the problems of
local school people.

Still, governments seem to be oblivious to one implementation fact:
The way in which they go about change *within* their own organizations is
a fundamental part of the implementation process. Stated another way, if
governments are poor at launching new programs or at bringing about
changes within their own ranks, how can they possibly criticize schools
for not changing? I suspect it is this more than anything else that turns
teachers, administrators, and others off in dealing with government personnel.

However, to continue our pursuit of the meaning of change, we
should attempt to understand the role of governments at least partly
from their perspective. They do have a responsibility to protect minorities
and to be concerned about the quality and equity of education at the local
level. Yet it is incredibly difficult to induce and support or monitor change
at a distance. Moreover, the vast majority of government personnel, like
the rest of us, are just cogs in the machinery. The daily demands and
pressures from superiors and peers in the world of politics are enormous.

Programs and politicians are frequently ephemeral. Before one policy has been completely formulated, the next one demands attention. Policy making is both more compelling and more exciting than policy implementation. When all is said and done there are many complaints and few satisfactions.

In order to examine the role of governments in educational change, this chapter is divided into four main sections. The first section considers the U.S. federal government; the next section, the role of state departments in the United States, the third section, the role of the federal and especially provincial departments of education in Canada; and the final section, a summary of the implications of the chapter in the form of "guidelines for governments."

THE UNITED STATES FEDERAL GOVERNMENT

Reflecting the short history of implementation concerns, the U.S. federal government has been involved heavily in the business of educational change only since the Elementary and Secondary School Act of 1965 and its various Titles.[1] The intention of this act and other programs soon to be identified is essentially to improve the quality and equality of education in the country. My interest from the point of view of the initiation (adoption) and implementation of change is in two areas: What programs and activities have they promoted? What are the main issues with respect to implementation and impact?

Educational Policies and Programs

The federal government is involved in two types of programs—one concerns federally funded educational policies and programs usually administered through states and departments to local districts; the other involves national laboratories and R&D centers focusing on research, development, and dissemination services operating from the Office of Educational Research and Improvement (OERI).

Federally Sponsored Educational Programs. It will not be possible to identify and report on every federally sponsored educational program, but we can provide a brief overview. Federal involvement in educational reform is significant but has been declining in relative terms since President Reagan's administration. The impact of the change has been toward greater deregulation from the federal to state and district levels, devolution, and budget reductions (Clark & Astuto, 1989; Elmore & McLaughlin, 1988). The federal share of expenditures for elementary and secondary education declined from 8.7% in 1981 to 6.2% in 1989; the

FIGURE 13.1.   Major U.S. Federal Education Programs, 1965 to Present

1965–1980 (ESEA)	*1981–Present* (ECIA)
Title 1 (assistance to disadvantage)	Chapter 1
Title IV–C (formerly Title III) (local development and adoption of exemplary programs)	Chapter 2
Basic Skills (formerly Right to Read) (upgrade basic skills especially re disadvantaged)	Chapter 2
Emergency School Aid Act (ESAA) (desegregation)	Chapter 2
Follow Through (model programs for low-income students)	Chapter 2
Title VII (Bilingual Education)	Bilingual Education
Bureau of Education Handicapped	Bureau of Education Handicapped
Vocational Education	Vocational Education

Department of Education budget decreased from 2.5% to 1.8% of the federal budget (Clark & Astuto, 1989). In real terms, adjusted for inflation, expenditures declined by 12% from 1980 to 1988 (Clark & Astuto, 1989). As we shall see in the next section, overall expenditure for education is greater because of dramatic increases in state budgets and activities since 1983.

Federal involvement in education can be divided into two periods. The first major participation began with the passage of the Elementary and Secondary Education Act (ESEA) of 1965 and continued for 15 years until Congress passed the Education Consolidation and Improvement Act (ECIA) of 1981. Figure 13.1 contains a listing of the main programs and relationships over the two time periods, which I will use as a guideline.

Chapter 1 (Title I) and Chapter 2 (block grant) can be used to discuss the nature and evolution of the programs (see Elmore & McLaughlin, 1988, and Shive & Eiseman, 1982, for more detailed analyses of federal policy involvement since 1965). Title I is by far the largest program in terms of money (over $3 billion annually), numbers of students (over 5 million), and educational personnel reached (Kirst & Jung, 1980). Its purpose is to provide financial assistance to districts for elementary schools with "concentrations of children from low-income families" (Public Law 89–10 Title I, Section 101). Specific proposals vary in emphasis but tend to concentrate on basic skills. There is an elaborate set of criteria, specifications, and requirements for reporting and evaluating programs, including data on progress in upgrading student achievement. As with other programs, noncompliance in the use of funds "theoretically" can lead to withdrawal of assistance (more about compliance later).

Almost 90% of the school districts in the United States receive at least some Title I funds. In California, for example, the 33 largest school districts receive more than 80% of the state's Title I funds (Kirst & Jung, 1980, p. 26). These funds provide for the salaries of district project staff and so-called Title I teachers in eligible schools, as well as other resources. Title I, in short, is a major source of federally sponsored educational reform representing close to 40% of the federal funds that end up at the district level.

While there has been considerable controversy over matters of wastage of funds, increased bureaucracy, and questions of impact, *Title I/ Chapter 1* has matured over the years to become a necessary and regular component of many district and state reform efforts. The Education Consolidation and Improvement Act of 1981 greatly streamlined the administration of Title I, but retained it as the major federal program.

The impact of Title I is difficult to assess. In reviewing evaluations of Title I, Elmore and McLaughlin note that the results of Title I vary from one setting to another. However, they conclude that

> Title I produced a wealth of practical insights at the school and district level into the special problems of educationally disadvantaged children . . . many states and localities developed positive ways of responding to Title I requirements that . . . encouraged effective educational practice . . . this maturity seemed to be a result of a two-step process of, first, adjusting to new federal priorities and funding requirements, and second, learning how to capitalize on the developmental opportunities presented by those requirements and translate those requirements into effective educational practice. (Elmore & McLaughlin, 1988, pp. 27–28)

As we turn to Chapter 2, a word is necessary about categorical vs. block grant funding. Categorical programs, like Title I, have the advantage of targeting money to specific usages, backed up by regulatory monitoring. They have the disadvantage of requiring elaborate and expensive bureaucracies and paper-work requirements to monitor compliance. They require an increase in local bureaucracy to fulfill reporting requirements, and when there are numerous categorical programs, fragmentation becomes a problem at the local level. Block grants, like Chapter 2, greatly reduce the paper work and provide lump sums of money to states and districts. This procedure permits more flexible use of funds geared to local needs, but it also allows for aimless or diffuse expenditures that squander resources.

In the period 1965 to 1980 Congress created a host of small and medium-sized competitive grant programs. Henderson (1986) describes the problem of the proliferation of categorical grants, which led to Chapter 2. "Each [categorical program] had its own application cycle, set of guidelines, and funding procedures. Taken together, they represented a maze that only the most sophisticated school districts could negotiate successfully" (p. 597). The response was Chapter 2, established as part of the ECIA. Chapter 2 is a block grant (currently $450 million a year) that combined a number of categorical programs (see Table 13.1) into a single grant to each state. As part of the strategy for devolution of authority *and* costs, funds were reduced by 25 percent and states were required to allocate at least 80 percent of their allotments by formula to localities (Elmore & McLaughlin, 1988).

Title III had provided funds to local districts for the development of innovative educational practices. This arrangement had two problems— it bypassed the state, and there was no mechanism to implement and disseminate the practices once developed. In 1974 Title III was consolidated into a new Title IV; the innovative program component, IV–C, became a state-administered project grant program for the development or adoption of innovative local projects.

Title IV disappeared into the block grant in 1981, along with 26 other programs, the most notable of which was the Emergency School Aid Act (ESAA) for desegregation, which accounted for 30 percent of the funding of all the old programs. Chapter 2 is not an unconditional block grant because it has to be used for certain broad purposes. It is divided into three parts.

> The state and local agencies may select from *any or all* of the three categories:
> (1) Basic Skills Development;
> (2) Improvement and Support Services (including books and instructional materials; guidance, counseling, and testing; computers; staff and management training; and desegregation); and
> (3) Special Projects (including community education, gifted and talented education, career education, and ethnic heritage). (Henderson, 1986, p. 598, emphasis in original)

There are several consequences of Chapter 2. First, there is a major shift of funding among states away from those with large urban areas (which were favored by the ESAA formula) toward those with greater suburban and rural areas (Henderson, 1986). Second, depending on the state's capacity, expenditure at the local level (80% of the funds) is not necessarily monitored. For example, ESAA provided direct incentives and pressures to districts to both develop and implement desegregation plans, which is absent from Chapter 2 (Henderson, 1986). Third, there is the tendency for Chapter 2 money to go to the purchase of equipment (e.g., computers) without support for implementation; using the money to support the development of innovative programs (as in Title IV–C) has virtually come to an end according to Elmore and McLaughlin (1988, p. 24). Fourth, of course, there was a major budget reduction of 25 percent, which affected all programs.

There is no need to examine the other programs listed in Table 13.1 unless one has a special interest in a particular program area (see Elmore & McLaughlin, 1988, and Shive & Eiseman, 1982, for program by program analyses). Nor have I attempted to report on all federally sponsored activities. The federally funded National Science Foundation, for example, is systematically involved in the development, implementation, and assessment of science teaching (see Elmore & McLaughlin, 1988).

To summarize the current status of federal involvement: Overall funding has decreased, but is still substantial. Paper work, regulation, targeting, and monitoring have decreased. On balance, aside from the budget reduction, the streamlining of programs and procedures is likely an improvement. The new system needs refinement in order to restore some of the focus on competitive grants for local improvement (Henderson, 1986, recommends that 10% of the funds in Chapter 2 be allocated for such a purpose) and to strengthen possibilities for follow-up and support for implementation. As we shall see shortly, however, the role of the states in reform has increased dramatically during the 1980s. The states are better placed than the federal government to influence local reform for better or for worse.

Research, Development, and Dissemination.   I will not attempt to trace the short but complex history of the rise and fall of The National Institute of Education (NIE). Begun in 1972, it had hopes of an initial budget of $150 million, which never rose above half that amount. Its budget peaked at $75 million by 1980, and was reduced to $55 million in 1981. It had three major divisions—Teaching and Learning, Educational Policy and Organization, and Dissemination and Improvement of Practice. During its formative decade (1972–1982), specific projects and programmatic themes produced significant research knowledge relevant to several chapters in this book—instructional practices, organizational leadership and change, role of the principal, parent involvement, staff development, characteristics of effective change programs, and so on. The system of R&D laboratories and centers was also passed on to NIE in the form of mandates to allocate certain portions of their funds to lab and center programs.

In 1985, NIE was phased out and its programs, along with other activities, were reorganized into the Office of Educational Research and Improvement (OERI) within the Department of Education. The OERI oversees six areas of programs or projects.

1. the Regional Educational Laboratories,
2. National Research & Development Centers,
3. Educational Resources Information Center (ERIC),
4. National Educational Longitudinal Study,
5. National Assessment of Educational Progress, and
6. the National Diffusion Network (U.S. Department of Education, 1990).

At the time of the reorganization in 1985, the original system of labs and centers was also reorganized and recompeted, that is, a system of open competition was established to decide on the new configuration. The labs, for example, were reorganized so that they were more geographically representative and had clearer mandates. Proposals were invited and adjudicated to establish a new set of labs across the country. The mission and function of the labs is stated as follows:

Laboratories plan programs through an ongoing assessment of regional needs, a knowledge of the current trends in research and practice, and interaction with the many other agencies and institutions that assist communities and schools with educational improvement. Improving schools and classrooms is the goal of the laboratories, a goal they carry out through a common set of five tasks or functions. (U.S. Department of Education, 1990, p. 50)

The five common tasks focus on: governance, school improvement, state policy, R&D resources, and collaboration. Each lab has a different set of specific projects depending on regional interest and lab capacity. Typical project titles include: classroom instruction, rural and small schools, improving teacher and administration performance, facilitating student achievement, improving writing skills, dropout prevention, assessment and evaluation, literacy and language, and so on. The nine funded labs, which are nearing the end of their first five-year term of operation (and will have to recompete in the early 1990s), are

- Appalachia Educational Laboratory
- Far West Laboratory for Educational Research and Development
- Mid-Continent Regional Educational Laboratory
- North Central Regional Educational Laboratory
- Northwest Regional Educational Laboratory
- Regional Laboratory for Educational Improvement of the Northeast and the Islands

- Research for Better Schools
- Southeastern Educational Improvement Laboratory
- Southwest Educational Development Laboratory

The laboratories are involved in development and implementation support as well as research. Funded with an average budget of approximately $2 million, and designed as they are to integrate theory and practice through partnership, they appear to be quite successful, although the major review at the end of the first five-year cycle will provide detailed evidence.

Also in the mid 1980s the National R&D Centers were reconfigured to map out priority domains of research. As stated by OERI,

> The National Research and Development Centers. . . conduct research on topics of national significance to educational policy and practice. Each center works in a defined field on a multi-year (and usually multi-disciplinary) program of research and development. Each center's role is to:
> - Exercise leadership in its mission area.
> - Conduct research and development that advance theory and practice.
> - Attract the sustained attention of expert researchers to concentrate on problems in education.
> - Create a long-term interaction between researchers and educators.
> - Participate in a network for collaborative exchange in the education community.
> - Disseminate research findings in useful forms to education policymakers and practitioners.
> (U.S. Department of Education, 1990, p. 36)

The centers were established on the belief that a "critical mass of scholarly effort cannot be mustered by individual researchers and individual research projects" (Finn, 1988, p. 129). Currently, OERI funds 19 research centers. They typically involve five-year grants ranging from $500,000 to $1.5 million annually. There are too many centers to name, but they can be illustrated through the following five examples: National Center on Effective Secondary Schools (University of Wisconsin), Center for Policy Research in Education (Rutgers University, in affiliation with University of Wisconsin–Madison, Michigan State University, and Stanford University), National Center for Research on Teacher Education (Michigan State University in affiliation with University of Wisconsin–Madison, Education Matters Inc., and Teachers College, Columbia University), Center for the Study of Writing (Carnegie-Mellon University), and Research Synthesis Center for the Teaching, Learning and Assessment of Science (The Network, Inc. in affiliation with Biological Sciences Curriculum Study).

It is virtually impossible to measure the impact of these national centers, but activities based on the sixfold mandate stated above have already resulted in a number of highly valuable research projects and synthesis of knowledge, which are used by researchers, practitioners, and policy-makers. Most of the centers are finishing their five-year cycle, and are just now being redefined and are about to be recompeted in what is a highly charged political process among institutions and coalitions (see also Kennedy, 1989, for a critical analysis of dilemmas and alternatives in funding national R&D centers). I should also note in passing that, while not federally funded, there has been a proliferation of university-based education policy centers. MacCarthy and Hall (1989) identify and describe 16 such centers operating in 1988, half of which were established in 1988 and 1989.

The Educational Resources Information Center (ERIC) established in 1966 has grown to be the world's largest research database in education. ERIC is an information system responsible for developing, maintaining, and providing access to research and practice-oriented data. The ERIC system includes a network of clearinghouses, "each of which acquires, indexes and abstracts documents and journal articles for entry into the ERIC database" (U.S. Department of Education, 1990, p. 3). There are 16 clearinghouses contracted to educational institutions across the country. The titles of the clearinghouses are similar to the R&D centers; for example, Clearinghouse on Elementary and Early Childhood Education, Clearinghouse on Teacher Education, Clearinghouse on Languages and Linguistics, etc. The total ERIC database contains over 650,000 abstracts, accessed through microfiche, online databases, reference publications, and hard-copy reproduction services. Over the past several years ERIC has placed more emphasis on dissemination, reaching wider audiences (practitioners and policy-makers as well as researchers), and adding practical information in concentrated areas (see Horn & Clements, 1988; Stone-hill, 1989).

OERI also oversees two tracer research studies. The National Education Longitudinal Study of 1988 began with a national survey in 1988 of grade 8 students. The study will track the students as they progress through junior high, high school, post-secondary education, and work. It is a comprehensive study designed to yield policy information about effective schools, dropouts, course-taking patterns, labor force training and participation, family patterns and changes, and just about anything that could affect the future of this cohort of students. The National Assessment of Educational Progress focuses on the educational attainment of students in grades 4, 8, and 12 in such areas as career and occupational development and citizenship, as well as in the basic subject areas.

Finally, the National Diffusion Network (NDN) is of special interest to us because of its direct impact on innovation. NDN was created in 1974, at the time of the consolidation of Title III into Title IV, in order to identify and spread exemplary innovations. Potential exemplary projects are validated through a central review process originally called the Joint Dissemination Review Panel but now referred to as the Program Effectiveness Panel. Once validated, the programs become part of the NDN system of dissemination and assistance for local districts in selecting and using programs that meet their needs. The program funds an NDN State Facilitator in each state. Facilitators are responsible for

- assisting educators to assess needs and to match needs and interests with appropriate exemplary education programs;
- arranging for program developers to train educators that want to implement their programs;
- identifying and assisting other programs that have been developed to submit evidence to the Department of Education's Program Effectiveness Panel; and
- providing information on ERIC, the OERI-supported Research and Development Centers and Regional Educational Laboratories, and the schools recognized by the Secretary's School Recognition Program (U.S. Department of Education, 1990, p. 30).

The NDN system of promoting the identification and adoption of educational programs of proven merit has been very effective in facilitating the successful implementation of new educational practices. This is not surprising, since it incorporates many of the principles of effective change: high-quality proven innovations, personal linkages through State Facilitators, local needs identification and decision making, access to expertise, ongoing support, etc. (Crandall et al., 1982). The main difference in the post-1981 period is that the federal government is almost out of the business of providing direct funding for the development of innovative programming. The current federal emphasis in NDN is on the identification and adoption of programs, not on producing some of the programs themselves (Elmore & McLaughlin, 1988, p. 24). Ironically, the NDN was originally formed specifically to spread the word on federally funded innovative programs (Title III).

Implications

Governments cannot mandate implementation, and the more remote they are from the local scene the less influential they will be. Thus, we cannot expect the federal government to have a direct impact on local implementation, although many of the categorical programs in the 1970s attempted to do just that, without much success. I will formulate some guidelines for action at the end of this chapter, but the main implications should be noted now.

The first is that the federal government is still a significant source of resources and networking for the particular programs and activities outlined in the previous section. Longitudinal analyses of the major programs have indicated important successes (Crandall et al., 1982; Elmore & McLaughlin, 1988).

Second, as Elmore and McLaughlin (1988) stress, "lags in implementation and performance are a central facet of reform" (p. 36). It takes time, they observe, "for reforms to mature into changes in resource allocation, organization, and practice" (p. 36). Related to this, the time lines of policy-makers and practitioners are radically different: Policy reforms are generated on "electoral time," but they are implemented on "administrative time" and "practice time" (p. 36).

Third, the symbolic role of the federal government in educational innovation and reform should not be underestimated, but it is difficult to assess. Certainly *A Nation at Risk,* as we have seen, galvanized and indirectly spawned massive amounts of reform efforts across the United States. On the other hand, the federal government has greatly reduced its share of the education budget, so its actual contribution is less.

Fourth, the need for reform is greater than ever before. Clark and Astuto (1989) provide an alarming analysis of national needs in education for the 1990s: poor children, inadequate education, wide variations in state fiscal and leadership capacity. Clark and Astuto conclude that some increased federal role is essential because of "the criticalness of the problem, the urgency of its solution, and the inability of standard political structures to respond" (p. 21).

President Bush in his State of the Union address on January 31, 1990, delivered some bold statements on the nation's education goals. By the year 2000, he said, every child must start school ready to learn; the high school graduation rate must increase from its current 70 percent to 90 percent; achievement and assessment as marked in the fourth, eighth, and twelfth grades must stand for high performance, and by the year 2000, the United States must be first in the world in mathematics and science; every adult must be a skilled, literate worker; and every school must be a disciplined and drug-free environment.

We know enough about political promises and the "hyperrationalization of educational reform" (Wise, 1977, 1988, and Chapter 6) to know that wishful thinking in the absence of knowing how or even whether something can be accomplished has over the years unwittingly given reform a bad name—the more things change the more they remain the same. Federal resources for education have declined in relative terms, although we know from the 1960s that large sums of money are not the

answer if implementation capacity is limited. The answer to national reform lies not in money (although an increase will be needed), and not in
the federal role per se, but in the federal–state relationship and, in turn,
in the role of the states in their own right.

THE STATE EDUCATION DEPARTMENT

The biggest development on the educational scene in the last five
years has been the increased presence and activity of the state in educational reform. There has been more reform activity led by states since
1985 than ever before. State structures for education consist of a department of education headed by a chief state school officer (the commissioner or state superintendent), who is responsible to a state board of
education and to the governor. The commissioner and board members
are either elected or appointed, depending on the state.

Leaving aside Hawaii, the District of Columbia, and the territories,
which have unique structures (such as single educational agencies with no
local districts), nearly all other states have intermediate service units. In a
very few cases (e.g., New Jersey) the units are regional offices of the department of education and thus perform a regulatory administrative
function. In the majority of cases, however, the intermediate units are
service agencies funded by states (using some federal program money) to
coordinate and provide supplementary assistance (staff development,
evaluation, curriculum development, etc.) to districts that could not otherwise afford the services. There are many different patterns. New York,
for example, is organized into Boards of Cooperative Education Services
(boces), Texas has its Regional Education Service Centers (resc) and
Kentucky its Educational Development Regions (edr), and so on.

States vary in their degrees of centralization. In 1976 van Geel classified 20 states as centralized, 23 as decentralized, and 6 as mixed. Centralized states tend to prescribe minimum competencies; some approve
textbooks for statewide use, take more interest in the content of courses
of study, and collect and make public achievement and other evaluative
data. Decentralized states are more inclined to favor local discretion in
deciding on the precise nature of school programs. Since 1983 there has
been a strong movement toward greater state involvement. For centralized states, this has meant greater intensification of requirements and of
monitoring systems. For less centralized states, it has entailed greater intervention and interaction with local districts. In all cases more legislation
and finances have accompanied the reforms.

In the early 1980s, the recognition of the growing educational crisis
in most states (poor academic performance, high dropouts, declining
quality and morale of the teaching force, weak and uncoordinated curric-

ulum) had already created a momentum for state-led reform. The federal government's decision to deregulate reinforced state orientations to action. And act they did, more often than not led by governors and other state legislators rather than by state departments of education. State funds rose dramatically. Between 1982–83 and 1986–87 state funding climbed over 21%, adjusted for inflation, although it has since leveled off (Firestone, Fuhrman, & Kirst, 1989a). The share of state funding of local school revenues has risen to a high of 50.7% (compared with 40% in 1970), with local districts at 42.5% and the federal government at 6.8% (p. 43). Part and parcel of greater funding was increased legislation and policy requirements.

In the rest of this section I analyze the new presence of states in education reform, from several perspectives.

1. What is the general content and direction of the reforms, and how do individual states differ in their approaches?
2. What is the nature of state–district relationships concerning the factors and processes related to successful implementation at the local level? and
3. What conclusions can be drawn about the capacity of states to bring about reform?

The Direction of the Reforms

The federally funded Center for Policy Research and Education (CPRE) has been conducting research on state reform initiatives (Firestone et al., 1989a). Firestone and associates report that nearly every state joined in the movement to address the concerns raised in *A Nation at Risk*. The two major areas of activity have been upgrading the academic curriculum, linked to higher standards and achievement testing, and improving teaching through changes in certification and compensation of teachers (see Chapter 14 for more detail on policy changes affecting teachers). Forty-five states for the first time further specified or increased their graduation requirements. Twenty-seven states instituted a minimum grade point average for entering teachers.

This initial "narrow" response was quickly followed (although not necessarily in the same states) by a second wave of reform called restructuring, which has also taken on the status of a national movement (see Chapter 1). Restructuring broadens in radical ways the first wave's focus on academics and teaching. Academics becomes redefined as success for all students, especially those at risk. Thus, equity as well as excellence has become a major concern receiving emphasis in new policies and programs for early childhood, dropout prevention, and coordination of social agencies, communities, and businesses. The priority on teaching also becomes restructured to give teachers more training and status and to give principals and teachers greater authority and support through site-based councils and other school improvement themes to empower schools (Harvey & Crandall, 1988; Murphy, in press).

We can examine these developments more closely through CPRE's study of six states: Arizona, California, Florida, Georgia, Minnesota, and Pennsylvania. CPRE began a five-year tracer study in 1986 of the implementation and effects of the reforms in these six states, which were chosen for their diverse approaches to reform. The states were selected to differ on scope of reform (comprehensive vs. small pieces), strategies used (mandates vs. other approaches like building local capacity), and geographical location (representative of regions). Firestone and associates (1989a) report that

> California, Florida and Georgia undertook comprehensive reform, symbolized by one major piece of legislation. . . . Reform in the other states was more incremental. . . . Florida, Georgia and Pennsylvania counted on state mandates to change local behavior. California used inducements and Minnesota favored strategies that build local capacity and broadened the State system of service providers. Arizona's plan balanced mandates and inducements. (p. 1)

Among the main interim findings, after three years of study, are the following:

- All six states passed special legislation focusing on student standards (and curriculum), teacher policies, and corresponding finances.
- Strategies and policy instruments varied according to tradition and state political culture. For example, California used comprehensive reform and incentives; Georgia mandated reform.
- Most state reform packages lacked coherence. It was not that specific provisions conflicted, but that they were unrelated. The exception, as we shall see, was California, where the state superintendent orchestrated the integration of existing and new provisions and co-ordinated implementation requirements.
- First-order changes involving graduation requirements, curriculum specifications, and the like, were more likely to occur and be retained than second-order changes involving career ladders, new decision-making structures, etc.
- District responses were crucial and varied greatly.

State–District Implementation

The more telling criterion, of course, is the effect of state initiatives on local school districts (see Chapter 10 on the role of the district). Several studies provide insights into these dynamics (Anderson et al., 1987; Firestone, et al., 1989a; Fuhrman, Clune, & Elmore, 1988; Marsh, 1988; Odden & Marsh, 1988).

In addition to state-level data gathering, CPRE researchers also visited 24 school districts in the 6 states and 59 schools within these districts. In those situations where student testing was a major feature of the reform, the researchers found what we have noted before. The amount of time students spent being tested, and the amount of time staff spent coordinating, administering, and interpreting the various tests, increased substantially. Many school personnel not only saw this as a burden, but also did not find the information useful and/or there was no mechanism linking the information to a process of instructional improvement (see also Corbett & Wilson, 1990; Lutz & Maddirala, 1988; Neill & Medina, 1989; Wise, 1988).

There were, however, a number of surprises in the CPRE findings. The three main ones were

1. There was very little resistance to reforms that involved increasing academic content. In fact, in some cases, district requirements exceeded state requirements.
2. Much of the progress on the restructuring agenda resulted from district initiatives.
3. Some districts are actively using state policies to promote local priorities (Firestone et al., 1989a, pp. 14–15).

As stated by Fuhrman, Clune, and Elmore (1988),

One of our most interesting and important discoveries is that many local districts are going far beyond compliance; they are responding very actively to state reforms. In over half of our local districts, administrators saw in the state reforms opportunities to accomplish their own objectives, particularly as the state reforms provided significant funding increases. Local districts are actively orchestrating various state policies around local priorities, strategically interacting with the state to achieve goals. For example, one major urban district coordinates almost all state teacher policies, including its mentor-teacher and alternate-route programs, to meet the prime objective of hiring a large number of new teachers. (p. 247)

Much as I discussed in Chapter 5, the appropriate model is not an innovation one, but rather an institutional capacity or developmental model. Fuhrman and associates conclude that it is more limiting to view districts as reactive, first to federal and then to state policy, than it is to understand where districts are and where they are heading. District capacity varies greatly (Chapter 10), and without it little serious improvement will occur vis-à-vis state reforms.

Another ongoing cross-state program of research and development on the role of states is being carried out by the Education Commission of the States (ECS). Ecs is a compact among states, which has been operating since 1965. Its primary purpose "is to assist governors, state legislators, state education officials and others to develop policies to improve the quality of education at all levels" (Anderson et al., 1987). In one major study, Anderson and associates investigated programs in 10 states, conducting field work in 4 to 7 schools within 2 to 4 districts in each state. The programs studied focused on instructional improvement (e.g., Arkansas' Program for Effective Teaching) or school-wide improvement (e.g., Connecticut's School Effectiveness Project).

In explaining variations in implementation success at the school level, the ECS researchers identify a combination of state and local factors in interaction. They highlight two broad conditions at the state level. One cluster involves state pressure and support outside the state department of education, including

1. state pressure for accountability and reform,
2. support from political leaders (governors, legislators),
3. respect for the balance between state and local control in policy and program design, and
4. discretionary money available to districts and schools.

The other cluster of factors operates within the state department, constituting its capacity to influence local improvement.

1. active advocacy and political support from leadership within the department;
2. a collegial, positive working relationship with districts;
3. adequate resources;
4. an emphasis on developing local capacity through technical assistance and structure; and
5. organization within the department (assigned staff with links to other efforts supported over time).

At the district level four environmental factors were found to inhibit implementation—the degree of turmoil (conflict within the district), innovation overload (too many innovations simultaneously), large school size, and large district size and complexity. Two variables positively associated with implementation were stability of staffing and leadership, and good labor relations (Anderson et al., 1987).

I have already referred to the findings of the research study of California's comprehensive reform legislation (see Chapter 10; Marsh, 1988;

Odden & Marsh, 1988). California's major reform legislation, S.B. 813, was enacted in 1983 and contained 14 major reform programs. The reform effort contained many of the state-level features identified above in the ECS research. The major findings, as stated by Odden and Marsh (1988), were

- Virtually all schools implemented key provisions of S.B. 813 in a manner consistent with state purposes.
- Education reform legislated at the state level can be an effective means of improving schools when it is woven into a cohesive strategy at the local level.
- Successful implementation of reforms at the local level reflects several key themes (district leadership, school collegiality, concern for all students, ongoing staff development, etc.).
- Attention to the substance of curriculum and instruction and to the process of school change correlates with high test scores and improved learning conditions for all students.
- Students with special learning needs—the poor, those with limited proficiency in English, and those at risk of dropping out—received increased services and attention. Unfortunately, the services were generally of a type that has produced insufficient levels of academic achievement in the past. Sample schools lacked appropriate strategies for mounting more effective interventions for at risk students.
- Sample schools wanted to engage in even more complex school improvement, such as focusing the curriculum on problem solving and on higher order skills (pp. 595–96).

Consistent with other research, Odden and Marsh found that a coordinated state-level strategy of pressure and support influences district and school implementation, especially for first-order changes; that district leadership, vision, and knowledge of effective change processes, when they exist, enable local districts to engage proactively in shaping implementation and often going beyond state requirements; and that more complex second-order changes in instruction for higher order skills and reorganization at the school level have not yet been accomplished, although many districts and schools are interested or have begun to move in this direction.

Bringing About Effective State-Mandated Reform

I have only scratched the surface of the role of states, partly because it is a complex one, with many levels, and partly because it is an active, changing target. The new post-1983 role of states is still emerging through the testing, assessing, and redefining of strategies that work.

Probably the best general analogy to the state–district relationship is the district–school relationship we considered in Chapter 10. Louis (1989) and others found that district–school relationships varied on two dimensions—the degree of bureaucratization (i.e., degree of regulation) and the degree of engagement (i.e., interaction, communication). We can see analogous patterns in the role of states. High regulation and high monitoring can achieve minimal compliance at best. This may be necessary in situations that are so bad that the most basic conditions do not exist, but regulatory approaches cannot accomplish basic reform. Laissez-faire, leave-it-to-the-districts orientations are also not the answer. The research we have reviewed, and the theory of meaning, which we hold as the key to real reform, strongly suggest that low to medium regulation (guidelines more than prescriptions), combined with high engagement (negotiation, technical assistance, monitoring, feedback, problem solving), works better.

The capacity of state departments to perform this more active role requires more attention, as does the interrelationship between state departments, intermediate service agencies, and districts. And there is great variation in resources devoted to education. The top five states in the country spent approximately $6,000 per pupil in 1987, while the bottom six spent $2,600 (Clark & Astuto, 1989).

The current trends are difficult to discern in terms of impact, as the tension between intensification and restructuring plays itself out. Many states that expected rapid reform through legislative order are now rethinking their approaches (Firestone et al., 1989a; see also Bellon, Bellon, Blank, Brian, & Kershaw, 1989b, on Tennessee; Routh, 1989, on Florida). Accountability mechanisms combined with support can be effective in highlighting issues, increasing expectations, and influencing local action (Wohlstetter, 1989). Individual states are also much more inclined to support restructuring experiments at the district level (David, 1989b). The Education Commission of the States is sponsoring a fundamental experiment, in which it is colloborating with the Coalition of Essential Schools in a project called Re-Learning (ECS, 1989). The purpose is to work with participating schools and states to redesign learning from "schoolhouse to statehouse."

It is too early to tell what the impact of the new development will be. Certainly a number of governors are committed to continuing educational reform, and new alliances between governors and President Bush are forming to define and act on national goals. National and state pushes for reform, as we have seen, can at best provide opportunities for improvement. How states relate to their districts, and how districts capitalize on or ignore the opportunities, are the crucial variables in statewide reform.

CANADIAN FEDERAL AND PROVINCIAL GOVERNMENTS

Before taking up the main implications of the role of governments in school reform, I turn to a consideration of the Canadian scene.

Education reform in Canada is less complex to explain than that in the United States, but no more manageable. Three general observations should be made at the outset: (1) the federal role is very limited; (2) each of the provinces and territories has become increasingly concerned about school improvement, restructuring, and the like; and (3) there is a dearth of policy research and development.

The Federal Government

The best introduction to the federal role in education is by way of money and policy. The federal government provides some of the former and extremely little of the latter, being explicitly discouraged from doing so by the provinces and by its own reluctance. The British North America Act (1867) states that provinces "may exclusively make laws in education" (Section 93).

For all intents and purposes there is no federal involvement in elementary and secondary education in Canada, except for specialized populations: Indians and Inuits, armed forces and dependants, members of penal institutions, and direct aid to the Yukon and the Northwest Territories (Hodgson, 1988). There is some indirect funding, most of which is in general revenues. The Established Programs Financing Act (EPF) provides revenue to provinces for post-secondary education, with no policy conditions. Most provinces receive Equalization Payments as revenue to provincial budgets, but there is no necessary link to education expenditures, let alone policy. Other revenues or programs exist in the areas of the two official languages, multiculturalism and job training, and employment programs (Hodgson, 1988). Nearly all of these programs operate outside the elementary and secondary education system.

What it all amounts to is that the federal government provides necessary revenues to support the education system, but hardly influences educational policy. An external review of Canadian educational policy by the Organization for Economic Cooperation and Development (OECD, 1976) put it this way: "Officially there is *no* federal presence in the area of educational policy . . . no federal authority with the word 'Education' in its title" (p. 89, emphasis in original). But the OECD examiners also note that there is a federal presence in education "as long as nobody calls it educational policy, and as long as there are no overt strings attached to the money coming from Ottawa" (p. 89). It is interesting to note that both levels of government—the federal and the provincial—are reluctant to talk about the federal role. There are suggestions from time to time, usually from people outside government, to establish a federal ministry in this direction. One of the results of this avoidance of educational policy discussion, according to OECD reviews, is the lack of a national policy or set of goals for education. The Council of Ministers of Education in Canada (CMEC) is a forum for broad discussion and liaison, but does not play a national policy role. There is some growing pressure to establish a national federal-provincial department or entity, but nothing has happened as yet.

The situation in Canada, then, is very different from that in the United States. Even with some reductions of federal funds, the U.S. federal government, as we have seen, has an important impact on state and local reform. And the national system of education laboratories, research centers, and agencies like the National Science Foundation provides direct funds for program innovation, critical policy analysis, focused research, and synthesis and dissemination of knowledge, as well as support for implementation. By contrast, in Canada as a whole, there is a glaring absence of innovation development, policy research, and evaluation in education. While there is not much more policy research at the provincial level, it is at this level that we see policy formation and implementation action.

The Provincial Governments

There are fewer than 1,000 school districts in Canada. Among the 10 provinces, Quebec has the largest number of districts (255), and Prince Edward Island the smallest (2); the rest range between 33 and 188. The numbers include Catholic school districts, which under the constitution are part of the public system. On average, school districts in Canada are larger in size (geographically and in numbers of students) than those in the United States. Educational policy is the responsibility of each provincial ministry of education, with certain responsibilities defined for local boards of education. Most provinces have regional offices, which, unlike most intermediate units in the United States are formally an arm of the provincial ministry.

Despite provincial autonomy, the goals, educational trends, and problems of implementation in all provinces are similar in many respects. Program and curriculum policy come in the form of official curriculum guidelines for each subject area, produced by the provincial ministry. These guidelines are usually developed by provincial committees or task forces with membership drawn from among teachers, administrators, university professors, and ministry personnel. The guidelines are developed, disseminated, reviewed, and revised on a cyclical basis every several years. In addition to the main curricula, ministries develop other educational policies governing all aspects of education—special education legislation, programs mandating or supporting parent advisory councils, work-education programs, and so on. Recently, major comprehensive restructuring initiatives have been undertaken in many provinces, usually originating from the Premier's office rather than from the Ministry of Education.

To better understand the orientations and impact of provincial departments or ministeries of education, I summarize the issues from two perspectives. One is to examine the curriculum policy guideline process, which is the mainstay of regular curriculum and school improvement activities. The other is to examine some recent restructuring examples that are more radical in nature.

The Curriculum Policy Process

Initiation. Until the early 1960s, curriculum guidelines in most provinces were highly content-specific. Since that time they have gone through a period of general statements or suggestions (approximately 1965 to 1975) to the current trend of increasing specificity of goals and expected outcomes. In the period of general guidelines there were enormous problems. The guidelines were deliberately left general on the assumption that local boards and teachers would develop the details. The main problem faced by districts and teachers was that it was not at all clear what the proposed policies really meant in practice. Nearly every province in the past fifteen years has taken to defining the curriculum more carefully. Guidelines typically include a list of objectives, topics, and content to be covered, and ideas and resource suggestions for teaching activities and evaluation. Most guidelines are by subject area and cover several grade levels according to the particular province's organization of the grade-level divisions. Thus, they do not constitute courses of study and leave two major dilemmas. First, even with further definition, the latest curriculum guidelines and documents are not in "implementable" form. Goal statements are more clear, content to be covered is set down more specifically, and reference to expected learning outcomes is tighter; but the *means* of implementation (e.g., teaching strategies and activities) are not well developed or integrated. Resource or support documents are frequently produced, but serve as a range of suggestions only. This lack of direction is not in itself a bad thing, however, as it allows decisions to be made at other levels (e.g., the district and the classroom).

The second set of problems at the development stage arises because the process is beset with political and ideological difficulties—many of them quite innocent, but just as consequential. The task forces or committees that develop the guidelines are formally representative of different groups. The fact that there is selectivity on committees is only a small part of the problem. Unrealistic time lines (politically driven and in many ways inevitable), value conflicts within the committees and certainly outside them, and insufficient resources, skills, or time to develop details and a reluctance to do so—all add up to an inauspicious start for many guidelines. Fowler (1979) comments on his experience in working with committees in Saskatchewan.

> Chief decision-makers pressure committees to produce a "final" product at the earliest possible date. Sometimes these work schedules produce undue stress on the working committee. With the introduction of such stress, decisions unfortunately often become based on unsubstantiated evidence and complex problems become oversimplified or glossed over in the rush to produce an end product. (p. 7)

Governments can't win. If they encourage widespread debate during the development phase, the policy gets delayed and the discussions bog down in abstract goals (not on what changes in practice are at stake). By the time the new guideline hits the streets it may be discredited for some and insufficiently developed for others.

There are positive features to this process, depending on one's viewpoint. It allows for debate at the development phase and great latitude at the implementation phase (since the policies usually are not highly specified). Moreover, in most provinces guideline revision is just reaching its second or third major cycle, so that there is some *cumulative* development occurring in terms of greater clarity of and agreement on goals, and better materials and resources for implementation.

Implementation.   Regardless of what happens at the policy formation or initiation phase, a lot of things can be done or undone when a guideline is introduced for use. There are no studies available that describe the details of what ministry personnel do in introducing and providing for or facilitating implementation. A picture of some of the main issues can be derived from research on how school people perceive the role of ministries of education, and from some inferences based on (1) what is known on the surface about the role of the ministry, and (2) what implementation theory and research tell us.

The problems of implementation are essentially the same as those examined in Chapter 5. At this point, I am more interested in the particular role of the ministries of education. Two aspects that stand out relate to *guidelines/materials development* itself, and *how the ministry goes about implementation*.

Curriculum guidelines are not (and are not intended to be) the actual curriculum materials to be used. Depending on the subject area and the province, they can go some distance in providing sources of ideas and activities, but they are not the intact curriculum for use. And many teachers do not use them. For example, in the province-wide assessment of reading in British Columbia, Tuinman and Kendall (1980, pp. 140, 152) found that two-thirds of the elementary school teachers and one-half of the secondary school teachers had not consulted the Curriculum Guide in the previous six months; only 17% and 26% of elementary and secondary school teachers, respectively, reported that the guide had a "significant impact" on their teaching. In other curriculum areas in British Columbia similar results were found: In social studies, for instance, almost 50% of the teachers responded at the low end of a helpfulness scale in rating the guide on "helpful teaching suggestions" (Aoki et al., 1977, pp. 62–66).

For most teachers the "curriculum in use" is derived from one or more of the following sources: textbooks from commercial publishers, materials developed by their local districts, materials borrowed or adapted from other districts that have developed curriculum, or piecemeal planning and use of resources by individual teachers. There are several problems with this approach. Textbooks by themselves, although they are approved by the ministry, are incomplete matches to the curriculum guidelines; districts that produce curricula do not necessarily have the resources to develop products of high quality; and there is often limited knowledge across districts about what has been developed in other locations, little money for obtaining the materials, and less for engaging in in-service education to use them. Put more generally, provincial governments have not put much money into the development of validated exemplary curriculum materials or innovative projects. Minor amounts have been provided for learning materials development in some provinces, but these add up to only a pittance. Nor am I suggesting that large amounts of money should have been directed to curriculum materials. Development without a system of access to information and people (e.g., in-service assistance) would have been a waste of resources. The problem remains, however, that Canadian-based curriculum materials are not widely available, and ways of aligning appropriate materials of high quality from whatever source with curriculum guidelines have not yet been well worked out.

A further aspect of implementation concerns how ministries go about introducing and following through on new and revised guidelines. They may do this either directly (using their own staff) or indirectly (providing resources for implementation). In the direct role, most ministries of education provide orientation sessions throughout the province about the nature of the particular curriculum. This approach presents at least two problematic issues: geographical distances and the fact that the number of districts may allow for only brief orientation sessions to district *representatives;* thus, the individual teacher may receive *no* orientation. Over 45 percent of the secondary school teachers in the Reading Assess-

ment Survey said that they received no formal orientation to the Curriculum Guide (Tuinman & Kendall, 1980, p. 152). And the ministry person
conducting the sessions may not be thoroughly knowledgeable about the
guideline and how to implement it, since it was probably developed by
another group or another department.

Even if the orientation goes well, the real implementation difficulties
lie beyond the introduction. In some cases, ministries have funded regional orientation workshops conducted by teachers, consultants, and
others who had participated in developing the new guideline—that is, by
those who were most knowledgeable about it. These pre-implementation
workshops, no matter how stimulating, are at best limited to producing
awareness, ideas, and interest in *attempting* implementation. As we have
seen so often, it is *during* the initial attempts at implementation that assistance is most needed and is frequently unavailable. The primary assumption about follow-up is that implementation is the responsibility of
school districts, schools, and individual teachers. But whether they accept
this responsibility depends on their priorities and processes, as described
in the relevant chapters in Part II. The ministries' role in follow-up has
varied over time and across provinces—from providing technical assistance, to clarifying and monitoring implementation, to conducting reviews
for further policy revision. Not the least of the difficulties is vacillation
and ambiguity as to whether ministry personnel are there to assist or to
monitor implementation; more fundamentally, there may be disagreement among ministry personnel about what should be emphasized in a
curriculum guideline. Assistance is problematic for reasons already
stated: numbers of people to be reached, lack of knowledge about the
change and/or the change process, and overlap or ambiguity—either in
the minds of ministry personnel or in the views of school people—about
the assistance vs. regulation roles.

Research studies asking teachers how helpful they find external
groups confirm the relatively limited impact of ministry personnel. A representative sample of teachers in the British Columbia Social Studies Assessment rated the ministry of education lowest of eight external sources:
on a helpfulness scale of 1 to 5 the mean rating for ministry personnel
was 1.56 (Aoki et al., 1977, p. 55). Similar findings are reported in other
surveys (Leithwood & MacDonald, 1981). The limited impact of ministry
personnel on local implementation is not surprising. Their numbers and
resources are small in the face of the overwhelming number of schools
and personnel within their jurisdiction. And it is a thankless task to bear
responsibility for policies and programs that by virtue of the inherent
difficulties in the implementation process never go smoothly.

Regulation or monitoring of implementation is just as difficult as providing assistance, since for many guidelines it is not at all clear exactly
what implementation would look like, and it is not easy to obtain valid

implementation information concerning what is really happening in the classroom. In short, ministry personnel have their own problems of meaning about educational change.

Provinces have, however, focused increasingly on implementation and school improvement during the 1980s. My own review in the mid-1980s reported a number of such policies and projects across the country (Fullan, 1986), which has been confirmed and updated by Wideen (1988). Saskatchewan's *Directions'* initiative, British Columbia's Program Implementation Unit, and Ontario's Curriculum Review Development and Implementation (CRDI) process are three among several efforts aimed directly at implementation (Fullan, 1986; Wideen, 1988). Many ministries of education have also had an indirect effect on implementation by sponsoring provincial and regional conferences, workshops, and projects on school improvement, principal leadership, the change process, and so on. They have also raised expectations and provided guidelines that expressly highlight implementation as the responsibility of districts. This has created an aura of implementation expectations, although, as I said in Chapter 10, the district should be seen as the unit that sorts out these expectations (see also Fullan, Anderson, & Newton, 1986).

Despite the focus on implementation during the 1980s, the current trend is away from implementation per se toward monitoring, testing, and restructuring. Provincial governments maintain high expectations for local implementation by districts, but are shifting their own attention to assessment and major new policy development.

Monitoring/Evaluation.   The third major responsibility of ministries of education is to assess the use and impact of public policy in education. There has been the familiar "accountability" trend in defining core subjects and testing student achievement, but it reaches nowhere the degree of specificity or compulsion that the "competency-based" movement has in the United States (see Corbett & Wilson, 1990; Wise, 1988). Until recently there were no compulsory provincial examinations. However, most ministries have now geared up for more evaluation data gathering. One of the first examples was the British Columbia Learning Assessment Program (LAP). Mussio and Greer (1980, p. 29) state that the main objectives are to

1. Monitor student achievement over time;
2. Assist curriculum developers at the provincial and local levels in the process of improving curriculum and developing suitable resource materials;
3. Provide information that can be used in determining the allocation of resources at provincial and district levels;

4. Provide direction for change in teacher education and professional development;
5. Provide direction for educational research; and
6. Inform the public of some of the strengths and weaknesses of the public school system.

Province-wide data are gathered on student attitudes and achievement and on attitudes and perceptions of parents, teachers, administrators, and other district staff on a wide variety of matters relating to the curriculum and its use. The assessments are carried out by teams. The general results are made public to all concerned; student achievement data by district are fed back to the districts for information value and possible use to make improvements. The assessments began in 1976 and operate on a cyclical schedule.

The other provinces conduct regular reviews of curriculum and are moving in the direction of collecting more detailed, systematic information. Ontario has developed the Ontario Assessment Instrument Pool (oaip), which is designed to provide an inventory of testing instruments to assess the achievement of objectives in the curriculum guidelines in each subject area. Program reviews are conducted in the various curriculum areas by ministry personnel, although most of the reviews are not seen as impactful by school people. Cooperative reviews may also be carried out by agreement between a school system and the ministry, and seem to be more successful. Whatever the case, all of the ministries of education in Canada are engaged in developing procedures for reviewing curriculum needs and quality, and are considering the question of how best to assess student learning. The latest trends involve more explicit student achievement testing to provide province-wide and district "benchmarks" for the main subject areas across several grade levels (see the next section on restructuring).

The collection of evaluation data presents difficulties. The field of educational evaluation has burgeoned over the past two decades, and in the same period has come the recognition that it is a very complicated business. There are three major interrelated problem areas that seem to plague provincial curriculum assessments (and any program evaluation): what information to collect, how to gather it, and above all how to use it. I can only highlight some of the main issues. In simple terms the question of what information to collect can be divided into two categories: data on student achievement or what we might call *implementation outcomes,* and information on *implementation practice* and difficulties (e.g., teacher use in the classroom, quality of materials, forms of help available). The "what" question, then, concerns the range of information that is targeted for collection. Information on learning outcomes without other implementation data is very difficult to interpret and use; on the other hand, implementation data are very difficult to collect, particularly because it is not always clear what implementation would look like in practice.

The question of how to gather information raises another set of issues. I leave aside the more technical methodological matters and mention what might be called "relationship" questions. These include questions of who does the review, of validity, and of ethics. The ministry may take greater or less control over the review, conducting the review itself or contracting it to a third party. Validity refers to whether the information obtained is an accurate reflection of what is actually happening (e.g., in terms of practices and outcomes). Ethics refers to several delicate issues concerning how the information is to be used fairly and justly (see House, 1980).

The final key question—how to use the information—ties together the three sets of questions. What information is collected obviously shapes what can be potentially used. Information on learning outcomes, for example, without information on implementation practices/difficulties can create pressure for reform but not very constructive pressure, because it indicates only what the problem is, not how to address it. Additional information would be needed to confront the latter. How the data are collected affects validity (for example, people don't usually provide accurate responses if they think the information might be used against them). If the information is not valid or is too general, it will be either ignored or misused.

Even if reasonably accurate data have been obtained, the real problem lies in figuring out how the information can be used. Frankly, this gets us back to the *beginning* of the implementation process. Stated another way, the evaluation system must be related to implementation strategies for acting on the results. While finding ourselves back at "GO" sounds discouraging, evaluations can and do have an impact. Evaluators frequently make a distinction between summative and formative evaluation. The summative impact of provincial assessments is more visible, because the information can be used to revise policy, i.e., the curriculum guidelines or materials. This use of data does not directly affect *practice*—it alters policy and development, which may or may not lead to subsequent implementation (depending on the presence or absence of other factors). Formative impact occurs when the evaluation data are used to improve practice. Linking evaluation data to instructional improvement, as we saw earlier, requires a sophisticated system of relationships and activities. A large part of the problem relates to the lack of attention to the "black box" of implementation. Testing data provide information on the achievement of desired educational objectives. Implementation involves questions of which *instructional* activities would best address objectives.

Unfortunately, much of the conflict and debate in education focuses on objectives and outcomes without attending to the critical intervening activities (i.e., instruction and learning activities) that link them together.

Restructuring. Recently provinces have made a qualitative shift toward more fundamental change. Dissatisfied with the performance of the educational system and the glacial pace of change through normal curriculum cycles, governments (not just the education ministries) are introducing comprehensive reforms. I use the cases of British Columbia and Ontario to illustrate.

British Columbia has embarked on *Year 2000: A Curriculum and Assessment Framework for the Future* (British Columbia Ministry of Education, 1988). The new policy revamps the entire education system based on a set of 23 principles in four areas: Learning and the Learner (3), Curriculum (12), Assessment and Evaluation (5), and Reporting (3). Selected principles include

- Learning requires the active participation of the learner. (Learning)
- The provincial curriculum will be organized according to four strands: humanities, sciences, fine arts, and practical arts. (Curriculum)
- The provincial curriculum will include a common curriculum which incorporates elements of all four strands. (Curriculum)
- The provincial curriculum will emphasize intended learning outcomes rather than learning activities. (Curriculum)
- Alternative pathways to complete the common curriculum will be available . . . but streaming is not appropriate. (Curriculum)
- Assessment should be done regularly and frequently. (Assessment)
- Certification of learner achievement should be done on the broadest possible assessment base. (Assessment)
- Reporting to students and parents should be done regularly and frequently. (Reporting)
- Reporting to students and parents should be based on a learner profile system. (Reporting)
(B.C. Ministry of Education, 1988)

Learning dimensions (knowledge, skills, and attitudes), goals (intellectual, human and social, and career development), and curriculum strands (humanities, sciences, fine arts, practical arts) are outlined in a single integrated curriculum model. Learning profiles will be developed according to the model. The four-year Primary Program (P1–P4) will be nongraded, the seven-year Intermediate Program (I1–I7) will integrate the traditional subjects into the four strands, and the two-year Graduation Program (G1–G2) will have three broad options (career programs, college/university preparation programs, and an exploration program), with all students required to participate in work experience, and the curriculum and learning subject to provincial standards of assessment.

A *Policy Directions* document (British Columbia Ministry of Education, 1989a), adopted as official policy, commits the province to the curriculum and states the teaching profession, governance, financial implications, and time lines for full implementation. It is stated that $1.4 billion in additional funds will be allocated for implementation over the next 10 years. The 10-year time line, including detailed target dates by year and within year, and responsibilities of the ministry, schools, districts, and provincial organizations (e.g., universities, teacher union) are outlined in a companion document entitled *Working Plan #1 1989–1999: A Plan to Implement Policy Directions* (British Columbia Ministry of Education, 1989b). Finally, a revised document—*Year 2000: A Framework for Learning*—provides a basic focus for the 1990s (British Columbia Ministry of Education, 1989c).

The Ontario Ministry of Education's *Restructuring the Education System* (1989) is less explicit, but equally radical in its direction. The system is reorganized into four components: the Early Years (junior and senior kindergarten), the Formative Years (grades 1–6), the Transition Years (grades 7–9), and the Specialization Years (grades 10–12). The offering of junior kindergarten will be a requirement for all school boards. Commitment at all four levels is made to new policy and program development, and to funds for learning materials and staff development. The curriculum will be "revitalized," a new core curriculum will be developed for grades 7–9, and streaming will be eliminated in grade 9. New diploma requirements will be introduced for grades 10–12. Within these specialization years, a major priority will be placed on the redesign of technological studies, including new approaches to program delivery and new partnerships with business, industry, and the community. A parallel set of tasks will be undertaken "to develop and coordinate teacher education policies to meet the needs created by these restructuring initiatives" (p. 3).

The restructuring document contains an *Action Plan 1989–94*. A Ministry of Education Steering and Management Committee oversees a Learning Program Advisory Council (LPAC). Reporting to LPAC will be small "Work Teams" in six areas (Early, Formative, Transition, and Specialization as well as Technological and Teacher Education), which have been established to complete the tasks. Reaction Groups for each work area will provide formative input. The action plan, as in British Columbia's plan, lays out the tasks and subtasks by year, primary responsibility, and start and end time lines.

Three observations about these restructuring trends in Canada stand out. First, one can see rather clearly the legitimate state role in forging new societal images of educational reform. Without such intervention the impetus for major change would be much less, if not absent. Second, the models and strategies are overly rational. We can predict massive implementation problems, which the policy documents ignore or gloss over. Third, there is no national capacity and limited provincial capacity to conduct systematic policy research on the evolution of these reforms.

GUIDELINES FOR GOVERNMENTS

Governments get lots of advice, and I will not attempt to add another long list of the ills of governments and what they should do differently. It is easy to treat governments as distant villains in the educational change process. While it is the case that government agencies and personnel should do some things differently if they wish to maximize their influence, our theory of meaning and change should generate considerable sympathy for their lot. The multilevel implementation process is, in a word, capricious. Government staff cannot abdicate their responsibility to oversee changes called for through legislative policy making. Local educational personnel do not see the constant pressures on government staff to get a high-priority program delivered and to balance countless competing demands from above and below, when the total amount of time and resources is not nearly equal (and getting less equal) to the requirements of doing the job. There is no reason to believe that civil servants are any less virtuous than the rest of us in wanting to see school improvements made.

Within this context of the difficulties of bringing about large-scale change, I will suggest a small number of major guidelines to highlight some of the things governments will have to do and emphasize, if they expect their policies and programs to stand a better chance of becoming implemented in practice. In the most general sense, of course, the advice is to understand the principles and processes of what makes for effective change (as, for example, described in this book) as a basis for generating particular approaches and follow-through support for implementation. Beyond this I will suggest six broad mutually reinforcing guidelines relating to

1. compliance vs. capacity,
2. state–district relationships,
3. implementation planning and resources,
4. the preparation of government staff,
5. a focus on second-order change, and
6. an appreciation of complexity and persistence in the change process (see also Anderson et al., 1987; Elmore & McLaughlin, 1988; Fuhrman, Clune, & Elmore, 1988).

Understanding the Difference Between Compliance and Capacity

The most insightful and simply stated version of this guideline is contained in Elmore's (1980) booklet. He writes: "There is a critical difference between the ability or willingness of implementors to comply with rules and their capacity to successfully deliver a service. Implementation depends more on capacity than it does on compliance" (p. 37). Governments are legally responsible for ensuring compliance with policies, but there are limits to what can be accomplished through regulation. If governments confine themselves to a regulatory role, two things happen, which actually interfere with implementation.

First, because the levels and parts of educational systems are "loosely coupled," and because program change is not simple to assess, it requires tremendous energy to find out what is happening; the more preoccupied governments become with surveillance, the more energy must be spent at all levels on administrative paper work, reporting, and other compliance-type information. Hill, Wuchitech, and Williams (1980) and Lutz and Maddirala (1988) found that district and school administrators spend enormous amounts of time complying with state and federal paper-work and reporting requirements (see also Corbett & Wilson, 1990 for the dysfunctions of compliance requirements).

The second and related reason why preoccupation with compliance hinders implementation is that it diverts energies and attention away from developing local capacity to make improvements. Elmore (1980, p. 12) suggests that policy-makers should be more concerned with the state of local capacity for program delivery and with figuring out ways of supporting, guiding, and prodding its further development. As we have seen, some government agencies are primarily concerned with their regulatory and bureaucratic role, while others take a more direct interest in the substance of the program and whether it is actually working. To illustrate the importance of this distinction, information on how many children participated in a program, how many teachers were involved in in-service sessions, and the like, tells nothing about whether the program is working to bring about the intended changes. I said earlier in this chapter that evaluation information frequently does not have an impact; it requires a sophisticated evaluation system for program improvement to be effected, and this system is related more to capacity-building than to control through compliance.

Stated another way, if a program is not working in certain settings, governments should know whether the reasons have more to do with competing priorities and lack of resources, skills, and leadership (i.e., capacity issues) or with diversion of funds, outright resistance, etc. (i.e., compliance). If capacity is the problem, increased surveillance will not help and may hinder actual implementation. Cowden and Cohen (1979,

p. 91) observe that for the odd major program, governments can pour in tremendous resources (money, power, and knowledge) and have an impact, but it is not feasible to do this very often, because the resources required to enforce the change in this manner are prohibitive. There is no simple solution, because governments must be concerned with both compliance and capacity; it will be necessary to decide on the balance of attention and resources to be devoted to each of these two aspects.

Focusing on capacity, as Elmore indicates, is more challenging, difficult, and interesting than only gathering compliance information. The implication of guideline 1 is that federal government program grantors should pay attention to how the capacity of state education agencies can be supported and further developed. (The move to block grants *may* facilitate this stance, since less federal resources are required for regulatory information gathering.) State agencies, in turn, should determine how they could relate to intermediate and local agencies. In Canada provincial ministries of education would consider how they can work with local districts more effectively in this regard.

Guideline 1, then, advises governments to concentrate on helping to improve the capacity of other agencies to implement changes.

State–District Relationships

It may seem as if de-emphasizing compliance is tantamount to allowing receiving agencies to do as they please. Paradoxically, concentrating on capacity requires more interaction and yields greater knowledge of what local agencies are attempting to do. We have seen several problems in the federal/state/local and provincial/local relationships. Ambitious and vague goals, unclear expectations, and episodic or nonexistent contact characterize government/local relationships in many program change efforts.

Guideline 2 stresses the importance of governments being clear about what the policy is and spending time interacting with local agencies about the meaning, expectations, and needs in relation to local implementation. There are some cases of outright rejection of change when local districts simply do not value or actively dislike certain policies; but in most of the research studies cited in this chapter, local districts (or state agencies vis-à-vis federal departments) desired *more* clarification and *more* assistance in implementing adopted programs, which government personnel were often reluctant to provide (perhaps because they did not really understand how the policy could be implemented). At the outset, Elmore (1980, p. 29) recommends, the smart policy-maker will say, "Before we go too far with this idea, can you tell me what it will look like in practice?" Once a policy is on its way, it is necessary for government personnel to devote time to interacting with implementers and to demonstrating that program change in practice is a priority. The benefits are in both directions. First, since the problem of meaning is inevitable when people first contend with a new policy, there must be plenty of opportunities to ask for clarification and assistance. When federal or state agencies clarify expectations and respond to requests for assistance, it increases the likelihood of implementation. Second, through this interaction government personnel find out about the realities and needs of implementation. But it is a more challenging role, because it requires going beyond the superficial piety of espousing new social policies into the reality of the implementation quagmire.

We have also seen that district variability is a fact, and that many districts are out in front of state policy (Chapter 10 and Fuhrman et al., 1988). "Variability is the rule and uniformity is the exception in the relationship among policy, administration and practice," observe Elmore and McLaughlin (1988, p. 34). They recommend that reforms must adapt to and capitalize on variability, and that adaptation is not simply acquiescing to local desires, but is *"more fundamentally, active problem-solving"* (p. 36, my emphasis).

Implementation Planning and Resources

Guideline 3 is implicit in the other guidelines; namely, the underlying assumption is that an explicit but flexible implementation plan is needed to guide the process of bringing about change in practice. One of the foundations for such a plan, as Williams (1980, p. 101) observes, is that top leaders must really *want* better implementation to the point of continually asking staff and local personnel about implementation, committing resources to support implementation, and being realistic but insistent about progress. "At basic issue," says Williams, "is whether the agency can alter its orientation and style of decision making to develop the resources and the organizational structure needed for *implementing* the implementation perspective" (p. 101, emphasis in original).

A few writers have offered more specific guidelines as to how "implementation analysis" and planning may be carried out. Elmore (1980) talks about the importance of "reasoning through implementation problems *before* policy decisions are firmly made" (p. 3, his emphasis). He outlines a set of guiding questions for doing "backward mapping": "Instead of beginning at the top of the system with a new policy and reasoning through a series of actions required to implement it, begin at the bottom of the system, with the most concrete set of actions, and reason backward to the policy" (p. 29).

As implementation gets under way, the critical supporting elements are those identified in other guidelines: balancing the relative emphasis on compliance and capacity; setting up information-gathering procedures that are most likely to influence local action; fostering interaction between local personnel and government staff and others external to the local district; promoting program development and technical assistance resources; and enhancing the capabilities of in-house staff to work effectively among themselves and with local and regional agencies.

Anderson and associates (1987) are quite clear about the main implications for state action derived from their large-scale study of implementation.

1. make school improvement a high priority,
2. get support for school improvement,
3. select valid school improvement programs,
4. facilitate implementation at the local level, and
5. highlight success and build networks (see Anderson et al., 1987, pp. 83–85 for more detailed strategies).

For more complex changes like restructuring, additional steps will be necessary to assist the development and networking of prototypical solutions. Careful evolutionary planning will be of the essence (Chapter 6).

The Preparation of Government Staff

The previous three guidelines assume that the government has its own house in order. If this is not the case, we can hardly expect government staff to extend clarity and support to others. Gideonse (1980, p. 67) comments on the problem: "What is needed is a consciousness on the part of top management on down, that the daily life of the organization is at least as important as the deliberations on high policy, for it is in the daily life that that policy is implemented. If the atmosphere is sour, so will be the implementation." Middle- and lower-level government staff are the ones who are more directly responsible for implementation, and, says Gideonse, "they are often quite unknowledgeable about the background rationale that shaped the thinking of key decisions" (p. 68). The problem can be especially acute when there are regional as well as central offices (as is the case in most provinces in Canada and most states in the U.S.). Williams (1980, p. 112) stresses the importance of knowledge and competence among field (regional) staff for implementation. Guideline 4 is constantly violated through frequent government reorganizations and shifting of personnel without proper preparation or sufficient longevity in a role to be effective.

Guideline 4 suggests that whether central or regional staff are being considered, government agency leaders should take special steps to ensure that their own staff, especially those who have the most direct contact with the field, have the opportunity to develop knowledge and competence regarding the policy and pro-

gram, as well as in how to facilitate implementation (again, competence in the *content of the change* and in the *change process,* respectively). This is not just a matter of having periodic workshops or other training opportunities for staff; it must be accomplished in the daily decision-making, communication, planning, and implementation activities engaged in by government staff. (See also Berman's 1978 description of macro implementation.)

Focus on Second-Order Change

We have seen that first-order changes focusing on spelling out objectives and competencies are easier to legislate than are second-order changes, which require altering organizational structures, patterns, and practices of individuals (Cuban, 1988c, pp. 228 ff). *The fifth guideline suggests that governments should become preoccupied with achieving more basic changes in the teaching profession in the practice and organization of teaching, and in the learning patterns and experiences of all students.* Without this fundamental focus, new policies and reforms will become ends in themselves. Questions of how do we implement or avoid particular policies will displace the underlying purposes that policies purport to address. The problem of coherence is very much embedded in this guideline. State policies, as observed earlier in this chapter, are often unconnected and fail to achieve any coordinated impact. Focusing on second-order change means that integration of policies, aimed at basic changes in teaching and learning, will become a raison d'etre of policy formation, follow-through, and revision. Such synergy is essential for addressing the complex reform agenda before us (see Elmore, 1988, for specific strategies focusing on second-order changes). Supporting and stimulating school districts to restructure is very much a part of guideline 5, but states should be wary of superficial structural changes.

Combine an Appreciation of Complexity With Persistence of Effort

The change process is complex. Simple solutions do more harm than good. We know a great deal about the ins and outs of successful reform. Putting this knowledge to use, however, is not straightforward. What is clear, as Wilson and Corcoran (1988) advise, is that "policy-makers must temper their desires for immediate and total change with an understanding of the complexity of the change process" (p. 159). This does not mean reducing expectations and attempting less. On the contrary, comprehensive multifaceted, interrelated, short-, medium- and long-term strategies are required, and must be persistently applied and continuously amplified and reshaped (for one example, see Honig, 1988). *Guideline 6 says that complexity and persistence go hand in hand.*

The length of this chapter gives some indication of just how entangled and dilemma-ridden the role of governments in implementation really is. Federal/state/regional/local relationships in the United States and federal/provincial/regional/local relationships in Canada represent intimidating challenges for those who wish to comprehend—let alone influence—educational reform. Opportunity for input into shaping reforms is needed at all levels. Inequality of education is not likely to be addressed adequately at the local level, either because of discrimination (intended or not) or because of lack of resources for developing and learning to use needed changes. Similarly, acceptable solutions are not likely to be designed at the policy level, because variations in local situations and priorities require variations in solutions and/or because local institutions vary in their commitment and capacity to implement new policies. In either case governments have a legitimate and essential role in educational reform because *problems of equity and program quality are unlikely to be resolved at the local level.*

As a final word of advice, we should be wary of local dependency. Districts whose main stance in relation to state reform is to seek only the literal meaning of a given policy are involved in a form of goal displacement and dependency. The policy becomes an end in itself, and the search for meaning tends to be confined inside the policy instead of in relation to local problems and needs. Effective districts actively engage and exploit state policies as part of local problem solving. The role of governments is to enlarge the problem-solving arena and to provide the kinds of pressure and support that force and reinforce local districts to pursue continuous improvements.

Chapter 14

Professional Preparation
of Teachers

The fact is that our primary value concerns our need to help ourselves change and learn, for us to feel that we are growing in our understanding of where we have been, where we are, and what we are about, and that we are enjoying what we are doing. . . . To help others to change without this being preceded and accompanied by an exquisite awareness of the process in ourselves is "delivering a product or service" which truly has little or no significance for our personal or intellectual growth.

—Sarason (1972), p. 122

Educational change involves *learning* how to do something new. Given this, if there is any single factor crucial to change it is professional development. In its broadest definition professional development encompasses what teachers bring to the profession and what happens to them throughout their careers.

In the next two chapters, I consider the professional preparation of teachers (this chapter), and the continuing professional development of teachers and administrators (Chapter 15). Guidelines for action are suggested at the end of Chapter 15. The education of educators is a burgeoning business that has much promise, but a poor track record. These two chapters should be read together because the educator as life-long learner is the key to future reform.

There are two fundamental assumptions underlying Chapters 14 and 15:

- Teacher education, or teacher as learner, from day one, must be thought of as a career-long proposition. Teacher education or teacher development is a continuum of learning.
- Teacher development and school development must go hand in hand. You cannot have one without the other.

On the positive side, teacher education has been receiving enormous attention over the past five years. There are many potentially powerful elements currently in the mix. On the other hand, teacher education policy and practice is still in bad shape, lacking coherence or simply wrong-headed, and squandering the many pockets of success that are cropping up more and more frequently. Teacher development is the nexus for so many of the issues of meaning, change, and improvement addressed throughout this book, and as such is absolutely fundamental to any long-lasting solution.

The 1990s represent a crucial time in teacher development, and hence in prospects for reform. For the first time in 20 years there is a growing need and indeed a shortage of teachers in North America. It is estimated that more than one-and-a-half million new teachers will have to be hired in the United States in the seven-year period from 1988 to 1995—involving a turnover of more than one-half of the total teaching population now in schools (Darling-Hammond & Berry, 1988, p. 4). All through the 1990s more than 200,000 new teachers will be hired each year—double the annual rate of hirings in the late 1970s (see also Darling-Hammond, 1990). In Ontario, the 20-year period from 1988 to 2008 will see similar increases in the need for new teachers (Smith, 1989). In Ontario almost one-half of the current teaching force will be replaced between 1988 and 1995. What happens by way of selection and teacher development during this period and its immediate aftermath in schools will determine the success or failure of educational reform for the next half century. Teacher education is an opportunity and a crisis of enormous proportion.

In this chapter we are going to consider what it means to become a teacher. I examine new developments in the initial preparation and certification of teachers, including the critical induction period of the first year or two of teaching, and alternative certification programs. The perspective introduced in this chapter is one that views educational development as part and parcel of a professional continuum from preservice to induction, to middle and later years of a career, including administrative and consulting roles. Ideally, the phases would be interrelated and cumulative so that relevant "stakeholders" (i.e., universities, schools, teacher unions, state or federal bodies) would engage in collaborative efforts in support of the generation and use of best practices as part of a "whole" rather than focusing on segmented pieces (see Fullan & Connelly, 1990; Hoffman & Edwards, 1987). The prospects are daunting. If it is hard to get two people to cooperate, imagine trying to get huge institutions like governments, universities, districts, schools, and unions to work together on complex matters. There are, however, as we shall see, case examples moving in this direction. And there are many day-to-day ways of forging links in the continuum. In any case, the solution lies in the domain of multiplying the instances of *interactive professionalism* at the one-to-one and cross-institutional levels, and all levels in between.

In 1962, Sarason, Davidson, and Blatt published a book entitled *The*

Preparation of Teachers: An Unstudied Problem in Education. Almost 25 years later thay released a revised edition in which they explicitly and sadly could not change the subtitle (see also Lanier & Little, 1986).

> . . . the fundamental question we address in this book: what is the relationship between the preparation of teachers and the realities they experience when they embark on their careers? That question is as unstudied today—as superficially discussed today—as in previous decades when the quality of education was a source of national concern. (Sarason et al., 1986, p. xiv)

Coincidentally in the same year the Carnegie Task Force on Teaching as a Profession released *A Nation Prepared* (1986), and several other policy manifestoes followed (e.g., the Holmes Group, 1986; the American Association of Colleges for Teacher Education's *Task Force on Teacher Certification,* 1986; the Ontario Ministries of Colleges and Universities, and of Education, *Final Report of the Teacher Education Review Steering Committee,* 1988). As we shall see in this section, virtually for the first time, careful research on teacher preparation and teacher development has begun to take place. It is still very much in its infancy, allowing the editors in the just released *Handbook of Research on Teacher Education* to lament that researchers and other writers on teacher education have a tendency to substitute "glowing accounts of what might be" for actual findings (Houston, Haberman, & Sikula, 1990). But at least "the unstudied problem" is receiving attention for the first time.

One final introductory comment. I have deliberately relegated to the next chapter a consideration of the big issue of recruitment and retention of quality teachers. While recruitment and retention do not chronologically come at the end, it is necessary to understand the whole career of teaching from beginning to end before one can intelligently discuss the kinds of policy incentives and actions currently being debated, which are aimed at attracting and retaining teachers of high quality.

UNIVERSITY PRESERVICE

In considering university preparation programs, I will not attempt to do justice to the many specialized and alternative programs that can be found among the nearly 1,400 teacher education institutions in the United States and the 50 faculties of education in Canada. Instead I will take up several themes related to the university and field experiences of students on their way to becoming teachers. Generally, researchers have found that teacher education programs lack overall coherence and that the purposes of many courses are "complex and hazy" (Floden, McDiarmid, & Werners, 1989; Kennedy, 1990; Lanier & Little, 1986).

Zeichner and Gore (1990) state that there are three major components in preservice education that can influence initial teacher socialization.

1. general education, that is, university liberal arts and science courses completed outside faculties and colleges of education;
2. methods and foundations courses usually completed within education faculties; and
3. field-based experiences usually carried out in elementary and secondary school classrooms.

It turns out that we don't know very much about the actual impact of the above three components, but there are intriguing issues emerging. First, there is a trend toward strengthening academic subject-matter preparation and other liberal arts components such as social science and humanities. However, as Zeichner and Gore (1990) and others have observed, there is a lack of empirical data about the impact of these academic courses on students relative to teaching. Sarason and associates (1986) agree: "Would there be a high relationship between teaching effectiveness and the degree of liberal arts and science background? We consider teacher training an unstudied problem precisely because these kinds of questions have not been investigated" (p. 32).

In any case, the emphasis on academic preparation and other attempts to professionalize teaching by lengthening the total preparation time have resulted in a move from integrated or concurrent four-year undergraduate education programs in favor of fifth year programs or other versions of post-liberal arts consecutive programs. This does not mean that professional components (both on campus and field) could not occur earlier in collaboration with liberal arts and science faculties. Indeed, we and others believe that such pre-education development is essential (Fullan & Connelly, 1990; Sarason et al., 1986). Thus, academic subject courses and social science courses as well as field practice could be geared to arts and science undergraduate students potentially interested in teaching as a career. While such cooperative endeavors between liberal arts and science faculties and education faculties are not unheard of, their development is greatly hampered by the lack of contact, low mutual respect, low status of education within the university, and a host of other disincentives and diversions existing on university campuses (Clifford & Guthrie, 1988; Lanier & Little, 1986). Until these barriers to collaboration are addressed liberal arts and science courses will continue to serve as a general, but largely unknown, backdrop to the preparation of teachers.

Second, the issues get more interesting as we move to the professional components of preservice teacher education progress, which normally include college of education courses (subject methods and foundations) and field-based elements, increasingly, as I have said, in a one-year, post-liberal arts program. Again, we know very little about the impact of these courses on students. This is not to say that they have no impact, only that there is little information on the topic. The learning theories in psychology; the socialization, organization, and community theories in sociology; the philosophies of education; and the application of theory-based teaching techniques across the subject areas, have all remained sources of promise, frustration, and confusion. Most student teachers will say that they get too much theory, that it is irrelevant and a waste of time. Many professors of education, especially those in the social science disciplines, will argue that students get too little theory, that they are uninterested in developing a solid grounding in theories of education and teaching. Most seem to agree, however, that the *integration* of theory and practice is a desirable, if elusive, goal. For example, in a Canadian nationwide survey of faculty and students in 11 English-speaking faculties of education (25% of the total number in Canada), we asked a sample of 1,400 students and 500 faculty members for their assessment of how much importance was actually attached to certain goals in their institutions, and how much importance they thought should be attached to them. One of these goals was "to prepare teachers who can integrate theory and practice." Students and faculty had essentially the same views: While about 30 percent of each group (calculated as those who responded "great" or "very great" on a five-point scale) thought that their institution actually attached a strong emphasis to this goal, about 90 percent thought that this goal should receive a strong emphasis (Fullan, Wideen, Hopkins, & Eastabrook, 1983). This discrepancy between the real and the ideal was one of the largest among the nine goal areas we asked about.

The relationship between theory and practice involves subject matter and methods, as well as foundation courses such as psychology. There is little research on the impact of subject methods courses or psychology courses on teaching effectiveness. Sarason, himself a psychologist of some renown, reports that one of the most frequent criticisms of psychology courses by students "was the lack of opportunity to observe in a live situation, how psychological principles, concepts, and generalizations could be derived" (Sarason et al., 1986, p. 100). Sarason and associates also note that "much that teachers learn is derived from a psychology of *the individual*" (p. ix, their emphasis), which often misses the complexities of classroom interaction, which is a group phenomenon. Indeed one of the most common complaints of student and new teachers is that they haven't been taught to cope with the variety and range of individual students in a group (classroom) setting. Further complicating the matter, Sarason and associates observe that psychology courses often focus on how children learn, not on "how teachers learn" (p. 118). In short, the role of foundations—psychology, history, philosophy, and sociology—in teacher education is fundamentally unconnected with what it means to become an effective teacher (for recommended solutions see Peterson, Clark, & Dickson, 1990; Shulman, 1990; Soltis, 1990).

Even with subject-matter methods courses, Sarason and associates describe three problems.

> First, the emphasis is on how to teach certain subject matter (reading, arithmetic, etc.), but this rarely is accompanied by opportunities for the student to try out the methods. Second, where the student does have such opportunity, it is usually of short duration, and supervision is minimal or nonexistent. Third, and this is felt most keenly by students, what the students obtain in these courses too often has little relevance for teaching a class of children who vary considerably (as is almost always the case) in their achievement in any particular subject matter or skill. (p. 102)

The third component of teacher preparation—field-based or practice teaching—has always been more valued by students, and its presumed practicality has led to increases and extensions of the practicum component of nearly all programs. Yet there are disturbing questions about the actual impact of this move. Over 10 years ago, Tabachnick, Popkewitz, and Zeichner (1979–80) reported on an intensive study of 12 student teachers in a four-semester program that had one semester devoted to practical work in the classroom and seminar discussions about it. They noted: "Student teaching typically involved a very limited range of classroom activities. When student teachers were observed, they were most often engaged in the rather routine and mechanical teaching of precise and short-term skills, in testing and grading children, or in 'management procedures'" (p. 14).

Tabachnick and associates (1979–80) also observed that student teachers frequently worked with prepackaged curriculum materials: "Typically, the students tended to follow the lessons contained in these materials somewhat rigidly rather than using them as guides" (p. 15). The student teachers' work was determined by several factors: "the structure of the school day; the pre-determination of curriculum and content and materials; an emphasis on order, control and busyness" (p. 14). The finding is similar to what Clifton (1979) reports in his Canadian study—that practice teaching is very much a question of "survival in a marginal situation." Tabachnick and associates conclude: "There is no justification in our results for the naive notion that practical experience *must* be useful in introducing students to a wide range of teaching abilities" (p. 27, their emphasis). They recall Dewey's (1975) admonition: "It is a mistake to assume that any experience is intrinsically desirable, apart from its ability to evoke a certain quality of response in individuals" (p. 75).

In his detailed case studies of student teaching Griffin (1989a) also found that student teachers tended to be in a relatively passive role, experienced a narrow range of opportunities to learn to teach, and were isolated from other school activities, and that there was fragmentation and lack of clarity of purpose between the university and school educators governing student teaching. He concludes rhetorically, "If novices are introduced to teaching as individualistic and particularized practice, what consequences are in store for those same teachers who may be called upon to engage in mentor programs, induction schemes, and peer evaluation procedures?" (p. 363). Sarason, Davidson, & Blatt (1986) also summarize the problem of practice teaching.

> The practice-teaching experience, which could be of paramount significance in the training of the student as a psychological observer and tactician, usually involves everything but training in problems of observation and individual differences. There are many reasons for this unfortunate situation, but one of the major ones is that the master, critic, or supervising teachers have no special qualifications for the supervisory role, that is, they are chosen because they are considered good teachers and not because they have had special training in supervision. Perhaps more to the point is that the master teacher, coming from identical or similar training program as the student teacher, pays far more attention to matters of lesson plans and classroom housekeeping problems than to problems which are far more difficult to communicate to the student teacher. (p. 35)

Among the problems are the criteria (or lack thereof) for selection of supervising teachers, the limited or nonexistent in-service available for supervising teachers in their role, and the often hit-or-miss experiences of student teachers, who can end up at various times with wonderful mentors, drill sergeants, or laissez-faire neglectors. At a minimum, as Zeichner and Gore (1900) observe, the knowledge base related to the impact of practice teaching on students is "notoriously weak."

The point of all this is not that initial teacher preparation has no effect. Rather it is that the quality of program experiences probably varies greatly, and until very recently we have had little information on the particular characteristics of programs that might make a difference. Some examples will show the value of these more specific investigations, which reflect a trend toward more precise research in the 1990s.

Hollingsworth (1989), for example, is engaged in a longitudinal study of changes in preservice teachers' knowledge and beliefs involving 14 student teachers in a fifth year program. In a first report, Hollingsworth compares pre- and postprogram beliefs. She claims that there are at least three knowledge bases that teachers need to acquire to be effective: (a) subject matter—both the content and how to teach the content, (b) general management and instruction pedagogy, and (c) knowledge of the ecology of the classroom—knowledge of how pupils learn, and the ability to diagnose and evaluate the learning process and outcomes. Concerning the question of subject knowledge and how to teach it, Hollings-worth found that preprogram beliefs served as "filters" for processing program content. Half of the 14 students initially believed that learning was accomplished by teacher-directed information. Others believed that children learned by constructing their own knowledge (which in fact was the basis of the program being offered). The impact of the program var-ied, but not necessarily in predictable ways. By the end of the program all student teachers expressed the belief that students should be respon-sible for their own learning, but the *depth* of the students' knowledge and convictions varied. Some reaffirmed their predispositions that student construction is important, but stayed at a superficial level. Alice was a case in point.

> When she received positive feedback for her modelling, it reaffirmed her notion of being on track in learning to teach. The result was satisfaction in terms of her performance, but not a deepening understanding of her own beliefs that might have resulted from confronting and examining her pre-program ideas about education. (p. 171)

Some entered the program with a stated philosophy that was in con-trast to the program, and reacted as follows:

> Although Margaret, like all other credential candidates, professed to believe by the end of the program that children constructed their own knowledge, she was not able to demonstrate—through her talk, writing, or teaching per-formances—that her beliefs had changed to a sufficient depth to transform the new ideas into an instructional repertoire. Her preprogram beliefs ap-pear to limit her understanding of the constructivist concept to a memory or copying level. (p. 172)

Others went beyond their predispositions in a compatible direction to deepen their knowledge and skills, while still others broke away from their initial stances to discover new ideas of what teaching meant for them. In short, the relationship between prior beliefs and program ex-periences is crucial, complex, and not straightforward.

Hollingsworth also found that 7 of the 14 student teachers success-fully reached a balanced managerial style during the 9-month program. Four factors contributed to this outcome.

> (a) a role image of themselves as learners and critics of teaching, which al-lowed for error and change; (b) an awareness that they needed to change their initial beliefs to come to terms with classroom organization; (c) the co-operating teacher and/or university supervisor as role models and facilitators of that change; and (d) a notion of having something worth teaching that demanded student cooperation. (p. 174)

The sequence was important—classroom management knowledge had to be sorted out before or in conjunction with attending to subject specific pedagogy.

In addition, a number of student teachers (5 of 14) revealed a new level of understanding that was a function of discrepancies and experiences that enabled them to transcend their initial predispositions as a result of

> (a) a disequilibrium set up by differences between their own beliefs and those of the cooperating teacher, (b) substantive cognitive integration of managerial and subject knowledge, and (c) an opportunity to try their own ideas across different contexts. (Hollingsworth, 1989, pp. 181–82)

One student, Chris, typified this experience. In the first semester he was placed with a teacher of like-minded philosophy from whom he learned new examples compatible with his approach. In the second semester he was with a cooperating teacher with whom he strongly disagreed. He was forced to rethink and clarify his approach in order to have the opportunity to use certain strategies and assess their impact. After discussion, Chris' cooperating teacher was willing to let him try certain approaches. Under these kinds of conditions, says Hollingsworth, student teachers learned new ideas; supervisors who coached or intervened informatively had an impact. She concludes with this revealing claim.

> Results clearly indicate that preservice programs should come to understand the incoming beliefs of their students along with other screening criteria in order to direct their placements in school settings, inform their supervision, and understand their learning. Further, it appears that contrasting viewpoints were helpful in clarifying complex aspects of classroom life and promoting comprehensive learning when accompanied by an expectation and support for preservice teachers to try out their own and program-related ideas. The study challenges the common sense notion that preservice teachers should be placed with teachers with whom they agree and that cooperating teachers should be chosen who are model teachers according to program philosophy. Such teachers tended to promote rote copying or modeling of their behavior, limiting the depth of preservice teachers, processing of information and change in beliefs. The matched pairings, in other words, hindered knowledge growth. (p. 186)

Stoddart and Gomez' (1990) research also clearly shows that the personal beliefs and perspectives of student teachers in both traditional and alternative certification programs have a powerful influence on how they go about teaching. In short, personal beliefs are a critical part of teacher education that has been neglected both in the design of programs and in research on how teachers develop.

Liston and Zeichner (1989) propose one method of addressing the issue of personal perspectives through an action research and reflective teaching preservice program. They argue that "a reflective orientation to teaching should stress the giving of good reasons for educational actions" (p. 1). Action research, for Liston and Zeichner, consists of documenting the effects of strategic teaching activities over a period of time, while reflecting on and altering practices accordingly within the context of a support group of teacher action researchers. Liston and Zeichner indicate that students working with an action research focus report that "they became more aware of their own practices, of the gaps between their beliefs and their practices and of what their pupils were actually learning and thinking" (p. 22; see also Grimmett & Erickson, 1988; Noffke & Zeichner, 1987). Other valuable research is now being conducted on how the different subject areas—math, English, writing, science, and so on—are and can be best taught (Ball & McDiarmid, 1990; Borko & Livingston, 1989; Grossman, 1989; Loucks-Horsley & associates, 1990; Shulman, 1987; Zeichner, 1989).

Not only has there been little research on preservice teacher education, but also basic descriptions and analyses of existing programs have been unavailable. Two recent exceptions are Howey and Zimpher's (1989) studies of preservice teacher education programs, under the auspices of the North Central Regional Educational Laboratory, and Goodlad and associates' major study of the education of educators (Goodlad, 1990a, 1990b). Howey and Zimpher provide valuable case descriptions of programs at six universities—Lutheran College, Ball State University, the University of Toledo, the University of Wisconsin–Eau Claire, Indiana University, and Michigan State University. Howey and Zimpher confirm in some detail the great variety of alternative programs across (and within) many colleges of education. They were not able to assess program effectiveness, but in a cross-program analysis devised 14 attributes that they suggest contribute to much-needed program coherence, including such factors as: programs based on clear conceptions of teaching and schooling; programs that have clear thematic qualities; faculty coalescing around experimental or alternative programs that have distinctive qualities; working with student cohort groups; adequate curriculum materials and a well-conceived laboratory component; articulation between on campus programming and field-based student teaching; direct linkage to research and development knowledge bases, and regular program evaluation (Howey & Zimpher, 1989, Ch. 7).

In addition to the continuing work of Howey and Zimpher, John Goodlad and his colleagues are in the midst of a massive research investigation called *Studying the Education of Educators* (Goodlad, 1990a). Twenty-nine colleges of education (and their universities) in eight states were selected to represent different types of colleges and universities.

Data are being gathered through site visits, observations, interviews, document analyses, and questionnaires to students, faculty, and administrators. Based on a number of assumptions and postulates, Goodlad and colleagues have set out to address just about all the major issues, and more, that we have identified so far in this chapter.

Goodlad and associates (1990a) proposed four sets of expectations for teacher education programs:

> 1) That they will prepare teachers to enculturate the young into a political democracy, 2) that they will provide teachers with the necessary intellectual tools and subject-matter knowledge, 3) that they will insure that teachers have a solid initial grounding in pedagogy, and 4) that they will develop in teachers the beginning levels of the knowledge and skills required to run our schools. (p. 699)

They found that the programs they studied fell far short of these expectations. Among their main findings:

> 1. The preparation programs in our sample made relatively little use of the peer socialization processes employed in some other fields of professional preparation. There were few efforts to organize incoming candidates into cohort groups or to do so at some later stage. Consequently, students' interactions about their experiences were confined for the most part to formal classes (where the teaching is heavily didactic). The social, intellectual, and professional isolation of teachers, so well described by Dan Lortie, begins in teacher education. This relatively isolated individualism in preparation seems ill-suited to developing the collegiality that will be demanded later in site-based school renewal.
>
> 2. The rapid expansion of higher education, together with unprecedented changes in academic life, have left professors confused over the mission of higher education and uncertain of their role in it. Although the effects of these changes in academic life transcend schools and departments, the decline of teaching in favor of research in most institutions of higher education has helped lower the status of teacher education. In regional public universities, once normal schools and teachers colleges, the situation has become so bad that covering up their historic focus on teacher education is virtually an institutional rite of passage. Teaching in the schools and teacher education seem unable to shake their condition of status deprivation.
>
> 3. There are serious disjunctures in teacher education programs: between the arts and sciences portion and that conducted in the school or department of education, from component to component of the so-called professional sequence, and between the campus-based portion and the school-based portion. . . . It is also clear from our data that the preparation under way in the programs we studied focused on *classrooms* but scarcely at all on *schools*.
>
> 4. Courses in the history, philosophy, and social foundations of educa-

tion ... have seriously eroded. (Goodlad, 1990a, pp. 700–701, emphasis in original)

Detailed descriptions of the above and other findings can be found in Goodlad (1990a), Goodlad, Soder, and Sirotnik (1990), Edmundson (1990), Sirotnik (1990), Soder (1990), and Su (1990). Goodlad concludes: "The disappointing results we found in the programs we examined are to a considerable degree the legacy of well over a century of neglect—for which we all are culpable" (p. 701).

One needs also to consider the teachers of teachers—education professors and the university context. Clark (in Howey & Zimpher, 1989, p. 2) observes that more than 70 percent of the four-year colleges and universities in the United States operate state-approved teacher education programs and that "their faculty members are typically not involved in the production of knowledge about teacher education" (p. 117). Howey and Zimpher (1989) in their six case studies discovered among faculty a sense of pride, personal caring, and heavy involvement in teaching, with corresponding limited research activity and almost nonexistent inquiry into programs (pp. 223–33). Judge (1982) found that education professors were held in low regard at universities, and that *within* research-based colleges of education, professors involved in the graduate school (i.e., research) distanced themselves from their teacher education colleagues and from practicing educators (see especially Clifford & Guthrie, 1988; and Lanier & Little, 1986 for additional analyses).

It is clear that universities and their faculties of education have not yet "got it right." Faculties of education in the past have lost on both fronts—university respectability and field effectiveness. The demographics of faculty—with large numbers of retirements in the 1990s—provide an opportunity to revamp the roles of colleges of education through renewal strategies, but the difficulties, including the shortage of professors and the incentive systems of universities, present formidable obstacles. In Chapter 15 we will examine some promising new developments in university–school partnerships, which indicate that research and knowledge, and teacher and school effectiveness not only can, but must, go together if either is to be effective.

Finally, let us return to our interest in change per se. To implement educational changes, teachers have to be able to assess the potential need for and quality of the changes; have certain basic skills in a range of teaching methods, planning, diagnosing, and evaluation; and be able to modify instructional activities continually in an attempt to meet the needs of diverse individual students. More broadly, they must have abilities that are barely (if at all) touched by the formal teacher education program: interacting with and learning from peers, using and relating to subject consultants, relating to the principal, talking to and working with parents. In short, not only are there difficulties in learning how to use new methods (such as applying theory to practice), but there is also an almost total neglect of the phenomenon of how changes are and can be introduced and implemented. In our national survey in Canada we asked student teachers and faculty to what extent the program did and should "prepare teachers who have the perceptions and skills to implement changes in the schools." There was agreement in the two groups: Only 15% in each group indicated that this goal was receiving "great" or "very great" emphasis, while 73% of the faculty and 64% of the students thought that it should. The 15% was the lowest percentage among nine different goals we asked about. Goals that were viewed as actually receiving the highest emphasis involved preparing teachers "who were knowledgeable in subject areas" and "who can adapt to and work within existing school systems."

If one reviews the many goals and difficulties discussed in this section, it becomes crystal clear that a five-year, let alone a nine-month, preservice program cannot possibly produce the complete starting teacher. Two conclusions seem warranted. First, we do not know nearly enough about the structure and sequence of preservice programs, but alternatives are now being attempted and researched (e.g., Hollingsworth, 1989). Second, and more fundamental, we are better off to recast the preservice question to "What is the strongest possible start, and how can one productively build on it?" Hence, induction.

INDUCTION

Two assumptions introduced this chapter—the teacher education continuum must become a reality, and teacher development and school improvement must be intimately reciprocal. Induction—deliberate support programs for beginning teachers—represents one of the most potentially powerful strategies for realizing these assumptions. Let us start from the perspective of the first-year teacher. It used to be said, not entirely facetiously, that the main goal of the first-year teacher is to become a second-year teacher. These days the main goal of many first-year teachers is to find another occupation. In either case, a struggle for survival characterizes the experience of many first-year teachers.

Ten years ago McDonald and Elias (1980) carried out a detailed four-volume study of beginning teachers and induction programs. The title of the first volume tells the story: *The Problems of Beginning Teachers: A Crisis in Training.* In this volume the authors review the research literature on the beginning teacher. They describe what they call some "facts" of their investigation.

1. Almost all teachers experience the transition period into teaching as the most difficult aspect of their teaching life and career. There apparently are some teachers who move into teaching smoothly and efficiently, but the majority report the period is one of great difficulty and even trauma.
2. The major kinds of problems and difficulties that teachers experience are readily identifiable. Most of them relate to the management and conduct of instruction. These problems are so critical that it is easy to overlook the equally obvious fact that the range of problems includes difficulties with evaluating pupils, being evaluated by the administration, working with parents, developing a consistent teaching style, finding out how the school functions, knowing the rules that must be followed, and a variety of other problems.
3. The least studied aspect of this transition period is the fear, anxiety, and feelings of isolation and loneliness that appear to characterize it. There is sufficient information in existing reports to indicate that these feelings are not uncommon; however, individual conversations with teachers are far more revealing than the current literature.
4. Almost all teachers report that they went through this transition period "on their own." They had little or no help available, and found help only through their own initiative. This help usually took the form of seeking out some other teacher in whom they could confide. . . .
5. There is probably a strong relationship between how teachers pass through the transition period and how likely they are to progress professionally to high levels of competence and endeavor. (see McDonald & Elias, 1980, Vol. I, pp. 42–43)

Veenman's (1984) systematic review of beginning teachers produces the same litany of problems. Studies at the individual level reveal the incredibly personal nature of these early experiences of teaching. Aitken and Mildon's (1991) longitudinal study of a group of teachers from a fifth year program is a case in point.

Samantha: But there are kids with chips on their shoulders and they're not going to like you no matter what you do. There was one boy who did badly on a math test and you can't be subjective about marking a math test. You either do well or you don't and it's not a question of grey areas where maybe he could have gotten another mark but he just, he hated me and he was such a problem and I couldn't reason with him, like I couldn't make him see that he had failed the math test, it wasn't me it was him, but no, it was my fault that he had failed the math test, and because I'd failed him, he couldn't be a prefect for the school and he couldn't, like he blamed me for everything and it got to the point where I couldn't even have him in my class, like he'd come in and I'd say, "George, get out" without any or very little provocation and it was hard 'cause I'd never been disliked by a kid before this. (pp. 14–15)

Shelagh: It is so much harder than I thought. And we run into more road-blocks and difficulties than I thought possible. I'm so much more tired when I get home than I anticipated. I'm cheerful by nature but sometimes I get mad having so many classes to deal with. . . . The principal just showed me my room and didn't tell me anything. He was completely indifferent to me and I am not used to that. Then I found this wonderful old teacher who knows everything and who took me under her wing. . . . I'm determined never to quit, but it's not easy. (p. 24)

And Jason: Look, of course we're not ready for teaching. We're kidding ourselves, but the way the system is we have to pretend we are ready. (p. 26)

The need to develop support systems for beginning teachers is a matter both of humanity (to beginning teachers *and* to the pupils they teach) and of teacher quality. Schlechty and Vance (1983) estimate that up to an incredibly high 30% leave the profession during their first two years on the job, compared with an overall turnover rate of 6% a year. Of all beginning teachers who enter teaching, up to 40%–50% will leave during the first seven years of their career. For some it could be said that they never should have entered teaching in the first place; for many, however, there is evidence that we are losing some of the potentially best teachers (in academic talent and other qualities) as they find the occupation and working conditions unsatisfactory (Hart & Murphy, 1990; Schlechty & Vance, 1983).

And, we haven't even introduced the problem of working in difficult urban multicultural schools. In a U.S. national survey of students in teacher education programs conducted in 1987 by the American Association of Colleges for Teacher Education (AACTE), reported in Zimpher (1988), the number of minority teacher education students was shown to be actually falling: 6% black and 1.7% Hispanic in the 1985 survey, to 4.3% black and 1.5% Hispanic in 1987. Students in teacher education programs were typically white and female, from a small town or suburban home community, and attended a local university (Zimpher, 1988). While they tended to have positive views of the teaching profession, they are conservative in their aspirations. Given that one characteristic of life for beginning teachers has often been taking on work that would challenge even the most skillful veteran teachers, it would seem this discrepancy alone would limit retention. The AACTE study makes the suggestion that one important preservice and in-service need is to develop skills for teaching in multiracial/multilingual settings to offset cultural insularity.

In a word, the situation faced by first-year teachers is overwhelming.

Whether those teachers experience the sink-or-swim individualism characteristic of traditional school cultures (Chapter 7) or the inbuilt support of collaborative work cultures makes a huge difference in whether they stay in the profession and how good they will become if they do. Induction programs, as we shall soon see, are not without their problems, but there are few things as deterministic of the entire career of a teacher as getting off to a disastrous or a strong start.

The goals of induction programs, according to Huling-Austin's (1990) review, vary greatly but typically include

1. to improve teaching performance,
2. to increase the retention of promising beginning teachers,
3. to promote the personal well-being of beginning teachers by improving teachers' attitudes toward themselves and the profession,
4. to satisfy mandated requirements related to induction and certification, and
5. to transmit the culture of the system to beginning teachers. (p. 539)

Induction programs usually involve reduced teaching time for beginning teachers (e.g., 80% teaching and released time and/or stipends for mentors). Program components include some or all of the following:

1. printed materials of employment conditions and school regulations,
2. orientation meetings and visits,
3. seminars on curriculum and effective teaching topics,
4. observations by supervisors/peers/assessment teams and/or videotaping of beginning teachers in the classroom,
5. follow-up conferences with observers,
6. consultations with experienced teachers,
7. support (helping/buddy/mentor) teachers,
8. opportunities to observe other teachers (in person or through subject-specific videotapes),
9. released time/load reduction for beginning teachers and/or support teachers,
10. group meetings of beginning teachers,
11. assignment to a team teaching situation,
12. credit courses for beginning teachers (university and/or local credit), and
13. beginning teacher newsletters and other publications designed to provide helpful teaching tips for the novice teacher (Huling-Austin, 1990, p. 539).

Cole and McNay (1989) identify four major goals of induction programs in Ontario.

1. orientation: integrating beginning teachers, and teachers new to the setting, into the professional and social fabric of the school, school district, and neighborhood community;
2. psychological support: promoting teachers' professional and personal self-esteem and well-being;
3. acquisition and refinement of teaching skills: attending to the development of knowledge, skills, and attitudes in those areas related to daily classroom teaching in which teachers feel in most need of support;
4. development of a philosophy of education: including habits of reflective practice and a commitment to continued professional growth (p. 9).

Proposals for induction programs have been around for at least 20 years, and are only now beginning to receive serious attention. As far back as 1972, the James Report in the United Kingdom recommended that probationary teachers have a reduced teaching load (75%) and additional release time to attend induction workshops within their schools or at regional centers; that professional tutors be appointed within schools to provide training and support for probationers; and that external centers be developed in teacher education institutions and teacher centers to conduct workshops and other support activities. Evaluation of pilot projects found that the program had very positive effects on the new teachers, and that tutor and other staff members benefited, as did interagency cooperation between the local authority, teachers centers, and teacher education institutions (Bolam, Baker, & McMahon, 1979). The program was never expanded due to financial costs and other educational political priorities that superseded it.

In the United States induction has received increasing attention but is still not well established. As of 1986, at least 39 states had induction policies and programs in the planning, development, pilot, or implementation stages (Darling-Hammond & Berry, 1988; Huling-Austin, 1990). By 1987 only 12 states reported no activity at the state level related to teacher induction. Virtually all the programs were established by mandate. In 15 of the 17 states' operating programs, induction is linked to certification (Huling-Austin, 1990). Thus, the most common form of induction in the United States involves assistance and assessment of beginning teachers. Included in these programs are such initiatives as the Kentucky Beginning Teacher Internship Program, the California Mentor Teacher Program, the Georgia Teacher Certification Program, the Florida Beginning Teacher Program, the Virginia Beginning Teacher Assistance Program, the North Carolina Initial Certification Program, the University of New Mexico/Albuquerque Public Schools Program, and the Richardson ISD (Texas) Program (Huling-Austin, 1990). Many of these programs are collaborative in nature and involve two or more sponsoring agencies representing different branches of the teacher education system (see Huling-Austin & Murphy, 1987, and Moore, 1989, for case study examples of a number of specific programs; the special issue on beginning teachers of *The Elementary School Journal*, March 1989; and a major policy research study recently launched, the California New Teacher Project, by Wagner, Ward, & Dianda, 1990).

In Canada, Andrews (1986) correctly characterized the approach to induction as "laissez-faire." Since 1986 Alberta has reported on its "Initiation to Teaching Project" (ITP) (Ratsoy, Friesen, & Holdaway, et al., 1987). The ITP was a pilot project funded by the provincial government, which provided employment as interns in 1985–86 and 1986–87 for 900 recent graduates. The purpose was twofold: to provide employment for recent graduates who might otherwise be unemployed (there was a teacher surplus at the time), and to assess the utility of a year-long intern program to assist the transition into teaching. A large-scale evaluation found that the many positive features of the program and the support by all major educational groups far outweighed the negative features, such as lack of role clarity of interns and supervisory teachers' lack of preparation time, low salary for interns, etc. (Ratsoy et al., 1987). The evaluators recommended that a "Teacher Residency Program" be mandatory for all beginning teachers.

In Ontario, the Teacher Education Review Steering Committee (Ontario Ministries of Education, and Colleges and Universities, 1988) recommended that an induction phase become mandatory by 1995, and that pilot projects be funded in the interim (Fullan & Connelly, 1990). Several individual school boards have initiated induction programs of their own, sometimes in cooperation with local universities (Cole & McNay, 1989; McNay & Cole, 1989). Other provinces have conducted similar policy reviews on teacher education that make major recommendations across the continuum, including induction. The major difference between the programs in the United States and Canada is that Canadian programs focus on support uncoupled from evaluation of beginning teachers, while most U.S. programs, as stated above, are linked to assessment as well as to assistance. As the majority of programs are still in the early stages, it is difficult to determine their success. Huling-Austin (1990) concludes her review by strongly advocating continued research and evaluation concerning the effects not only on beginning teachers, but also on support teachers (see also Moore, 1989). Several critical issues and preliminary implications can, however, be identified.

First, the research and evaluation that are available indicate that by

and large induction programs are valuable. New teachers who are assisted, are more likely to stay in teaching than comparison groups, and
participants and supervisors have positive views (Huling-Austin, 1990).
But Huling-Austin cautions

> While there is evidence to suggest that induction programs can be successful,
> it is important for those who develop and implement programs to realize
> that desired outcomes will rarely be achieved "by accident" just because a
> program exists. In order for the goals to be achieved, program activities spe-
> cifically targeted toward identified outcomes must be carefully designed and
> implemented appropriately. (pp. 28–29)

Second, the preoccupation with the basic competency of (beginning)
teachers as exemplified by the "intensification" movement I described in
earlier chapters tends toward *minimum* competencies and sets a course of
keeping teachers, however unwittingly, at the lower limits of professionalism. Shulman's (1989) examination of the knowledge base of teaching,
and his and his colleagues' longitudinal research on the growth of pedagogy and content in teachers, leads him to the following observation:

> Assessments of teachers in most states consist of some combination of basic-
> skills tests, an examination of competence in subject matter, and observations
> in the classroom to ensure that certain kinds of general teaching behavior
> are present. In this manner, I would argue, teaching is trivialized, its com-
> plexities ignored, and its demands diminished. (p. 6)

Assessment-based induction schemes run the risk of reducing teaching to less significant goals and of repelling the best teacher prospects
and teacher-leaders (while not on induction per se, see Hart & Murphy,
1990). Put positively, induction programs must be part and parcel of a
continuum that contributes to the growing sophistication and effectiveness of the teacher (Fullan & Connelly, 1990). And, they must contribute
to and be supported by the kinds of collaborative schools described in
Chapter 7. If induction programs do not foster continuous growth and
development, and greater meaning and capacity for improvement both
individually and with others, they will be a step backward.

Third, induction has helped to propel the mentoring phenomenon,
opening up new opportunities for professionalism, while also exposing
logistical and normative constraints to changing the culture of schools
and teaching as a profession. Anderson and Shannon (1988) trace the
concept of mentoring and offer the following definition:

> [Mentoring is] a nurturing process in which a more skilled or more experi-
> enced person, serving as a role model, teaches, sponsors, encourages, coun-
> sels, and befriends a less skilled or less experienced person for the purpose

of promoting the latter's professional and/or personal development. Mentoring functions are carried out within the context of an ongoing, caring relationship between the mentor and the protege. (p. 40)

The formal designation of mentor in education is being applied in many states, provinces, and local jurisdictions to refer to school associates working with student teachers, and to those working with beginning teachers in induction schemes and with new teachers in alternative certification programs (it has also been used in "career ladders" or other special designations to include other leadership roles). Here the potential benefits shift to the mentor and the school as an organization. Behind mentoring is the goal of developing and retaining skillful teacher-leaders close to the classroom, and generally providing opportunities for teachers to have more fulfilling and impactful careers—possibilities that remain underdeveloped or lost in the traditional individualism of teaching and schools.

Although there is not a great deal of research, most mentors, when asked, report satisfaction and benefits to their own professional development. There are a number of problems limiting the effectiveness of mentoring programs, some related to difficulties of implementation, others more fundamental (for the best review, see Little, 1990b). One set of problems concerns selection criteria, training, and support for mentors. Mentors should be selected on the basis of expertise and credibility—both as classroom teachers and as colleagues with track records of working successfully with other teachers. Little reports that hasty implementation of new mentor programs has not been conducive to careful selection. Little also found that pre-implementation training for mentors was variable, often focusing only on general process skills. Relative to post-selection support, Bird and Alspaugh (1986) found that 40 percent of districts participating in the first two years of California's mentor program allocated no resources to support mentors during implementation.

A more fundamental issue is that the formal role of mentor is new and clashes with some of the individualistic traditions of teaching. As Little states: "Those who would implement mentor roles are confronted with a two-part challenge: to introduce classroom teachers to a role with which they are unfamiliar; and to introduce the role itself to an institution and occupation in which it has few precedents" (pp. 9–10). The ambiguity of the role often left mentors to "invent their roles as they went along" (Hart, 1989, p. 24). According to Little, lack of clarity and ambivalency in the role tend to produce a lower rate of direct teacher-to-teacher involvement of the very sort needed to make the role credible and effective. Smylie and Denny (1989) report the same finding—lower incidences of direct classroom and instructional exchanges—for teacher-leadership roles they studied. Mentoring is a powerful strategy for improvement, but to be effective it must go beyond one-to-one relationships; it must, in other words, be supported by and contribute to the development of "collaborative work cultures" (Chapter 7; Fullan, 1990).

Fourth, financial and political factors inhibit the expansion of induction programs. The costs are large, and the political payoff is unclear. One need only start calculating salary costs if all new teachers have an 80 percent timetable, not to mention costs related to mentoring. Since more teachers would be needed, and there already is a shortage, it is not a feasible proposition.

Despite all of these difficulties induction is expanding across North America. And the reason is simple. Induction support is powerfully sensible, and the many potential and actual benefits for new teachers, mentors, and their schools are soon intuitively, if not actually, realized as people try out induction programs. A final critical point should be made. Induction programs should not be seen simply as an add-on. It is vitally important that the preservice year of fifth year programs and the induction year be considered *in tandem* in order to strengthen the developmental links between the two. Put another way, faculties of education should be involved in induction programs, just as school people should be involved in preservice programs. Induction provides a golden opportunity to make part of the teacher education continuum a reality.

This brings us to one of the most intriguing developments in teacher education, namely, the increasing presence of alternative certification schemes. Nothing calls into question the reputation of the entire teaching profession as emphatically as the suggestion that anyone with good content knowledge can be rapidly prepared for teaching. But the matter of alternative certification is not at all simple.

ALTERNATIVE CERTIFICATION

Alternative certification (AC) programs bypass traditional teacher education programs in favor of more direct routes to certification and are usually district- rather than university-based. The two extreme sides of the argument are as follows: (a) on the pro AC side is a growing teacher shortage combined with a perception that traditional university teacher education programs are not that effective anyway; it is concluded that more streamlined field-based programs will meet the need without any loss in quality. Further, AC programs are often aimed at attracting mid-career people from business and industry into science, mathematics, and other speciality fields, making it possible for them to switch careers (Lutz & Hutton, 1989); (b) those opposing alternative certification claim that it undermines the advance of teacher professionalism at the very time that the deepening and lengthening of teachers' preparation is being advocated, and that AC programs will reduce quality control at the entry level and otherwise result in "weak, poorly prepared counterfeits" (Watts, 1986, p. 29).

I agree with Lutz and Hutton's assessment: "Although some might argue that the perceived lack of quality of traditionally trained teachers has contributed to the development of AC programs, it is likely that the compelling force behind AC programs is the current teacher shortage, particularly serious in urban school districts" (p. 238). The growing shortage in urban areas has required emergency certificates or letters of permission to teach, which waive, at least temporarily, teacher education requirements altogether. As far back as 1982–83, a U.S. survey in Texas, Ohio, California, Florida, Colorado, and New Jersey reported that more than 10 percent of all new teachers hired had been issued emergency or substandard credentials (Darling-Hammond & Berry, 1988, p. 21). A survey in 1985 by the National Center for Education indicated that over 12 percent of all newly hired teachers were not fully certified. In some large cities the problem is of crisis proportions. In Los Angeles, 50 percent of the 1,500 teachers hired annually over the past few years are on emergency credentials (Shulman, 1989). In Toronto, the number of letters of permission for uncertified teachers is seriously on the rise.

Alternative certification is then a response to the shortage of teachers in urban areas, and to the perception of some that it is a more flexible way of attracting good people to certain subject areas. The number of states that passed alternative certification legislation jumped from 8 in 1984 to 23 in 1986 (Darling-Hammond & Berry, 1988). In analyzing 12 alternative certification programs, Adelman (1986) found that compared with standard programs: (a) AC programs feature more field experience and more direct supervision at least for a brief period of time; (b) formal coursework is a compressed version of regular programs, offered in the evenings and/or summers; and (c) well-educated individuals are being attracted to the programs but their classroom competence cannot yet be assessed.

California's alternative route to certification, for example, involves (1) possessing a bachelor's degree; (2) passing the state basic skills proficiency test; (3) passing a subject-matter knowledge exam; (4) obtaining a teacher trainee certificate; (5) teaching satisfactorily for two years with a mentor, while completing a professional development plan formulated by the district in consultation with a college; and (6) obtaining a permanent teaching credential (McKibbin, Walton, & Wright, 1987). New Jersey's alternative certification requires 200 contact hours in pedagogical training while teaching, compared with two-and-one-half times that amount for standard programs.

Part of the problem is that data-based support for either regular or alternative programs is weak, and because of the acuteness of teacher shortages in some areas, coverage understandably takes precedence over teacher development. The value of good empirical studies is not so much that they provide all the answers, but that they ask the right questions, thereby keeping inquiry focused on the central issues. There are very few studies, but the most informative is Lutz and Hutton's (1989) assessment of the AC program operated by the Dallas Independent School District (DISD). I report on four of the several questions Lutz and Hutton addressed.

1. What are the characteristics of the DISD AC program?
2. What are the characteristics of the AC intern recruits?
3. How do the AC interns perform as teachers?
4. Did the AC program provide DISD with qualified teachers?

I can only summarize briefly their main findings and conclusions. First, 110 interns were selected in 1986 for training (1,300 applied, 691 took a basic skills test, 557 passed and were interviewed, and 110 were selected). The program was in response to critical areas of shortage in English as a second language, general elementary, and secondary math and science. The program consisted of formal instruction in August, five follow-up sessions throughout the year (led by DISD consultants and staff from East Texas State University) on various aspects of classroom management and teaching methods, and classroom observation during September, followed by teaching in October. Teacher mentors had "direct and intensive" involvement with interns throughout the year. The interns were evaluated using a number of instruments used by the state.

Second, relative to the characteristics of the interns, the average age was 31; 38% were white, 34% black, and 28% Hispanic. The interns were older and included a higher representation of minority groups (which was the intention of the program), compared with other first-year teachers. About 31% were unemployed at the time of application, with 35% from business, and 20% from public services.

Third, concerning performance, using a number of rating forms and sources, interns were rated as performing as well as or superior to typical first-year teachers. Of the 110 interns who started the year, 59 were recommended for certification by May, 24 were placed in a pending category with a few requirements still to be met, 15 were required to do an additional year of internship, 1 was recommended for termination, while 11 had dropped out. Lutz and Hutton note that the best case scenario is that the district will have some 83 (59 plus 24) newly certified teachers from the original 110 (75%) a year after the program began.

Fourth, did the alternative certification program solve the teacher shortage problem? Lutz and Hutton are clear that AC does not now, and will not likely, represent more than a minor contribution to a solution to this problem. The DISD hired about 1,200 new teachers in 1987–88, of whom the interns represented at best 8%. Furthermore, in the entire state there were only 305 interns in 1986–87, including DISD's 110. Over the past three years DISD's intern program has declined from 350 (1985–86), to 110 (1986–87), to 52 (1987–88). Lutz and Hutton point out that the high financial costs of running such programs is one reason for the decline.

McKibbin, Walton, and Wright (1987) report on their findings in California. Between 1984 and 1986, over 400 entered the state's alternative teacher trainee program, nearly all in one major district. After two years 20% had not completed the program, compared with an attrition rate of over 30% for a comparable group of beginning teachers. They also found that a higher percentage of trainees were prompted to become teachers because jobs were available or for financial reasons, compared with other novices (34% vs. 18%). Mentor teachers provided assistance to the trainees over the two-year period. An observation instrument was used to assess classroom effectiveness on six dimensions. There were no significant differences in performance comparing teacher trainees with a group of probationary teachers. Interestingly, during the same period 18 of the teacher trainees also entered a university teacher preparation program, and as a group their classroom effectiveness scores were significantly higher. Obviously, there may be a selectivity factor, but McKibbin and his colleagues suggest that university preparation along with internship support is likely the best combination (see the discussion on university–district partnerships in Chapter 15). Without the university connection, alternative certification programs can end up being employer focused, missing the wider range of experiences and preparation necessary for teacher development.

In brief, alternative certification programs can assist in a small way in alleviating teacher shortages by attracting selected candidates. In the few studies available, alternative candidates are perceived as doing as well as typical beginning teachers. But the information on both alternative and typical new teachers is superficial and begs the main question of how to identify and build the knowledge base and habits needed for the continuous development of teachers.

Good teaching, as researchers are discovering, is complex (Rosenholtz, 1989; Shulman, 1987). Shulman (1989) found that the alternative-route teachers she studied experienced serious problems and dilemmas, which required a foundation in teaching methods and guided experience by mentors that she recommends should be across a variety of situations in which outstanding instruction is being used. Grossman (1988, 1989) studied six first-year English teachers—three who were teaching without teacher certification, and three with formal teacher preparation. All six had a strong subject background in English. The teachers without teacher preparation based their teaching almost wholly on content, without being able to take into account student variability or to adjust to it when it was encountered. The three teachers with formal training were more likely to plan instruction with ranges in student ability in mind.

> What they learn from experience is shaped by their conceptions of teaching English, which they constructed in the process of teacher education. The frameworks they were exposed to concerning the teaching of writing and literature helped these teachers interpret student misunderstanding and difficulties within both the language and philosophy of this work. (pp. 47–48)

The three trained teachers were more likely to make effective adjustments when they encountered difficulties—as all six teachers did. For those untrained, Grossman says that "learning that something doesn't work is not the same as learning what to do about it" (p. 48). Grossman (1988, 1989) provides many specific examples of how the six teachers taught literature differently. She concludes

> While subject-matter knowledge, good character, and the inclination to teach are important characteristics of beginning teachers, they do not necessarily lead to a pedagogical understanding of subject matter nor to a theoretical understanding of how students learn a particular subject. (Grossman, 1989, p. 207; see also Grossman & Richert, 1988; Clarridge, 1989)

Grossman's untrained teachers did not have the benefit of an alternative scheme, which would include some training in pedagogical skills, but this is beside the main point I should like to make about teacher preparation. Short-term survival skills and support, and/or superficial theorizing characterize the experiences of many prospective and beginning teachers. Expert subject-matter knowledge is only one among several key components of effective teaching. As Sarason and associates (1986) state,

> It is obvious to all who have attended college that knowledge of subject matter bears no simple relationship to the effectiveness of teaching. One would have no difficulty pointing to a host of college professors whose command of their subject matter is unquestioned but whose effectiveness in teaching is sad indeed. (pp. 2–3)

The overriding conclusion of this chapter is abundantly clear. All aspects of initial preparation—academic knowledge, general and specific pedagogy, foundations, and field experiences—need strengthening and above all require *coherence and greater integration*. We have seen promising proposals and examples in this chapter that are explicitly moving in this direction (Feiman-Nemser, 1989; Goodlad, 1990a, 1990b; Goodlad, Soder, & Sirotnik, 1990; Griffin, 1986; Howey & Zimpher, 1989; Kennedy, 1989). Induction and mentoring programs are taking huge chunks out of the walls of privatism that have traditionally surrounded bad and excellent teaching. The beginning of teaching is crucial—to get the right people in, to stop wasting talent and resources through high rates of early attrition, and to establish best possible initial skills and habits.

CHAPTER 15

Professional Development of Educators

For our schools to do better than they do we have to give up the belief that it is possible to create the conditions for productive learning when those conditions do not exist for education personnel.

—Sarason (1990), p. 13.

Regardless of one's starting point, the evidence is that beginning teachers will get better or worse depending on the schools in which they teach. Continuous development of all teachers is the cornerstone for meaning, improvement and reform. Professional development and school development are inextricably linked. This means that teacher development depends not only on individuals, but also on the teachers and administrators with whom he or she works. In this chapter I first take up the question of the development of teachers throughout their careers. Second, I turn to the preparation, selection and professional development of administrators and consultants to see how these would-be change agents learn or don't learn to manage, lead and support improvement and reform. In the final section I summarize the main implications of Chapters 14 and 15 in the form of a set of guidelines for effective preparation and continuous development of educators.

How often do you hear statements to the effect that the continuous professional development of teachers is the key to school improvement? Like so many other single-factor solutions to multifaceted phenomena, the *general* endorsement of in-service education means nothing without an accompanying understanding of *the characteristics of effective as compared with ineffective in-service education efforts.* Nothing has promised so much and has been so frustratingly wasteful as the thousands of workshops and conferences that led to no significant change in practice when the teachers returned to their classrooms. Neither teacher participants nor workshop leaders are satisfied with the results of their efforts. I start with a brief consideration of why most professional development programs fail. I then describe four case examples of successful staff development, which in effect confirm that effective change processes and effective teacher development are one and the same. I conclude by discussing opportunities for staff development, which are as ubiquitous as they are difficult to harness in a sustained way.

Why Most Professional Development Fails

In a review of in-service education over 10 years ago, I summarized the reasons for failure:

1. One-shot workshops are widespread but are ineffective.
2. Topics are frequently selected by people other than those for whom the in-service is intended.
3. Follow-up support for ideas and practices introduced in in-service programs occurs in only a very small minority of cases.
4. Follow-up evaluation occurs infrequently.
5. In-service programs rarely address the individual needs and concerns.
6. The majority of programs involve teachers from many different schools and/or school districts, but there is no recognition of the differential impact of positive and negative factors within the systems to which they must return.
7. There is a profound lack of any conceptual basis in the planning and implementing of in-service programs that would ensure their effectiveness (Fullan, 1979, p. 3).

We can take college extension courses and school district staff development as cases in point. The college of education extension course is a common form of in-service education for individual teachers seeking upgrading, master's degrees, recertification, and so on. There is the usual criticism that many of the courses are too theoretical or impractical. But even in cases where the course is stimulating and contains many valuable ideas, it is difficult to use them. If the individual attempts to put the ideas into practice, there is no convenient source of help or sharing when problems are encountered. It is hard to be a lone innovator.

School district-led staff development is one of the largest and potentially strongest forms of staff development, but represents another instance of frequently missed opportunities. Based on his study of four urban improvement projects, Pink (1989) found 12 factors that acted as barriers to effective staff development.

1. an inadequate theory of implementation, resulting in too little time for teachers and school leaders to plan for and learn new skills and practices;
2. district tendencies toward faddism and quick-fix solutions;
3. lack of sustained central office support and follow-through;

4. underfunding the project, or trying to do too much with too little support;
5. attempting to manage the projects from the central office instead of developing school leadership and capacity;
6. lack of technical assistance and other forms of intensive staff development;
7. lack of awareness of the limitations of teacher and school administrator knowledge about how to implement the project;
8. the turnover of teachers in each school;
9. too many competing demands or overload;
10. failure to address the incompatibility between project requirements and existing organizational policies and structure;
11. failure to understand and take into account site-specific differences among schools; and
12. failure to clarify and negotiate the role relationships and partnerships involving the district and the local university (pp. 21–22).

All of this sounds rather depressing, but it is the norm. I will turn in a moment to a description of successful examples, but we should realize what an effort it will take to overcome the patterned obstacles that characterize the present system (see Wallace, LeMahieu & Bickel, 1990, for an excellent example that demonstrates that it can be done).

Little's (1989) comprehensive study of staff development in California yielded a number of findings that indicate that progress toward effective staff development is slow. She and her colleagues found fewer instances of one-shot activities than they had anticipated (of all participant hours, only 19% were spent in one-time sessions of six hours or less). But they also found few examples of serious follow-up, and in those cases where follow-up occurred it was rare for teachers to observe one another. Only 8 of the 30 districts were engaged in systematic program evaluation. Most staff development was not linked to other curriculum and program improvement efforts ongoing in the school. Most districts provided "a lengthy menu of short term workshops." Professional development, observes Little, can be best described as "service delivery."

> It is expressed by (a) a range of activity determined largely by a marketplace of packaged programs and specially trained presenters, (b) uniformity and standardization of content, with a bias toward skill training and (c) relatively low intensity with regard to teachers' time, teachers' involvement, and the achieved fit with specific classroom circumstances. (p. 173)

Moreover, "staff development remains largely dissociated from other personnel policies (teacher selection, tenure decisions, evaluation, promotion), from program evaluation, and from program development" (p. 177).

Why should a teacher engage in professional development anyway? Presumably, a teacher would be attracted to the idea that professional development would expand knowledge and skills, contribute to growth, and enhance student learning. But what are the costs? Will professional development make the job easier or harder? The rhetoric of innovation underestimates, if it does not totally ignore, the real costs of attempting something new. Consider a few of them. Especially at the beginning, innovation is hard work. It takes extra time and energy, even when release time is provided. It can add significantly to the normal workload. As for increased competence on the job—another incentive—it is more likely that our competence actually *decreases* during first attempts at trying something new. Our tendency is to return to familiar ways of doing things, or to practice the new ways privately so as not to expose our inadequacies to peers and supervisors. It is exactly the opposite that is needed—exchanges among peers and others about the *natural* problems of learning new skills. All of this is compounded by the possibility that the particular change may not necessarily be well developed or be the most appropriate one for the situation.

In short, professional development, one of the most promising and powerful routes to growth on the job, to combating boredom and alienation, to school improvement, and to satisfaction, has gotten a bad name. Despite poor experiences (and possibly because of a few good experiences), however, people still seem to have faith in its potential, probably because it makes such obvious, intuitive good sense.

The majority of staff development experiences do not work because they fail to incorporate the characteristics of effective change processes. The bottom line is one of change, development, improvement. Staff and professional development *is* change—in learning materials, in skills and practices, in thinking and understandings (Chapter 3). There is no single strategy that can contribute more to meaning and improvement than ongoing professional development. Successful staff development (and we are seeing more examples of it, as described in the cases below), like successful change, requires great skill, sophistication, and persistence of effort. As Loucks-Horsley, Harding, Arbuckle, Murray, Dubea, and Williams (1987) state,

> Teacher development is a complex process whose success depends upon a favorable context for learning and practical, engaging activities. Availability of resources, flexible working conditions, support, and recognition can make all the difference in the desire of teachers to refine their practice. Similarly, staff development experiences that build on collegiality, collaboration, discovery, and solving real problems of teaching and learning summon the strength within a staff, instead of just challenging them to measure up to

somebody else's standard. The focal point for staff development is the individual, working with others, trying to do the best possible job of educating children. When staff development emphasizes an idea or an approach without considering the person(s) who will implement it, the design and results are weakened. (p. 7)

Successful Staff Development

I view staff development in two different but complementary ways. First, it can be seen as (and is) a powerful strategy for implementing specific improvements. Second, for long-term effectiveness it must be seen as part and parcel of the development of schools as collaborative workplaces. Staff development, then, is both a strategy for *specific, instructional change*, and a strategy for *basic organizational change* in the way teachers work and learn together (Fullan, 1990). This distinction will become clearer as we build an understanding of what constitutes effective professional development.

Case One: Staff Development and the Improvement of Reading Practices. In several settings using different designs, Stallings (1989) and her colleagues set out to improve teaching and student achievement relative to reading practices in secondary schools. Stallings identified research findings on effective reading practices (i.e., the innovation), as well as research on critical factors related to effective staff development. Relative to the latter, Stallings (1989) states that teachers are more likely to change their behavior and continue to use new ideas under the following conditions:

1. they become aware of a need for improvement through their analysis of their own observation profile;
2. they make a written commitment to try new ideas in their classroom the next day;
3. they modify the workshop ideas to work in their classroom and school;
4. they try the ideas and evaluate the effect;
5. they observe in each other's classrooms and analyze their own data;
6. they report their success or failure to their group;
7. they discuss problems and solutions regarding individual students and/or teaching subject matter;
8. they need a wide variety of approaches; modelling, simulations, observations, critiquing video tapes, presenting at professional meetings;
9. they learn in their own way to set new goals for professional growth. (pp. 3–4)

The cornerstones of the model, according to Stallings, are:

- Learn by doing—try, evaluate, modify, try again.
- Link prior knowledge to new information.
- Learn by reflecting and solving problems.
- Learn in a supportive environment—share problems and successes. (p. 4)

Over the years, Stallings was able to compare the effects of three different training designs. The question was, what would the effect be on secondary students' reading scores,

1. if only reading teachers were trained and their students tested?
2. if all language arts teachers and reading teachers in a school were trained—hence reaching all students—and all students are tested?
3. if all teachers in a district were trained . . . over a three-year period?. (pp. 1–2)

Without going into all the details, the first design involved 47 teachers in 7 districts, along with a control group. Teachers in the treatment group, compared with the control group, changed their behavior in the classroom, and their students gained six months in reading scores over the control group. In the second design, all teachers in two schools were trained and compared with a control group of two schools. The differential gain in reading scores was eight months. In the third study, all teachers in the district were provided with the training, with no control group. Each group of ninth-grade students across three years of testing steadily improved their reading scores.

These impressive results demonstrate the power of a carefully designed staff development strategy for implementing single innovations.

Case Two: Staff Development for Implementing Instructional Models of Teaching. Joyce and associates (1989), in their recent work in Richmond County, Georgia, provide further confirmation of the link between staff development, implementation, and student outcomes. Working with summer institutes and follow-through support, and with school teams of administrators and teachers, Joyce and his colleagues have been applying their well-known model of theory-demonstration-practice, feedback, and continuous follow-through (Joyce & Showers, 1988). As stated by Joyce and Murphy (1990),

Our setting has been able to support a major project. Twenty-six schools are involved thus far, with about 10 to be added annually until all 50 are connected and the district administration has easily handled conflicts, logistics, and the procedures for orienting personnel. Nearly a thousand teachers are regularly using research-based models of teaching that were completely new to them. Cooperative learning pervades the schools that have been involved for a year or more. Implementation has been substantial enough that in some areas there is evidence of notable increases in student learning. (p. 245)

After 18 months of intensive training and follow-up with teams of teachers focusing on models of teaching, Joyce and his colleagues were able to claim considerable (but variable) implementation in the classroom, which in turn was related to a dramatic impact on student achievement and student promotion rates (Joyce & Murphy, 1990).

It is important to emphasize that both the Stallings and Joyce initiatives required considerable sophistication, skill, and effort to accomplish what they did. Most staff development activities do not measure up to these standards. And when they do, the initial successes may not be sustained beyond the tenure or energy of those who started the projects.

Case Three: District–University Partnerships. Staff development for specific instructional improvement (as in the previous two cases) is not sufficient for substantial and sustained improvement. The latter requires changes in the culture of the school as a workplace and changes in the culture and role of the university. Significant new strategies involving district–university partnerships have arisen over the past five years and represent a potential powerful force for change for the future (Sirotnik & Goodlad, 1988). These new approaches attempt to refocus teacher development so that it becomes part of an overall strategy for professional and institutional reform. I provide here one illustration taken from our current work in The Learning Consortium (Fullan, Bennett, & Rolheiser-Bennett, 1990).

The Learning Consortium is a three-year renewable partnership among four major school districts in the greater Toronto area—the Duferrin-Peel Roman Catholic Board, and the Durham, North York, and Halton Public Boards—and two higher education institutions—the Faculty of Education, University of Toronto, and The Ontario Institute for Studies in Education. The districts are large, ranging in size from 45,000 students to 60,000 students. I will not describe the various activities being undertaken, but they involve Summer Institutes and follow-up, cadre staff development and support, leadership in-service for lead-teachers and administrators, field-based preservice teacher education programs, and the like. The goal is to design and carry out a variety of activities that make the professional and staff development continuum a reality, and that link classroom and teacher development with school development by coordinating and focusing the efforts of the districts and the universities.

Classroom management, cooperative learning strategies, coaching, mentoring, collaborative work cultures, management of change at the school level, and coordination, coherence, and consistency at the district and university levels characterize the activities of the consortium. The consortium is committed to the initiation of new programs and practices, conducting research and inquiry on activities undertaken, use of the latest knowledge, and contribution to the knowledge base through dissemination.

Our goal, pursued through coordinating and linking the above activities, is to understand and bring about both classroom and school improvement, and to foster relationships between the two. The Learning Consortium has been operating for two years and has been successful in mobilizing hundreds of teachers, administrators, and university staff to action that they and others agree has resulted in teacher development, classroom improvement, school improvement, and greater coordination and integration of efforts within each district, across districts, and between districts and the university. Data gathered up to this point confirm the success of the project, but it is too early to draw firm conclusions (Fullan, Bennett, & Rolheiser-Bennett, 1990; Fullan & Watson, 1991).

School–university partnerships are on the rise, but we should not underestimate what enormously complex social experiments they are (Sirotnik & Goodlad, 1988). Goodlad (1988) stresses that "schools and universities are markedly different cultural entities" (p. 14). But they do have overlapping interests and need each other to be most effective. Goodlad suggests that there must be three minimum conditions for such symbiotic partnerships: "dissimilarity between or among the partners; mutual satisfaction of self-interests; and sufficient selflessness on the part of each member to assure the satisfaction of self-interests on the part of all members" (p. 14). The best partnerships integrate teacher development and school development through such activities as "the creation of exemplary sites in which future teachers are educated . . . the cultivation of site-based staff development activities designed to foster continual school renewal, particularly of the curriculum and accompanying pedagogical practices . . . the restructuring of schools to assure increased continuity of students' programs"; "the continuous infusion of knowledge relative to provision of good education in schools and in programs preparing educators," and so on (Goodlad, 1988, p. 27).

Goodlad also lays down a dozen essentials for structuring the relationship, including: a governing board; a modest-sized secretariat; an operating budget; top-level endorsement and support; task forces or working parties; an orderly process for deciding on projects and activities; an ongoing effort to document, analyze, and communicate or disseminate success and failures and associated reasons; establishing linkages with other partnerships; additional funds; reduction of existing funds; a formal time commitment of at least five years; and arrangements for sharing information ideas and resources within and across partnerships (Goodlad, 1988, p. 28–9). Goodlad and his colleagues have created a National Network for Educational Renewal (NNER), which currently consists of 14 different partnerships (involving a total of 17 higher education institutions and 115 school districts). Each of the 14 partnerships has a separate identity and is a member of NNER committed to the activities and exchanges just described (Sirotnik, 1987; Sirotnik & Goodlad, 1988; see also Brookhart & Loadman, 1988). Other major partnership experiments are being launched. The Holmes Group (1990) has published its manifesto, *Tomorrow's Schools*, and the ambitious multi-million dollar *Michigan Partnership for New Education* (1990) has begun to establish professional development schools.

University–district partnerships, if they are to work, are a new way of life, not just another project. In the process, the culture of the school and the culture of the university change and begin to overlap in organic ways. Conducting inquiry, for example, becomes the interest of teachers as well as of researchers, and implementing new school-based professional development practices becomes the concern of college professors as well as of lead-teachers and administrators. All of the knowledge of the change process we have been talking about will be required to make these partnerships work. We can predict that many instances of so-called partnerships will be non-events, because they are not built on the essentials identified by Goodlad and the fundamentals of change described in this book. We need powerful strategies for powerful change; the university–district partnership is one such strategy.

Case Four: Teacher Supervision and Appraisal for Growth.   Teacher appraisal, teacher evaluation, clinical supervision, career ladders, and similar terms abound in confusion of meaning and variability in practice. Research reveals that most teacher evaluation systems are pro forma wastes of time. Lawton and associates (1986) examined appraisal systems in 30 Ontario school boards. They found that most boards in the province had appraisal systems, but there was little evidence of impact. For example, 84 percent of the over 3,000 teachers surveyed indicated little or no improvement as a result of the appraisal process. Darling-Hammond (1986) also observes that teacher evaluation is often a superficial bureaucratic requirement, which can be "utterly unimportant." I will refer to some successful examples in a moment, but by and large the reforms in the United States since 1983 have generated a massive, bureaucratic proliferation of teacher accountability schemes, which are enormously expensive and yield few results relative to the costs (Darling-Hammond & Berry, 1988). They serve to undercut rather than enhance teacher development.

One can sort out many of the successes from the failures by going back to the roots of the change process and of the purposes of accountability. Successful cases of effective teacher appraisal are described in Wise, Darling-Hammond, McLaughlin and Bernstein's (1985) major study, and in McLaughlin and Pfeiffer's (1988) analysis of four exemplary school districts. Wise and associates found that the form of successful evaluation systems does not vary as much as "their seriousness of purpose and intensity of implementation" (p. 104). Many district systems identify minimum competency or at best "effective teaching behaviors," and in either case do not have a process or the capacity to help change teaching behavior. The successful districts in Wise and associates' study had top-level commitment and resources, evaluator competence through training, administrator–teacher collaboration, and compatible and linked evaluation and support systems (Wise et al., 1985).

In their case studies of four exemplary district evaluation systems, McLaughlin and Pfeiffer (1988) found that a major "triggering event," such as new leadership, a managerial crisis, or external pressure, prompted initial action. Beyond that, active leadership and teacher involvement were critical enabling conditions. In the evaluation procedures themselves six factors were key: joint training for administrators and teachers, a system of checks and balances, accountability structure for evaluation, effective feedback procedures, flexible instrumentation, and integration of evaluation and staff development.

McLaughlin and Pfeiffer (1988) state emphatically that accountability must be more than an inspection of minimal performance to identify incompetent teachers. The districts they studied linked accountability and improvement, providing highly interactive systems that identified poor performance, and in the vast majority of cases served to recognize and support the development of good performance. The basic value system in these districts—and this is crucial—was based on a climate of improvement through reflection (recognition of potential areas of growth) and motivation to change (resulting in involvement in learning activities). A minor but important part of the system was what happened to teachers receiving consistent negative feedback who did not show improvement. In these districts between 3 and 4 percent of the teachers over a several-year period resigned on the basis of evaluation evidence. Three of the four districts had not instituted any formal dismissal proceedings for incompetence.

Lest the implications be lost, there are two very important lessons here. First and foremost the evaluation systems were geared toward and supported development and improvement, which was seen as the natural order of things for over 95 percent of the teachers. The systems were credible and valued by teachers and functioned *primarily* for staff development and promotion. Second, and not unrelated, negative evaluations focused on a very small percentage of teachers and used multiple sources of data. The overall climate was positive, overwhelmingly seeking excellent performance. Without a climate valuing growth, such as when evaluation schemes are preoccupied with assessing minimal competence, we may find not only that people don't improve significantly, but also that the "wrong" people leave the profession, that is, those who find the conditions for professionalism and excellent performance missing (Hart & Murphy, 1990).

This is also the time to recall the roots of clinical supervision. Gitlin and Smyth (1989) go back to some of the original tenets of clinical supervision, which were to confront the complexities of teaching and to provide means whereby teachers in interaction (among themselves and with others) could observe, analyze, discuss, reflect on, confront, and do something to improve the effectiveness of teaching and learning (see also Glickman & Bey, 1990). Many modern versions of clinical supervision, as observed by Gitlin and Smyth, bear no resemblance to these original purposes, as they have been transformed into schemes for imposing on teachers in narrowly concerned ways.

Once one opens up the definition of teacher development to the more basic notions of interactive professionalism, it is possible to consider a range of approaches by asking how well they accomplish these more radical aspects of inquiry and improvement. Redefined approaches to clinical supervision (Gitlin & Smyth, 1989), reflective and action research practices (Grimmett & Erickson, 1988; Kemessis, 1987; Liston & Zeichner, 1989; Oja & Smulyan, 1989; Schön, 1987), life histories and narratives (Connelly & Clandinin, 1989; Goodson, 1991), strategies such as peer and cognitive coaching (Sparks, 1990; Joyce & Showers, 1988) all become assessable (see also Wideen & Andrews, 1988). The point is not that these alternatives are identical, but that they all have a potential role to play and can be evaluated in terms of the value and clarity of their stated purposes, how well they go about implementing their approaches, and what results they obtain.

To say the least, there are many complexities associated with sorting out the above menu. We must be clear, however, that the primary purpose of teacher evaluation should be teacher development. We also should clearly separate appraisal schemes for development from procedures for evaluation decisions. I, as others, believe that peer and supervisory tracks for development should be separated as clearly as possible from decision-making procedures for termination, promotion, and the like. Stiggins and Duke (1988) recommend three parallel evaluation systems—one for induction, one for competent experienced teachers, and one for the small number of cases of "experienced teachers in need of remediation." There will always be some overlap, but evaluation for improvement and evaluation for decision making do not mix well. Paradoxically, establishing interactive peer and administrator professional development practices is more effective at weeding out incompetent teachers along the way than seemingly more direct bureaucratic forms of evaluation (Darling-Hammond, 1986; Rosenholtz, 1989).

The four cases just described differ in some of their underlying premises. Some, like Joyce and Showers (1988), focus on instructional theory and skill development. Others, like Gitlin and Smyth (1989), take up a critical analysis and action perspective. I do not advocate choosing one over the other. We have argued elsewhere that teacher education should foster the development and integration of several aspects of teacher effectiveness—technical skill development, critical reflection, inquiry, and collaboration (Fullan, Bennett, & Rolheiser-Bennett, 1990; Fullan & Connelly, 1990). The total teacher in interaction with others should be able to make critical assessments in sorting out what actions to take in given instances. Incorporating the different perspectives minimizes the likelihood of partial and one-sided solutions, providing built-in checks and balances, and enabling ever more enlightening decisions.

The teacher as learner is central to transcending the dependency now faced by teachers as they attempt to cope with streams of innovations and reforms constantly coming at them. Figure 15.1 portrays our image of the professional educator as learner. Educational reform will never amount to anything until teachers become simultaneously and seamlessly inquiry oriented, skilled, reflective, and collaborative professionals. This is the core agenda for teacher education, and the key to bringing about meaningful, effective reform.

We have not been able to address all the issues related to what is needed for successful professional development. We know that professional development needs and situations are different depending on age, stage of career, and gender (Huberman, 1988; Krupp, 1989). Professional development opportunities are different at the secondary compared with the elementary level (Little, 1988). Philosophical and value questions must be sorted out even among the seemingly successful cases relative to power and gender biases (for example, see Apple & Jungck, 1991; Robertson, 1991). All in all, however, we have more and more examples of effective professional development approaches, which allow us to pose these more pointed critical questions, putting us in a position to refine and build on the successes.

Opportunities for Professional Development

I define professional development as the sum total of formal and informal learning experiences throughout one's career from presevice teacher education to retirement. The impact of professional development depends on a combination of *motivation* and *opportunity* to learn. I will

FIGURE 15.1.   Teacher as Learner

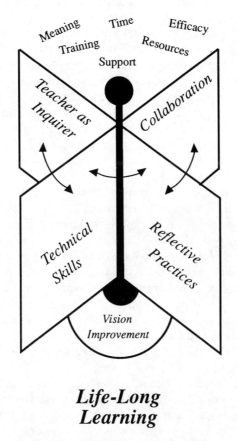

Source: Fullan, Rolheiser-Bennett, and Bennett, 1989.
Used with permission.

leave the matter of motivation to learn until the end of this section. I use the word *opportunity* in an active sense to refer both to the availability of professional development and to how the educational system is organized structurally and normatively *to press* for continuous teacher development. The former is decidedly stronger than the latter.

The sheer availability of staff and professional development is substantial and has increased in the past five years. When we start adding up the number and variety of professional development opportunities for teachers, what we find is considerable potential, although by corporate standards the investment in service is not high. Starting with the university, preservice, in-service, and graduate work presents a wide range of individual opportunity. We have seen, in Chapter 14, that preservice requirements have lengthened and deepened, including induction programs. Moving to in-service, formal university coursework has declined in the United States over the last decade (Little, 1988, p. 26). In Ontario, however, with its Additional Qualifications system tied into university delivery, some 25,000 participants—the equivalent of one in four teachers—each year take courses to upgrade their positions (Fullan & Connelly, 1990). Graduate-level education, already considerable in numbers at the master's level, is receiving renewed impetus through various plans for increased standards of teacher preparation, including master's level qualifications for lead-teachers such as mentors, master teachers, and the like (Carnegie Task Force, 1986; Holmes Group, 1986; Woolfolk, 1989).

Whatever changes are occurring at the university level, the real boom in staff development has been at the district and state levels, with teacher unions getting more involved in staff development, either independently or in collaboration with districts. Turning first to school districts, we do not have much precision. We know that district and school staff development is considerable, that it varies in investment from district to district, and that it typically lacks coherence and coordination. Two studies have attempted to analyze and provide specific information on the amount and configuration of school/district staff development. The findings are revealing (but also show what a morass it is).

Moore and Hyde (1981) set out to "make sense of staff development" in three urban school districts, which were selected on the basis of apparent levels of staff development activity (high, medium, and low). Staff development was defined as "any school district activity that is intended partly or primarily to prepare paid staff members for improved performance in present or possible future roles in the school district" (Moore & Hyde, 1981, p. 9). In all three districts they found that the actual costs of staff development were *fifty* times more than district staffs estimated. One reason for the discrepancy related to the hidden costs of personnel time for staff development; another reason was that the responsibility for staff development was dispersed among a large number of people and departments, so that much of the work was not commonly known.

> Frequently staff leaders were unaware of the activities of their colleagues, even when these activities placed demands of time and energy on the same teachers. In general, offices designated to coordinate staff development played a minor role in this swirl of activity. (Moore & Hyde, 1981, p. 4)

There were marked differences among the three districts in the proportion and type of monetary incentives used. The total budgets of the three districts were $163.6 million for Seaside district, $122.4 million for Riverview district, and $123.9 million for Union district (the three names

are pseudonyms). The amount (and proportion) of the budget spent on
staff development was $9.3 million (5.7%), $4.6 million (3.8%), and $4.0
million (3.3%), respectively (Moore & Hyde, 1981, p. 33)—not small
amounts by any reckoning.

There is a wealth of detail in the report, and it is worth describing
some of the specific findings. In two of the three districts (Seaside and
Union) five major types of activities were found: (1) conducting seminars
and workshops, usually in local schools; (2) providing individual assistance to teachers; (3) administering and coordinating staff development;
(4) conducting district-wide conferences; and (5) training resource teachers to carry out staff development (p. 39). Staff development activities
were conducted in each of several departments or divisions. For example,
in Seaside six departments/divisions were all involved substantially in professional development work: career education department, in-service department, compensatory education department, curriculum department,
student services division, and personnel division. Riverview district had
substantial federal funds because of higher proportions of minority and
poor students. They had nearly two dozen different federal programs
each containing specific staff development components (30 staff members
altogether), as well as a curriculum department, a special education department, a vocational education department, a magnet schools division
(to facilitate racial desegregation), a personnel division, and a teacher
corps project.

A more specific breakdown of the source of funds is interesting. The
vast majority of the monies supporting staff development came from district general funds in Seaside (92%) and Union (85%), while in Riverview
only 56% came from general funds and the remainder was largely from
federal grants. When these percentages are linked to the earlier information on percentage of revenue spent on staff development, Seaside,
with hardly any external funds, spent proportionately about one-third
more than did Riverview, which had substantial external funds (5.7% vs.
3.8%); Union spent about the same as Riverview.

Moore and Hyde (1981) also calculated the total amount of time
spent on staff development and found that Seaside, at an average of 108
hours per teacher each year, devoted more than twice as much time as
Union, at 50 hours. This, of course, does not indicate how well the time
was spent. And these are averages; some teachers spend a great deal of
time, while others are uninvolved. Moore and Hyde estimate that from
$1,000 to $1,700 per teacher is invested annually by the districts. The
pattern of staff development also varied considerably. In Riverview, for
example, a high proportion of funds went to central office personnel
doing staff development and to external consultants, compared with Seaside, in which there was a balance of district-initiated and school-initiated
staff development.

Moore and Hyde found significant variations, as noted, across the three districts, and also found great differences comparing schools within districts. In Seaside, for example, the highest activity school spent almost four times the number of hours on staff development than did the lowest school (the familiar explanation was a principal and staff collaborating to make use of every opportunity). They conclude

> The amount of time that can be gleaned from the regular workday by committed teachers and administrators is clearly demonstrated in our study. Through early dismissal policies, the creative use of teacher preparation periods and staff meetings, and concerted efforts to build a spirit of collaboration among the members of a particular school staff, greatly heightened participation has been achieved in individual schools without dramatic cost increases. If the staff development aspect of central office administrative roles is emphasized and these administrators are trained to support school-based staff development, and if in addition school building administrators are trained to make maximum use of non-instructional salaried worktime, it appears that the resources for staff development can be increased substantially. (Moore & Hyde, 1981, p. 116)

I have already referred to Little and colleagues' (Little, 1989; Little et al., 1987) study of staff development in California. She and her associates found that the average annual direct expenditure for local staff development (excluding university courses) was $1,360 per teacher. For every dollar that districts spent, another 60 cents was contributed by teachers in uncompensated (after hours) time. But she also found that 90 percent of the total investment went to central district staff development salaries and other district-controlled activities, as distinct from investment at the school and teacher level. The amount of money for staff development coming from the state had also increased, representing approximately 1 percent of the state education budget—a fourfold increase over the past few years.

States, through various categorical and block grants and other investments in teacher development, have been a major contributor to the expansion of teacher development opportunities since 1986 (Chapter 13). Teacher-leader in-service programs for mentors, coaches, etc., while weak or nonexistent in the early stages, are now receiving direct attention at some district and state levels. Teacher centers, which have all but disappeared in their original form, in a few cases have been incorporated and funded as part of district professional development, and have left some general legacy for teacher involvement in restructuring efforts (Yarger, 1990). Teacher unions, as noted in Chapter 7, have been increasingly active in promoting professional development as part of district and school reform efforts (e.g., McDonnell & Pascal, 1988; Rauth, 1990; Shanker, 1990). Finally, the rapid expansion of the National Staff Development Council and its *Journal of Staff Development* attests to the widespread interest and opportunities available.

The current investment in professional development is not enough, nor is it guaranteed to stay. There is a vicious cycle at work. Most professional development activities do not lead to changes in practice. If improvement in practice is not seen as an outcome, policy-makers, the public, and senior administrators will be more likely to reduce resources for staff development in favor of other priorities. Diminished resources in turn reduce opportunity and incentive to become involved. Without continuous professional development, improvement, let alone reform, will not happen.

Underlying all of the discussion in this chapter, is the assumption that staff development cannot be separated from school development. Staff development will never have its intended impact as long as it is grafted onto schools in the form of discrete unconnected projects (Fullan, 1990). Rosenholtz' (1989) study illustrates how the fabric of the school and the fabric of the continuous development of the school are one and the same. The point is nowhere more clearly made than in comparing the attitudes toward teacher learning in the collaborative or "learning-enriched" schools with those in the isolated or "learning-impoverished schools" (Chapter 7). In the collaborative schools "80% of the teachers responded, first, that their own learning is cumulative and developmental, and second, that learning to teach is a life-long pursuit" (Rosenholtz, 1989, p. 80).

Typical of the teacher comments was "You never stop learning. . . . It's important to learn how to teach something in as many different ways as possible to reach all these students. I'm always on the search for new ideas" (p. 80).

By contrast, only 17 percent of the teachers in learning-impoverished schools expressed a sustained view of learning for themselves. Teachers in these schools estimated that it takes only two to three years to learn how to teach—as in the following teacher's comments: "I learned by my third year. How to handle kids so they pay attention, when you're going to teach them and how, take a little time. You also need to be familiar with the text books you use, without them you'd be lost" (p. 82). Rosenholtz observes

> Missing in more learning-impoverished settings is the sense of teaching as a complex undertaking that requires an ever expanding repertoire of strategies, that takes into account differing student needs based on contextual or population differences, and matches particular teaching strategies with different requirements and purposes. . . . Social organizations establish and maintain a self-fulfilling prophecy: *The more impoverished the school's opportunities to learn, the less about teaching there is to learn, and the less time teachers require to learn it.* (pp. 82–83, emphasis in original)

Rosenholtz found that the majority of teachers in learning-impoverished schools tended to believe that their skills were either largely instinctive or acquired or not at the beginning of the teaching career, whereas the majority in learning-enriched schools tended to believe that their skills were continually acquired and that "they can therefore develop, perfect, and add to their fund of new skills by expending more time and effort" (p. 99).

Teachers in the collaborative schools sought more ideas from colleagues, professional conferences, and workshops. When troubles were encountered with students or parents, they were far more likely to seek and receive advice and assistance from other teachers and the principal. Teachers in collaborative schools had greater confidence and commitment to improvement. They expected students could learn and they got results (see also Ashton & Webb, 1986) Their attitude to colleagues in general carried over to beginning teachers. In noncollaborative schools, beginning teachers were left on their own, as norms of sink-or-swim self-reliance prevailed. In collaborative schools, learning to teach was seen as something that one would get better and better at with sufficient support. In short, in collaborative schools, "continuous self-renewal is defined, communicated, and experienced as a taken-for-granted fact of everyday life" (p. 74).

This brings us full circle back to teaching as an occupation. The quality of the teaching force depends on how attractive the profession looks from a distance, and what it is like once you get there. Better compensation, preservice programs that link theory and practice in clinical settings, supportive induction programs, more integrated continuous professional development, opportunities for leadership, and restructuring-type reforms that put teachers in a position to make a difference in the lives of children and adolescents, all contribute to attracting and retaining excellent teachers. Intensification-type reforms focusing on narrowly defined and imposed curriculum and teacher competencies repel good people from entering and/or staying. Bureaucratic reforms may be able to guarantee minimal performance, but not excellence in teaching. As Rosenholtz (1989, p. 215) puts it, "efficacious teachers are not likely to long tolerate the paternalistic will of a distant bureaucracy." It is also clear that the absence of such a bureaucracy by itself is not the solution. In its place, there must be the highly charged and accountable press of collaborative work cultures supporting both individual and collective efficacy.

Professionalism of teachers is at the crossroads (Chapter 7) because the political desire to improve the educational system is high (or, if you prefer, political dissatisfaction is high) and the solution could go either way—toward the technocracy of intensification, or the critical reflection and action of advanced forms of restructuring. Hart and Murphy's (1990) study brings the problems into bold relief. They interviewed teachers with five or fewer years of experience concerning their response to the work redesign implications of a career ladder reform being implemented by the district. Teachers in the sample were grouped according to high, medium, and low academic ability and promise (based on a combination of academic average and principal rating of promise). Hart and Murphy's findings are revealing and disturbing. They found that teachers with high promise and ability used different criteria in assessing their work and teaching as an occupation. Specifically, for high promise/ability teachers

1. Security was less important compared with professional growth opportunities, access to power and leadership, and a focus on student outcomes. Work structures emphasizing student performance rather than rules and regulations were more important to the high group.
2. While teacher empowerment appealed to all groups of new teachers, the high group saw this feature as an opportunity to provide leadership and influence student learning, while the other group saw it in terms of a predictable "step and lane system" in career terms.
3. The status of the teaching profession and the esteem in which teachers are held in the community was a source of dissatisfaction for the high group teachers.
4. Job satisfaction of the high group teachers was related to clear linkages between work structures, incentives, teaching and learning, and performance outcomes; inequalities in work assignments and reward structures, and make-work projects that only increased earning power were devalued.
5. Professional development and growth through leadership and a chance to prove themselves were more attractive to high group teachers, while more formalized supervision, feedback, and in-service appealed to medium and low group new teachers. The low group respondents liked the security of the salary step system through the earning of college credits and other predictable activities.
6. High group teachers felt less constrained in their future career opportunities. They were more likely to be unsure about their plans and showed less concern about leaving teaching. They were committed to making a difference, but only if the school was organized to do so. Teachers in the other groups who were dissatisfied were more likely to feel locked into their career choice.

Above I used the term "advanced forms" of restructuring advisedly. Hart and Murphy comment that many restructuring reforms have concentrated on "promotion to new ranks, mentor and supervision tasks, and site-based management or decision making" (p. 33). Restructuring that alters decision making but does not fundamentally refocus efforts on teaching and learning will not be attractive to the best teachers. As Hart and Murphy state, "If the top new teachers in this sample are to be believed, proforma or procedural compliance [structural changes] results in contempt for reform" (p. 32).

In the 1970s there was a decline in the United States in the quality of people entering teaching (Schlechty & Vance, 1983). Although there is some distance to go, especially for minority groups, gender composition, and certain subject areas, I believe that the downward trend was reversed in the 1980s. Compensation levels and the opportunity to bring about reforms and make a contribution to the learning experiences of students have improved significantly in many jurisdictions since 1983. Incentive schemes and other strategies are still very much needed in order to build on this momentum, especially to attract ethnic minorities. (The Carnegie Task Force, 1986, estimates that as many as 50,000 ethnic minority new teachers per year are needed in the United States.) But the trend to making teaching more attractive has begun. Its growth will depend very much on whether conditions for interactive professionalism and continuous teacher development are established at universities and schools.

There are a number of issues related to recruitment and selection, which I will not be able to analyze in detail in this chapter. The quality and number of applicants have already been mentioned. In overall terms, as I have said, greater numbers of teachers are needed. The question of the quality of teacher education applicants is still being debated in the United States, and there appear to be a number of myths as well as somewhat of a moving target (Cross, 1988).

In Canada, where the salary and prestige of teachers have always been comparatively better, the total number of applicants is not the problem. In Ontario, for example, there are over 20,000 applicants being considered for the 5,500 places for 1990–91. Here as in many other jurisdictions across North America the additional question is selection criteria. Academic grades, experience profiles, and aptitude for teaching, including personality traits, have all figured in a long and largely fruitless debate about who make the best teachers. Now that more focused research in teacher education has finally begun to occur, I expect that we will have better data to inform the policy considerations, but at this point we do not know much for sure about how to make these choices.

An equally serious problem concerning teacher shortage is regional disparity. Incentives for teaching in one state compared with another, one province vs. another, one city or another, vary greatly. Title's (1989) analysis of "incentives that matter" illustrates this point rather clearly (see also Bartell, 1988; Dorman & Bartell, 1988). Title compared incentive profiles in the seven northeast states (Connecticut, Maine, Massachusetts, New Hampshire, New York, Rhode Island, and Vermont). Salary levels varied significantly, as did working conditions (attendance rates, per pupil expenditures, pupil/teacher ratios and the like) and compensation benefits. Quality of life indicators, a factor looming larger and larger for people in the 1990s, represented another set of major differences. Using nine factors—climate and terrain, housing, health care and environment, crime, transportation, education, arts, recreation, and economy—Title carried out a series of revealing analyses. The attractiveness of particular configurations will depend on individual values and preferences, but there is little doubt that the factors influence where people choose to teach, especially when there is a surplus of jobs.

Within provinces or states there are also great differences. In the Toronto area, the seven Metropolitan Public School Boards and the large Roman Catholic School Board are having great difficulty attracting and retaining teachers, compared with the rapidly growing school boards immediately outside Toronto and beyond. The reasons relate to quality of life and working conditions, including housing costs, urban congestion and related stress, places to raise families, chances of promotion, and the like.

As vexing as these particular problems are, there is a more fundamental message contained in this chapter. The worst case scenario explains why Huberman (1988, 1991) found so many disillusioned older teachers. It goes like this.

1. Some excellent people interested in teaching do not apply.
2. Many excellent people do apply and their first experiences at the preservice level are less than exhilarating.
3. In the critical first five years of teaching, the better candidates are more likely to leave (as well as a few of the worst) because schools are alienating, unfulfilling places for both teachers and students. Average or other teachers experiencing dissatisfaction do not leave.
4. As the years unfold, dissatisfied teachers become more and more disillusioned, cynical, and less motivated to participate in improvements.
5. Schools don't improve and remain alienating, unfulfilling places for teachers and students.
6. Full circle: Because schools are alienating places to have a career, some excellent people interested in teaching do not apply. But some do, etc.

I said this is the worst case scenario. It does not say anything about the thousands and thousands of dedicated teachers doing an excellent job, positively influencing the life-chances of the students they encounter— except that they are doing this despite the system. As stark as the above scenario is, it should be abundantly clear what the agenda of reform is about. It is creating more and more best case scenarios of the kind seen in Rosenholtz' (1989) learning-enriched schools and other success stories we have seen throughout this book. It is not just a matter of imagining better solutions, or even finding them in existence, but of engaging in sophisticated strategies and persistent processes of change to accomplish them. There is far, far more to reform than most people suppose.

THE PROFESSIONAL DEVELOPMENT OF ADMINISTRATORS AND CONSULTANTS

So far I have concentrated on the professional development of teachers. Equally important in a strategic sense are the certification and professional development opportunities designed for those who lead and facilitate the change process.

We can start with a generalization about the formal training received by administrators and consultants prior to entering their positions: With a few recent exceptions they do *not* receive much preparation for their roles as change leaders. Let us consider the kind of preparation received by administrators and district consultants, respectively.

Administrators

To become a principal or district administrator, candidates are typically required to take advanced degrees or courses, usually in educational administration, and more recently specific training and experiences in "leadership academies" and leadership centers, which have been established over the past five years throughout North America. The preparation and professional development of administrators have evolved from the university-based educational administration tradition to a variety of forms that tend to cluster around the intensification and restructuring themes. I will briefly characterize and assess the essence of this development.

Murphy and Hallinger (1987), Daresh and LaPlant (1985), Pitner (1987), and many others have described the limitation of the traditional educational administration route. Abstract theorizing, lack of problem and skill focus, distance from actual settings, and absence of mechanisms for application and follow-through have made university-based programs relatively ineffective. As the pressure for improvements intensified during the 1980s, and as research and practice repeatedly identified effective leadership as a key to reform, the university model came under increasing fire. It did not contribute to the improvement of administrative practice, which was desperately needed.

Given its strategic importance, and given that professional development for leaders had even further to go than staff development, there has been an enormous expansion of leadership preparation and training activities since 1983. In the United States, 18 states passed new legislation between 1983 and 1986 concerning certification requirement; 24 states enacted legislation for in-service training for administrators, establishing leadership academies, administrative training centers, and the like (Murphy & Hallinger, 1987). In Canada, there has not been as much new legislation, but similar rapid expansion of government, district, and university programs and centers has occurred (Fullan, Park, Williams, et al., 1987; Leithwood, Armstrong, & Kelly, 1989; Leithwood & Avery, 1987). Leithwood and Steinbach's (1990) training in problem-solving expertise is one good example of the kind of professional development needed by administrators for coping with complex matters of improvement. The certification, assessment, and competency-based models in the United States suffer from the same problems (and more) as those described in Chapter 14 for teacher competency, certification, and training. Chapters 8 and 10 discussed what is needed for effective leadership at the school and district levels, respectively. Leaders must manage and lead sophisticated, persistent, and continuous improvement processes. They must derive meaning for themselves and enable others to obtain meaning in a sea of reform, which, to say the least, is not all that clear. They are being asked to lead restructuring efforts involving radical change and associated complexities (Elmore, 1988; Sykes & Elmore, 1989). They are not simply implementers of policy, but leaders in sorting out the multiple priorities and possibilities continually being generated inside and outside the systems in which they work. Assessment, certification, and other competency-based approaches are insufficient, and may even be retrogressive for the kind of leadership that is needed, which is closer to what Bennis and Nanus (1985) so aptly described as *perpetual learning*. Bennis and Nanus interviewed a diverse group of highly effective leaders, and were struck by the fact that "above all, they talked about learning."

> Nearly all leaders are highly proficient in learning from experience. Most were able to identify a small number of mentors and key experiences that powerfully shaped their philosophies, personalities, and operating style. . . . Learning is the essential fuel for the leader, the source of high-octane energy that keeps up the momentum by continually sparking new understanding, new ideas, and new challenges. It is absolutely indispensable under today's conditions of rapid change and complexity. Very simply, those who do not learn do not long survive as leaders. (Bennis & Nanus, 1985, p. 188)

The movement toward new leadership approaches is still at the early stages. Murphy and Hallinger's (1987) volume contains descriptions of a number of the new programs in question, which they group into three categories: (1) *state models* (the Maryland Professional Development Academy, the North Carolina Leadership Institute); (2) *laboratory and university centers* (the Far West Lab's Peer-Assisted Leadership program [PAL], Harvard's Principals' Center, IDEA's Principals' Collegial Support Group, Lewis and Clark's College Summer Institute); and (3) *professional association programs* (the American Association of School Administrator's [AASA] Model for Preparing School Leaders, the Center for Advancing Principalship Excellence [APEX]). In addition, school districts across North America have developed thousands of in-district programs for future and present leaders.

The best of the new programs appear to incorporate much needed new designs and experiences—knowledge bases that include research findings and school-based and district cases, support groups among participants, adult and staff development learning principles, skill and application focuses, and so on.

There are still, however, a host of problems related to our earlier discussion of why professional development programs often fail to live up to their promise. Hallinger and Wimpelberg (1989), among many others, have observed that despite a greater relevance of the content of programs, there is still "a relative infrequency of substantive program follow-up in the forms of coaching, on-site technical assistance, or support groups" (p. 11). Martin and Johnson (1989) report that while 92 percent of the districts in Colorado have administrator staff development programs, "almost no districts followed-up their . . . programs with subsequent observations, coaching, surveys, analyses, or technical assistance" (p. 10). Murphy and Hallinger (1987) state that there is an overall "lack of assessment of program effects" (p. 271). Little and associates (1987) found widespread involvement of administrators in district in-service, in the California School Leadership Academy (with 14 regional centers) and in professional conferences, but they also note that lack of follow-up was the prevailing pattern.

There are a number of conclusions that we can draw about administrator staff development. First, there has been a proliferation of development, training, and support programs, especially for school principals. If teaching is a "lonely profession" by tradition, principaling is more so, since there are fewer colleagues and greater physical distance between them. Some leadership and support programs are beginning to address this problem. Most new approaches described above built in collegiality and professional exchange at least during the course of the program. A few go beyond this. Barnett and Mueller (1989) found both short-term and longer-term (two to three years) effects from the PAL program for principals, which continued to meet in problem-solving groups. Daresh (1988) describes the potential of a new program to provide future principals with mentors and other development support. But there is a long way to go, especially in linking leadership programs to follow-up and improvement on the job.

Second, there is even further to go if we consider instructionally focused restructuring reforms. Here principals are expected to lead teams and schools in wholesale revamping of the school (Elmore, 1989). As Little and associates (1987) found, even the new pattern of staff development activities "maintains a long tradition of separating the training of administrators from the training of teachers" (p. 97). Some team development approaches are beginning to emerge, but we have not yet made much headway in establishing collaborative work cultures (Fullan, 1990).

Third, I have not made a distinction in this discussion between school and district administrators. There are new certification and staff development requirements and opportunities for superintendents, but they are much, much less developed than those for principals. Little and associates (1987) state that "there are few instances of professional development that prepared school boards, superintendents, and other district administrators to do an effective job of supporting site administrators in their work with teachers" (p. 97). In Ontario, we found few intensive professional development opportunities to prepare and support superintendents for their leadership roles (Fullan et al., 1987).

Fourth, the focus on leadership development has resulted in the establishment of new units as well as inter-agency cooperation. University faculties of education have adapted by creating new centers for leadership, participating in the running of regional leadership academies, and otherwise collaborating in new field-based leadership initiatives.

Fifth, I will not be able to delve in to the crucial issues related to the identification and development of leadership candidates, or selection procedures. It is only recently that some districts have been attempting to identify and support the early and continuous development of potential future leaders within the system. There is still a serious shortage of ethnic minority candidates. Women are beginning to be appointed in numbers, but their particular pre- and on-the-job professional development and support needs are not being addressed (see Bell & Chase, 1989; Shakeshaft, 1987, 1989). Irrespective of ethnicity and gender, and leadership training opportunities, selection criteria and procedures for promotion are notoriously vague and ad hoc in most districts (Baltzell & Dentler, 1983; Lawton, Hickcox, Leithwood, & Musella, 1986).

Finally, it should be recognized that teacher, principal, and superintendent learning and development go together. It is obvious that the principles of effective professional development apply to all three groups. More fundamentally, effective systems treat professional development of all groups as intimately interrelated. Rosenholtz (1989) identified "moving" and "stuck" schools, but she also discovered that school districts could be classified in the same way. The moving districts systematically concentrated on teacher, principal, and superintendent "selection and learning." Rosenholtz stresses: "In district efforts at continuous improvement, superintendents' own learning cannot be overestimated" (p. 183). And in moving districts, "superintendents make clear through their actions that above all else, principals must be continuous learners, and through their leadership, entice teachers to be learners, too" (p. 185). In short, school and system improvement in the long run depends on the constant generation of leaders who are expert at self-learning and at promoting individual and collaborative learning in others (see also Barth, 1990; Schlechty, 1990).

Consultants

District, regional, and state curriculum and program consultants; project directors; and the variety of people concerned with providing technical assistance, linkage, and training are directly involved in attempting to bring about change. While the depth of skills in different areas may vary depending on the job, I have suggested that consultants need some degree of knowledge and skills in both the *content* of changes being considered and in the *process* of change (Chapter 11). The latter, in reference to this chapter, is none other than the consultant's ability to establish effective professional development activities with his or her clientele. The formal preparation of consultants for their role as change agents is, to overstate the case, not well developed. Most do not receive any special training other than the preservice and in-service courses available to teachers and administrators. Consultants can develop considerable expertise in the substance of the curriculum or program area in which they work. However, the capacity to plan, conduct, and follow through on professional development activities and other aspects of the change process is much more rare.

The number of teacher-leadership roles, as noted, has greatly expanded in the last few years—resource teachers, mentors, coaches, and staff developers have been added to the list of other district and school specialists charged with facilitating improvements. With experience, district and school consultants can become effective at introducing new programs and practices, but it is a trial-and-error process (Fullan, Anderson, & Newton, 1986). The professional development needs of these teacher-leaders is greater than ever. Even staff developers whose forte is designing and conducting training, may at best be good at providing staff development to assist in the implementation of innovations, but may not be prepared for the more basic tasks of implementing new roles (their own included) into the institution, or helping to bring about collaborative work cultures and other organizational changes (Fullan, 1990).

A number of resources and professional development opportunities available are for consultants, but few of them include on-the-job follow-up and other principles of effective staff development. Saxl, Miles, and Lieberman (1990) with their ACE materials (Assisting Change in Education) have recently designed one of the most thorough and relevant training series available for change facilitators. Ironically, the problem remains that there are a great and increasing variety of change agents—curriculum consultants, staff developers, mentors, coaches, etc.—who themselves need pre- and in-service professional development on change lead-ership.

GUIDELINES FOR EFFECTIVE PROFESSIONAL DEVELOPMENT

We have covered very considerable ground in Chapter 14 and in this chapter, precisely because continuous early learning and development—in this case for adults in the system—is the key to long-term reform. A number of suggestions for action are already embedded in the various sections and associated references. In addition, Arbuckle and Murray (1989), Caldwell (1989), Levine (1989), Loucks-Horsley and colleagues (1987), Murphy and Hallinger (1987), and Orlich (1989) all contain guidelines and ideas for effective staff development.

With the caution that particular professional development ap-proaches should be based on the knowledge of the role, people, and set-tings in question, as well as on an overall understanding of the change process and the meaning of change, I confine myself here to three major thematic guidelines that emerge from Chapters 14 and 15.

Starting with the university as we did in Chapter 14, faculties and schools of education should re-orient themselves fundamentally to align themselves with the profession of teaching and the improvement of schools rather than with abstract academe (Clifford & Guthrie, 1988, Ch. 8). This does not mean that they should eschew the university; on the contrary, it requires closer collaboration with arts and science, but from a clearer and stronger primary base of professionalism. More specifically, *Guideline 1 recommends that faculties and schools should use three interrelated strategies—faculty renewal, program innovation, and knowledge production—to establish their new niche as respected and effective professional schools.*

Faculty renewal involves taking advantage of current opportunities by restaffing schools of education with individuals and combinations of in-dividuals who can interrelate inquiry and teacher development across the continuum, through collaborative activities inside and outside the univer-sity. We need people who are *equally* at home in universities and schools. The same principles of selection *and* continuous learning on the job that we have been talking about apply to school of education professors.

Program innovation is multifaceted and continuous. Foundation, methods, and practice teaching—hitherto islands unto themselves—must be fundamentally interrelated through experimental programs explicitly designed for that purpose. Preservice programs now lack coherence. Al-ternative and experimental programs may very well be the norm over the next decade, but in any case focused programs with small cohorts of stu-dents are needed that are designed so that *individuals* can achieve mean-ing in their own minds. Program coherence, after all, is not an objective phenomenon; it is only subjective integration that really counts. New forms of collaborative programming with arts and science, and joint activities with the field relative to the entire continuum (pre-preservice, preservice, induction, in-service) will be required. Prospective new teachers would be involved in a number of purposeful teaching settings in order to acquire the skills and habits of working with a variety of situations and strategies. Clinical observation and supervised reflective practice should be featured in all models (Fullan & Connelly, 1990; Goodlad, Soder, & Sirotnik, 1990; Sarason et al., 1986; Schön, 1987). Arts and science and faculty of education collaboration, and school–university partnerships would be directed at making the teacher education continuum an early reality. Such partnerships would embrace the continuing development of leaders through programs for mentors, coaches, principals, superintendents, and other school leaders.

Knowledge production suggests that the proper role of the university is to foster constant inquiry within the profession, starting with itself. This means three interrelated things: (1) using the knowledge base to design programs, (2) conducting collaborative research and evaluation on programs with those in school systems, and (3) contributing to a growing body of knowledge through dissemination and continuous exchange with the broader community of field and university professionals. All of this implies that coherent alternative models, constantly being assessed in a checks-and-balances manner, would be the pattern, rather than monolithic all-purpose programs (for more systematic guidelines congruent with the recommendations here, see Goodlad, 1990a; Griffin, 1986; Howey & Zimpher, 1989).

As we move to school districts and schools, induction programs linked to faculties of education would serve several purposes simultaneously by breaking down isolation between the two sets of institutions, by providing developmental support for new teachers, and by stimulating and stretching mentors and those (e.g., principals) supporting mentors. It is a high-payoff strategy, but we have also seen that professional development in school districts and schools is fragmented, lacks follow-through, and fails to contribute to the continuing development of teachers or of schools as institutions. *Guideline 2 is that learning—in this case of adults—must permeate everything the district and school does; it must be held as equally important for all staff regardless of position; districts and schools must strive to coordinate and integrate staff development.*

Mortimore and associates (1988), it will be recalled, found that the most effective schools in their sample highly valued in-service education. However, it was not the amount of staff development that made the difference; it was the extent to which schools were *selective* as to which in-service opportunities they would take up among the vast array of possibilities. Teacher, principal, and central office selection must all be geared to identifying, promoting, and supporting a community of purposeful learners (Barth, 1990; Rosenholtz, 1989). At the school level, principals and teachers would work together in establishing instructionally focused collaborative work cultures, which would put them in a position to be critical consumers of the considerable professional development resources available to them. Collaborative work cultures, as we have seen, not only use staff development more effectively, but they create and generate resources such as time and access to the expertise of others. Districts in collaboration with unions would be responsible for establishing an environment of preservice and support conducive to the development, maintenance, and evaluation of such schools and the people in them. Effective districts are highly engaged with their schools, which they see as centers of learning and development of both staff and students. Synergy of professional development—the sum total of formal and informal learning—is the hallmark of effective districts and the schools within them.

The final overall guideline is directed at any and all agencies or groups involved in professional development. *Guideline 3 is that all promoters of professional development should pay attention to and worry about two fundamental requirements: (1) incorporating the attributes of successful professional development in as many activities as possible, and (2) ensuring that the ultimate purpose of professional development is less to implement a specific innovation or policy and more to create individual and organizational habits and structures that make continuous learning a valued and endemic part of the culture of schools and teaching.*

Loucks-Horsley and associates (1987) summarized what they saw as the 10 characteristics of successful teacher development (which apply to all professional development).

1. collegiality and collaboration;
2. experimentation and risk taking;
3. incorporation of available knowledge bases;
4. appropriate participant involvement in goal setting, implementation, evaluation, and decision making;
5. time to work on staff development and assimilate new learnings;
6. leadership and sustained administrative support;
7. appropriate incentives and rewards;
8. designs built on principles of adult learning and the change process;
9. integration of individual goals with school and district goals; and
10. formal placement of the program within the philosophy and organizational structure of the school and district. (p. 8)

Districts, schools, universities, unions, governments, professional associations, and staff developers of all types should strive to incorporate what we know about successful professional development. The second aspect of guideline 3 is a reminder that in-service education is not an end in itself, nor is implementing a proven innovation. The ultimate goal is changing the culture of learning for both adults and students so that engagement and betterment is a way of life in schools. We will have arrived when professional development as the workshop or the course gives way to how the teacher and the administrator go about seeking and testing improvements as part of their everyday work inside and outside the school. In this way the variety of formal and informal learning experiences would merge—training and sharing workshops, teacher–teacher interaction, one-to-one assistance through coaching and mentoring, meetings, trying out new approaches, observing and being observed, individual and team planning, monitoring results and other inquiry, and the like. Thus, learning by educators would not just occur during formal workshops, but would become a natural part of the work setting.

As long as there is the need for improvement, namely, forever, there will be the need for professional development. Problems of teaching in modern society are getting ever more complex. In-built professional development of the type described in this chapter is *the* premier strategy for coping with this growing complexity. People change by doing new things in conjunction with others, while obtaining new insights and commitments to do even better. If the lessons of this chapter are to be learned, people in the education profession will have more contact with each other, with other agencies, and with their clients; there will be more support, but also more pressure and vulnerability, as what people do becomes the subject of observation, discussion, and action. Staff development coordinators and leaders, whether consultants, teachers, principals, union members, government personnel, or university professors, will be involved in designing more thorough professional development. They will seek better ways to support follow-through application of ideas, which achieve improvement in practice while simultaneously contributing to the establishment of new structures and norms.

Imagine the cumulative effect, for better (or for worse), of attracting the right (or the wrong) people to the profession, and then of providing from the beginning a series of uplifting (or dulling) daily experiences over a 40-year period. We need a broader and more intensely developmental conception of teaching from day one onward—a conception backed up by structures and practices that integrate continual development into the regular work of becoming and being a teacher and administrator. Sustained improvements in schools will not occur without changes in the quality of learning experiences on the part of those who run the schools.

CHAPTER 16

The Future of
Educational Change

Caveat implementor.

The shame of educational change is the squandering of good intentions and the waste of resources in light of personal and societal needs of great human consequence. The capacity to bring about change and the capacity to bring about improvement are two different matters. Change is every-where, progress is not. The more things change the more they remain the same, if we do not learn our lessons that a different mind- and action-set is required.

Striving for progress has both good and bad features. All change, including progress, contains ambivalence and dilemmas because, when we set off on a journey to achieve significant change, we do not know in advance all the details of how to get there, or even what it is going to be like when we arrive. And in most cases we are not setting off but more being swept along by the forces of change. Positive change is highly excit-ing and exhilarating as it generates new learning, new commitments, new accomplishments, and greater meaning, but anxiety, uncertainty, exhaus-tion and loss of confidence also mark the way, especially at the early stages. What we are faced with is how to appreciate the good and bad of change and to approach it with a view to altering the mix by strengthen-ing the good features and reducing the bad.

There is one pragmatic reason why this challenge is worth taking seriously. It is not as if we can avoid change, since it pursues us in every way. We might as well, then, make the best of it. The answer is not in avoiding change, but in turning the tables by facing it head-on. The new mind-set is to exploit change before it victimizes us. Change is more likely to be an ally than an adversary, if it is confronted. We can learn to reject unwanted change more effectively, while at the same time becoming more effective at accomplishing desired improvements.

Grappling with educational change in self-defeating ways has been the modal experience over the last 30 years. We know that people often don't learn from their own experiences, let alone from the experience of others (i.e., from history). The response of many has been to redouble their efforts. For those in authority this has meant more advocacy, more legislation, more accountability, more resources, etc. For those on the receiving end the response has been more closed doors, retreats into isolationism or out of education altogether, and in some cases collective resistance. We have seen that these seemingly rational political solutions, while perfectly understandable if one is in a hurry to bring about or avoid change, simply do not work. In fact, they do more harm than good as frustration, tension, and despair accumulate.

At the same time, when a problem is important and solutions are not forthcoming some people begin to take different tacks, reframing their approaches however consciously or intuitively. This is how new paradigms are forged, and I have tried in the chapters of this book to provide insights into this new way of thinking about educational change as applied to the key roles, constituencies, and functions of schools and their environments. The building blocks of improvement will be found in the combination of insights and actions of differently placed individuals. For that reason the point of departure for new approaches is contained in the analyses and corresponding recommendations in the different chapters, and these will not be repeated here.

We have seen many case examples and pockets of success. While still in the minority, the successes seem both more frequent and more robust over the past five years. Less piecemeal and more wholistic approaches to reform are becoming evident. We are also seeing clear parallels with successful cases in business and industry. Block (1987), Kanter (1989), and Peters (1987)—to name a few—have arrived at essentially the same conclusions and recommendations.

The immediate future of educational change is at a particularly strategic juncture. The life-chances of large segments of society are increasingly dismal. Educational reform, especially designed with at risk students in mind, obviously represents one major solution. At the same time, we are in the midst of a temporary opportunity to take substantial action on many interrelated fronts—the retirement and corresponding new hiring of up to one-half of the teaching and administrative educational force between 1988 and 1995, political resources of power and money on a scale not seen for 25 years, a greatly expanded knowledge base related to teaching new programs and change processes that are increasingly thorough and powerful, and more people and constituencies inside and outside the educational system willing and committed to working on the solutions. What we do in the 1990s to exploit or abuse these powerful levers for reform will determine the quality of education for the next half-century. This confluence of factors will not be available after 1995.

I will not attempt to predict the future of educational change, except to identify six themes central to the emerging new paradigm that will be needed to cope with and turn change to our advantage. The six involve moving from an old, unsuccessful way of managing change to a new mind-set.

1. from negative to positive politics,
2. from monolithic to alternative solutions,
3. from innovations to institutional development,
4. from going it alone to alliances,
5. from neglect to deeper appreciation of the change process, and
6. from "if only" to "if I" or "if we."

FROM NEGATIVE TO POSITIVE POLITICS

People at all levels of the educational system have power—power most often used *not* to do things. Negative politics from below means constantly resisting changes; from above it means attempting to impose reform through fiat. These negative modes are understandable given that changes are not normally introduced with much sensitivity and that there is little time to be considerate. The result is a decidedly negative vicious cycle. Resistance, cajoling, blaming others, self-protection, avoidance, and caution all become habitual strategies for coping. It is possible, of course, to survive in such a negative environment through self-serving manipulation, but Peter Block (1987) cuts to the core when he challenges, "Why get better at a bad game?" What's the percentage?

If we are going to use power, we might as well use it to do good. Positive politics means focusing on a few important priorities by implementing them especially well, while keeping other potential priorities in perspective. We have seen that not all proposed policy change can or should be implemented. While we continue to say no to changes that do not make sense or that come when we are overloaded, we should always be able to point to valued change priorities we are working on. It is not acceptable to say, "I cannot implement X" unless we can continue the sentence by saying, "because I am bringing about improvements in Y and Z." The burden of positive politics is to work continually on shaping and pursuing what *is* valuable. Block summarizes in these words.

The key to positive politics, then, is to look at each encounter as an opportunity to support autonomy and to create an organization of our own choosing. It requires viewing ourselves as the primary instrument for changing the culture. Cultures get changed in a thousand small ways, not by dramatic announcements emanating from the boardroom. If we wait until top management gives leadership to the change we want to see, we miss the point. For us to have any hope that our own preferred future will come to pass, we provide the leadership. We hope that the world around us supports our vision, but even if it doesn't, we will act on that vision. Leadership is the process of translating intentions into reality. (pp. 97–98)

Like-minded individuals and small groups of individuals can create their own critical masses, even if it is only two people. Positive politics is not a sure-fire way out of the dilemmas of change, and it is not risk free, but it is a much more powerful and satisfying route to reform. In short, one aspect of the new mind-set is to increase the proportion of effort devoted to positive politics: to use power to bring about improvements in our own immediate environment.

FROM MONOLITHIC TO ALTERNATIVE SOLUTIONS

Another dilemma in educational reform concerns uniformity vs. variation of solutions. Neither centralization nor decentralization seems to work. Meaning cannot be masterminded at a global level. It is found through small-scale pursuits of significant personal and organizational goals. The school is the "center" of change. Thus, we must allow for and foster variation across schools. I argued in Chapter 10 that this does not mean that anything goes. Constant communication and negotiations between districts and schools, for example, can honor both variation and mutual shaping. Statewide intensification systems tightly designed to align curriculum, teaching, and student performance cannot work without reducing the educational enterprise to a low common denominator.

The alternative that I have suggested is planned variation with the priority placed on building individual and school capacity to bring about changes. Any time we focus on capacity-building, we create systems that to some extent have minds of their own. From the point of view of the external authority certain priorities and means may be selected that are not of their choosing. This does not represent as much of a loss of control as might be expected, since, as just noted, people have always exercised the right not to implement priorities selected by external authorities. Uncontrolled variation is prevented because the process of interaction and negotiation described in previous chapters operates in a checks-and-balances fashion. Sustained interaction around the goals and means of reform generates more ideas in the aggregate, but it also limits random individual variation. Norms of collaboration and continuous improvement enable us to pursue reforms through drawing on and contributing to the pool of ideas and solutions. The emphasis on figuring out alternative solutions close to home (albeit drawing widely on ideas) reduces the propensity to seek or accept ready-made external solutions.

FROM INNOVATIONS TO INSTITUTIONAL DEVELOPMENT

The innovation paradigm has provided considerable insights into the do's and don'ts of implementing single innovations. We should continue to use this knowledge any time we are working on particular valued priorities. But there is a more fundamental message in the new mind-set that says that thinking in terms of single innovations is inherently limiting, because we are in reality faced with attempting to cope with multiple innovations simultaneously. We have also concluded that it is impossible to implement all these innovations, even if we wanted to. The solution has to be found in making sense of this multiplicity by reducing it—through prioritizing, timing, and synthesizing—to manageable proportions.

Instead of tracing specific policies and innovations, we turn the problem on its head, and ask what does the array of innovative possibilities look like, if we are on the receiving or shopping end. Thus, institutional development—changes that increase schools' and districts' capacity and performance for continuous improvements—is the generic solution needed (Fullan, 1990).

Taking on one innovation at a time is fire fighting and faddism. Institutional development of schools and districts increases coherence and capacity for sorting out and integrating the myriad of choices, acting on them, assessing progress, and (re)directing energies. The greatest problem faced by school systems is not resistance to innovation but taking on too many changes indiscriminately. Selectivity and synergy replace ad hocism in institutionally developed organizations (Rosenholtz, 1989).

We cannot develop institutions without developing the people in them. This is why teacher development and professionalism, along with student engagement and active involvement of each of the constituencies, have figured so prominently in the earlier chapters. Combining individual and institutional development has its tensions, but the message in this book should be abundantly clear. You cannot have one without the other.

FROM GOING IT ALONE TO ALLIANCES

Interactive professionalism has been another core theme throughout the analysis. It serves simultaneously to increase access to and scrutiny of each other's ideas and practices. We have seen the debilitating effect of the tradition of individualism in teaching. All successful change processes are characterized by collaboration and close interaction among those central to carrying out the changes. If we are to accomplish change in education, we have to, in Bruce Joyce's coruscating phrase, "crack the walls of privatism." Privatism and professional development are closely and inversely linked. Alliances provide greater power, both of ideas and of the ability to act on them.

Alliances are not only across individuals. We have also seen that some of the most powerful strategies involve inter-institutional partnerships—between school districts and universities, businesses and districts, coalitions of schools, and so on.

These individual and social experiments are not problem free. One can collaborate and do bad and wasteful things as well as good things. In each of the chapters in Parts II and III, I have made recommendations to assist individuals and groups to take productive action with others. There is no question that the problems of reform are insurmountable without a dramatic increase in the number of alliances practicing positive politics.

FROM NEGLECT TO DEEPER APPRECIATION OF THE CHANGE PROCESS

It is so easy to underestimate the complexities of the change process. There is in fact a lot of common sense in successful change processes. Looked at one day, in one setting, successful change seems so sensible and straightforward. But on another day, in another situation, or even the same situation on another day, improvement cannot be obtained with the most sophisticated efforts. Change is difficult because it is riddled with dilemmas, ambivalences, and paradoxes. It combines steps that seemingly do not go together: to have a clear vision and be open-minded; to take initiative and empower others; to provide support and pressure; to start small and think big; to expect results and be patient and persistent; to have a plan and be flexible; to use top-down and bottom-up strategies; to experience uncertainty and satisfaction. Educational change is above all a very personal experience in a social, but often impersonal, setting.

Coping with change effectively requires that we explicitly think and worry about the change process. We should constantly draw on knowledge about the factors and insights associated with successful change processes (see Chapter 5). But we must employ this knowledge in a nonmechanical manner along with intuition, experience, and assessment of the particular situation, each time adding to our store of common knowledge. Respecting the change process means seeking common patterns while being prepared for uniqueness. This amounts to being self-conscious about the change process as it affects us, and promoting collective self-consciousness about how the process affects others.

There are no short-cuts, and there is no substitute for directly engaging in improvement projects with others. Like most complex endeavors, in order to get better at change we have to practice it on purpose. What makes this guideline all the more important is that we can be assured that countless others around us will not be respecting the change process in their hurry to impose or avoid change. "Pursuing fast-paced innovation" and "learning to love change" are central to the new paradigm (Peters, 1987).

FROM "IF ONLY" TO "IF I" OR "IF WE"

Another example of looking for solutions in the wrong places is the "if only" problem. Patterson, Purkey, and Parker (1986) identified this reinforcer of the status quo by comparing what they called "rational" and "nonrational" models.

> The central difference between the two models lies in their interpretation of reality. Proponents of the rational model believe that a change in procedures will lead to improvement in educational practice. In short the rational model begins with an "if–then" philosophy. If A happens, then B will logically follow. When reality fails to validate this "if–then" perspective (i.e., when B doesn't happen) the argument shifts to an "if–only" position. If only schools will tighten up rules and regulations, improved discipline will follow. If only teachers are given clear directives, then improved teaching will follow. Advocates for the nonrational model claim that the "if–then and if–only" model is wishful thinking; organizations do not always behave in a logical, predictable manner. Acknowledging this reality, the nonrational model attempts to turn it to the advantage of those in the system. Rather than spending organizational energy trying to conform to wishful thinking, the nonrational model allows us to invest our energy into devising solutions that will work, given reality. (Patterson, et al., 1986, p. 27)

If only statements beg the question, externalize the blame, and immobilize people. Expecting others to act first, or "waiting for clear instructions before acting" (Block, 1987, p. 16) is self-defeating. Far from letting others off the hook, taking action for oneself puts *greater pressure* on others to respond than do reams of wishful thinking and verbal advocacy. Using the principles and ideas of change in this book, every individual can take some effective action in collaboration with one or more other individuals. Organizations do not get healthy by themselves, and we would be extremely lucky if our organization got better through someone else's efforts other than our own. The more "if I" action that takes place in conjunction with the other themes in this chapter, the more "if we" participation will be generated.

Acting on change is an exercise in pursuing meaning. Selected educational reform that takes individual meaning and development seriously not only stands a better chance of being implemented; it also offers some hope for combating the stagnation, burnout, and cynicism of those in schools—which in the long run will lead to the desiccation of all promising change.

One of the impressive features of viewing change from the perspective of meaning lies in the realization that there are problems and responsibilities at every level in the educational system. We should recognize our own responsibilities, and at the same time attempt to understand the conditions faced by those in other roles as a precondition for engaging them in change. We should approach educational change with the renewed respect that comes from the realization that it demands multilevel responsibilities.

Opportunities for reform have never been more abundant. But opportunities can be squandered. A healthy respect for the change process will not eliminate problems, because significant change and learning are always accompanied by tension. As Block (1987) says,

> Almost every important learning experience we have ever had has been stressful. Those issues that create stress for us give us clues about the uncooked seeds within us that need our attention. Stress and anxiety are an indication that we are living our lives and making choices. (p. 191)

Respecting change and working for meaning in ourselves and others will, however, make the tension more productive. We must first count on ourselves, but do so through constant interaction with others in order to broaden the range of ideas and influence. Paradoxically, counting on oneself for a good cause in a highly interactive manner is the key to *system change*. New meaning and reform are created in a thousand small ways that eventually add up to a new order of things. Systems do not change by themselves. People change systems through their actions. It is time to change the way we change.

THE MESSAGE

How will I think and behave differently because I have read this book? First, I will have come to the realization that most changes, even the big restructuring ones, have a pacifier effect because they give the appearance that something substantial is happening when it is not. Second, I will have concluded that countless efforts at change are failing because they do not impact the culture of the school and the profession of teaching.

Thus, the workplace itself is key. Reform cannot be achieved without working with school sites. But school sites are going to need a massive change. Everyone inside and outside the school is going to have to put great energy over a period of time into changing the culture of the school. This means new values, norms, skills, practices and structures. As Goodlad (1990c) observes:

> Renewal—whether of ponds, gardens, people, or institutions—is an internal process, whatever the external concerns and stimulants. It requires motivation, dedication, systematic and systemic evolution, and *time*. A second or

third reform wave calling on teachers as the prime actors will be no more successful than a first wave pushed by policymakers if the conditions necessary to renewal are not developed. Teachers employed for 180 days and required to teach 180 days simply will not renew their schools. . . . The answer is not 160 days of teaching with 20 additional days of employment for planning. It is 180 days of teaching and 20 or more additional days for institutional renewal. (pp. 25–26, emphasis in original)

The answer is not to tack on 20 additional days at the end of the school year. It is to redesign the workplace so that innovation and improvement are built into the daily activities of all teachers. One aspect of the main message, then, is to identify what we are up against, namely, institutional renewal with new forms of leadership, collegiality, commitment to, and mechanisms for continuous improvement. But this is not the full message because it has been stated or implied before without much effect. Sarason's (1971) and Lortie's (1975) analyses of these matters, as brilliant as they are, have stopped short of recommending a way ahead. The main message in this book, in addition to identifying the focus of change (institutional renewal at the school level), is that as individuals we cannot wait for or take as sufficient the actions or policy decisions of others. It would be a mistake to conclude that the solution is for policymakers and administrators to become experts in the change process. By itself, this would be manipulative and ineffectual. Administrators and other change managers have organizational power, but not educational power, because the use of organizational power is not how things get done in schools. As we have seen, decision-makers can make organizational and curriculum change, but still not make any progress.

The only solution is that the whole school—all individuals—must get into the change business; if individuals do not do this, they will be left powerless. The current school organization is an anachronism. It was designed for an earlier period for conditions that no longer hold. It constrains the creation of a new profession of teaching that is so badly needed. Massive effort is required but it must come from individuals putting pressure on themselves and those around them.

Reform is badly needed, yet people's experience with change is overwhelmingly negative—imposition is the norm, costs outweigh benefits, the few successes are short-lived. The only way out of this dilemma is for individuals to take responsibility for empowering themselves and others through becoming experts in the change process. The main message of this book is that individuals must begin immediately to create a new ethos of innovation—one that has the ability to permit and stimulate individual responsibility, and to engage collectively in continuous initiative, thereby preempting the imposition of change from outside. Put another way: successful individuals will be highly involved with their environments, influencing and being influenced in this continuous exchange. The solution lies in critical masses of highly engaged individuals working on the creation of conditions for continuous renewal, while being shaped by these very conditions as the latter evolves. Once some momentum has been established, new organizations will have some generative capacity to select and help renew future members, but it will always require the careful and constant attention of individuals to ensure that renewing organizations continue to develop.

We have a huge negative legacy of failed reform that cannot be overcome simply through good intentions and powerful rhetoric. Paradoxically, the way ahead is through melding individual *and* institutional renewal. One cannot wait for the other. Both must be pursued simultaneously and aggressively. This means that individuals, regardless of their institutions, will have to take affirmative action to make positive changes in their own situations, affecting as many as possible around them. And it means that institutions will have to provide both pressure on and support for individuals: pressure on individuals and organizations to take into account wider societal perspectives, and corresponding action; support, by being responsive to individual and school initiatives encouraging variation as well as convergence on recognized solutions.

It is time to produce results. Individual and institutional renewal, separately and together, should become our raison d'être. We need to replace negativism and Pollyanna-ish rhetoric with informed action. Armed with knowledge of the change process, and a commitment to action, we should accept nothing less than positive results on a massive scale—at both the individual and organizational levels.

Endnotes

CHAPTER 1

1. For a first-rate and fascinating discussion see Robert Nisbet's *The History of the Idea of Progress* (1980). He concludes that societies are deteriorating rather than progressing.

CHAPTER 2

1. These factors, of course, can be separated, for people can value a specific program that is not well developed, or a program that we do not value can be very well developed.

2. See Gold and Miles (1981) for a powerful example of how the community of a middle-class school successfully thwarted an open-education school that they did not value; few working-class communities would have attempted or succeeded in similar opposition.

3. As we shall see later I am not suggesting that testing and monitoring of achievement have no place in improvement efforts. We are dealing in this chapter with the unintended consequences of one-sided or partial solutions.

CHAPTER 3

1. The description of subjective meaning tries to capture the modal individual in a given group. There is no sociologism that all individuals in the same role have the same orientation. There are great differences of course in subjective reality depending on one's gender and career-life stage (Huberman, 1988; Krupp, 1989; Levine, 1989). I will discuss variations in Part II, which deals with specific roles.

2. See Lighthall's (1973) brilliant critique of Smith and Keith's (1971) failure to recognize "the multiple realities" in their otherwise fine case study. Firestone (1989) notes that the problem of multiple realities is especially true if pre-existing conflicts exist between teacher or building staff and district administration. Conflict will spill over into the planning and implementation process and divert attention from the reform to these other matters.

3. See Fullan and Park (1981, p. 6), Crandall et al. (1982), and Hall and Hord (1987) for more elaborate discussions of the notion of different dimensions of implementation. Werner (1980) discusses the role of beliefs in implementation. It is possible to add a few other dimensions, but the three referred to here are central.

4. For a discussion of the two different perspectives on implementation that elaborates on the above issues and contains other ideas on what is a very complex topic, see Berman (1980), Farrar et al. (1979), Majone and Wildavsky (1978), and Fullan and Pomfret (1977). If we were to get into a finer-grained debate, there is some argument for distinguishing between adaptation and evolution.

CHAPTER 4

1. It bears repeating that I am not implying that all members of a group function the same way. There are many individuals who are exceptions, but the sociological pressure is otherwise and eventually exerts its influence on the majority of people in the role.

CHAPTER 7

1. Philip Jackson (1980) quoted Henry Adams as writing, "A teacher affects eternity, he can never tell where his influence stops." As the title of Jackson's paper (*The Uncertainties of Teaching*) indicates, and as Lortie and others have so clearly demonstrated, the obverse is also true. Teachers can never tell when or even whether their influence *starts*, or whether or not it will ever become evident after the student leaves them.

CHAPTER 10

1. By district administrator I mean the chief executive officer and those immediate subordinates who are in *authority* line positions at the district level. The chief executive officer is called Superintendent in most school districts and Director of Education in some jurisdictions in Canada. Immediate subordinates are variously called Assistant Superintendent, Area Superintendent, Superintendent of Program, Director of Instruction, Director of Curriculum, etc. District curriculum consultants (who are in staff positions) are discussed in Chapter 11.

CHAPTER 12

1. Epstein and her colleagues identify a fifth type of parent involvement, which focuses on "parenting" or helping families establish positive home conditions for learning. I do not discuss this in detail, but it is especially important for parents of children at the preschool and early grade stages.

CHAPTER 13

1. There was some ad hoc prior involvement, most notably in the 1954 *Brown* v. *Board of Education* segregation decision and its civil rights aftermaths.

Some large-scale curriculum development projects were also launched with major federal backing with the passage of the National Defense Education Act in 1958 following Sputnik I, when national concern with deficiencies in the country's scientific capabilities was intensified (see Atkins & House, 1981).

References

American Federation of Teachers. (1982). *AFT educational research and dissemination program*. Washington, DC: AFT.

Adelman, N. E. (1986). An exploratory study of teacher alternative certification and retraining programs. Washington, DC: U.S. Department of Education.

Aitken, J. L., & Mildon, D. (1991). Teacher education and the developing teacher: The role of personal knowledge. In M. Fullan & A. Hargreaves (Eds.), *Teacher development and educational change*. East Sussex, United Kingdom: Falmer Press.

Allison, D. J. (1988). *Ontario directors and American superintendents: A study of contrasting cultures and contexts*. Division of Educational Policy Studies, University of Western Ontario, London.

American Association of Colleges for Teacher Education. (1986). *Task Force on teacher certification*. Washington, D.C.: Author.

Anderson, B. (1989). *Reformation of the full education system*. Denver: Education Commission of the States.

Anderson, B., and associates. (1987). State strategies to support local school improvement. *Knowledge: Creation, Diffusion, Utilization, 9*(1), 42–86.

Anderson, B., & Cox, P. (1987). *Configuring the education system for a shared future: Collaborative vision, action, reflection*. Andover, MA: Regional Laboratory for Educational Improvement of the Northeast and the Islands.

Anderson, E. M., & Shannon, A. L. (1988). Toward a conceptualization of mentoring. *Journal of Teacher Education, 39*(1), 38–42.

Anderson, S. (1989). *The management and implementation of multiple changes in curriculum and instruction*. Unpublished doctoral dissertation, University of Toronto.

Anderson, S., Stiegelbauer, S., Gerin-LaJoie, D., Partlow, H., & Cummins, A. (1990). *Project excellence: Evaluation of a student centered secondary school*. Toronto: Ontario Ministry of Education.

Andrews, I. H. (1986). *An investigation of the academic paradigms underlying education programs in five countries*. Paper presented at American Educational Research Association annual meeting.

Aoki, T., et al. (1977). *British Columbia social studies assessment*, Vols. 1–3. Victoria: British Columbia Ministry of Education.

Apple, M. W. (1988). What reform talk does: Creating new inequalities in education. *Educational Administration Quarterly, 24*(3), 272–81.

Apple, M. W., & Jungck, S. (1991). You don't have to be a teacher to teach in this unit: Teaching, technology and control in the classroom. In A. Hargreaves & M. Fullan (Eds.), *Understanding teacher development*. London: Cassell.

Arbuckle, M. A., & Murray, L. B. (1989). *Building systems for professional growth: An action guide*. Andover, MA: Regional Laboratory for Educational Improvement of the Northeast and Islands and the Maine Department of Educational and Cultural Services.

Armour, D., et al. (1976). *Analysis of the school-preferred reading program in selected Los Angeles minority schools.* Santa Monica, CA: Rand Corporation.

Ashton, P., & Webb, R. (1986). *Making a difference: Teachers' sense of efficacy and student achievement.* New York: Longman.

Atkins, J., & House, E. (1981). The federal role in curriculum development, 1950–1980. *Educational Evaluation and Policy Analysis, 3*(5), 5–36.

Bacharach, S. B., Conley, S. C., & Shedd, J. B. (1987). A career developmental framework for evaluating teachers as decision-makers. *Journal of Personnel Evaluation in Education, 1*, 181–94.

Ball, D., & McDiarmid, G. W. (1990). The subject-matter preparation of teachers. In R. Houston, M. Haberman, & J. Sikula (Eds.), *Handbook of research on teacher education* (pp. 437–49). New York: Macmillan.

Baltzell, D., & Dentler, R. (1983). *Selecting American school principals.* Cambridge, MA: Abt Associates.

Barnett, B. G., & Mueller, F. L. (1989). Long-term effects of the peer-assisted leadership program on principals' actions and attitudes. *The Elementary School Journal, 89*(5), 559–74.

Bartell, C. A. (1988). *Policy perspectives on teachers incentive planning.* Paper presented at American Educational Research Association annual meeting.

Barth, R. (1979). Home based reinforcement of school behavior: A review and analysis. *Review of Educational Research, 49*(3), 436–58.

Barth, R. (1990). *Improving schools from within: Teachers, parents and principals can make the difference.* San Francisco: Jossey-Bass.

Bass, G., & Berman, P. (1979). *Federal aid to rural schools: Current patterns and unmet needs.* Santa Monica, CA: Rand Corporation.

Bass, G., & Berman, P. (1981). *Analysis of federal aid to rural schools, Part II: Special needs of rural districts.* Santa Monica, CA: Rand Corporation.

Becker, H. (1981). *Teacher practices of parent involvement at home—A statewide survey.* Paper presented at American Educational Research Association annual meeting.

Bell, C. S., & Chase, S. E. (1988). *Women as district leaders in a male-dominated context: An analysis of gender issues.* Unpublished paper, University of Tulsa.

Bell, C. S., & Chase, S. E. (1989). *Women as educational leaders: Resistance and conformity.* Paper presented at American Educational Research Association annual meeting.

Bellon, E. C., Bellon, J. J., Blank, M. A., Brian, D. J. G., & Kershaw, C. A. (1989a). *Alternative incentive programs for school based reform.* Paper presented at American Educational Research Association annual meeting.

Bellon, J. J., Bellon, E. C., Blank, M. A., Brian, D. J. G., & Kershaw, C. A. (1989b). *Refocusing state reform: The Tennessee experience.* Paper presented at American Educational Research Association annual meeting.

Bennis, W., & Nanus, B. (1985). *Leaders.* New York: Harper & Row.

Bereiter, C., & Scardamalia, M. (1987). An attainable version of high literacy: Approaches to teaching higher-order skills in reading and writing. *Curriculum Inquiry, 17,* 9–30.

Berger, P., & Luckmann, T. (1967). *The social construction of reality.* New York: Anchor Books.

Berman, P. (1978). The study of macro- and micro-implementation. *Public Policy,* *26*(2), 157–84.

Berman, P. (1980). Thinking about programmed and adaptive implementation: Matching strategies to situations. In H. Ingram & D. Mann (Eds.), *Why policies succeed or fail* (pp. 205–27). Beverly Hills, CA: Sage.

Berman, P. (1981). Toward an implementation paradigm. In R. Lehming & M. Kane (Eds.), *Improving schools* (pp. 253–86). Beverly Hills, CA: Sage.

Berman, P., & McLaughlin, M. (1977). *Federal programs supporting educational change: Vol. VII. Factors affecting implementation and continuation.* Santa Monica, CA: Rand Corporation.

Berman, P., & McLaughlin, M. (1978a). *Federal programs supporting educational change: Vol. VIII. Implementing and sustaining innovations.* Santa Monica, CA: Rand Corporation.

Berman, P., & McLaughlin, M. (1978b). Implementation of educational innovation. *Educational Forum, 40*(3), 345–70.

Berman, P., & McLaughlin, M., with Pincus, J., Weiler, D., & Williams, R. (1979). *An exploratory study of school district adaptations.* Santa Monica, CA: Rand Corporation.

Bird, T., & Alspaugh, D. (1986). *1985 survey of district coordinators for the California mentor teacher program.* San Francisco: Far West Laboratory for Educational Research and Development.

Block, P. (1981). *Flawless consulting.* Austin, TX: Learning Concepts.

Block, P. (1987). *The empowered manager.* San Francisco: Jossey-Bass.

Blumberg, A. (1985). *The school superintendent: Living with conflict.* New York: Teachers College Press.

Blumberg, A., & Greenfield, W. (1980). *The effective principal.* Boston: Allyn & Bacon.

Boich, J., Farquhar, R., & Leithwood, K. (1989). *The Canadian school superintendent.* Toronto: OISE Press.

Bolam, R., Baker, K., & McMahon, A. (1979). *The T.I.P.S. project national evaluation report.* Bristol, United Kingdom: University of Bristol, School of Education.

Borko, H., & Livingston, C. (1989). Cognition and improvisation: Differences in mathematics instruction by expert and novice teachers. *American Educational Research Journal, 26*(4), 473–98.

Bossert, S., Dwyer, D., Rowan, B., & Lee, G. (1982). The instructional management role of the principal. *Educational Administration Quarterly, 18,* 34–64.

Bowles, D. (1980). *School-community relations, community support, and student achievement: a summary of findings.* Madison, University of Wisconsin, R&D Center for Individualized Schooling.

Bowles, S., & Gintis, H. (1976). *Schooling in capitalist America.* New York: Basic Books.

Boyd, W. (1978). The changing politics of curriculum policy making for American schools. *Review of Educational Research, 48*(4), 577–628.

Brandt, R. (1989). On parents and schools: A conversation with Joyce Epstein. *Educational Leadership, 47*(2), 24–27.

Bridge, G. (1976). Parent participation in school innovations. *Teachers College Record, 77*(3), 366–84.

British Columbia Ministry of Education. (1988). *Year 2000: A curriculum and assessment framework for the future.* Victoria, BC: Author.

British Columbia Ministry of Education. (1989a). *Mandate for the school system of the province of British Columbia*. Victoria, BC: Author.

British Columbia Ministry of Education. (1989b). *Working plan #1 1989–1999: A plan to implement policy directions*. Victoria, BC: Author.

British Columbia Ministry of Education. (1989c). *Year 2000: A framework for learning*. Victoria, BC: Author.

Brookhart, S., & Loadman, W. (1988). *School-university collaboration: Why it's multicultural education*. Paper presented at American Educational Research Association annual meeting.

Brookover, W. (1981). *Effective secondary schools*. Philadelphia: Research for Better Schools.

Brophy, J., & Good, T. (1986). Teacher behavior and student achievement. In M. Wittrock (Ed.), *Handbook of Research on Teaching* (pp. 328–75). New York: Macmillan.

Brown, S., & Lueder, D. C. (1989). *The emerging roles of the home/school coordinator*. Paper presented at American Educational Research Association annual meeting.

Bryk, A. S., & Thum, Y. M. (1989). *The effects of high school organization on dropping out: An exploratory investigation*. New Brunswick, NJ: Center for Policy Research in Education.

Burke, P., Christensen, J., Fessler, R., McDonnell, J., & Price, J. (1987). *The teacher career cycle: Model development and research report*. Paper presented at American Educational Research Association annual meeting.

Bussis, A., Chittenden, E., & Amarel, M. (1976). *Beyond surface curriculum*. Boulder, CO: Westview Press.

Cadena-Munoz, R., & Keesling, J. (1981). *Parents and federal education programs: Vol. IV. Parental involvement in Title VII projects*. Santa Monica, CA: System Development Corporation.

Caldwell, S. D. (Ed.). (1989). *Staff development: A handbook of effective practices*. Oxford, OH: National Staff Development Council.

Canadian Education Association. (1979). *Results of a Gallup poll of public opinion in Canada about public involvement in education decisions*. Toronto: Author.

Carlson, R. (1972). *School superintendents: Career and performance*. Columbus, OH: Charles Merrill.

Carnegie Forum on Education and the Economy. (1986). *A nation prepared: Teachers for the 21st century* (Report of the Task Force on Teaching as a Profession). New York: Author.

Charters, W., & Jones, J. (1973). *On the neglect of the independent variable in program evaluation* (Occasional paper). Eugene: University of Oregon.

Charters, W., & Pellegrin, R. (1973). Barriers to the innovation process: Four case studies of differentiated staffing. *Educational Administration Quarterly, 9*(1), 3–14.

Cherniss, C. (1980). *Staff burnout: Job stress in the human services*. Beverly Hills, CA: Sage.

Clark, C., & Yinger, R. (1977). Research on teacher thinking. *Curriculum Inquiry, 7*(4), 279–304.

Clark, C., & Yinger, R. (1980). *The hidden world of teaching*. Paper presented at American Educational Research Association annual meeting.

Clark, D., & Astuto, T. A. (1989). The disjunction of federal education policy and educational needs in the 1990s. *Journal of Educational Policy, 4*(5), 11–26.

Clark, D., Lotto, S., & Astuto, T. (1984). Effective schools and school improvement: A comparative analysis of two lines of inquiry. *Educational Administration Quarterly, 20*(3), 41–68.

Clark, D., Lotto, S., & MacCarthy, M. (1980). Factors associated with success in urban elementary schools. *Phi Delta Kappan, 61*(7), 467–70.

Clarridge, P. B. (1989). *Alternative perspectives for analyzing expertise in teaching.* Paper presented at American Educational Research Association annual meeting.

Clifford, G. J., & Guthrie, J. W. (1988). *Ed school: A brief for professional education.* Chicago: University of Chicago Press.

Clifton, R. A. (1979). Practice teaching: Survival in a marginal situation. *Canadian Journal of Education, 4*(3), 60–74.

Cohen, M. (1987). Improving school effectiveness: Lessons from research. In V. Koehler (Ed.), *Handbook of research on teaching* (pp. 474–90). New York: Longman.

Cohen, M. (1988). Designing state assessment systems. *Phi Delta Kappan, 70*(8), 583–88.

Cole, A., & McNay, M. (1989). Induction programs in Ontario schools: Raising questions about pre-service programs and practice. *Education Canada, 29*(2), 4–9, 43.

Coleman, J. (1966). *Equality of educational opportunity.* Washington, DC: U.S. Government Printing Office.

Conley, S., Bacharach, S., & Bauer, S. (1989). The school work environment and teacher career satisfaction. *Educational Administration Quarterly, 25*(1), 58–81.

Connelly, F. M., & Clandinin, D. J. (1989). *Teachers as curriculum planners: Narratives of experience.* New York: Teachers College Press.

Cooper, M. (1988). Whose culture is it, anyway? In A. Lieberman (Ed.), *Building a professional culture in schools* (pp. 45–54). New York: Teachers College Press.

Corbett, H. D., Dawson, J., & Firestone, W. (1984). *School context and school change.* New York: Teachers College Press.

Corbett, H. D., & Wilson, B. (1990). *Testing, reform and rebellion.* Norwood, NY: Ablex.

Corwin, R. (1973). *Reform and organizational survival—The teacher corps as an instrument of educational change.* New York: Wiley.

Cowden, P., & Cohen, D. (1979). *Divergent worlds of practice.* Cambridge, MA: Huron Institute.

Cox, P. L. (1983a). *Inside-out and outside-in: Configurations of assistance and their impact on school improvement efforts.* Paper presented at American Educational Research Association annual meeting.

Cox, P. L. (1983b, November). Complementary roles in successful change. *Educational Leadership*, pp. 10–13.

Crandall, D., and associates. (1982). *People, policies and practice: Examining the chain of school improvement* (Vols. 1–10). Andover, MA: The Network.

Crandall, D., Eiseman, J., & Louis, K. (1986). Strategic planning issues that bear on the success of school improvement efforts. *Educational Administration Quarterly, 22*(3), 21–53.

Cross, L. H. (1988). *Teacher crisis: Myth or reality revisited.* Paper prepared for American Educational Research Association annual meeting.

Crowson, R., & Porter-Gehrie, C. (1980). *The school principalship: An organizational stability role.* Paper presented at American Educational Research Association annual meeting.

Cuban, L. (1988a). Why do some reforms persist? *Educational Administration Quarterly, 24*(3), 329–35.

Cuban, L. (1988b). A fundamental puzzle of school reform. *Phi Delta Kappan, 70*(5), 341–44.

Cuban, L. (1988c). *The managerial imperative and the practice of leadership in schools.* Albany: State University of New York Press.

Cusick, P. (1973). *Inside high school.* Toronto: Holt, Rinehart & Winston.

Cusick, P. (1983). *The egalitarian ideal and the American high school.* New York: Longman.

Daft, R., & Becker, S. (1978). *The innovative organization: Innovation adoption in school organizations.* New York: Elsevier North-Holland.

D'Amico, J., & Corbett, D. (1988). *Role of the district in school improvement.* Paper presented at American Educational Research Association annual meeting.

Danzberger, P., Carol, L., Cunningham, L., Kirst, M., McCloud, B., & Usdan, M. (1987). School boards: The forgotten players on the education team. *Phi Delta Kappan, 68*(1), 53–59.

Daresh, J. C. (1988). *The role of mentors in preparing future principals.* Paper presented at American Educational Research Association annual meeting.

Daresh, J. C., & LaPlant, J. (1985). *Inservice for school administrators: A status report.* Paper presented at American Educational Research Association annual meeting.

Darling-Hammond, L. (1986). Proposal for evaluation in the teaching profession. *Elementary School Journal, 86*(4), 531–51.

Darling-Hammond, L. (1990). Teachers and teaching: Signs of a changing profession. In R. Houston, M. Haberman, & J. Sikula (Eds.), *Handbook of Research on Teacher Education* (pp. 267–90). New York: Macmillan.

Darling-Hammond, L., & Berry, B. (1988). *The evolution of teacher policy.* Santa Monica, CA: Rand Corporation.

Datta, L. (1981). Changing times: The study of federal programs supporting educational change and the case for local problem-solving. *Teachers College Record, 82,*(1), 111–116.

Dauber, S. L., & Epstein, J. L. (1989). *Parents' attitudes and practices of involvement in inner-city elementary and middle schools.* Paper presented at American Educational Research Association annual meeting.

David, J. L. (1989a). Synthesis of research on school-based management. *Educational Leadership, 46*(8), 45–53.

David, J. L. (1989b). *Restructuring in progress: Lessons from pioneering districts.* Washington, DC: National Governors' Association.

Davies, D. (1989). *Poor parents, teachers and the schools: Comments about practice, policy and research.* Paper presented at American Educational Research Association annual meeting.

Dewey, J. (1916). *Democracy and education.* Toronto, Ontario: Collier-Macmillan.

Dewey, J. (1975). *Experience and education.* New York: Collier.

Dorman, A., & Bartell, C. A. (1988). Incentives for teaching: LEA programs and practices in seven states. In North Central Regional Educational Laboratory, *Attracting Excellence: The Call for Teacher Incentives.* Elmherst, IL: Author.

Downey, L., & Associates. (1975). *The social studies in Alberta—1975.* Edmonton, Alberta: L. Downey Research Associates.

Doyle, W., & Ponder, G. (1977–78). The practicality ethic in teacher decision making. *Interchange, 8*(3), 1–12.

Drucker, P. (1985). *Innovation and entrepreneurship.* New York: Harper & Row.

Duignan, P. (1979, November). The pressures of the superintendency: Too many deadlines, not enough time. *The Executive Educator,* pp. 34–35.

Duke, D. L. (1986). The aesthetics of leadership. *Educational Administration Quarterly, 22*(1), 7–27.

Duke, D. L. (1988). Why principals consider quitting. *Phi Delta Kappan, 70*(4), 308–13.

Duttweiler, P. C. (1988). *Organizing for excellence.* Austin, TX: Southwest Educational Development Laboratory.

Dwyer, D. (1984). The search for instructional leadership routines and subtleties in the principal's role. *Educational Leadership, 41,* 32–37.

Eastabrook, G., & Fullan, M. (1978). *School and community: Principals and community schools in Ontario.* Toronto: Ontario Ministry of Education.

Edmonds, R. (1979). Effective schools for the urban poor. *Educational Leadership, 39,* 15–27.

Edmundson, P. (1990). A normative look at the curriculum in teacher education. *Phi Delta Kappan, 71*(5), 717–722.

Edu-con. (1984). *The role of the public school principal in the Toronto Board of Education.* Toronto: Edu-con of Canada.

Education Commission of the States. (1989). *Maintaining the momentum for educational reform.* Denver, CO: Author.

Educational Leadership. (1989). [Special issue on strengthening partnerships with parents and community], *47*(2).

The Elementary School Journal. (1989). [Special issue on beginning teachers], *89*(4).

Elmore, R. F. (1980). *Complexity and control: What legislators and administrators can do about implementing public policy.* Washington, DC: National Institute of Education.

Elmore, R. F. (1988). *Contested terrain: The next generation of educational reform.* Paper prepared for Commission on Public School Administration and Leadership, Association of California School Administrators.

Elmore, R. F. (1989). *Models of restructured schools.* Paper presented at American Educational Research Association annual meeting.

Elmore, R. F., & McLaughlin, M. W. (1988). *Steady work: Policy, practice and the reform of American education.* Santa Monica, CA: Rand Corporation.

Emrick, J., & Peterson, S. (1978). *A synthesis of findings across five recent studies in educational dissemination and change.* San Francisco: Far West Laboratory for Educational Research and Development.

Epstein, J. L. (1986). Parents' reactions to teacher practices of parent involvement. *Elementary School Journal, 86*(3), 277–94.

Epstein, J. L. (1988). Effects on student achievement of teachers' practices for parent involvement. In S. Silvern (Ed.), *Literacy through family, community, and school interaction.* Greenwich, CT: JAI Press.

Epstein, J. L., & Dauber, S. L. (1988). *Teacher attitudes and practices of parent involve-*

ment in inner-city elementary and middle schools. Paper presented at the American Sociological Association annual meeting.

Evans, C. (1979). *The micro millennium.* New York: ashington Square Press.

Fantini, M. (1980). *Community participation: Alternative patterns and their consequence on educational achievement.* Paper presented at American Educational Research Association annual meeting.

Farrar, E., DeSanctis, J., & Cohen, D. (1979). *Views from below: Implementation research in education.* Cambridge, MA: Huron Institute.

Feiman-Nemser, S. (1989). *Teacher preparation: Structural and conceptual alternatives.* East Lansing: National Center for Research on Teacher Education, Michigan State University.

Finn, C. (1988). Lessons learned: Federal policy making and the education research community. *Phi Delta Kappan, 70*(2), 127–33.

Firestone, W. (1989). Using reform: Conceptualizing district initiative. *Educational Evaluation and Policy Analysis, 11*(2), 151–64.

Firestone, W., & Bader, B. (1990). *Restructuring teaching: Form, process and outcome.* Paper presented at American Educational Research Association annual meeting.

Firestone, W., & Corbett, H. D. (1987). Planned organizational change. In N. Boyand (Ed.), *Handbook of research on educational administration* (pp. 321–40). New York: Longman.

Firestone, W., Fuhrman, S., & Kirst, M. (1989a). *The progress of reform: An appraisal of state education initiatives.* New Brunswick, NJ: Rutgers University, Centre for Policy Research in Education.

Firestone, W., Fuhrman, S., & Kirst, M. (1989b). *An overview of education reform since 1983.* New Brunswick, NJ: Rutgers University, Centre for Policy Research in Education.

Firestone, W., & Rosenblum, S. (1988). *The alienation and commitment of students and teachers in urban high schools.* Washington, DC: Rutgers University and Office of Educational Research and Improvement.

Flinders, D. J. (1988). Teacher isolation and the new reform. *Journal of Curriculum and Supervision, 4*(1), 17–29.

Floden, R., McDiarmid, G., & Werners, N. (1989). *What are they trying to do? Perspectives on teacher educators' purposes.* East Lansing: National Center for Research on Teacher Education, Michigan State University.

Fowler, R. H. (1979). *The politics of curriculum development problems in bureaucratic decision-making.* Paper presented at the Canadian Society for Studies in Education annual meeting.

Fowler, R. H. (1989). Curricular reform in social studies: An analysis of the cases of Saskatchewan and British Columbia. *Canadian Journal of Education, 14*(3), 322–37.

Fuhrman, S., Clune, W., & Elmore, R. (1988). Research on education reform: Lessons on the implementation of policy. *Teachers College Record, 90*(2), 237–57.

Fullan, M. (1979). *School-focused in-service education in Canada.* Report prepared for Centre for Educational Research and Innovation (o.e.c.d.), Paris.

Fullan, M. (1985). Change process and strategies at the local level. *The Elementary School Journal, 84*(3), 391–420.

Fullan, M. (1986). *School improvement efforts in Canada.* Paper prepared for the Council of Ministers of Education, Toronto.

Fullan, M. (1987). *Implementing educational change: What we know.* Paper prepared for the World Bank, Washington, DC.

Fullan, M. (1988). *What's worth fighting for in the principalship: Strategies for taking charge in the elementary school principalship.* Toronto: Ontario Public School Teachers' Federation.

Fullan, M. (1990). Staff development, innovation and institutional development. In B. Joyce (Ed.), *Changing school culture through staff development* (pp. 3–25). Alexandria, VA: Association for Supervision and Curriculum Development.

Fullan, M. (1991). *Productive educational change.* East Sussex, United Kingdom: Falmer Press.

Fullan, M., Anderson, S., & Newton, E. (1986). *Support systems for implementing curriculum in school boards.* Toronto: OISE Press and Ontario Government Bookstore.

Fullan, M., Rolheiser-Bennett, C., & Bennett, B. (1989). *Linking classroom and school improvement.* Paper presented to American Educational Research Association annual meeting.

Fullan, M., Bennett, B., & Rolheiser-Bennett, C. (1990). Linking classroom and school improvement. *Educational Leadership, 47*(8), 13–19.

Fullan, M., & Connelly, M. (1990). *Teacher education in Ontario: Current practices and options for the future.* Toronto: Ontario Ministries of Colleges and Universities and of Education.

Fullan, M., & Eastabrook, G. (1973). *School change project.* Unpublished report. Toronto: Ontario Institute for Studies in Education.

Fullan, M., Eastabrook, G., & Biss, J. (1977). The effects of Ontario teachers' strikes on the attitudes and perceptions of grade 12 and 13 students. In D. Brison (Ed.), *Three studies of the effects of teachers' strikes* (pp. 1–170). Toronto: Ontario Ministry of Education.

Fullan, M., & Hargreaves, A. (1991). *What's worth fighting for in your school.* Toronto: Ontario Public School Teachers' Federation.

Fullan, M., & Park, P. (1981). *Curriculum implementation: A resource booklet.* Toronto: Ontario Ministry of Education.

Fullan, M., Park, P., Williams, T., Allison, P., Walker, L., & Watson, N. (1987). *Supervisory officers in Ontario: Current practice and recommendations for the future.* Toronto: Ontario Ministry of Education.

Fullan, M., & Pomfret, A. (1977). Research on curriculum and instruction implementation. *Review of Educational Research, 47*(1), 335–97.

Fullan, M., & Watson, N. (1991). Beyond school-university partnerships. In M. Fullan & A. Hargreaves (Eds.), *Teacher development and educational change.* East Sussex, United Kingdom: Falmer Press.

Fullan, M., Wideen, M., Hopkins, D., & Eastabrook, G. (1983). *The management of change in teacher education: Vol. II. A comparative analysis of faculty and student perceptions.* Final Report to Social Sciences and Humanities Research Council.

Gaines, E. (1978, May 23). School superintendents describe the job: Short and sour. *Educational Dailey,* (Washington, DC), p. 5.

Galton, M., Simon, B., & Croll, P. (1980). *Inside the primary classroom.* London: Routledge & Kegan Paul.

Gersten, G., Carnine, D., Zuref, L., & Cronin, D. (1981). *Measuring implementation of educational innovations in a broad context.* Paper presented at American Educational Research Association annual meeting.

Gideonse, H. (1980). Improving the federal administration of education programs. *Educational Evaluation and Policy Analysis, 2*(1), 61–70.

Gitlin, A., & Smyth, J. (1989). *Teacher evaluation: Educative alternatives.* Philadelphia: Falmer Press.

Glickman, C., & Bey, T. (1990). Supervision. In R. Houston, M. Haberman, & J. Sikula (Eds.), *Handbook of Research on Teacher Education* (pp. 549–66). New York: Macmillan.

Gold, B., & Miles, M. (1981). *Whose school is it anyway? Parent-teacher conflict over an innovative school.* New York: Praeger.

Goldhammer, K. (1977). Role of the American school superintendent. In L. Cunningham et al. (Eds.), *Educational administration.* Berkeley, CA: McCutchan.

Goodlad, J. I. (1975). *The dynamics of educational change.* Toronto: McGraw-Hill.

Goodlad, J. I. (1984). *A place called school: prospects for the future.* New York: McGraw-Hill.

Goodlad, J. I. (1988). School-university partnerships for educational renewal: Rationale and concepts. In K. Sirotnik & J. I. Goodlad (Eds.), *School-university partnerships in action* (pp. 3–31). New York: Teachers College Press.

Goodlad, J. I. (1990a). Studying the education of educators: from conception to findings. *Phi Delta Kappan, 71*(9), 698–701.

Goodlad, J. I. (1990b). *Teachers for our nation's schools.* San Francisco: Jossey-Bass.

Goodlad, J. I (1990c). The occupation of teaching in schools. In J. Goodlad, R. Soder, & K. Sirotnik (Eds.), *The moral dimensions of teaching* (pp. 3–34). San Francisco: Jossey-Bass.

Goodlad, J. I., Klein, M., & associates (1970). *Behind the classroom door.* Worthington, OH: Charles A. Jones.

Goodlad, J. I., Soder, R., & Sirotnik, K. A. (Eds.). (1990). *The moral dimensions of teaching.* San Francisco: Jossey-Bass.

Goodson, I. (1991). Teachers' lives. In A. Hargreaves & M. Fullan (Eds.), *Understanding teacher development.* London: Cassell.

Gorton, R., & McIntyre, K. (1978). *The senior high school principalship: The effective principal, Vol. 2.* Reston, VA: National Association of Secondary School Principals.

Griffin, G. (1986). Clinical teacher education. In J. Hoffman & S. Edwards (Eds.), *Reality and reform in clinical teacher education* (pp. 1–24). New York: Random House.

Griffin, G. (1989a). A descriptive study of student teaching. *The Elementary School Journal, 89*(3), 343–64.

Griffin, G. (1989b). A state program for the initial year of teaching. *The Elementary School Journal, 89*(4), 395–405.

Grimmett, P. P., & Erickson, G. L. (Eds.). (1988). *Reflection in teacher education.* New York: Teachers College Press.

Gross, N., Giacquinta, J, & Bernstein, M. (1971). *Implementing organizational innovations: A sociological analysis of planned educational change.* New York: Basic Books.

Grossman, P. L. (1988). *Does teacher education make a difference?* Paper presented at American Educational Research Association annual meeting.

Grossman, P. L. (1989). Learning to teach without teacher education. *Teachers College Record, 91*(2), 191–208.

Grossman, P. L., & Richert, A. E. (1988). Unacknowledged knowledge growth: A re-examination of the effects of teacher education. *Teaching & Teacher Education, 4*(1), 53–62.

Hall, G. E. (1988). The principal as leader of the change facilitating team. Four studies using different disciplinary perspectives of the principal's role in change. *Journal of Research and Development in Education, 22*(1), 49–59.

Hall, G. E., & Hord, S. (1984). A framework for analyzing what change facilitators do: The intervention taxonomy. *Knowledge: Creation, Diffusion, Utilization, 5*(3), 275–307.

Hall, G. E., & Hord, S. (1987). *Change in schools: Facilitating the process.* Albany: State University of New York Press.

Hall, G. E., Hord, S., & Griffin, T. (1980). Implementation at the school building level: The development and analysis of nine mini-case studies. Paper presented at American Educational Research Association annual meeting.

Hall, G. E., & Loucks, S. (1977). A developmental model for determining whether the treatment is actually implemented. *American Educational Research Journal, 14* (3), 263–76.

Hall, G. E., & Loucks, S. (1978). *Innovation configurations: Analyzing the adaptations of innovations* (Report No. 3049). Austin: The University of Texas at Austin, Research and Development Center in Teacher Education.

Hall, G. E., Putnam, S., & Hord, S. (1985). *District office personnel: Their roles and influence on school and classroom change: What we don't know.* Paper presented at American Educational Research Association annual meeting.

Hallinger, P., Bickman, L., & Davis, K. (1989). *What makes a difference? School context, principal leadership, and student achievement.* Paper presented at American Educational Research Association annual meeting.

Hallinger, P., & Richardson, D. (1988). *Models of shared leadership: Evolving structures and relationships.* Paper presented at American Educational Research Association annual meeting.

Hallinger, P., & Wimpelberg, R. (1989). *New settings and changing paradigms for principal preparation.* Paper presented at American Educational Research Association annual meeting.

Hargreaves, A. (1989). *Curriculum and assessment reform.* Milton Keynes, United Kingdom: Open University Press.

Hargreaves, A., & Dawe, R. (1989). *Coaching as unreflective practice: contrived collegiality or collaborative culture.* Paper presented at American Educational Research Association annual meeting.

Hart, A. W. (1987). A career ladder's effect on teacher career and work attitudes. *American Educational Research Journal, 24*(4), 479–504.

Hart, A. W. (1989). *Role politics and the redesign of teachers' work.* Unpublished manuscript, University of Utah, Salt Lake City.

Hart, A. W., & Murphy, M. J. (1990). New teachers react to redesigned teacher work. *American Journal of Education,* May.

Harvey, G., & Crandall, D. P. (1988). *A beginning look at the what and how of restruc-*

turing. Andover, MA: The Network, and Regional Laboratory for Educational Improvement of the Northeast and the Islands.

Havelock, R., & Havelock, M. (1973). *Educational innovation in the United States: Vol. 1. The national survey*. Ann Arbor: Institute for Social Research, University of Michigan.

Henderson, A. T. (1986). For better or worse? *Phi Delta Kappan, 67*(4), 597–602.

Herriott, R., & Gross, N. (Eds.). (1979). *The dynamics of planned educational change: An analysis of the rural experimental schools program*. Berkeley, CA: McCutchan.

Hill, P., Wuchitech, J., & Williams, R. (1980). *The effects of federal education programs on school principals*. Santa Monica, CA: Rand Corporation.

Hodges, W., et al. (1980). *Follow through: Forces for change in the primary schools*. Ypsilanti, MI: High Scope Press.

Hodgson, E. D. (1988). *Federal involvement in public education*. Toronto: Canadian Education Association.

Hoffman, J. V., & Edwards, S. A. (Eds.). (1987). *Reality and reform in clinical teacher education*. New York: Random House.

Hollingsworth, S. (1989). Prior beliefs and cognitive change in learning to teach. *American Educational Research Journal, 26*(2), 160–90.

Holmes Group. (1986). *Tomorrow's teachers*. East Lansing, MI: Author.

Holmes Group. (1990). *Tomorrow's schools: Principles for design of professional development schools*. East Lansing, MI: Author.

Honig, B. (1988). The key to reform: Sustaining and expanding upon initial success. *Educational Administration Quarterly, 24*(3), 257–71.

Hopkins, D. (1990). Integrating teacher development and school improvement: A study in teacher personality and school climate. In B. Joyce (Ed.), *Changing school culture through staff development* (pp. 41–67). Alexandria, VA: Association for Supervision and Curriculum Development.

Hord, S. M. (1988). *Riding the coat-tails of mandates: Gaining entry and developing trust in rural effective schools projects*. Paper presented at American Educational Research Association annual meeting.

Hord, S. M., Stiegelbauer, S. M., & Hall, G. (1984). How principals work with other change facilitators. *Education and Urban Society, 17*(1), 89–109.

Horn, S. K., & Clements, S. K. (1988). *ERIC: The past, present, and future federal role in education dissemination*. Paper presented at American Educational Research Association annual meeting.

House, E. (1974). *The politics of educational innovation*. Berkeley, CA: McCutchan.

House, E. (1980). *Evaluating with validity*. Beverly Hills, CA: Sage.

House, E., & Lapan, S. (1978). *Survival in the classroom*. Boston: Allyn & Bacon.

Houston, W., Haberman, M., & Sikula, J. (Eds.) (1990). *Handbook of research on teacher education*. New York: Macmillan.

Howey, K. R., & Zimpher, N. L. (1989). *Profiles of preservice teacher education, inquiry into the nature of programs*. Albany: State University of New York Press.

Huberman, M. (1978). *Microanalysis of innovation implementation at the school level*. Unpublished paper, University of Geneva.

Huberman, M. (1981). *Exemplary center for reading instruction (ECRI), Masepa, North Plains: A case study*. Andover, MA: The Network.

Huberman, M. (1983). Recipes for busy kitchens. *Knowledge: Creation, Diffusion, Utilization, 4*, 478–510.

Huberman, M. (1988). Teacher careers and school improvement. *Journal of Curriculum Studies, 20*(2), 119–32.

Huberman, M. (1990). *The social context of instruction in schools.* Paper presented at American Educational Research Association annual meeting.

Huberman, M. (1991). Teacher development and instructional mastery. In A. Hargreaves & M. Fullan (Eds.), *Understanding teacher development.* London: Cassell.

Huberman, M., & Miles, M. (1984). *Innovation up close.* New York: Plenum.

Huguenin, K., Zerchykov, R., & Davies, D. (1979). *Narrowing the gap between intent and practice.* Boston: Institute for Responsive Education.

Huling-Austin, L. (1990). Teacher induction programs and internships. In W. R. Houston, M. Haberman, & J. Sikula (Eds.), *Handbook of research on teacher education* (pp. 535–48). New York: Macmillan.

Huling-Austin, L., & Murphy, S. (1987). *Assessing the impact of teacher induction programs: Implications for program development.* Paper presented at American Educational Research Association annual meeting.

Hull, C., & Rudduck, J. (1980). *Introducing innovation to pupils.* Norwich, United Kingdom: Centre for Applied Research in Education, University of East Anglia.

Hulsebosch, P. L. (1989). *Beauty in the eye of the beholder: Teachers' perspectives on parent involvement.* Paper presented at American Educational Research Association annual meeting.

Jackson, B. L., & Cooper, B. S. (1989). *What role for parents in urban high schools? The New York City experience.* Paper presented at American Educational Research Association annual meeting.

Jackson, P. (1968). *Life in classrooms.* New York: Holt, Rinehart & Winston.

Jackson, P. (1980). *The uncertainties of teaching.* Paper presented at American Educational Research Association annual meeting.

James Report [Great Britain Department of Education and Science, Committee of inquiry into teacher training, Lord James Rusholme, Chair]. (1972). *Teacher Education and Training.* London: Her Majesty's Stationery Office.

Jencks, C., Smith, M., Ackland, H., Bane, M., Cohen, D., Gintis, H., Heyns, B., & Micholson, S. (1972). *Inequality: A reassessment of the effect of family and schooling in America.* New York: Basic Books.

Johnson, D. W., & Johnson, R. T. (1989). *Leading the cooperative school.* Edina, MN: Interaction Book Company.

Johnson, D. W., & Johnson, R. T. (1990). *Cooperation and competition: Theory and research.* Hillsdale, NJ: Lawrence Erlbaum.

Johnson, F. L., Brookover, W. B., & Farrell, W. C. (1989). *School personnel and students' view of parent involvement and their impact on students' academic sense of futility.* Paper presented at American Educational Research Association annual meeting.

Joyce, B. (Ed.). (1978). *Involvement: A study of shared governance of teacher education.* Syracuse, NY: Syracuse University.

Joyce, B. (Ed.). (1990). *Changing school culture through staff development.* Alexandria, VA: Association for Supervision and Curriculum Development.

Joyce, B., & Murphy, C. (1990). Epilogue: The curious complexities of cultural change. In B. Joyce (Ed.), *Changing school culture through staff development* (pp.

243–50). Alexandria, VA: Association for Supervision and Curriculum Development.

Joyce, B., & Showers, B. (1988). *Student achievement through staff development.* New York: Longman.

Joyce, B., Murphy, C., Showers, B., & Murphy, J. (1989). School renewal as cultural change. *Educational Leadership, 47*(3), 70–78.

Judge, H. (1982). *American graduate school of education: A view from abroad.* New York: Ford Foundation.

Kanter, R. M. (1989). *When giants learn to dance.* New York: Simon & Schuster.

Katz, E., Lewin, M, & Hamilton, H. (1963). Traditions of research on the diffusion of innovation. *American Sociological Review, 28*(2), 237–52.

Keesling, J. (1980). *Parents and federal education programs: Some preliminary findings from the study of parental involvement.* Santa Monica, CA: System Development Corporation.

Keidel, G. (1977). *A profile of public school superintendents of the state of Michigan.* Lansing: Michigan Association of School Administrators.

Kemessis, S. (1987). Critical reflection. In M. Wideen & I. Andrews (Eds.), *Staff development for school improvement* (pp. 73–90). East Sussex, United Kingdom: Falmer Press.

Kennedy, M. M. (1989). *Federally-funded research centers as links between research and practice.* Paper presented at American Educational Research Association annual meeting.

Kennedy, M. M. (1990). Choosing a goal for professional education. In R. Houston, M. Haberman, & J. Sikula (Eds.), *Handbook of Research on Teacher Education* (pp. 813–25). New York: Macmillan.

King, A. J. (1986). *The adolescent experience.* Toronto: Ontario Secondary School Teachers' Federation.

King, A. J., Warren, W., & Peart, M. (1988). *The teaching experience.* Toronto: Ontario Secondary School Teachers' Federation.

Kirst, M., & Jung, R. (1980). The utility of a longitudinal approach in assessing implementation: A thirteen year view of Title I, ESEA. *Educational Evaluation and Policy Analysis, 2*(5), 17–34.

Krupp, J. A. (1989). Staff development and the individual. In S. D. Caldwell (Ed.), *Staff development: A handbook of effective practices* (pp. 44–57). Oxford, OH: National Staff Development Council.

Laing, R. D. (1970). *Knots.* London: Tavistock.

Lanier, J., & Little, J. (1986). Research on teacher education. In M. Wittrock (Ed.), *Handbook of research on teaching* (pp. 527–69). New York: Macmillan.

LaRocque, L., & Coleman, P. (1989a). Quality control: School accountability and district ethos. In M. Holmes, K. Leithwood, & D. Musella (Eds.), *Educational policy for effective schools* (pp. 168–191). Toronto: OISE Press.

LaRocque, L., & Coleman, P. (1989b). *The politics of excellence: Trustee leadership and school district ethos.* Paper presented at American Educational Research Association annual meeting.

Lawton, S. B., Hickcox, E., Leithwood, K., & Musella, D. (1986). *Development and use of performance appraisal of certificated educational staff in Ontario School Boards.* Toronto: Ontario Ministry of Education.

Lawton, S. B., Leithwood, K., Batcher, E., Donaldson, E. L., & Stewart, R. (1988).

Student retention and transition in Ontario high schools, policies, practices, and prospects. Toronto: Ministry of Education.

Leavitt, H. (1986). *Corporate pathfinders.* Homewood, IL: Dow Jones-Irwin.

Leithwood, K. (1981). The dimensions of curriculum innovation. *Journal of Curriculum Studies, 13*(1), 25–36.

Leithwood, K. (1989). School system policies for effective school administration. In M. Holmes, K. A. Leithwood, & D. F. Musella (Eds.), *Educational policy for effective schools* (pp. 73–92). Toronto: OISE Press.

Leithwood, K. (1990). The principal's role in teacher development. In B. Joyce (Ed.), *Changing school culture through staff development* (pp. 71–90). Alexandria, VA: Association for Supervision and Curriculum Development.

Leithwood, K., Armstrong, M., & Kelly, F. (1989). The pre-service preparation of school administration in Ontario: Centre for principal development. In R. E. Blum & J. A. Butler (Eds.), *School leader development for school improvement* (pp. 61–80). Leuven, Belgium: ACCO (Academic Publishing).

Leithwood, K., & Avery, C. (1987). Inservice education for principals in Canada. In K. Leithwood, W. Rutherford, & R. van der Vegt (Eds.), *Preparing school leaders for educational improvement* (pp. 132–54). London: Croom Helm.

Leithwood, K., & Jantzi, D. (1990). *Transformational leadership: How principals can help reform school culture.* Paper presented at American Educational Research Association annual meeting.

Leithwood, K., & MacDonald, R. (1981). Decisions given by teachers for their curriculum choices. *Canadian Journal of Education, 6*(2), 103–6.

Leithwood, K., & Montgomery, D. (1982). The role of the elementary school principal in program improvement: A review. *Review of Educational Research, 52*(3), 309–39.

Leithwood, K., & Montgomery, D. (1986). *The principal profile.* Toronto: OISE Press.

Leithwood, K., & Steinbach, R. (1989a). *A comparison of processes used by principals in solving problems individually and in groups.* Paper presented at Canadian Association for the Study of Educational Administration annual meeting.

Leithwood, K., & Steinbach, R. (1989b). *Characteristics of secondary school principals' problem solving: A comparison with the problem solving of elementary principals and chief education officers.* Paper presented at Canadian Association for the Study of Educational Administration annual meeting.

Leithwood, K., & Steinbach, R. (1990). *Improving the problem-solving expertise of school administrators: theory and practice.* Paper presented at the Canadian Society for Studies in Education annual meeting.

Leithwood, K., et al. (1978). *An empirical investigation of teachers' curriculum decision making processes and strategies used by curriculum managers to influence such decision making.* Unpublished report, Ontario Institute for Studies in Education, Toronto.

Levin, H. (1976). Educational reform: Its meaning. In M. Carnoy & H. Levin (Eds.), *The limits of educational reform.* New York: McKay.

Levine, D., & Eubanks, E. (1989). *Site-based management: Engine for reform or pipedream? Problems, pitfalls and prerequisites for success in site-based management.* Manuscript submitted for publication.

Levine, D., & Leibert, R. E. (1987). Improving school improvement plans. *The Elementary School Journal, 87*(4), 397–412.

Levine, D., & Lezotte, L. (1990). *An interpretive review and analysis of research and practice in unusually effective schools.* Madison: University of Wisconsin Press.

Levine, S. (1989). *Promoting adult growth in schools.* Boston: Allyn & Bacon.

Lezotte, L., Hathaway, D., Miller, S., Passalacqua, J., Brookover, W. (1980). *School learning climate and student achievement.* East Lansing: Michigan State University, Center for Urban Affairs.

Lighthall, F. (1973, February). Multiple realities and organizational nonsolutions: An essay on anatomy of educational innovation. *School Review,* pp. 255–87.

Lindblom, C. (1959). The science of muddling through. *Public Administration Review, 19,* 155–69.

Lindblom, C., & Cohen, D. (1979). *Usable knowledge.* New Haven, CT: Yale University Press.

Lindquist, K., & Mauriel, J. (1989). School-based management: Doomed to failure? *Education and Urban Society, 21*(4), 403–16.

Lippitt, G., & Lippitt, R. (1986). *The consulting process in action* (2nd ed.). LaJolla, CA: University Associates.

Liston, D., & Zeichner, K. (1989). *Action research and reflective teaching.* Paper presented at American Educational Research Association annual meeting.

Little, J. W. (1981). The power of organizational setting (Paper adapted from final report, *School success and staff development*). Washington, DC: National Institute of Education.

Little, J. W. (1982). Norms of collegiality and experimentation: Workplace conditions of school success. *American Educational Research Journal, 19,* 325–40.

Little, J. W. (1987). Teachers as colleagues. In V. Richardson-Koehler (Ed.), *Educators' handbook* (pp. 491–518). White Plains: Longman.

Little, J. W. (1988). *Conditions of professional development in secondary schools.* Stanford, CA: Center for Research on the Context of Secondary Teaching.

Little, J. W. (1989). District policy choices and teachers' professional development opportunities. *Educational Evaluation and Policy Analysis, 11*(2), 165–80.

Little, J. W. (1990a). The persistence of privacy: Autonomy and initiative in teachers' professional relations. *Teachers College Record, 91*(4), 509–36.

Little, J. W. (1990b). The "mentor" phenomenon and the social organization of teaching. In C. Cazden (Ed.), *Review of Research in Education* (Vol. 16, pp. 297–351). Washington: American Educational Research Association.

Little, J. W., Gerritz, W. H., Stern, D. S., Guthrie, J. W., Kirst, M. W., & Marsh, D. D. (1987). *Staff development in California: Public and personal investments, program patterns, and policy choices.* San Francisco: Joint publication of Far West Laboratory for Educational Research and Development and Policy Analysis for California Education.

Lortie, D. (1975). *School teacher: A sociological study.* Chicago: University of Chicago Press.

Lortie, D. (1987). Built in tendencies toward stabilizing the principal's role. *Journal of Research and Development in Education, 22*(1), 80–90.

Loucks, S., & Hall, G. (1979). *Implementing innovations in schools: A concerns-based approach.* Paper presented at American Educational Research Association annual meeting.

Loucks-Horsley, S., & Hergert, L. (1985). *An action guide to school improvement.* Alexandria, VA: Association for Supervision and Curriculum Development.

Loucks-Horsley, S., Harding, C., Arbuckle, M., Murray, L., Dubea, C., & Williams, M. (1987). *Continuing to learn: A guidebook for teacher development.* Andover, MA: Regional Laboratory for Educational Improvement of the Northeast and Islands and National Staff Development Council.

Loucks-Horsley, S., & associates. (1990). *Developing and supporting teachers for middle school science education.* Andover, MA: National Center for Improving Science Education and The Network.

Louis, K. (1989). The role of the school district in school improvement. In M. Holmes, K. Leithwood, D. Musella (Eds.), *Educational policy for effective schools* (pp. 145–67). Toronto: OISE Press.

Louis, K., & Miles, M. B. (1990). *Improving the urban high school: What works and why.* New York: Teachers College Press.

Louis, K., & Rosenblum, S. (1981). *Linking R & D with schools: A program and its implications for dissemination.* Washington, DC: National Institute of Education.

Louis, K., & Sieber, S. (1979). *Bureaucracy and the dispersed organization.* Norwood, NJ: Ablex.

Lucas, B., Lusthaus, C., & Gibbs, H. (1978–79). Parent advisory committees in Quebec: An experiment in mandated parental participation. *Interchange, 10*(1), 26–39.

Lueder, D. (1989a). *Effects of parent education and pre-kindergarten on disadvantaged student achievement.* Paper presented at American Educational Research Association annual meeting.

Lueder, D. (1989b). Tennessee parents were invited to participate—And they did. *Educational Leadership, 47*(2), 15–17.

Lutz, F. W., & Hutton, J. B. (1989). Alternative teacher certification: Its policy implications for classroom and personnel practice. *Educational Evaluation and Policy Analysis, 11*(3), Fall, 237–54.

Lutz, F. W., & Maddirala, J. (1988). *Stress, burnout in Texas teachers and reform mandated accountability.* Paper presented at American Educational Research Association annual meeting.

Lyon, C., Doscher, L., McGrahanan, P., & Williams, R. (1978). *Evaluation and school districts.* Los Angeles: Center for the Study of Evaluation, U.C.L.A.

MacCarthy, M., & Hall, G. (1989). *The emergence of university-based education policy centers.* Eugene, OR: ERIC Clearinghouse on Educational Management.

MacDowell, M. (1989). Partnerships: Getting a return on the investment. *Educational Leadership, 47*(2), 8–11.

Majone, G., & Wildavsky, A. (1978). Implementation as evolution. In H. Freeman (Ed.), *Policy studies annual review, Vol. II.* Beverly Hills, CA: Sage.

Manasse, L. (1985). Improving conditions for principal effectiveness. *The Elementary School Journal, 85,* 439–63.

Mann, D. (1981). *Education policy analysis and the rent-a-troika business.* Paper presented at the American Educational Research Association annual meeting.

Marris, P. (1975). *Loss and change.* New York: Anchor Press/Doubleday.

Marsh, D. (1988). *Key factors associated with the effective implementation and impact of*

California's educational reform. Paper presented at the American Educational Research Association annual meeting.

Marsh, D., & Bowman, G. (1988). *State initiated top-down versus bottom-up reform in secondary school.* Madison: National Center on Effective Secondary Schools, University of Wisconsin—Madison.

Marshall, C., & Mitchell, B. (1989). *Women's careers as a critique of the administrative culture.* Paper presented at American Educational Research Association annual meeting.

Martin, J., & Zichefoose, M. (1979). *The school superintendent in West Virginia.* Unpublished report, West Virginia University.

Martin, M., & Johnson, C. (1989). Let's evaluate the impact of administrator staff development programs. *The Journal of Staff Development, 10*(1), 8–13.

Martin, W., & Willower, D. (1981). The managerial behavior of high school principals. *Educational Administration Quarterly, 17*(1), 69–90.

McDonald, J., & Elias, P. (1980). *The problems of beginning teachers: A crisis in training* (Vol. 1). Princeton: Educational Testing Service.

McDonnell, L. M., & Pascal, A. (1988). *Teacher unions and educational reform.* Santa Monica, CA: Rand Corporation.

McKibbin, M., & Joyce, B. (1980). *An analysis of staff development and its effects on classroom practice.* Paper presented at American Educational Research Association annual meeting.

McKibbin, M., Walton, P., & Wright, D. (1987). *An evaluation of an alternative route into teaching in California.* Paper presented at American Educational Research Association annual meeting.

McLaughlin, M., & Marsh, D. (1978). Staff development and school change. *Teachers College Record, 80*(1), 69–94.

McLaughlin, M., & Pfeiffer, R. S. (1988). *Teacher evaluation: Improvement, accountability, and effective learning.* New York: Teachers College Press.

McNay, M., & Cole, A. L. (1989). Induction programs in Ontario: Current views and directions for the future. *Education Canada, 29*(1), 9–15

Melaragno, R., Lyons, M., & Sparks, M. (1981). *Parents and federal education programs: Vol. 6. Parental involvement in Title I projects.* Santa Monica, CA: System Development Corporation.

Mertz, N. T., McNeely, S. R., & Venditti, F. P. (1989). *The changing profile of school leadership: Women in administration.* Paper presented at American Educational Research Association annual meeting.

Metropolitan Life. (1985). *Former teachers in America.* New York: Author.

Metz, M. H. (1990). *Teachers' ultimate dependence on their students: Implications for teachers' responses to student bodies of differing social class.* Paper presented at American Educational Research Association annual meeting.

Michigan partnership for new education. (1990). East Lansing: Michigan State University.

Miles, M. (1987). *Practical guidelines for school administrators: How to get there.* Paper presented at American Educational Research Association annual meeting.

Miles, M., Farrar, E., & Neufeld, B. (1983). *Review of effective schools: Vol. 2. The extent of adoption of effective schools programs.* Cambridge: Huron Institute.

Miles, M., & Kaufman, T. (1985). A directory of programs. In R. Kyle (Ed.), *Reaching for excellence: An effective schools sourcebook.* Washington, DC: National Institute for Education.

Miles, M. B., Louis, K. S., Rosenblum, S., Cipollone, A., & Farrar, E. (1988). *Improving the urban high school: A preliminary report: Lessons for managing implementation.* Boston: Center for Survey Research, University of Massachusetts.

Miles, M., Saxl, E., & Lieberman, A. (1988). What skills do educational "change agents" need? An empirical view. *Curriculum Inquiry, 18*(2), 157–93.

Moore, B. (1989). *Descriptions of induction programs.* Paper presented at American Educational Research Association annual meeting.

Moore, D., & Hyde, A. (1981). *Making sense of staff development progress and their costs in three school districts. Final report to National Institute of Education.* Chicago: Designs for Change.

Moore, D., Hyde, A., Blair, K., & Weitzman, S. (1981). *Student classification and the right to read.* Chicago: Designs for Change.

Moore, D., Soltman, S., Steinberg, L., Manar, U., & Fogel, D. (1983). *Child advocacy and the schools.* Chicago: Designs for Change.

Moorehead, R., & Nediger, W. (1989). *Behaviours of effective principals.* Paper presented at Canadian Society for Studies in Education annual meeting.

Morgan, G. (1989). *Riding the waves of change.* San Francisco: Jossey-Bass.

Mortimore, P., Sammons, P., Stoll, L., Lewis, D., & Ecob, R. (1988). *School matters: The junior years.* Sommerset, United Kingdom: Open Books.

Murphy, J. (in press). *Restructuring schools: Capturing the phenomena.* New York: Teachers College Press.

Murphy, J., & Hallinger, P. (1986). The superintendent as instructional leader: Findings from effective school districts. *Journal of Educational Administration, 24*(2), 213–36.

Murphy, J., & Hallinger, P. (Eds.). (1987). *Approaches to administrative training in education.* Albany: State University of New York Press.

Mussio, J., & Greer, N. (1980). The British Columbia assessment program: An overview. *Canadian Journal of Education, 5*(4), 22–40.

National Commission on Excellence in Education. (1983). *A nation at risk.* Washington, DC: Author.

National Education Association. (1979). *Nationwide teacher opinion poll 1979.* Washington, DC: Author.

National Education Association. (1986). *The learning workplace.* Washington, DC: Author.

National Education Association. (1988). *Mastery in learning project.* Washington, DC: Author.

National Education Longitudinal Study. (1988). Washington, DC: Office of Educational Research and Improvement.

National Governors' Association. (1986). *A time for results.* Washington, DC: Author.

National Governors' Association. (1989). *The Governors' 1991 report on education—time for results.* Washington, DC: Author.

Nelson, M., & Sieber, S. (1976). Innovations in urban secondary schools. *School Review, 84,* 213–31.

Neill, D., & Medina, N. (1989). Standardized testing: Harmful to educational health. *Phi Delta Kappan, 70*(9), 688–97.

Newmann, F. M., & Thompson, J. A. (1987). *Effects of cooperative learning on achievement in secondary schools: A summary of research.* Madison: National Center on Effective Secondary Schools, University of Wisconsin.

Nias, J. (1989). *Primary teachers talking, a study of teaching as work.* New York: Routledge.

Nias, J., Southworth, G., & Yeomans, R. (1989). *Staff relationships in the primary school.* London: Cassell.

Nisbet, R. (1969). *Social change and history.* New York: Oxford University Press.

Nisbet, R. (1980). *The history of the idea of progress.* New York: Basic Books.

Noffke, S., & Zeichner, K. (1987). *Action research and teacher thinking.* Paper presented at American Educational Research Association annual meeting.

Odden, A., & Marsh, D. (1988). How comprehensive reform legislation can improve secondary schools. *Phi Delta Kappan, 69*(8), 593–98.

Ogawa, R., & Malen, B. (1989). *Site-based governance councils: Mechanisms for affirming rather than altering traditional decision making relations in schools.* Presented at American Educational Research Association annual meeting.

Oja, S. N., & Smulyan, L. (1989). *Collaborative action research: A developmental approach.* Philadelphia: Falmer Press.

Ontario Ministries of Education, and Colleges and Universities. (1988). *Final report: Teacher Education Review Steering Committee.* Toronto: Author.

Ontario Ministry of Education. (1989). *Restructuring the education system.* Toronto: Author.

Ontario Ministry of Education. (1990). *Information statistics, 1988–89.* Toronto: Author.

Organization for Economic Cooperation and Development. (1976). *Review of national policies for education: Canada.* Paris: Author.

Orlich, D. C. (1989). *Staff development, enhancing human potential.* Boston: Allyn & Bacon.

Paddock, S. (1979). *The myth of parent involvement through advisory councils.* Paper presented at American Educational Research Association annual meeting.

Patterson, J., Purkey, S., & Parker, J. (1986). *Productive school systems for a nonrational world.* Alexandria, VA: Association for Supervision and Curriculum Development.

Peters, T. (1987). *Thriving on chaos: Handbook for a management revolution.* New York: A. Knopf.

Peters, T., & Waterman, R. (1982). *In search of excellence.* New York: Harper & Row.

Peterson, K. (1981). *Making sense of principal's work.* Paper presented at American Educational Research Association annual meeting.

Peterson, P. L., Clark, C. M., & Dickson, W. P. (1990). Educational psychology as a foundation in teacher education: Reforming an old notion. *Teachers College Record, 91*(3), 322–46.

Pincus, J. (1974). Incentives for innovation in public schools. *Review of Educational Research, 44,* 113–44.

Pink, W. T. (1989). *Effective staff development for urban school improvement.* Paper presented at American Educational Research Association annual meeting.

Pitner, N. (1987). Principles of quality staff development. In J. Murphy & P. Hallinger (Eds.), *Approaches to administrative training on education* (pp. 28–44). New York: State University of New York Press.

Powell, A., Cohen, D., & Farrar, T. (1985). *The shopping mall high school.* New York: Houghton Mifflin.

Prawat, R. S. (1989). Promoting access to knowledge, strategy, and disposition in students: A research synthesis. *Review of Educational Research, 59*(1), 1–41.

Purkey, S. C., & Smith, M. S. (1985). School reform: The district policy implications of the effective school literature. *The Elementary School Journal, 85*(3), 353–89.

Ratsoy, E., Friesen, D., Holdaway, E., & others. (1987). *Evaluation of the initiation to teaching project.* Alberta Education Final Report. Edmonton: University of Alberta.

Rauth, M. (1990). Exploring heresy in collective bargaining and school restructuring. *Phi Delta Kappan, 71*(10), 781–90.

Rees, R., Warren, W., Coles, B., & Peart, M. (1989). *A study of recruitment of Ontario teachers.* Toronto: Ontario Public School Teachers' Federation and Ontario Secondary School Teachers' Federation.

Rhine, R. (Eds.). (1981). *Making schools more effective: New directions from follow through.* New York: Academic Press.

Robbins, A., & Dingler, D. (1981). *Parents and federal education programs: Vol. 3. Parental involvement in ESAA projects.* Santa Monica, CA: System Development Corporation.

Robertson, H. J. (1991). Teacher development and sex equity. In A. Hargreaves & M. Fullan (Eds.), *Understanding teacher development.* London: Cassell.

Robinson, F. (1982). Superordinate curriculum guidelines as guides to local curriculum decision-making. In K. Leithwood (Ed.), *Studies in curriculum decision-making* (pp. 132–160). Toronto: OISE Press.

Rosenblum, S., & Louis, K. (1979). *Stability and change: Innovation in an educational context.* Cambridge, MA: ABT Associates.

Rosenholtz, S. (1987). Workplace conditions that affect teacher quality and commitment: Implications for the design of teacher induction programs. *The Elementary School Journal, 89*(4), 421–40.

Rosenholtz, S. (1989). *Teachers' workplace: The social organization of schools.* New York: Longman.

Ross, J. A., & Reagan, E. M. (1990). Self-reported strategies of experienced and inexperienced curriculum consultants: Exploring differences. *The Alberta Journal of Educational Research, 36*(2),157–80.

Routh, D. (1989). The case for restructuring. *Florida ASCD Journal.*

Rumberger, R. (1987). High school dropouts. *Review of Educational Research, 57*(2), 101–21.

Rutter, M., Maugham, B., Mortimer, P., Ouston, J., & Smith, A. (1979). *Fifteen thousand hours: Secondary schools and their effects on children.* Cambridge, MA: Harvard University Press.

Sarason, S. (1971). *The culture of the school and the problem of change.* Boston: Allyn & Bacon.

Sarason, S. (1972). *The creation of settings and the future societies.* San Francisco: Jossey-Bass.

Sarason, S. (1978). The nature of problem-solving in social action. *American Psychologist, 33*, 370–380.

Sarason, S. (1982). *The culture of the school and the problem of change* (rev. ed.). Boston: Allyn & Bacon.

Sarason, S. (1983). *Schooling in America.* New York: The Free Press.

Sarason, S. (1990). *The predictable failure of educational reform.* San Francisco: Jossey-Bass.

Sarason, S. B., Davidson, K. S., & Blatt, B. (1986). *The preparation of teachers: An unstudied problem in education* (rev. ed.). Cambridge, MA: Brookline Books.

Sarason, S. B., & Doris, J. (1979). *Educational handicap, public policy, and social history.* New York: Free Press.

Saxl, E., Miles, M., & Lieberman, A. (1990). *Assisting change in education (ACE).* Alexandria, VA: Association for Supervision and Curriculum Development.

Scardamalia, M., & Bereiter, C. (1989). Schools as knowledge-building communities. In S. Strauss (Ed.), *Human development.* Norwood, NJ: Ablex.

Scardamalia, M., Bereiter, C., McLean, R., Swallow, J., & Woodruff, E. (1989). Computer-supported intentional learning environments. *Journal of Educational Computing Research, 5*(1), 51–68.

Schlechty, P. (1990). *Schools for the 21st century.* San Francisco: Jossey-Bass.

Schlechty, P., & Vance, V. (1983). Recruitment, selection and retention: The shape of the teaching force. *The Elementary School Journal, 83*(4), 469–87.

Schneider, G. (1988). *Reaching for the top—Are women interested?* Paper presented at American Educational Research Association annual meeting.

Schön, D. (1971). *Beyond the stable state.* New York: Norton.

Schön, D. (1987). *Educating the reflective practitioner.* San Francisco: Jossey-Bass.

Shakeshaft, C. (1987). *Women in educational administration.* Beverly Hills, CA: Sage.

Shakeshaft, C. (1989). The gender gap in research in educational administration. *Educational Administration Quarterly, 25*(4), 324–37.

Shanker, A. (1988). Reforming the reform movement. *Educational Administration Quarterly, 24*(4), 366–73.

Shanker, A. (1990). Staff development and the restructured school. In B. Joyce (Ed.), *Changing school culture through staff development* (pp. 91–103). Alexandria, VA: Association for Supervision and Curriculum Development.

Sharan, S., & Shaulov, A. (1989). Cooperative learning, motivation to learn, and academic achievement. In S. Sharan (Ed.), *Cooperative learning: Theory and research.* New York: Praeger.

Sharan, Y., & Sharan, S. (1989). Group investigation expands cooperative learning. *Educational Leadership, 47*(4), 17–21.

Sharon, D. (1988). The Renfrew quality education project: Teachers' views after the first year. *Canadian Journal of Educational Communications, 17*(1), 53–62.

Sharp, R., & Green, A. (1975). *Education and social control: A study in progressive primary education.* London: Routledge & Kegan Paul.

Shive, G., & Eiseman, J. (1982). *People, policies and practices: Vol. 5. Dissemination for school improvement: An analysis of nine federal education programs.* Andover, MA: The Network.

Shulman, J. (1989). Blue freeways: Traveling the alternative route with big-city teacher trainees. *Journal of Teacher Education, 40*(5), 2–8.

Shulman, L. S. (1987). Knowledge and teaching: Foundations of the new reform. *Harvard Education Review, 57*(1), 1–22.

Shulman, L. S. (1990). Reconnecting foundations to the substance of teacher education. *Teachers College Record, 91*(3), 301–10.

Sieber, S. (1979). *The solution as the problem.* Paper presented at Society for the Study of Social Problems annual meeting.

Silberman, C. (1970). *Crisis in the classroom.* New York: Vintage Books.

Simms, J. (1978). *The implementation of curriculum innovation.* Unpublished doctoral dissertation, University of Alberta, Edmonton.

Sirotnik, K. A. (1987). *The school as the center of change* (Occasional Paper No. 5). Seattle, WA: Center for Educational Renewal.

Sirotnik, K. A. (1990). On the eroding foundations of teacher education. *Phi Delta Kappan, 71*(5), 710–716.

Sirotnik, K. A., & Goodlad, J. (Eds.). (1988). *School-university partnerships in action: Concepts, cases, and concerns.* New York: Teachers College Press.

Smith, B., & Nerenberg, S. (1981). *Parents and federal programs: Vol. 5. Parent involvement in follow through programs.* Santa Monica, CA: System Development Corporation.

Smith, L. (1989). *Perspectives on teacher supply and demand in Ontario, 1988–2008.* Toronto: Ontario Ministry of Education.

Smith, L., & Keith, P. (1971). *Anatomy of educational innovation: An organizational analysis of an elementary school.* New York: Wiley.

Smith, W. F., & Andrews, R. L. (1989). *Instructional leadership: How principals make a difference.* Alexandria, VA: Association for Supervision and Curriculum Development.

Smylie, M. A., & Denny, J. W. (1989). *Teacher leadership: Tensions and ambiguities in organizational perspective.* Paper presented at American Educational Research Association annual meeting.

Soder, R. (1990). How faculty members feel when the reward structure changes. *Phi Delta Kappan, 71*(5), 702–709.

Soltis, J. F. (1990). A reconceptualization of educational foundations. *Teachers College Record, 91*(3), 311–21.

Sparks, D. (1990). Cognitive coaching? An interview with Robert Garmston. *Journal of Staff Development, 11*(2), 12–5.

Stallings, J. A. (1989). *School achievement effects and staff development: What are some critical factors?* Paper presented at American Educational Research Association annual meeting.

Stiegelbauer, S., & Loucks-Horsley, S. (1987). *Putting research to work: Utilizing field-based research on implementation to develop a training program for principals.* Paper presented at American Educational Research Association annual meeting.

Stiggins, R. J., & Duke, D. (1988). *The case for commitment to teacher growth: Research on teacher evaluation.* Albany: State University of New York Press.

Stoddart, T., & Floden, R. (1990). *Traditional and alternative forms of teacher certification: Issues, assumptions and misconceptions.* Paper presented at American Educational Research Association annual meeting.

Stoddart, T., & Gomez, M. L. (1990). *The balancing of personal and professional perspectives: Learning to teach writing in traditional and alternative routes to teacher certification.* Paper presented at American Educational Research Association annual meeting.

Stonehill, R. M. (1989). *How ERIC can better serve the consumer: Prospects for program improvement.* Paper presented at American Educational Research Association annual meeting.

Su, Z. (1990). The function of the peer group in teacher socialization. *Phi Delta Kappan, 71*(5), 723–727.

Sykes, G., & Elmore, R. F. (1989). Making school manageable: Policy and administration for tomorrow's schools. *Journal of Education Policy, 3*(5), 77–94.

Tabachnick, R., Popkewitz, T., & Zeichner, K. (1979–80). Teacher education and the professional perspectives of student teachers. *Interchange, 10*(4), 12–29.

Teddlie, C., Kirby, P. C., & Stringfield, S. (1989). Effective versus ineffective schools: Observable differences in the classroom. *American Journal of Education, 97*, 221–236.

Thierbach, G. (1988). *Reaching for the top—are women interested? A study of career aspirations of women in educational administration.* Paper presented at American Educational Association annual meeting.

Timar, T. (1989). A theoretical framework for local responses to state policy: Implementing Utah's career ladder program. *Educational Evaluation and Policy Analysis, 11*(4), 329–41.

Title, D. (1989). *The critical role of teacher incentives in the northern states.* Andover, MA: Regional Laboratory for Educational Improvement of the Northeast and the Islands.

Toffler, A. (1970). *Future shock.* New York: Bantam Books.

Toffler, A. (1980). *The third wave.* New York: Bantam Books.

Tomkins, G. (1986). *A common countenance: Stability and change in the Canadian curriculum.* Toronto: Prentice-Hall.

Toronto Board of Education. (1976). *We are all immigrants to this place.* Toronto: Author.

Trider, D., & Leithwood, K. (1988). Influences on principal's practices. *Curriculum Inquiry, 18*(3), 289–311.

Tuinman, J., & Kendall, J. (1980). *The British Columbia reading assessment: General report.* Victoria: British Columbia Ministry of Education.

United States Department of Education. (1990). *Institutional projects funded by OERI.* Washington, DC: Author.

Van Geel, T. (1976). *Authority to control the school program.* Lexington, MA: D. C. Heath.

Veenman, S. (1984). Perceived problems of beginning teachers. *Review of Educational Research, 54*(2), 143–78.

Wagner, L., Ward, B., & Dianda, M. (1990). *California New Teacher Project.* Paper presented at American Educational Research Association annual meeting.

Wallace, R., LeMahieu, P., & Bickel, W. (1990). The Pittsburgh experience: Achieving commitment to comprehensive staff development. In B. Joyce (Ed.), *Changing school culture through staff development* (pp. 185–202). Alexandria, VA: Association for Supervision and Curriculum Development.

Waring, M. (1979). *Social pressures and curriculum innovation.* London: Methuen.

Watts, D. (1986). Alternate routes to teacher certification. *Action in Teacher Education, 8*(2), 25–29.

Watzlawick, P., Weakland, J., & Fisch, R. (1974). *Change.* New York: W. W. Norton.

Weatherley, R. (1979). *Reforming special education: policy implementation from state level to street level.* Cambridge, MA: MIT Press.

Weatherley, R., & Lipsky, M. (1977). Street-level bureaucrats and institutional innovation: Implementing special-education reform. *Harvard Educational Review, 47*(2), 171–97.

Wehlage, G., & Lipman, P. (1989). *Integrating school and community: The Annie E. Casey Foundation's new futures initiative for at-risk youth.* Paper prepared at the National Center on Effective Secondary Schools.

Wehlage, G., Rutter, R., Smith, G., Lesko, N., & Fernandez, R. (1990). *Reducing the risk: Schools as communities of support.* East Sussex, United Kingdom: Falmer Press.

Weinstein, R. (1983). Student perceptions of schooling. *The Elementary School Journal, 83*(4), 287–311.

Wellisch, W., MacQueen, A., Carriere, R., & Duck, G. (1978). School management and organization in successful schools. *Sociology of Education, 51,* 211–26.

Werner, W. (1980). *Implementation: The role of belief.* Unpublished paper, Center for Curriculum Studies, University of British Columbia, Vancouver.

Whiteside, T. (1978). *The sociology of educational innovation.* London: Methuen.

Wideen, M. F. (1988). School improvement in Canada. *Qualitative Studies in Education, 1*(1), 21–38.

Wideen, M., & Andrews, I. (Eds.). (1988). *Staff development for school improvement.* East Sussex, United Kingdom: Falmer Press.

Wigginton, E. (1986). *Sometimes a shining moment: The foxfire experience.* New York: Anchor Books.

Williams, W. (1980). *The implementation perspective.* Berkeley: University of California Press.

Willis, P. (1977). *Learning to labour.* Westmead, United Kingdom: Saxon House.

Wilson, B., & Corcoran, T. (1988). *Successful secondary schools: Visions of excellence in American public education.* Philadelphia: Falmer Press.

Wimpelberg, R. (1981). *Parent choice in public education: The preferences and behaviors of parents related to their children's schooling.* Paper presented at American Educational Research Association annual meeting.

Wise, A. (1977). Why educational policies often fail: The hyperrationalization hypothesis. *Curriculum Studies, 9*(1), 43–57.

Wise, A. (1979). *Legislated learning.* Berkeley: University of California Press.

Wise, A. (1988). The two conflicting trends in school reform: Legislative learning revisited. *Phi Delta Kappan, 69*(5), 328–33.

Wise, A., Darling-Hammond, L., McLaughlin, M. W., & Bernstein, H. (1985). Teacher evaluation: A study of effective practices. *The Elementary School Journal, 86*(1), 61–121.

Wohlstetter, P. (1989). *Accountability mechanisms for state education reform: Some organizational alternatives.* Paper presented at American Educational Research Association annual meeting.

Wolcott, H. (1973). *The man in the principal's office.* New York: Holt, Rinehart & Winston.

Woolfolk, A. E. (Ed.). (1989). *Research perspective on the graduate preparation of teachers.* Englewood Cliffs, NJ: Prentice-Hall.

Yarger, S. (1990). The legacy of the teacher center. In B. Joyce (Ed.), *Changing school culture through staff development* (pp. 104–116). Alexandria, VA: Association for Supervision and Curriculum Development.

Yin, R., Herald, K., & Vogel, M. (1977). *Tinkering with the system.* Lexington, MA: D. C. Heath.

Zeichner, K. (1989). *Learning to teach writing in elementary school.* Madison: University of Wisconsin-Madison.

Zeichner, K., & Gore, J. (1990). Teacher socialization. In W. Houston, M. Haberman, & J. Sikula (Eds.), *Handbook of Research on Teacher Education* (pp. 329–48). New York: Macmillan.

Ziegler, S. (1987). *The effects of parent involvement on children's achievement: The significance of home/school links.* Toronto Board of Education: Research Section, Library Services Department.

Zimpher, N. (1988). *1987 National survey of students in teacher education programs: Preliminary findings.* Paper presented at American Educational Research Association annual meeting.

Index

About the Authors

MICHAEL G. FULLAN is the Dean of Education, University of Toronto. He received his Ph.D. in Sociology from the University of Toronto in 1969. He spent a number of years conducting research, graduate teaching and in-service work on educational change at the Ontario Institute for Studies in Education, where he completed a term as Assistant Director (Academic) in 1987. Professor Fullan has participated as researcher, consultant, trainer, and policy advisor on a wide range of educational projects with school systems, teachers' federations, research and development institutes, universities and government agencies in Canada and internationally, and has written extensively on the topic of educational reform. Since joining the University of Toronto as Dean of Education in 1988 he has been involved in major innovations in teacher education and school improvement. In 1990, he became the first recipient of The Annual Award for Excellence of the Canadian Association for Teacher Educators.

SUZANNE M. STIEGELBAUER is an Assistant Professor of Education at the University of Toronto. She received her Ph.D. in Anthropology from the University of Texas in 1990. From 1979 to 1985 she was a Research Associate with the CBAM Program, Research and Development Center in Teacher Education, University of Texas, Austin. Since then she has participated in numerous research, consulting, and training projects in both the United States and Canada focusing on the issue of change.